# LIQUOR

### AND

# ANTI-LIQUOR

### IN

# VIRGINIA

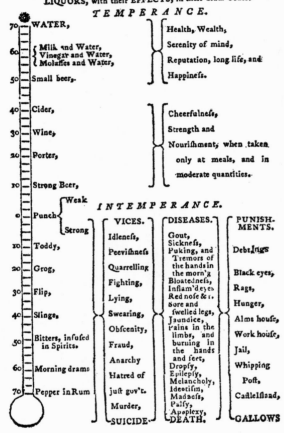

**12**

# A MORAL and PHYSICAL THERMOMETER

Or, a *Scale* of the *Progress* of TEMPERANCE and INTEMPERANCE.
LIQUORS, with their EFFECTS, in their usual Order.

### T E M P E R A N C E.

| | | |
|---|---|---|
| 70 | WATER, | Health, Wealth, |
| 60 | Milk and Water, Vinegar and Water, Molasses and Water, | Serenity of mind, Reputation, long life, and |
| 50 | Small beer. | Happiness. |
| 40 | Cider, | Cheerfulness, |
| 30 | Wine, | Strength and |
| 20 | Porter, | Nourishment, when taken |
| | | only at meals, and in |
| 10 | Strong Beer, | moderate quantities. |

### I N T E M P E R A N C E.

|  | | VICES. | DISEASES. | PUNISH-MENTS. |
|---|---|---|---|---|
| 0 | Punch {Weak / Strong} | Idleness, | Gout, Sickness, | |
| 10 | Toddy, | Peevishness | Puking, and Tremors of the hands in the morn'g | Debt, |
| 20 | Grog, | Quarrelling | Bloatedness, Inflam'd eyes | Black eyes, |
| 30 | Flip, | Fighting, Lying, | Red nose & f. Sore and swelled legs, | Rags, |
| 40 | Slings, | Swearing, Obscenity, | Jaundice, Pains in the limbs, and burning in the hands and feet, | Hunger, Alms house, |
| 50 | Bitters, infused in Spirits. | Fraud, Anarchy | Dropsy, Epilepsy, | Work house, Jail, |
| 60 | Morning drams | Hatred of just gov't. | Melancholy, Ideotism, Madness, | Whipping Post, |
| 70 | Pepper in Rum | Murder, | Palsy, Apoplexy, | Castle Island, |
| | | SUICIDE. | DEATH. | GALLOWS |

"A Moral and Physical Thermometer" from Benjamin Rush, *An Inquiry into the Effects of Spirituous Liquors on the Human Body* (Boston, 1790).

# "LIQUOR
## AND
# ANTI-LIQUOR
### IN
# VIRGINIA
## 1619-1919„

*C. C. Pearson*

*and*

**J. Edwin Hendricks**

DUKE UNIVERSITY PRESS
*Durham, N. C.    1967*

# PREFACE

*If the Temperance agitation were merely a morbid freak of human caprice . . . , it should yet be chronicled as a remarkable phenomenon in the history of mankind.*

Lucian Minor in the *Southern Literary Messenger,* July, 1850.

This chronicle of what has proved to be much more than a "morbid freak of human caprice" is the work of two authors from two generations. Dr. C. C. Pearson, professor of Political Science and the Social Sciences at Wake Forest College, 1916-1952, worked on the book for many years with interruptions coming as a result of World War I, the Depression, World War II, the veteran boom in the colleges, and various spells of ill health. On his death in 1956 some polishing and much deciphering of his appended notes remained to be done before the manuscript could be published. When I began work almost six years later the task was further complicated by the fact that numerous volumes had appeared on this subject in the intervening years. Also, the personal papers of such important temperance workers as Bishop Cannon, Carter Glass, and others were opened for public use either after Dr. Pearson's death or too late in his career for him to use them completely. The manuscript was invaluable for the records it contained of Dr. Pearson's conversations with many who were involved with the temperance movement of the late nineteenth and early twentieth centuries. He had access to many original records which are no longer available. These sources, combined with a piercing insight and a strong organizational capacity, made the manuscript of such a quality as to almost demand preparation for publication. My contribution, in addition to bringing the research up to date, has been to edit some portions and to revise and rewrite others.

There is no end to this "remarkable phenomenon in the history of mankind." The three centuries under consideration—and the years from 1919 to the present—portray above all else the persistence of the battle. The hostility to liquor among middle-class people was as constant as the determination of all other groups (and many of the middle class as well) to drink. Nowhere does there appear a totally satisfactory answer to the question used by Dr. Pearson as the title of a paper read to the North Carolina Historical Society: "Why can't you and I let people go to hell in their own way?" But, despite the lack of a solution, the study of the problem is an intriguing one.

J.E.H.

# CONTENTS

# ILLUSTRATIONS

# LIQUOR
### AND
# ANTI-LIQUOR
### IN
# VIRGINIA

*Chapter One*

# GENESIS OF THE REGULATORY SYSTEM

Legislative regulation of the distribution of liquor had its beginning in Virginia in 1619.[1] All the Southern states began in their earliest settlements to follow some program of regulation and continued until total prohibition was adopted,[2] but it was in Virginia that the system of regulation attained its greatest legal development. There were no ante bellum experiments in legal prohibition in the Old Dominion. Instead, for nearly three hundred years, the regulatory system was backed strongly by political theory and social prestige and had its fairest chance as a solution to the problem of drink in America.[3] In the twentieth century Virginia, and later the nation, turned to prohibition as an answer, but after the repeal of the Eighteenth Amendment Virginia returned to regulation.

## REGULATION: ITS EVOLUTION TO 1705

The early settlers brought with them to Virginia[4] and the later colonies the drinking tastes and habits of old England. To the familiar drinks (beer, wine, and gin) they added homemade cider, whiskey, and brandy as well as imported brandy and imported rum—all of them "hard" drinks and all

1. *Journals of the House of Burgesses of Virginia*, ed. H. R. McIlwaine and J. P. Kennedy (13 vols.; Richmond, 1905-1915), 1619-1658/59, 9 (hereinafter cited as *J.H.B.*). See Appendix I below.
2. Georgia began with prohibition but public opinion soon brought its government to a system of regulation.
3. Dr. John A. Krout in his *The Origins of Prohibition* (New York, 1925) conveys in chap. 3, "The Basis of Regulation," an impression of New England priority in regulation and in concern over excessive drinking. A better claim could be established for Virginia.
4. Notwithstanding the excellence of Philip Alexander Bruce, *Economic History of Virginia in the Seventeenth Century* (2 vols.; New York, 1896), this chapter is based on an independent study of the sources.

of them consumed with English heartiness. They also brought with them English laws and notions as to the legal control of drinks and drinking. As far as the Crown and Parliament were concerned English regulations were to be followed in the colonies unless local officials deemed alterations necessary.[5] Company and parliamentary authorities were the first to become interested and they viewed the matter as it concerned the colony's reputation and their own finances or trade. Occasionally, on their instruction, the governor took the initiative.[6] But the colonial legislators frequently acted independently and it was principally they who adapted the old ideas and the old words to the ever-changing practical situations. The Burgesses took their share of the initiative and interested private citizens and local public authorities undertook to influence them. By the end of the seventeenth century a regulatory system evolved that was English in spirit but essentially home-grown.[7] This system lasted almost two centuries.

The assumption underlying all legislation was the old

5. Under parliamentary acts of 1552 and 1553 alehouses and victualling houses operated under licenses granted by the county justices. The system was well worked out by 1618. Sidney Webb and Beatrice Webb, *The History of Liquor Licensing in England* (London, 1903), pp. 1-14.

6. Sir Francis Wyatt in his proclamation against drunkenness, 1622, mentions many proclamations on the subject by his predecessors. Susan M. Kingsbury (ed.), *Records of the Virginia Company of London* (4 vols.; Washington, 1906-1935), III, 658 (Document 247).

7. So also says Bruce, *Economic History*, II, 211-231. Part of the evidence of the governor's share is found in W. W. Hening (ed.), *Statutes At Large; Being a Collection of All the Laws of Virginia from the First Session of the Legislature in the Year 1619* (13 vols.; Richmond and Philadelphia, 1809-1823), I, 114; *Virginia Magazine of History and Biography*, II (1894-1895), 286, 395; III, 31; IV, 51; *Minutes of the Council and General Court of Colonial Virginia, 1622-1632, 1670-1676*, ed. H. R. McIlwaine (Richmond, 1924), pp. 5, 515; *J.H.B.* 1659/60-1693, 43; Virginia Historical Society, *Collections*, n.s. (Richmond, 1882-1892), I, 68. For the legislature's share see Hening, *Statutes at Large*, I, 226; *J.H.B.*, 1659/60-1693, 100, 308; 1758-1761, 69; 1761-1765, 81, 210; "Bacon's Laws," II, 167, 395; *Executive Journals of the Council of Colonial Virginia*, by H. R. McIlwaine and Wilmer L. Hall (5 vols.; Richmond, 1925-1945), I, 6; Jennings C. Wise, *Ye Kingdome of Accawmacke or the Eastern Shore of Virginia in the Seventeenth Century* (Richmond, 1911), p. 196; J. Lewis Peyton, *Augusta County* (Staunton, Va., 1892), p. 54. For the crudity of the laws and their revision see Herbert L. Osgood, *American Colonies in the Seventeenth Century* (3 vols.; New York, 1904-1907), I, 343.

English idea that liquor[8] is part of man's natural food and drink and therefore is *good*.[9] The Virginia legislators shared this view with England and the other colonies and expressed it clearly in the laws which were effective until long after the Civil War.

The ordinary consumption of liquor was never deemed a subject for legislation. No person was prohibited from drinking and none was limited as to quantity. No beverage was forbidden although there was some discrimination in favor of certain drinks.[10] On the other hand, after 1619 there was

8. "Liquor" here connotes whatever beverages were covered by the laws. In general these were all malt or spirituous drinks until 1819; from 1819 to 1854 "ardent spirits" with beer and cider not named; after 1854 beer and cider were specifically included. In the laws "any drink" was used in 1660 and "liquor" in 1705, but in other years the beverages were specified, usually with "or any mixture thereof" added and sometimes with any other "spirits" or "ardent spirits" or "drinks of any kind" added.

9. This attitude was held not only toward liquor but toward the "publick Diversions" which accompanied the purchase and consumption of the beverage. When the English in 1752 passed laws limiting the number of such public places, the editor of the Virginia *Gazette* commented: "The new Regulations for limiting places of publick Diversions, and by these Means the spreading of Vice amongst low People, are doubtless well intended to promote a General Reformation amongst the class, who never needed it more than now. Diversions are injurious, or not, according to their particular Nature, or the Circumstances of those who pursue them. Diversions which have no immoral Tendency, when purchased by those who can well afford it, unbend the Mind from severer Applications, promote a social Temper, and diffuse a general Satisfaction through the Ranks of Life. Pleasure is one of the greatest Springs of human Action; and were it not for this, there would be a general Stagnation of all Sorts of Business; for if the End for which Opulence is so much desired is once removed, nothing remains to animate Industry or excite a virtuous Emulation. Great Caution is necessary when new Restraints are to be laid, even on the lowest People, least their Spirit should be crushed by Authority; for if their necks are bended to the Yoke without Prospects of Relaxation, and reaping the Rewards of their Industry in their own clownish Jollity, their Tempers will be sowered, and their Nerves slackened in the Pursuit of Independence. Low People love low Diversions; they periodically go to it with as much Elevation of Spirit as the upper Ranks to Genteeler Recreations; and if they are to be indulged who enjoy Fortunes by the Accident of their Birth only, it would be somewhat hard to debar those from Pleasure who purchase the Means of Enjoyment by the Sweat of their Brow." Virginia *Gazette,* July 24, 1752. For additional intimations see the numerous references to drunkenness and the various beverages in the *Gazette* as indexed in Lester J. Cappon and Stella M. Duff [Mrs. Fraser Neiman] (eds.), *Virginia Gazette Index* (2 vols.; Williamsburg, Va., 1950).

10. See below, pp. 7-8, 24.

always a statute against drinking which resulted in drunkenness. At first the legislature seemed to think of drunkenness as an offense in itself—a "vice" and a "loathsome sinne" and an "abuse of God's creatures." Later the social consequences were emphasized: crime, poverty, and the "overthrow of many good acts and manuall trades."[11] The Virginia Company also disapproved of drunkenness and in 1622 called on Governor Francis Wyatt to "ernestly require the speedie redress" of excessive drinking, the "infamie" of which "hath spread itself to all that have but heard the name of Virginia."[12]

As the opinions of the seriousness of excess drinking varied so did the seriousness of the penalties prescribed. In 1619 the penalties ranged from a reprimand by the minister, first privately, then publicly, to imprisonment. These quickly and permanently gave way to a fine, usually of five shillings or the equivalent.[13] Though for a time legislators, ministers, and justices of the peace each had a special schedule of fines[14] for being "disguised with over much drink," the legislature's concern was for the lower classes. A fine of fifty pounds of tobacco or half a day's hire for a wagon and four horses[15] would obviously deter no well-to-do man. But, from 1691 to 1699, any man who could not pay faced the stocks and, from 1699 until 1831, ten sound lashes on the bare back. In the administration of these laws the growing tendency was to rely less on punishment and more on indirect control by regulating selling.[16]

11. *J.H.B.*, 1619-1658/59. 9; Hening, *Statutes at Large*, I, 126, 240; III, 73; Va. Hist. Soc., *Collections*, n.s. III, 36. A parliamentary act of 1620/21 "for repressing the odious and loathsome sinne of drunkenness" calls drunkenness the root of "other enormous sinnes" which it enumerated at length. Kingsbury, *Records of the Virginia Company*, III, 429.

12. Edward D. Neill, *History of the Virginia Company of London* (New York, 1869), p. 322.

13. Hening, *Statutes at Large*, I, 126, 193-194; III, 73, 170. The fine was 10s. from 1691 to 1699. From 1792 to 1831, 83 cents was designated; after that a dollar.

14. *Ibid.*, I, 508; II, 384.

15. Calculated from an act of 1676 fixing the hire of teams for public use.

16. Drunkenness is studied from different angles, below, pp. 44ff. See

Since under the English conception liquor was a good thing, colonial authorities sought to insure a proper supply.[17] Of prime importance were the shipments from British merchants. The legislators gave serious and continuous attention to the quality of liquors sent, the landing places, the outlets set up by factors and agents, and the terms of sale. Yet their great interest lay in encouraging domestic brewing and distilling as well as experiments with grape-growing and wine-making. Such encouragement included at one time a sort of patent on wooden vessels used in the wine-making process and at another a higher permissible selling price for "Virginia drams" than for comparable British products.[18] Monopoly and speculation were attacked by the legislatures and governors to the extent of taking a cask from ex-Governor Yeardley, who was speculating when the liquor supply was limited.[19]

At no time did the legislature handicap private initiative in effecting a proper supply by setting up any monopoly or by requiring a license to produce and sell or barter the product, nor did the duties levied upon some importations appreciably affect supply. Under this policy liquors rapidly became plentiful both in quantity and variety. Beers (except small beer) were hard to brew from available materials and were

---

Arthur P. Scott, *Criminal Law in Colonial Virginia* (Chicago, 1930), p. 258, for other laws which confirm this tendency. An interesting sidelight on the dangers of drinking parties in a frontier society is noted in an act of 1655/56. Although attacks by the Indians were rare after the mid-seventeenth century the danger was nonetheless ever present in the colonists' minds. The legislature decreed that since the only way to give prompt notice of sudden attacks was by firing guns, and since shootings at drinkings tended to spread false alarms, no person should "Shoot any gunns at drinkeing (marriages and funeralls onely excepted)." Richard L. Morton, *Colonial Virginia* (2 vols..; Chapel Hill, N. C., 1960), I, 178; Hening, *Statutes at Large*, I, 401-402.

17. Bruce, *Economic History of Virginia*, II, 211.

18. The economic soundness of such "encouragement" is questioned by Krout, *The Origins of Prohibition*, p. 16. His general criticism of the regulations seems to be unfounded.

19. *J.H.B.*, 1619-1658/59, 9; Hening, *Statutes at Large*, I, 229, 374, 489; II, 19-20; *Minutes of the Council and General Court*, p. 5; "Bacon's Laws," II, 286, 395; III, 31.

too bulky for cheap transportation, and wines were expensive when imported; yet both were always at hand. English brandy appeared in Jamestown very early, and with plentiful fruit and stills available on many plantations by 1643 there was no dearth of local pear and apple brandy. Rum from the West Indies or New England was popular everywhere. Whiskey, though known in Jamestown in 1620, was not popular until the Scotch-Irish arrived and does not appear in the price lists until the eve of the Revolution. Domestic cider and persimmon and other beers were abundant. The prices were not unreasonable, especially the prices of wines, when compared with prices in England.[20]

Producers and private dealers who channeled the commercial supply to the drinker were also regarded highly by the legislators and treated accordingly. In striking contrast, the legislators eyed the retailers of liquor-by-the-drink with suspicion and after a few years attempted to regulate this business. Retailing was never prohibited but from the early years some experiment in regulation was under way. Almost every conceivable device except governmental retailing was tried at one time or another. The last half of the seventeenth century is filled with examples of such experimental regulation. Although this period was one of party clashes between Puritan and Cavalier and between Baconites and Governor Berkeley[21] and his friends, the struggles had little if any effect on liquor regulation. As the colony grew in population and size the practical problems involved in retailing liquor demanded more attention. Three regulatory policies were developed to deal with the situation: price-fixing, limitation of credit, and selective licensing. They developed simultaneously and each influenced the other.

20. Bruce, *Economic History of Virginia*, II, 211-229. Duties ranged from 2d. to 6d. per gallon on distilled liquors and wine, with English and Irish goods free.
21. The influence of Berkeley, governor during half of this period, was great but not greater than would be expected from the length of his tenure and his status as royal governor.

A period of scarcity of liquors brought the first attempt to regulate selling prices. In 1623 the governor and Council considered the problem of speculation and increased prices which resulted from a temporary shortage of certain items. The result was a price-fixing proclamation which applied to liquor and vinegar and "sallet oyle." The reason given for issuing the proclamation was the "state" arising from the great increase in the price of commodities which would be purchased by "the como. sort at what rate soever."[22] By 1640 the legislature assumed jurisdiction over the matter (as it already had over drunkenness) and in an act of that year authorized "ordinary keepers to have instead of 6 lb. tobacco, or 18 d. in money for a meale or gallon of beer but 12 d." By 1645 the legislature was fixing the prices of all "retailing wines or strong waters." In 1659 it transferred this duty to the county courts and there the price-fixing authority remained, although several times prior to 1705 the legislature felt free to give directions and even set prices.[23]

Retailers opposed the price-fixing policy. They diluted their goods, gave short measure, and openly violated the price schedule even in Jamestown. The legislature in turn ordered their mixed liquors destroyed and their measures carefully tested, put them under bond, tried argument, compromise, coaxing, and even fined the purchaser who paid too much.[24] Still in 1667 it bewailed that "most persons" having business at court were so "exacted upon" for liquor that they were often "terrified and forced to desist in their suits lest they be ruined." The Royal Commission of 1676-1677, which in its inquiry found the costs of the legislature one of the two prin-

22. The price-fixing proclamation of 1623 was in effect eleven years before the first attempt at liquor regulation in the Massachusetts Bay Colony. Krout, *Origins of Prohibition*, p. 15; *Minutes of the Council and General Court*, p. 5.
23. Hening, *Statutes at Large*, I, 229, 234; II, 263, 287. These include fixing a maximum profit for dealers.
24. *J.H.B.*, 1619-1658, 9; Hening, *Statutes at Large*, I, 300, 489; II, 19-20, 384; III, 395. On Oct. 2, 1667, the House thanked Governor Berkeley for his attention to the excessive accounts of ordinary keepers and asked him to proceed further in the matter. *J.H.B.*, 1659/60-1693, 48.

cipal reasons for Bacon's Rebellion, gravely stated that the
liquor prices of the ordinaries seemed to be "the true reason
that members of the Assembly can not find their Account or
be content with a reasonable salary. . . ."[25]

This persistent clamor over price was not due to any
parsimony of the legislators, even though they were large
consumers themselves and had consumers among their constituents. Rather, their ideas that prices should reflect as
accurately as possible the supply of potables (that is, cheap
when supplies were plentiful and expensive only when in
short supply) and should vary directly with the price of tobacco (that is, cheapest when tobacco was selling at lowest
prices) seem both sensible and fair.[26] Their application of
these ideas allowed so great a profit spread that many were
attracted to the retailing business.[27]

The retailers felt that their prices were reasonable. Those
who operated at the county seats or in the capital village felt
that they ought to be allowed higher prices because their
business was occasional or seasonal. Most dealers suffered
losses from bad debts. And most important, the price of
tobacco, in terms of which rates were set and transactions
were ordinarily concluded, might go down during the (sometimes) long interval between times for price-setting or be-

25. *J.H.B.*, 1659/60-1693, 92. Bruce seems to have overlooked this remarkable statement. Petitions printed in the *Journal* indicate that the
delegates believed their salaries and expenses inadequate to cover the
costs of attending sessions of the legislature whereas the citizens believed
the tax levies to be too high. One of the primary factors in both instances
seems to have been excessive ordinary costs. A petition from Surry
County specifies "the ordinary Keepers Excessive Rates for drinke hath
been fownt by too sad experience to have much impoverished the inhabitants of this Colony." *Ibid.*, 1659/60-1693, 113.

26. See act of 1639-1640 ("because of the great plenty of provisions")
and act of 1658-1659 ("as the prices of tobacco shall rise or fall"). Hening,
*Statutes at Large*, I, 229, 522.

27. Bruce, *Economic History of Virginia*, II, 222 ff. The act of 1666
permitted retailers to charge treble what they paid provided they did not
exceed the rate set by law; "most of the inhabitants of Jamestown made
their living 'keeping ordinaries at extraordinary rates.' "—Mary Newton
Standard, *Colonial Virginia, Its People and Its Customs* (Philadelphia,
1917), p. 150, quoting a writer of Bacon's time. For illustrations of price
lists see Appendix IV; Bruce gives many more for the seventeenth century.

tween price-fixing and time of payment. The decline meant a loss of the profit. Even though many dealers obeyed the law when it was fair, when it ceased to be fair they found methods of adjustment.

Gradually the legislature introduced various devices to reduce the difficulties of regulation. These included annual rate-setting in each of the counties, revision of credit laws, and selective licensing of retailers. By the end of the seventeenth century, either because of such legislation or through the operation of ordinary economic laws, prices steadied, complaints ceased, and the foundation for another century of legal prices for liquors was laid.

Because the people were so economically dependent upon a single cash crop, the use of credit was essential in many businesses and was practiced widely. The extension of credit to those desiring drinks apparently was deemed unprofitable and in August, 1643, an order was issued (and made into law by the legislature in October, 1644) which stated that "noe debts made for wines or strong waters shall be pleadable or recoverable in any court of justice within the colony."[28] The law was repealed in February of the next year with the provision that such debts be collectable at a rate of "one-third of the said debt at the next cropp, And the other two-thirds at the next ensueing cropps proportionable."[29] In 1647 the sweeping prohibition of credit revived and was "made perpetual."[30] As with many such "perpetual" laws it soon outlived its usefulness and was repealed in 1666 in an attempt to induce tavern and ordinary keepers to abide by the price regulations of the day.[31]

The defense put forth by the legislature to justify such departure from the customary regulations on debt collection was "the wellfare of this collonie" since it was alleged that

28. Hening, *Statutes at Large*, I, 287.
29. *Ibid.*, I, 295.          30. *Ibid.*, I, 350.
31. The 1647 act presumably stood unaltered until 1666, as no record of other acts is found in the interval. The 1666 act states "by the present laws ordinary keepers accounts are not pleadable. . . ." *Ibid.*, II, 234.

the readiness of dealers to extend credit increased drunkenness and so injured the colony's reputation.[32] One may surmise that dealers had become unusually willing to extend credit in order to sell as much as possible at the high prices then prevailing. It is not known whether the law had achieved the desired effect before it was superseded in 1691.

Public policy was the main object of the legislature in the act of 1666 since the collection of debts incurred for drinks would be allowed only if the bill was created at legal prices. Protection for the individual was provided: the "party drinking" must know the price which he was being charged; he must be impleaded within one year after the debt accrued; and the suit must be begun during his lifetime. This was to discourage attempts to collect huge debts which might have been created while the debtor was on a spree or to discourage suits for old debts brought into court when the price of tobacco was high or when the debtor was no longer alive to challenge their accuracy.[33]

Interest in the social aspects of drinking and drinkers' debts reappeared when, after twenty-five years, the 1666 law was modified. Reciting that with "the unlimited credit given by ordinaries and tippling houses . . . to seamen and others, . . . they spend not only their ready money, but their wages and other goods, which should be for the support of their families," in 1691 the legislature proceeded to protect such persons. The lawmakers also worried about the "many persons newly free" who got in debt and ran away to neighboring colonies "to the great disadvantage of this country." Accordingly, legal collection of liquor debts for more than the

32. The preamble to the act of 1647 speaks of the "wellfare of this collonie," and Philip Alexander Bruce, *Social Life of Virginia in the Seventeenth Century* (2 vols.; Richmond, 1907), I, 183, cites a letter of Governor Berkeley concerning the increase of drunkenness.

33. In acts of 1661/62 the legislators specified that accounts of ordinary keepers or notes given them for drink were not valid evidence of debt unless signed by the purchaser and that the latter was not expected to remember such transactions "which it is impossible to keep in memory, or any part thereof." Hening, *Statutes at Large*, II, 112.

value of 300 pounds of tobacco was denied unless the debtor was master of two servants or visibly worth £50. Drawing on past experience, the legislators added severe penalties for dealers if they avoided the law by charging liquors as some other goods.[34]

The plan obviously was designed to restrain excessive drinking on credit terms for those of the laboring classes either to "keep them in their place" and get more work from them or to protect them and their families against their own folly and the exploitation of the retailers. Perhaps both ends were envisioned, although only the welfare of the lower classes is mentioned in the acts themselves. With slight alterations the law stood for forty-three years and after 1734 the credit limitation was continued but without restriction except for sailors and servants.[35]

In combination with price-fixing and the limitation of credit the legislature turned to selective licensing as a means of controlling ordinaries and tippling houses. The former was strictly a place where one could sleep and eat as well as drink, the latter, a mere drinking place.[36] Both were places where men were apt to assemble with drinking as an object. In 1644 keepers of ordinaries and "eating houses" were required to obtain licenses from the governor after "approbation of the court of the county."[37] The alleged reason for this was

34. *Ibid.*, III, 399-400. An order of 1669 had directed that ordinary keepers not trust seamen. *Minutes of the Council and General Court*, p. 513. But the act of 1691 originated in the House committee on propositions and grievances. *J.H.B.*, 1659/60-1693, 308.

35. Scott, *Criminal Law*, p. 257, thinks these laws "seem to have accomplished little." He gives no evidence, however, save an amusing letter to the Virginia *Gazette*, Nov. 26, 1772, showing how the Rev. Patrick Luman had taken advantage of the law to defraud the writer who kept an ordinary in Suffolk.

36. "Ordinaries" seem to correspond most closely to the "inns" of England. "Tavern" in England was strictly a wine shop though gradually it came to include all places where liquor was sold. The name "ordinary" continued to be used in Virginia until the nineteenth century. The use of "tavern" in the laws begins after the Revolution, though it was used in indexes earlier.

37. Hening, *Statutes at Large*, I, 287; Governor Harvey reported in 1638 that he had secured an act requiring the would-be purchaser to

"the excessive rates exacted" by them, which the legislature already was regulating. In 1660/61 the requirement was extended to all who "in their houses retayle any drinke"—that is, to tippling houses as well as ordinaries. The preamble states that by this time "many disorders and riotts" were occurring in such places. For any disorder the act placed responsibility on the retailers not only through the requirement of a license (which need not be renewed and could be revoked) but also by bonding them to maintain good order as well as to sell at legal prices.[38] Sources outside the laws[39] reveal that similar disorders continued to occur on court days and there is no reason for thinking that warrant-tryings and other assemblings were not occasions of drunken brawls then as later. Such doings could hardly be controlled by the retailer when they occurred principally outside his place. For this reason after 1677 the dealer's bond covered only specific offenses clearly within his control. His responsibility for disorders resulting from his sales was recognized only at licensing time.[40]

A second and distinctive[41] phase of the licensing policy consisted in the development of preferential treatment of ordinaries as distinguished from tippling houses. The first licensing act attempted to confer upon them an exclusive privilege of feeding and lodging people while withholding the right to sell liquors other than strong beer.[42] But apparently the ordinaries were selling without limitation and continued

procure a license. *Virginia Magazine*, III, 31. This may be the act referred to as repealed in 1640 in Hening, I, 226.

38. Hening, *Statutes at Large*, II, 19-20; in 1658/59 the retailer had to "give good security" to sell at legal prices (*ibid.*, I, 522) and the act of 1660/61 required "bond according to the laws of England." The amount of bond was not fixed; it rested with the court. It was later fixed at definite sums: 10,000 pounds of tobacco in 1705, $50 current money in 1748, $150 in 1803, $250 in 1819, $200 in 1858.

39. Wise, *Eastern Shore*, p. 109; Scott, *Criminal Law*, p. 259; Northampton Petition, see Appendix II.

40. Hening, *Statutes at Large*, II, 393-394.

41. England's policy apparently aimed at keeping those places with alehouse licenses (including inns) respectable social meeting places, but the laws by no means consistently favored them. See Webb, *History of Liquor Licensing*, pp. 9-14.

42. Hening, *Statutes at Large*, I, 229; Bruce, *Economic History*, II, 220.

to do so, and the restriction was repealed the next year. The situation is not entirely clear until tippling houses also were licensed (1660-1661),[43] at which time all distinction between them and ordinaries passed out of legislative and popular minds alike. Both were licensed and regulated by law and at both drink was the main consideration. Coincidentally the number of selling places increased greatly. Moreover, "cherishing idleness and debaucheries," they became havens for "a sort of loose and carelesse persons" whose number was recruited from the ranks of indentured servants. Facing this situation the legislature in 1668 ordered the county courts "to take speciall care for the suppressing and restraint of the exorbitant numbers of ordinaries and tippling houses in their respective counties, and not to permitt in any county more than one or two, and those neare the court house, and noe more, unles in publique places . . . where they may be necessary for the accomodation of travelers. . . ."[44] In this statute of 1668 and again in 1671, when setting rates in detail, the legislature made no distinction between ordinaries and tippling houses but made similar restrictions on both. No improvement in behavior at the drinking places resulted from these restrictions.

In June of 1676, in the midst of rebellion against the royal governor, the legislature again became concerned with the problem of too many drinking establishments. Finding that "the many ordinaries in severall parts of the county are very prejudicall," the assembly proceeded to include in Bacon's Laws an order "that no ordinaries, ale houses, or other tipling houses whatsoever" be kept in the colony except in the capital town and at the York River ferries, and these were restrained from selling any strong drink but beer and cider.[45] This was the most remarkable of all colonial liquor

---

43. Hening, II, 19.     44. *Ibid.*, II, 268-269.
45. *Ibid.*, II, 361-362; Bruce, *Economic History*, II, 225; Thomas Jefferson Wertenbaker, *Torchbearer of the Revolution: The Story of Bacon's Rebellion and Its Leader* (Princeton, 1940), p. 123. Wilcomb E. Washburn, *The Governor and the Rebel: A History of Bacon's Rebellion*

measures passed by Burgesses, which tried to remedy the accumulated evil of fifteen electionless years. Considered along with petitions referred to in Bacon's Laws and with a petition of the same year against permitting any ordinary in Northampton County, it suggests the existence of a popular "temperance" sentiment.[46] However, the object of the act was presumably to restrain and diminish drinking since it left untouched plantation production and sale as well as importation. Perhaps the purpose was not even to diminish drinking but by rigorous action to end the abuses which recent policies had only made worse.

Since Bacon's Laws never went into effect, this measure did not change things at all. Definitive action, however, was near at hand. In the act of 1668 the point was made that the selling places were "set up for a private gain" and it was ordered that public convenience be considered in permitting them.[47] Bacon's Laws carried this idea to the point of permitting only those which were clearly indispensable from a public viewpoint. Ostensibly from these suggestions came the law of 1676/77 for "Regulating Ordinaries, and the Prices of Liquors." Bacon's Laws were repealed and the new regulations for drinking places provided that the county courts should grant licenses for ordinaries. These licenses carried full liquor-selling privileges but were limited to only two persons in each county other than the one where the General Court was meeting. To hold a license a person must be able and give bond to provide accommodations for travelers. No

---

*in Virginia* (Chapel Hill, 1957), in the chapter devoted to this subject (pp. 49-67) does not consider the suppression of ordinaries. In his concern to prove that Bacon was not interested in reform, Mr. Washburn apparently ignores the possibility that the assembly was vitally interested in such measures.

46. The petition from Northampton County speaks of "the Detraction of time and the Rudeness of People where Drink is sold . . ." and of people supposedly at courts who were instead "neglecting their business, spending and wasting their estates, abusing themselves and Authority, Quarreling and fighting with all Imagenary Illconveniences, and evil consequences thereby accruing." Appendix II.

47. Hening, *Statutes at Large*, II, 268-269.

mention was made of tippling houses and these continued to do business with or without license.[48]

The completion of the late seventeenth-century trend to limit ordinaries came with the adoption of the code of 1705 in which tippling houses were especially forbidden and the courts were directed to license only such ordinaries as they "by their discretion shall judge" to be "convenient."[49] Thus after sixty years of experiment and discussion legislators were convinced not only that a policy of severe restriction in the number and quality of retail places was required in the interest of law and order but also that the profits of the business could be made to promote the development of places for public lodging, an ever-increasing necessity. The legislators hardly were unaware that the closing of the many convenient little drinking places would be resented by the masses as an unfair deprivation. Perhaps they were helped in their determination by the arguments of the more important innkeepers, a class at that time rising to considerable importance;[50] and perhaps they relied upon self-interest of those future retail monopolists to help enforce the law. At any rate, after 1705 tippling houses were outlawed and the ordinary became a quasi-public and monopolistic institution.[51]

## ADJUSTMENTS AND DEVELOPMENTS, 1705-1860

Thus the regulatory system came into the eighteenth century with its main principles agreed upon and embodied

48. *Ibid.*, II, 393-394; the act of 1691 speaks of the tippling houses being in operation and no regulatory act is found during this period. *Ibid.*, III, 45.

49. *Ibid.*, III, 395-401.

50. The House and the Council debated at length before passing the bill—an indication of the importance attached to it. *J.H.B.*, 1702-1712, 171, *passim*. Bruce, *Economic History*, II, 558, mentions the investments of several innkeepers in building lots in Yorktown; and Wise, *Eastern Shore*, p. 175, records the offer of one such individual to supply the materials for a new courthouse.

51. There seems to be no parallel course of regulation elsewhere during this period. Webb, *Liquor Licensing in England*, entitles the chapter dealing with this "A Period of Laxness."

in the statutes. With the exception of the supplanting of white servants by slaves no great internal change came to Virginia which would affect the liquor legislation and the legislators apparently deemed the work of their predecessors adequate. They were too occupied first with wars against the Spanish, Indians, and French and then with quarrels with the mother country to change the laws and no significant changes in the matter of liquor regulations appeared until after the Revolution. The task for the rest of the colonial period, as indicated in the revision of the laws in 1705, was "regulating Ordinaries, and restraint of Tippling houses."[52]

Regulations adopted for ordinaries disclosed not only that these places were becoming more and more social centers for men but also that they tended to attract whatever was currently deemed iniquitous in society. In each instance the responsibility for prevention was placed squarely upon the keeper and usually under the penalties commonly attached to the commission of the crime. A new requirement was that the keeper must not "on the sabbath day suffer any person to tipple and drink more than is necessary"—suggesting that the week-end drinker annoyed and perhaps disgusted other guests. This law was to stand long and unchanged.

Also of 1705 vintage was a specification against gaming at ordinaries.[53] This practice, it was disclosed in 1740, "of late, hath been very much used to the ruin of the health and corruption of the morals of the youth of this colony, who upon such occasions, frequently fall in company with lewd, idle, and dissolute persons, who have no other way of maintaining themselves, but by gaming."[54] This prohibition, which at first

52. The title of the act of 1705. The regulations following, unless otherwise noted, are taken from this act, Hening, *Statutes at Large*, III, 395-401.
53. Scott, *Criminal Law*, chap. 11, "Offenses against Public Morals," pp. 252-292, shows a close connection between English and Virginia laws against gambling in this period but without particular reference to the use of ordinaries for that purpose in the two countries.
54. Hening, *Statutes at Large*, V, 103. Important also is the idea still present in the mid-eighteenth century that ordinaries had a specific purpose to serve and that gambling and other excesses hindered fulfilling that

prevented even a game of cards (but not "back gammon"), was made in 1748 to cover evasion through use of the proprietor's "shed, booth, arbour, or stall either by night or day."[55]

The welfare of the youth of the colony was not the only point of concern; the act of 1705 struck at evils involving the lowest social groups. It forbade selling any drinks to servants or to seamen without permission from their masters. The goal of this and other laws was to eliminate the disorderly activities of these classes and most particularly the loss of their time and efficiency. Not only were the masters concerned about the Monday-morning aftereffects of a weekend of drinking but also about the problem of servants who stole to finance their tippling. Ordinaries tended to become trading centers for such stolen goods and those near the harbors became refuges for deserting sailors as well. The laws sought to correct these evils and, subject only to occasional modifications in penalty or in legal procedure to keep them enforceable, they stood throughout the colonial period.[56]

In the realm of legal credit there was a special discriminatory regulation applying to sailors after 1705. All credit for the purchase of liquors of any sort was prohibited to this group. For others the trend of seventeenth-century policy was

function. Cf. a letter from a clergyman relating to ordinaries: ". . . it is notorious, that Ordinaries are now, in a great Measure, perverted from their original intention, and proper Use; *viz.* the Reception, Accomodation, and Refreshment of the weary and benighted Traveller; (which Ends they least serve or answer) and are become the common Receptacle, and Rendezvous of the very Dreggs of the People; even of the most lazy and dissolute that are to be found in their respective Neighbourhoods, where not only Time and Money are, vainly and unprofitably, squandered away, but (what is yet worse) where prohibited and unlawful Games, Sports, and Pastimes are used, followed, and practised, almost without any intermission. . . ."

55. *Ibid.*, VI, 79.

56. For servants see *ibid.*, I, 240, 489; II, 19-20; VI, 74, 359. The act of 1753 (VI, 359) includes "Slave" with servants and is unusually severe. For seamen see *ibid.*, III, 45, 488; IV, 109; VI, 75; VII, 595. The act of 1710 (III, 488), which ran for two years, set very severe penalties on the sale of liquor to sailors. For this Governor Spotswood claimed credit; his interest arose from desertions from warships. Va. Hist. Soc., *Collections*, n.s., I, 68.

reversed: after 1743 debts created up to 20 shillings in one year were legally collectable without regard to the debtor's wealth; after 1762 the limitation on amount applied only to residents of the town or the county where the sales were made. As a reason for the change of 1743 the legislature alleged "the impoverishment and ruin of many poor families."[57] From this and from later allegations of ordinary keepers one may infer that retailers avoided obeying the spirit of the previous law by selling on credit to the poorer people of honest inclination and collecting what they could through their own devices. That the new law was effective seems clear; a petition from Yorktown and Williamsburg keepers of ordinaries in 1744 alleged that under it "great Inconveniences, as well as manifest Losses in their Way of Business, have arisen," including the inability of an executor to pay the bills of the deceased even "supposing his Inclination to be ever so honest whilst living."[58] In 1762 the law was changed because of alleged injury to ordinaries "with respect to debts, contracted with them by travellers, and other transient people," a point of view presented by the ordinary keepers that year.[59] These eighteenth-century changes defined more clearly the accepted idea of an ordinary—no place for servants or seamen or Sunday drunkards or gamblers or the impoverished local tippler, but a hospitable resort for transients with money or good names and for local men good in the courts for 20 shillings a year.

Restraint of regular tippling houses apparently was easy, but throughout the century unauthorized selling in other ways continued to be a problem.[60] First, "divers loose and disorder-

57. Hening, *Statutes at Large*, IV, 428.

58. Petitions of the 1740's, 1750's, and 1760's are in *J.H.B.*, 1742-1749, 94; 1758-1761, 69; 1761-1765, 81, 210. That of 1764 (1761-1765, 210) indicates an abiding interest in being allowed to extend credit to sailors.

59. Hening, *Statutes at Large*, VII, 595.

60. Scott, *Criminal Law*, p. 258, says: "The county records show many prosecutions for selling without license, with a fair proportion of convictions." He cites two Yorktown cases of 1715 and 1721 respectively. He says also: "Various courts found it necessary, in order to prevent 'disorders, misrules, and riots,' to issue orders that no liquor be sold in the

ly persons" took advantage of the phraseology of the law of 1705, which only forbade one to "keep a tiplin house," by "setting up booths, arbours, and stalls, at court-houses, race fields, general-musters, and other public places where, not only the looser sort of people resort, get drunk, and commit many irregularities, but servants and Negros are entertained, and encouraged to purloin their master's goods, for supporting their extravagencies." This practice was doubtless based on the ancient right of Englishmen to brew and sell in "brush houses" at fair times without license.[61] The legislature, however, promptly (1710) forbade anyone except licensed ordinaries to sell "either in houses . . . or any other place whatsoever."[62]

The flow of liquor into the hands of the populace by means other than those legally established was not stopped. With the same sort of ingenuity that was to mark the speakeasy operators and bootleggers of prohibition days, peddlers appeared, especially in Yorktown but presumably elsewhere also, selling liquor in small quantities, watered and at a cheap rate—to the detriment of the ordinaries and the general defeat of the law's purposes.[63]

Accordingly, in 1748 the legislature, disclosing its irritation at these petty offenders, directed that only ordinaries and merchants, including planters keeping stores, should retail

neighborhood during the sitting of the court without special permission." He cites Stafford records of 1691 and "elsewhere."

61. Webb, *History of Liquor Licensing*, p. 98, discusses the English practice.

62. Hening, *Statutes at Large*, III, 535-536. The act did not apply to "any merchant, or other person, to sell, in what quantity he pleases, any of the aforementioned liquors, not intended to be tippled or drunk out at the houses, stores, or plantations, where the same are sold." This is the first appearance in the laws of a clear distinction between sale for on-premise and off-premise consumption. Such a distinction was suggested in Bacon's Laws, however, and probably was generally accepted prior to 1710.

63. In 1736 the ordinary keepers of Yorktown protested against "the great Dimunition of their Profits, occasioned by the Retailing of Rum, and strong Liquors, in that Town, by Persons who mix water with those Liquors, and sell them to Servants and Slaves. . . ." *J.H.B.*, 1727-1734, 271; 1736-1740, 300.

anywhere. The penalties laid down were severe, being either
£10, current money, or "twenty-one lashes, well laid on, at
the public whipping post."[64]

As the colonial period ended the main features of the law
concerning liquor were approximately these: no regulation
of production and wholesaling; no regulation of consumption unless it resulted in drunken disorder; regulation of retailing for on-premise drinking through selected and licensed
privately owned ordinaries which must provide accommodations for transients, maintain good order, sell at prices fixed
under law to freemen only and on credit only to people not of
the neighborhood; limitation of retailing for off-premise drinking to ordinaries, merchants, or even planters on the plantation, and to houses devoted solely to the selling of liquor in
small quantities from door to door. The rigidness of such
regulations was softened by the fact that enforcement was
in the hands of the county courts and the courts and juries
were lax at times in their attitude toward these laws. This was
true despite the fact that the legislature normally offered at
least a part of the fines charged for violations to those who
informed on lawbreakers.

The Revolution brought no discovered change in underlying ideas concerning liquor legislation. It did bring excitement, crowds, and less respect for accustomed restraints.
Consequently tippling houses again became a "public nuisance," a "growing and dangerous evil" with which existing
laws could not adequately deal. Accordingly, in 1779 the
legislature increased the penalty for keeping such illegal
houses, made a second offense punishable by six months' imprisonment, and gave to the proper authorities unprecedented
powers in the matter. Strengthened thus, the old colonial system of regulation became the new state system.[65]

64. Hening, *Statutes at Large*, VI, 74.
65. *Ibid.*, X, 145. The manufacture of liquor was suspended in 1778
because of grain shortage but this, like the £50 additional penalty imposed in the act of 1779, soon disappeared. It is interesting to note that
neither the English temperance movement of the post-Revolutionary period

The post-Revolutionary period, though marked by legal reforms, saw no important change in liquor laws. The prohibition on sale to servants disappeared from the code[66] and so did the possible whipping penalty for prohibited selling; only a hopeless inebriate without money or friend could be whipped for drunkenness. Perhaps motivated by the same humaneness the laws included a stern though not new warning against gaming "which must often be attended with quarrels, disputes, the impoverishment of many people and their families, and the ruin of the health and the corruption of the manners of youth."[67] If there was any democratic urge for greater equality in drinking opportunity through the legalization of tippling houses, as in neighboring North Carolina, or otherwise, it did not materialize.[68] And the monopoly of the ordinaries remained with but one change of lasting importance: in incorporated areas the administration of the liquor laws was hereafter in the hands of the municipal courts.[69]

The entire problem of ordinaries and the services they were to provide was reconsidered in 1819. A group of legal and political specialists known as the revisers was selected by the legislature to overhaul the state's legal code and in their deliberations they considered certain abuses of the system for

nor the English agitation for a free-sale policy (1816-1830) or the experiment with free sale (1830-1869) found reflection in Virginia law. Cf. Webb, *History of Liquor Licensing*, pp. 49-126.

66. Disappearance of a law is taken to mean that it was no longer being enforced. For various authorized publications prior to 1819 see *The Revised Code of the Laws of Virginia* [1819] (2 vols.; Richmond, 1819), II, 323-325.

67. Contrary to colonial practice, the laws from this time forward rarely state the reasons for their enactment. See, however, Dunmore's efforts. Va. Hist. Soc., *Collections*, n.s., III, 30.

68. Daniel Jay Whitener, *Prohibition in North Carolina, 1715-1945* ("The James Sprunt Studies in History and Political Science," Vol. XXVII [Chapel Hill, N. C., 1946]), p. 34. If such a democratic tendency did appear, its effects were limited to allowing the unlicensed sale of beer and wine and even this extension of tippling privileges was again curtailed in 1854.

69. Hening, *Statutes at Large*, XIII, 200. Williamsburg and Norfolk received this privilege in 1748, and in 1752 it was transferred to the College of William and Mary. *Legislative Journals of the Council of Colonial Virginia* [1680-1775], ed. H. R. McIlwaine (3 vols.; Richmond, 1918-1919), II, 1073.

licensing ordinaries.[70] Here and there private homes were "entertaining" transients who could not conveniently or comfortably eat or lodge elsewhere. Hereafter those which were located so as to compete with the ordinaries had to secure license and pay a tax without acquiring the liquor privilege.[71] Pleasing to the ordinaries (and to some discriminating men) was the newly included permission to retail at a public auction or a muster as long as there was no ordinary within a mile. On the other hand, beer and cider were specifically excepted from the ordinary's monopoly, and "ardent spirits" instead of "spiritous liquors" became the law's definition of the liquors regulated—a change that was to last until 1854 when beer was again included. This, of course, would somewhat diminish the ordinaries' business. It pleased those who liked to sell and buy cakes and cider (perhaps under brush arbors) on open-air occasions and those who liked a swig from the bucket on the merchant's counter. It was important also as a reflection of the views of those who believed that a distinction should be made in favor of "unintoxicating" drinks. Here as in former changes the object was to render the law enforceable in all its parts.[72]

In two other provisions ordinaries appeared in an un-

70. The revisers, headed by Spencer Roan of the state's highest court, were appointed Feb. 18, 1817, and reported to the legislature, which passed the revised act pertaining to ordinaries Feb. 22, 1819. This act was embodied in the *Code* [1819]. References to past statutes and indications as to which portions are new are found in the *Code* [1819], II, 279. B. W. Leigh, one of the revisers, did the editing of the *Code*, with the assistance of W. W. Hening and William Munford. Further support of the idea that the revisions of 1819 contained little or nothing which could be interpreted to be a movement toward a more democratic position is found in Bruce E. Steiner, "The Prelude to Conservatism, 1781-1822; An Account of the Early Life, First Ventures into Politics, and Legal Career of Benjamin Watkins Leigh" (Master's thesis, University of Virginia, 1959), pp. 153-155.

71. *Code* [1819], II, 281. Those outside of towns or more than 800 yards away from a public highway were exempted.

72. England's move to free trade in beer did not come until an act of 1830. Later dealers in beer and wine alone paid a somewhat smaller tax. Discriminations before 1819 occurred only in the seventeenth century and favored beer and wine—especially the local production of wine. For contemporary Virginia sentiment see chap. 2, below.

favorable light. The "owner, master, keeper, or occupier" of ordinaries had long been charged with the prevention of gambling on the premises. Now if gambling was discovered his bond might be forfeited. In addition, the bond was made to cover a new requirement that the keepers prevent excessive drinking all week long instead of simply preventing excessive tippling on the Sabbath.[73]

As a sort of seal to all this the courts were not allowed to license without first awarding the applicant a "character certificate." For a century and a half the law had emphasized the convenience of the proposed place and the ability of the applicant to provide adequate accommodations. Once the license had been granted only the penalties set forth in the statutes insured compliance with the laws regulating order and good behavior. Under the new code the court had to certify that the applicant was "a man of good character, not addicted to drunkenness or gaming";[74] and this certificate had to be recorded and along with it the opinion of the court that he would keep "a useful and orderly house of entertainment." Moreover, violation of the "true spirit and intent of this act" by keeping a mere tippling house was made punishable as if sale had been made without license as well as by forfeiture of the bond. In this manner the legislators hoped to extend their control over the sale of alcoholic beverages by regulating not only the number but also the good behavior of the ordinary keepers.

The more widespread distribution of liquor to the mass of the people meant further difficulties in control. The methods chosen to deal with the problem were not those of further reductions in the number of selling places but rather stricter regulation of those involved. First came the licensing of those merchants who sold for off-premise drinking. Even in the seventeenth century selling liquor to be consumed elsewhere

73. The old limitation on Sunday selling appeared elsewhere in the *Code* [1819], I, 555.
74. *Ibid.*, II, 279-280.

was distinguished from consumption on the premises. The simple retailing of liquor other than by-the-drink was regarded as an auxiliary of production which was not to be restrained. It is very likely that none of the early laws was ever applied to the store owner. It seemed natural for him to sell spirits which came to him through barter or from his own plantation.[75] At any rate, the legislature in 1748 specifically exempted the merchant from licensing and other requirements as long as the liquors he sold were not consumed on the premises. The law remained through the revolutionary period despite the occasional complaints of ordinary keepers and the recommendations of some important public men.[76]

After the turn of the century the number of stores increased significantly and attracted legislators' attention as a source of revenue.[77] In addition to becoming more numerous they also became more popular, especially as gathering places for the gregariously minded lower classes. Provided for the first time with drinking facilities, these men flocked to the local stores, violated the restrictions concerning on-premise drinking, and created a highly objectionable situation. This picture was complicated by the Negro slaves, many of whom came to purchase for their masters, themselves, or for resale to others.

The legislature assumed that not all persons were capable of dealing with such problems and began its attempts to regulate those who sold liquors for off-premise use as well as those who sold for immediate consumption. In 1822 mer-

75. The act of 1822 specifically exempted any person selling spirits made from the produce of his own estate or distilled by him or those in his employ. *Acts of the General Assembly of Virginia, 1821-1822* (Richmond, 1822), p. 20.

76. Williamsburg ordinaries protested only to meet rebuff at the hands of the Council in 1730; *Legislative Journals of the Council*, II, 760. House committees studied the matter from time to time but rejected attempts to alter the situation; *J.H.B.*, 1752-1758, 70.

77. Licenses for merchants, applicable first to goods of foreign origin only, were required in 1784, repealed in 1790, and revised in 1799. See Edgar Sydenstricker, *A Brief History of Taxation in Virginia* (Richmond, 1915), pp. 13-14.

chant-sellers were required to secure a certificate of good character[78] and then—in 1833 in the counties and in 1848 in
the cities—a certificate of fitness and convenience of place
of sale.[79] In 1842 a license fee was imposed.[80] Such restriction had long been effective for the ordinary keepers, and the
legislature now attempted to control the package sale of
liquors and to regulate its use. The ordinary's ancient monopoly of the right to sell for on-premise drinking was not in-
fringed upon. The regulatory system was merely extended
so as to cover selling by merchants for off-premise drinking,
a business that had developed partly from ancient rights of
producers and partly from the desires of consumers, especially
those of the lower classes. The licensing of merchants to sell
for off-premise drinking simply supplemented the older and
preferred licensing of ordinaries.

Even in the earliest attempts at liquor regulation servants
and freedmen had occupied a special category against which
more rigid restriction existed. As the Negro slave came to
play a prominent role in Virginia society he found himself
possessing almost no rights in the matter of purchasing, consuming, or selling liquors. In 1705 all traffic with slaves
without the master's consent was forbidden.[81] Despite this
prohibition, selling to slaves and free Negroes was a fairly
common practice, so much so as to become a nuisance in the
early nineteenth century. No attempt at more rigid enforcement was made until the 1830's, when suddenly the wave of
fear of slave uprisings following Nat Turner's rebellion in
1831 brought a host of new restrictions on the slaves and
free Negroes.

78. *Acts of the Assembly, 1821-1822*, p. 20.
79. *Ibid., 1833-1834*, p. 10; *Code of Virginia* [1849] (Richmond, 1849),
pp. 443-444.
80. *Acts of the Assembly, 1842-1843*, p. 4.
81. This law was reaffirmed in 1792 and 1801 with changes in penalty
provisions. The original penalties were: for freedmen, forfeiture of four
times the value of the article traded, imprisonment for a month, and a
bond of £10 for good behavior; for slaves, whipping. If the bond was not
furnished, 39 lashes were required. Hening, *Statutes at Large*, III, 451-452.

In this atmosphere of fear the law of 1832 specifically forbade the sale of liquor to slaves without written permission from the master. Also prohibited was the selling of liquor by slaves or by free Negroes at any public meeting of either whites or blacks; this was strengthened by a provision for fining a master who gave a permit to buy knowing that the slave would resell.[82] None of these was successful. The legislature in 1858 again tightened the restriction on free Negroes, who themselves had become a problem in addition to the fact that they acted as intermediaries in the dealing with slaves. Moreover, the law required of all licensed sellers (merchants and ordinary keepers) an oath as well as a bond that they would obey the laws restricting Negroes.[83] As the nation drifted toward the Civil War the problem of liquor as well as most other problems of the day were intensified by attacks on the institution of slavery. In meeting the specific problem of drink in the hands of slaves and free Negroes the legislature employed some new methods, but the principal point of attack was still the retailer and the reasons for control were still the protection of property (slaves as well as real property), the preservation of public order, and the protection of the laboring classes.

In the colonial period the revenues derived from licensing were of little public interest.[84] The license fee, first imposed in 1661, went to the governor but was not of sufficient value to deserve mention as an ordinary source of revenue; it was merely a logical accompaniment of licensing. After the Revolution the state government appropriated such income

82. The editor of the *Supplement to the Revised Code* put the new law relating to the "manner of granting licenses to retail ardent spirits" along with the slave laws, explaining in a footnote that its apparent principal object was "to regulate the conduct of slaves." *Supplement to the Revised Code of the Laws of Virginia: Being a Collection of all the Acts of the General Assembly . . . Passed Since the Year 1819* (Richmond, 1833), pp. 249-250.

83. *Acts of the Assembly* (1857-1858), pp. 51-52.

84. The license fee was 350 lbs. tobacco in 1661, 35s. in 1748. Percy Scott Flippin, *Financial Administration of the Colony of Virginia* (Baltimore, 1915) does not mention it as an ordinary source of revenue.

for its own uses and the legislature concerned itself with the administrative details of collecting the revenue. The auditors enforced the law that license fees must be paid strictly in advance of sale and for a period ending with the next May court. Regulations for the liquor business came to be printed as part of the state's revenue laws and the commonwealth maintained the right to appeal cases from the sometimes easygoing county courts.[85] By degrees the licensing system was extended to include merchants and (quite a departure) wholesalers and manufacturers.[86] By degrees the fees charged were increased on a sliding scale until in 1856 the rate for an ordinary license or for the liquor-selling privilege of a merchant was a flat rate of $40 for the first year and then a tax of .5 per cent on gross receipts was added.[87] By 1857 ordinaries were paying a total of $66,235 annually and merchant retailers, $55,771. These developments were part of a general system of taxing business and perhaps reflect the farmer's suspicion and jealousy of the businessman.

By no means can it be said that revenue rather than regulation was the dominant consideration. At no time were the total fees exacted of ordinaries for their monopolistic privileges higher than those which the merchant paid for selling goods other than liquor. The legislature through its restrictions always held in check the number of selling places. A primarily fiscal policy would have secured earlier taxation of wholesaling and earlier and fuller taxation of manufacturing. The annual receipts of around $120,000 in 1857 were

85. *Supplement to the Code*, pp. 249-250; *Code* [1849], pp. 207-210. *Reports of Cases Decided in the Supreme Court of Appeals of Virginia*, reporter, Peachy R. Grattan, X (Richmond, 1855), 749. The commissioner of the revenue must supply to the local court annually the names of merchants or ordinary keepers whom he believed to be selling without license and the court must investigate through a grand jury and the commonwealth's attorney must prosecute those indicted. Penalties on the commissioner for neglect of his duties in this area were heavy.

86. An act of June 5, 1852, taxed stills if operated for four months in a year, also the manufacture of ale and porter. *Acts of the Assembly* (1852) pp. 15, 17.

87. Sydenstricker, *History of Taxation in Virginia*, pp. 17-20.

only about one-fifth of the total yielded by the license taxes and not one-twenty-fifth of the state's total revenues.[88] On the other hand, revenue considerations operated as a reason (or an excuse) for opposing experiments in regulation.

Following the English precedent, administration of the liquor laws was entrusted mainly to the county courts after 1654[89] except as the appearance of towns made other arrangements advisable.[90] The county court consisted of about a dozen resident gentlemen who collectively managed most of the county's affairs and served as a court of law in addition to being justices of the peace.[91] Until 1851 when they became elective by popular vote[92] they were virtually a self-perpetuating board although nominally appointed by the governor. The position was deemed one of importance and dignity and leading citizens did not disdain to fill it—even though incumbents did not always attend meetings. Members were apt to be independent,[93] aristocratic, autocratic, but also well acquainted with local conditions and opinions, including the sentiment of their neighbors on liquor matters.

While the price-fixing policy was in effect, it was their privilege and their obligation in the face of specified penalties to say what the prices should be. They also had wide discretion in the granting of licenses. They could license only for

88. *Biennial Report of the Auditor of Public Accounts 1858 and 1859* (Richmond, 1859), pp. 71 *et passim*. The figures were not ordinarily broken down—hence the use of the 1857 statistics included in the report of 1858.

89. Webb, *History of Liquor Licensing*, pp. 8 ff.

90. Beginning in 1748 with Williamsburg and Norfolk, licenses were granted in the cities, usually by the Hustings Court. After 1792 the law was ordinarily the same for the city and the county. Hening, *Statutes at Large*, VI, 75.

91. O. P. Chitwood, *Justice in Colonial Virginia* (Baltimore, 1905), chap. 3; *Code* [1819], I, 244-261; *Code* [1849], pp. 243-244.

92. N. M. Blake, "The Virginia Reform Convention of 1850-1851" (Master's thesis, Duke University, 1929), shows no change in the quality and membership of these courts such as might be expected after this democratizing convention.

93. Philip Alexander Bruce, "William Berkeley," *Dictionary of American Biography*, ed. Allen Johnson and Dumas Malone (20 vols.; New York, 1928-1936), II, 217-218.

one year and only those persons and those places that met the increasing requirements of the laws. But there was no official check if they were unduly lenient with respect to persons and places and no compulsion to grant a permit unless "they see fit" and from their judgment there was no appeal.[94] They could suspend or revoke licenses—for cause prior to 1831 and without named reason after that date.[95] Though no right to fix conditions of sale was legally vested in them, such power would flow from their control over licenses (as was deemed to be true in England) if they cared to avail themselves of it.

They could never license as individual magistrates (as was done in England prior to 1729) but the requirements as to which members or how many must be present to sit as a court were never severe. As individual magistrates it was incumbent upon them to make investigations where suspicion pointed to illegal selling. They could put the suspected person under bond and could direct the commonwealth's attorney to prosecute if they thought the suspicion well grounded.[96] As a court (rather than as an administrative board) they were required along with other courts from time to time to give special charges to grand juries concerning certain situations and also as a court they, with the aid of petit juries, tried those indicted in most of the liquor cases. All this was done without state supervision or encouragement.[97]

An accurate estimate of these courts' performance of

94. *Reports of Cases*, XI (1855), 655; XXII (1856), 454. In 1832 it was enacted that a rejected application could not be reheard during the license year save by a majority of members or by the same ones as had previously acted.

95. *Ibid.*, XXIX (1870), 708.

96. W. W. Hening, *The New Virginia Justice, Comprising the Office and Authority of a Justice of the Peace in the Commonwealth of Virginia* (1st ed.; Richmond, 1795), pp. 342-344, gives convenient legal forms for the magistrate's use.

97. Presentments made by church wardens came before these courts in colonial days. County clerks kept a list of those suspected of selling without license. In later days circuit courts also had jurisdiction. The right of private citizens to compensation for informing on violators seems not to be included in codes of 1819 and after.

their duties must await examination of many voluminous records. Some gleanings from their order books in fairly typical regions[98] and for rather long periods in the nineteenth century may be assumed to be illustrative. These disclose great variations in administrative practice. Price lists were made out everywhere though not with the regularity which the law required: why bother when there were no important changes to be made? Applications for license were passed on individually in court[99] and the entries required by the laws were carefully made at all times. Testimony was sometimes taken, rehearings were granted at times, an irregular licensing was occasionally "recinded." In the earlier nineteenth century licenses were continued without any record of application or decision, but not in later years. No case of revocation appeared but perhaps such cases were entered elsewhere.[100]

The work of the county courts was on the whole satisfactory. There were no appeals from their decisions to the highest court before 1837; after that they were sustained in all essentials.[101] The legislature rarely intimated disapproval, never threatened state supervision, and refused to limit the courts' discretion by permitting a popular vote on the matter of licensing or by requiring that a license be issued if the conditions imposed by statute were met. Even when organized temperance forces began their attack they did not impeach the work of the courts.

Conclusions as to other matters are less easily formed. Unlicensed selling undoubtedly did go on but the amount of it was not sufficient to raise any great protest from those who

98. The records in the clerk of the court's offices have been examined in Richmond, Lancaster, Rockbridge, Albemarle, Halifax, and Henry counties and in the cities of Richmond and Norfolk.

99. In Richmond and Norfolk in the late fifties, 30 or 40 were licensed in a batch.

100. Scott, *Criminal Law*, p. 258, says "Occasionally, though not often, licenses were suspended, but very few were permanently forfeited." He cites two Yorktown cases.

101. Most of these appeals were at the insistence of the commonwealth and because of the revenues involved. The points were usually technical. Appeals to circuit courts have not been studied.

were paying for licenses to sell. Gambling was at times rife, but in Richmond at least it was not reported as being associated with the selling of liquor.[102] The penalty for drunkenness was certainly not imposed in the very many cases which were known to the justices; however, this may have been due to the belief that the law on the subject was "dead."[103] Travelers sometimes asserted that "suitable" accommodations were not provided by the ordinaries, but the courts may well have thought that suitable meant "good enough." The number and quality of the travelers as well as the community standards had to be taken into consideration. The courts' "greatest fault" was failure to enforce in many places the law against licensed merchants' selling to anyone for on-premise drinking. It is difficult to estimate whether these evils could have been remedied—the desire to drink on the merchants' premises was certainly strong, and the election of justices by popular vote would not encourage resistance to popular wishes.

Since the whole realm of home drinking was untouched by law it is clear that there was little if any intent to curtail consumption. The regulations applied neither to the supply coming from the abounding stills (which required no license) nor to the supply coming from the stores of merchants who could sell for off-premise drinking. Only excessive drinking was punishable. This system, a product of the place and time, was and had always been distinctly aristocratic and paternalistic, for it vested control in the hands of a few, gave the

102. A sermon on the "Evils of Gaming" by J. B. Jeter in 1842 states that in Richmond there were from 25 to 35 gaming establishments "recently and splendidly furnished" with from 45 to 60 professional gamblers who lived in luxury and from 3,000 to 5,000 patrons of all ages and ranks. He in no way implicates liquor. *The Baptist Preacher*, I (1842), 47-62. Frederick Law Olmsted, *A Journey in the Seaboard Slave States* (New York, 1856), p. 52, similarly does not blame the selling places for disorderly conduct on a James River island of which he read.

103. Bruce, *Economic History*, II, 216-220, shows early enforcement. Peyton, *Augusta County*, p. 69, says: "In the early days the county court . . . sought by rigid exercise of the laws, to exterpate the evil" and points to the imposition of 53 fines in 1746; but compare Nicholas Cresswell's record, below, p. 41, at the same time. In the 1840's fines for drunkenness are occasionally reported in the Richmond *Dispatch*—perhaps an average of one a day.

master greater control over labor (whether slave or free), and, though adversely affecting the upper classes but little, practically denied to the poorer and lower classes equal opportunity to meet their supposed needs or gratify their follies. Concessions to the people appeared as time passed in the equalization of credit restrictions, the abolition of whipping as a penalty for drunkenness, the exemption of beer and cider from regulatory control, the intended improvement of the dispensing stores through licensing, and the late-coming popular election of the magistrates who controlled licensing and conduct. These are seen as concessions to democracy, for they went far toward equalization for white men. For blacks, slave or free, the trend was toward greater restriction. As the system became more democratic, finance in the form of revenues obtained from the licenses seemed to acquire increasing importance.

The outstanding factor is the persistent adherence to the main principles that had evolved by the beginning of the eighteenth century—a persistence too strong for either democracy or temperance to destroy. One cause for this was a conviction of the correctness of the old underlying principles and a general disinclination to change. Another cause was the strong position of the county court justices, which enabled them to obtain from legislatures modifications of the law which experience seemed to recommend. There were derelictions of legal duty in many places and at many times. It may well be, however, that the principal importance of these is their testimony to the flexibility of the regulatory system. The justices, being men of assured community standing, could yield to the transient moods of their neighbors without letting the situation get hopelessly out of hand. Perhaps it was this local application of the state's laws, partly popular and partly arbitrary, that gave stability and long life to the whole system. At any rate, law and public opinion never flaunted each other and the regulatory system never broke down.

Thus the Virginia liquor system came to 1860. For two and a half centuries the business was recognized by the law as supplying natural and legitimate necessities and desires. Production and wholesaling were rarely controlled and after much experimentation the law vested a monopoly of sale for on-premise drinking in highly regulated taverns for over a century and a half. This at once restricted and regulated this phase of the business and forced it to contribute to the public interest by providing accommodations for transients. For off-premise drinking one could buy in small as well as large quantities from the producer, from the tavern, and from the merchant's store. During the last forty years stores had been subject to laws which sought to make this practice increasingly more orderly and law-abiding.

The Civil War did what the Revolution had only threatened to do: it weakened prestige and fixed beliefs and so let loose democratic forces of many kinds. During the war and Reconstruction the old system was emasculated by pressure from the forces of democracy, exploitation, and revenue. Afterward it was patched up along old lines and continued as the principal means by which the state controlled liquor until 1904. And where the demand for liquor was greatest it was used until 1916, when it was contemptuously set aside for prohibition. But the revival of the old system was prompted by the enemies of liquor as much as by its friends and so may best be treated as part of the anti-liquor movement.

## Chapter Two

# THE BACKGROUND OF THE TEMPERANCE SOCIETIES

Long before organized anti-liquor activity began in Virginia in 1826, many individuals and small groups concerned themselves with the problems created by the misuse of the beverage. A look at this isolated opposition reveals that these attacks against liquor consumption were seminal to the development of the temperance organizations of a later period. To understand fully either this individual opposition or the opposition of the temperance societies it is necessary first to survey the social situation in Virginia which gave rise to both the Virginian's liquor habits and his attacks on its use.

Virginia society from the Revolution to the Civil War was distinguished by a class-consciousness. Certainly the distinction was not so clear as in the earlier days[1] but it was more evident in Virginia than in most of America at that time or than anywhere in the nation today. The highest rank contained the large landowners and their affiliates, particularly in the east to the Blue Ridge Mountains. These resident landowners, who for the most part were large slaveholders, dominated politics and society, usually with the aid of some of the professional and business men of the towns. The upper classes were not dependent upon their own efforts for their livelihood though most of them did work at some profession such as politics, general supervision of their plantations, shipping, banking, or manufacturing. By common consent they set the standards for the populace in addition to governing it, though their power was gradually diminishing. Their sentiments on liquor and its use formed the basis for the state laws and the decisions of the county courts.

The opposite extreme of society was composed of the

1. Hamilton J. Eckenrode, *The Revolution in Virginia* (Boston and New York, 1916), chap. 1.

Negroes, slave and free, and those whites who lived in hand-to-mouth fashion. In between were members of the middle class, most of whom owned land which they farmed personally, often supplementing their income by some shop work, handicraft, petty office, or profession. A man was rated as upper or lower middle class depending in part upon how much he worked with his hands, in part upon his accomplishments, and in part upon whether his connections were with the higher or the lower class. Intermarriage frequently improved one's status, as did business or professional success. In the west class-consciousness was not so elaborate but it was far from being unknown even there.[2]

The philosophy of the upper class was certainly not one of self-denial whether for the increase of fortune, the development of character, or the saving of one's soul. There were, of course, things that one did not do—lying or cheating, for instance. And there were things that one should always do—fight for country or for private honor, be chivalrous (to equals at least), courteous, and hospitable. Within such broad limits one lived life as one loved it. A member of the upper class read seriously and with enjoyment[3] though perhaps not too much. He hunted, dined and danced, drank, conversed, and, above all, enjoyed his household and the society of his friends. Such, at least, is the picture one gets from contemporary observers, novelists and historians,[4] and the old Virginia

2. Thomas Jefferson Wertenbaker, *Norfolk: Historic Southern Port* (Durham, N. C., 1931), and John Edward Massey, *Autobiography of John E. Massey*, ed. Elizabeth H. Hancock (New York and Washington, 1909), are both suggestive. U. B. Phillips, *Life and Labor in the Old South* (Boston, 1929), p. 339, counts those possessing from 5 to 19 slaves as "a middle class of large farmers and comfortable townsmen." Such people are classed here as "upper middle class." In the western parts of the state propertied people did not necessarily own slaves.

3. Eckenrode, *Revolution in Virginia*, pp. 6, 7. Henry Adams quotes the Duc de Liancourt: " 'In spite of the Virginian love of dissipation, the taste for reading is commoner there among men of the first class than in any other part of America; but the populace is perhaps more ignorant there than elsewhere.' " *History of the United States During the Administrations of Jefferson and Madison* (9 vols.; New York, 1890-1898), I, 133.

4. Of an earlier period but applicable here as well are the ideas of

gentlemen themselves. To the lowest class this seemed to be the ideal life. The middle class had less leisure time and money, which led them occasionally to voice objections to the social and sporting habits of the higher and lower classes, objections in which some thoughtful upper-class folk occasionally joined.[5] Some of them were greatly influenced by the teachings of the plain people's churches. None of this, however, prevented middle-class members from enjoying sports, home, and hospitality with the same zest for living evidenced by the upper class.

The dominant idea on liquor was that it was a good thing, a "creature of God."[6] Men generally thought that it was a preventive of disease, a remedy, and a tonic.[7] It modified both heat and cold. It relieved fatigue and assuaged pain. It tempered sorrow, stimulated work, and enlivened leisure. Drinks initiated and concluded business transactions and sealed solemn oaths. One had to have liquor to electioneer "on and with." Long associated with the hospitality which Virginians deemed their particular virtue,[8] its offer to guests was at once

the Virginia gentleman as expressed in the diaries of William Byrd. For a picture of the gentleman at a party at Nomini Hall see Philip V. Fithian, *Philip V. Fithian's Journal and Letters, 1767-1774*, ed. John R. Williams (2 vols.; Princeton, 1930-1934), I, 28. A similar party in Alexandria where the men were "chiefly Scotch and Irish" is described in Nicholas Cresswell, *The Journal of Nicholas Cresswell, 1774-1777* (New York, 1924), p. 52.

5. Phillips, *Life and Labor*, pp. 354-357; see especially Edmund Ruffin's complaint of loungers and spongers in *Farmers Register*, II (1834-1835), 96.

6. An idea which appears repeatedly. Cf. *Circular Letter of the Dover Baptist Association* (Richmond, 1801): "designed by Heaven as a blessing to man."

7. "A julep before breakfast was believed to give protection against malaria, and a toddy, a glass of wine, punch, or beer at almost any time of the day or night to be good for the body as well as cheering to the spirit. . . ." Mary Newton Stanard, *Colonial Virginia, Its People and Its Customs* (Philadelphia, 1917), p. 19.

8. William Logan recorded in 1745 that on the Eastern Shore when he bought feed for his horse, Mr. Smith, "being of a Virginia Disposition, would take nothing for them, although very poor, and very Drunk, but very generous." "William Logan's Journal of a Journey to Georgia, 1745," *Pennsylvania Magazine of History and Biography*, XXXVI (1912), 3. Stanard says that hospitality was recognized as a fixed habit of rich and poor alike by Beverly and Hugh Jones in their histories of 1700 and 1724. Stanard, *Colonial Virginia*, p. 18.

a mark of the host's respect for the guest and of his own respectability. The obligation to "treat" extended to auctions and funerals as well as to parties. Contemporary literature does not exploit these views as one might expect, though John Pendleton Kennedy comes near to doing so in his *Swallow Barn*, a picture of contemporary society which included all classes. Stanard quotes a well-known Negro rhyme:

> Christmas comes but once a year;
> Every man must have his *sheer*
> Of apple cider'n "simmon beer."[9]

Few Virginians failed to learn:

> When I go toiling on my farm
> I take little brown jug on my arm;
> Down I sit in the shade of a tree,
> Take little brown jug on my knee.
> Ha, ha, ha, you and me,
> Little Brown Jug, don't I love thee!

Drinking preferences varied with the status and locality as well as with the taste of the consumer. The wealthy and refined drinker always had several kinds of wine on hand, some of which were imported. The poorer sort often resorted to cider, "sweet" or "hard," and to various concoctions that went under the name of beer. New England or West Indian rum could be found at any retail place but as the distilling processes were mastered Virginia whiskey and brandy became the mainstays of most drinkers. Brandy was most used when and where the fruit crop was abundant, but whiskey appeared everywhere and at all seasons.[10] The potency, con-

9. Stanard, *Colonial Virginia*, p. 24. Other examples may be found in Armistead C. Gordon, *Virginian Writers of Fugitive Verse* (New York, 1923), and Authur Kyle Davis, *Traditional Ballads of Virginia* (Cambridge, Mass., 1929), *Folk Songs of Virginia* (Durham, N. C., 1949), *More Traditional Ballads of Virginia* (Chapel Hill, N. C., 1960).

10. Virginians never developed the exclusive fondness for corn whiskey which characterized the North Carolinians and others. See Daniel Jay Whitener, *Prohibition in North Carolina, 1715-1945* ("The James Sprunt Studies in History and Political Science," Vol. XXVII [Chapel Hill, N. C., 1946]), p. 8. This was notwithstanding the high approval to a drink

venience, and economy of these liquors combined to make them popular.

"Spirits" were sometimes taken "straight"; sometimes a little water was added.[11] Kennedy noted "the custom . . . about an hour before dinner, to prepare a bowl of toddy, which is generally made of the finest old Jamaica spirit, or rum of St. Croix, and being well brewed is iced almost to the freezing point . . . quite a pleasant thing to handle."[12] This was a precursor of the julep which in turn was progenitor of the mint julep, each glass of which was frosted and contained a spray of freshly picked mint.

Drinking was done most often in the home and this made the liquor "case" or "chest" of the poor and the side board and decanter of the well-to-do highly prized furnishings.[13] For drinking elsewhere there was the ordinary, the "grocery" (the merchant retailer who never was able to prevent drinking on or near the premises even if he tried), the still, and the plain bottle or jug, to be turned up, emptied of a hearty swallow, and then passed on to a friend.

Drinking was all but universal. This was true with the English settlers of two centuries before and with the Scotch and many of the German settlers of a century before. Whether because of inheritance, philosophy, or easy supply it re-

---

made from corn given by George Thorpe, president of the proposed Virginia college in 1621. Mathew Page Andrews, *Virginia, the Old Dominion* (2 vols.; New York, 1937), I, 33.

11. Phillips, *Life and Labor*, p. 352, "a son of the soil took his whiskey straight, with a shiver and a smack, disdaining water to check the scorch in his gullet." When mixed with water and sugar the result was "toddy." After an election in 1774, "Col. George Washington and Major Bedwater . . . gave the populace a Hogshead of Toddy (what we call Punch in England)." Cresswell, *Journal*, p. 28.

12. John Pendleton Kennedy, *Swallow Barn* (Philadelphia, 1832), p. 89. Phillips, *Life and Labor*, p. 364, says that around 1845 at the Greenbrier White Sulphur, most esteemed of resorts, toddy and julep were the most preferred drinks.

13. For references to the "chest" or "case" in less affluent homes see William E. Hatcher, *Life of J. B. Jeter, D.D.* (Baltimore, 1887), pp. 32-33; Richard McIlwaine refers to "the decanter on the sideboard" of his youthful home in *Memories of Three Score Years and Ten* (New York, 1908), p. 32.

mained so in all walks of life. The elder William Byrd once ordered a "hogshead of claret, with some more in bottles" for political uses and was commissioned by other members of the council to order for them also.[14] The exploring party of Spotswood carried several kinds of wine on horses from Fredericksburg to the summit of the Blue Ridge where, according to tradition, drink gave out and exploration ceased simultaneously.[15] Dinwiddie officially stated that a poll tax of two shillings "would not be much felt, if the poorer sort would only deny themselves punch for one day at the courts."[16] On the eve of the Revolution Nicholas Cresswell found company for drinking at all times of day or night; while among the poor "at the Grave the parents and friends wept and drank whiskey alternately."[17] During the Revolution spirits were part of the rations of soldiers and were charged as a factory expense in the Westham arms plant.

The Great Awakening, sweeping through Virginia both before and after the Revolution, greatly influenced the religous interests and practices of many but did not influence drinking habits.[18] Of the many sermons heard by Richard Dozier from 1771 to 1810 in the Northern Neck, not one concerned drinking, according to his "Text Book."[19] Back in 1787 the Valley Mill Creek Baptist Church suspended Elder John Gerard from his office not for drinking but for having

14. William Byrd, *The Writings of "Colonel William Byrd, of Westover in Virginia, esqr"* ed. John Spencer Bassett (New York, 1901), pp. xxxi, xxxii.

15. Tradition to the contrary, the explorations extended beyond the mountains and from accounts of the journey it would have been difficult for the plentiful supplies of wine and liquors to be exhausted. Cf. Richard L. Morton, *Colonial Virginia* (2 vols.; Chapel Hill, N. C., 1960), II, 445-449.

16. Va. Hist. Soc., *Collections*, n.s., III, 36, 468.

17. Cresswell's *Journal, passim.*

18. Wesley M. Gewehr, *The Great Awakening in Virginia, 1740-1790* (Durham, N. C., 1930), p. 260.

19. Richard Dozier, "Historical Notes Concerning the Planting of Baptist Principles in the Northern Neck of Virginia; Text Book from 1771. Sermons preached and heard by Richard Dozier, son of Thomas in (Westmoreland Co.) Virginia" (typed copy in the Wake Forest College Library). The sermons were by preachers of various faiths and cultures.

drunk too much.[20] The circular letter of the Baptist Dover Association,[21] including Richmond and the counties around, in 1801 spoke of the "general abuse of spiritous liquors, by our countrymen of every age and order"; young J. B. Jeter deemed the usage of strong drink "numbered among the privileges of the kingdom of heaven";[22] and Abner Clopton stated in writing a little later that Baptist ministers were afraid to say much against drunkenness because they themselves were lovers of strong drink.[23]

Among the churches only the Methodists had rules against drinking, but the numerous entries in the diary[24] of vigorous young John Early, later a bishop, show scarcely a word spoken against liquor in the southwest. Bishop Francis Asbury recorded at Amherst Court-house, March, 1815, ". . . a local preacher who keeps a public house: may he disappoint all my fears, and exceed all my hopes."[25] Lucian Minor speaking of these days declared that "church members, and none more freely than the followers of Wesley, bought, and sold, and drank strong waters almost as freely as the World's people."[26] Among Presbyterians, "Dr. Speece used to say that some men who were staid church members at home left their religion behind on the Blue Ridge" when they went to market their produce at Scottsville on the eastern side of the

20. Valley Mill Creek Baptist Church, *Minute Book*, Virginia Baptist Historical Society, University of Richmond, Richmond, Virginia. The church is located in what is now Berkley County, West Virginia.

21. *Minutes of the Dover Baptist Association, 1801* (Richmond, 1801).

22. Jeremiah Bell Jeter, *The Recollections of a Long Life* (Richmond, 1891), p. 34. Jeter was probably influenced by the doctrine of Christian liberty.

23. J. B. Jeter, *A Memoir of Abner W. Clopton* (Richmond, 1837), p. 137. "Formerly most of our ministers, lovers of strong drink themselves, and fearful of being hard upon others who had transgressed in drinking, lest they too might fall by the same snare, indirectly encouraged the sin of intemperance."

24. *Virginia Magazine of History and Biography*, XXXIII (1925), 166-174, 283-287.

25. Francis Asbury, *Journal of Rev. Francis Asbury* (3 vols.; New York, 1852), III, 447.

26. Lucian Minor, "The Temperance Reformation in Virginia," *Southern Literary Messenger*, XVI (1850), 427.

mountain.[27] Episcopalians were certainly no more abstemious than the others.

Politicians "treated" at elections (with no legal control) before and after the Revolution.[28] Evidence that liquor was an item of common consumption by the political leaders is supported by the "Virginian" writing later in the *Southern Literary Messenger* and stating that the "five gallon bowl of toddy was daily made in the Governor's house for their [the legislators'] refreshment after they had closed the day's labors in the Capitol."[29] The story of the early days of the University of Virginia indicates the prevalence of drink among all classes of Virginians. The proctor's reports of building expenses regularly included the cost of liquor for the laborers. When the institution was opened drinking went uncontrolled because the young men would not tolerate infringement upon the liberties to which they were accustomed in their homes.[30] Wertenbaker used newspaper citations to show extensive drinking and carousing of sailors and others in the Norfolk region.[31] A leading Baptist minister commented on conditions in the rural districts:

In that day the use of strong drink was universal, or limited only by the ability to obtain it. At every place of public resort—store, blacksmith's shop or mill—the liquid was freely offered for sale, and everywhere found a ready market. Most families kept it in their "case" and all, from the hoary-headed father to the little child, partook daily of the morning "dram" and the noontide

27. Joseph Waddell, *Annals of Augusta County, Virginia, from 1726 to 1871* (Staunton, Va., 1902), p. 406.

28. For excessive use of liquor in a Hanhover election in 1752 the two Burgesses returned were refused their seats. *J.H.B.* (1752-1758), 56-70. A bill to prevent giving or selling on election day failed passage. Cf. George Washington's treating *after* an election, above, and Edmund Pendleton's indictment of the customs, below, pp. 40n, 46.

29. *Southern Literary Messenger*, XVIII (1852), 4. James Monroe was then governor.

30. Philip Alexander Bruce, *History of the University of Virginia, 1819-1919; the Lengthened Shadow of One Man* (5 vols.; New York, 1920-1922), II, 276 ff.

31. Wertenbaker, *Norfolk: Historic Southern Port*, p. 138.

"grog" or "toddy." Families too poor to indulge in its daily use would drink it freely on holidays and festive occasions.[32]

Drunkenness was a serious problem throughout the state. For all the humor in them two contemporary descriptions showed what being drunk meant. On the title page of his *Drunkard's Looking Glass* Mason L. Weems of Dumfries near Alexandria gave the contemporary designations of the stages in getting drunk in the early 1800's: first, "a drop in his eye"; then "half-shaved"; then, "getting a little on the staggers or so"; "and so on till he is 'quite capsized' or 'snug under the table with the dogs' and 'can stick to the floor without holding on.' "[33] Lucian Minor said: "All classes of men thought themselves temperate, so long as they could walk without staggering, and avoided blunders glaringly ridiculous, and such atrocities as beating wives."[34] Drunkenness was equally prevalent everywhere. Dr. Conrad Speece is quoted as saying that the Charlottesville region had been reserved by the Devil for his own "special use";[35] it would seem that he had made additional reservations as well. Until the late thirties the practice of drink was freely admitted. On the other hand, as Jeter pointed out, "the excess was occasional rather than habitual. There were many drunkards but few sots." With most people lack of money and the demands of their work prevented "habitual inebriety." The practical consequences of drunkenness were sometimes very serious. But there was not a solid body of opinion against the practice. Men talked about getting drunk as men who have scruples about a thing do not talk. Some, especially young men, seemed to think that to get drunk was something of an accomplishment —perhaps a gentleman's accomplishment.

32. Jeter, *Recollections,* p. 14.
33. "Parson" Weems' title is here reproduced from a copy in the University of Virginia library.
34. Minor, "Temperance Reformation," p. 427.
35. William Spottswood White, *Rev. William S. White, D.D. and His Times (1800-1873): An Autobiography,* ed. Rev. H. M. White, D.D. (Richmond, 1891), p. 111.

THE

# DRUNKARD'S LOOKING GLASS,

REFLECTING A FAITHFUL

## LIKENESS OF THE DRUNKARD,

IN

SUNDRY VERY INTERESTING ATTITUDES,

WITH

*Lively Representations of the many strange Capers which he cuts at different Stages of his Disease;*

AS FIRST,

WHEN HE HAS ONLY "A DROP IN HIS EYE;"

SECOND,

WHEN HE IS "HALF SHAVED;"

THIRD,

WHEN HE IS GETTING "A LITTLE ON THE STAGGERS OR SO;"

AND FOURTH AND FIFTH, AND SO ON,

### TILL HE IS "QUITE CAPSIZED;"

OR

"SNUG UNDER THE TABLE WITH THE DOGS,"

AND

*CAN "STICK TO THE FLOOR WITHOUT HOLDING ON."*

### BY M. L. WEEMS,

Author of the Life of Washington, &c.

*SIXTH EDITION, GREATLY IMPROVED.*

PRINTED FOR THE AUTHOR.
1818.
(Price Twenty-five Cents.)

Title Page from "Parson" Mason Locke Weems' *The Drunkard's Looking Glass* (6th ed. 1818).

Drunkenness was "regarded by the Fathers as a palliating circumstance in almost every crime from failure to attend church to treason."[36] The laws against drunkenness were not enforced. To most folk it was at worst a "venial vice." To others it was a "loathsome sin." The cosmopolitan Jefferson praised the absence of drunkenness in France and was critical of American men who were seen "transforming themselves into brutes" by drinking.[37] Jefferson favored measures to spread the use of wine and beer among the "midling class" and thus help them avoid "the poison of whiskey, which is destroying them by wholesale."[38] Parson Weems's attacks on the excessive use of the beverage were well received, though his hearers' duplicity was indicated by Weems's observation that some had rather lie than admit drunkenness.[39] And the law stigmatizing such overindulgence stood unrepealed.

From the standpoint of reform the situation was by no means hopeless in the early 1820's. More than half of the people, and biologically the more important half, were not addicted to drinking at all. For though women habitually served wine or cider at social affairs and frequently took stronger drinks, their indulgence was generally known to be slight. Some men substantiated their arguments that liquor was not necessary for health with this fact. A drunken woman was a thing to be talked about and even set down in writing.[40]

36. Eckenrode, *Revolution in Virginia*, p. 148.
37. To Mr. Bellini, from France, 1785. Thomas Jefferson, *The Papers of Thomas Jefferson*, ed. J. P. Boyd et al. (Princeton, 1950——), VIII, 569.
38. Jefferson as a brewer is discussed at length in Stanley Baron, *Brewed in America: A History of Beer and Ale in the United States* (Boston, 1962), pp. 135-148. In 1818 he proposed lowering the tariff on wines to reduce the consumption of whiskey by making wine more easily obtainable. T. J. to W. H. Crawford [Monroe's Secretary of the Treasury], Nov. 10, 1818, Jefferson Papers, Library of Congress. He also favored the establishment of vineyards and breweries in Virginia for the same purpose.
39. Some "preach up sobriety like double sanctified saints and yet twig the whiskey bottle like distillers' swine . . . and yet after all will swear they were never drunk in all their lives! *never saw the day they could not walk a seam.*" Kellock, *Parson Weems*, p. 169.
40. William Byrd was "very much surprised to find Mrs. Blair the wife of Comissary James Blair drunk, which is growing pretty common with her. . . ." William Byrd, *The Secret Diary of William Byrd of*

Though a child was sometimes humored with a little drink and was acclimated to liquor deliberately, drinking by children was rarely a problem.[41] As for the other half, reformers never claimed that the men and lads were worse than those of other states; suggestions that they were worse in England remain to be sustained.[42] Bad as the practice was among the men the world seldom sees greater virility of body and mind than these men displayed.

The evils of the prevailing drinking customs attracted attention in post-revolutionary days. About 1785 Edmund Pendleton, then and for years the dominant member of the Supreme Court of Appeals, drew, and with the most respectable citizens of Caroline, signed a petition to the legislature for "an energetic law" against the custom of treating at elections; the signers pledged themselves to support such a law "by withholding our suffrage from all who infringe upon it."[43]

*Westover, 1709-1712*, ed. Louis Wright and Marion Tinling (Richmond, 1941), p. 11. Women of the lower classes got drunk. Richmond *Enquirer*, Dec. 15, 1858; Phillips, *Life and Labor*, p. 341. J. B. Taylor recorded in his diary in 1845 four deaths from drinking in or near Richmond; at least two were women. G. B. Taylor, *Life and Times of James B. Taylor* (Philadelphia, 1872), pp. 155-156.

41. William Logan traveling down the Eastern Shore and through the Norfolk region in 1745 found giving liquor to very young children prevalent. "William Logan's Journal of a Journey to Georgia, 1745," pp. 3, 5. If one included lads who technically have not yet reached adulthood then drinking among children need be considered as more prevalent.

42. Cf. Philip Alexander Bruce, *Institutional History of Virginia in the Seventeenth Century* (2 vols.; New York, 1910), I, 38-44. Sidney Webb and Beatrice Webb, *The History of Liquor Licensing in England* (London, 1903), pp. 85-126. Virginians' reputation for excess probably grew out of some much-quoted early writings. The Virginia Company, for example, is cited by John A. Krout, *The Origins of Prohibition* (New York, 1925), p. 3, as writing to Governor Wyatt in 1622 with respect to excessive drinking in the infant colony, "the dry whereof can not but have gone to Heaven, since the infamy hath spread itself to all that have heard the name of Virginia." Charles William Taussig, *Rum, Romance and Rebellion* (New York, 1928), p. 12, plays up a less well authenticated document. Perhaps, too, the talk of young men about the University of Virginia customs helped spread and perpetuate the idea.

43. William Meade, *Old Churches, Ministers and Families of Virginia* (Philadelphia, 1885), I, 416. The petitioners asked "Whether the best mode of enabling electors to judge a candidate's qualifications is to deprive them of their senses" and "Whether liberty will be considered inestimable by those who are in the habit of selling it for a bottle of rum." In North Carolina the practice of treating is viewed as having been "an

From France the same year Jefferson expressed his own strong condemnation of American social drinking customs.[44] Soon after the war of 1812 the newspapers of Norfolk and Richmond contained occasional items: complaints of the rowdiness of drinkers; the death of a distinguished topographical engineer in Richmond "while in a moment of intemperance"; a case of "Insanity Produced by Drink" in New York; a resolution of selectmen in Massachusetts against gratuitous distribution of liquor on public occasions.[45] To General John H. Cocke in 1816 Joseph C. Cabell, just removed from Illinois, wrote: "I believe that in the manner in which it [the drinking habit] prevails even in our polite circles, it is productive of present inconvenience, and lays the foundation for most of the pains and ills of old age."[46] For a decade Mason L. Weems had written and sold temperance tracts even to the habitués of the drinking places. "Drink no longer water," said Weems in *Golden Recipes Against Drunkenness*, "but use a *little* wine for thy stomach's sake. Also cyder, ale, beer, etc. . . . Hot coffee in the morning is a good cure for dram-craving. And a civic crown to him who will set the fashion of *coffee* at dinner."[47] At New Market, in the Valley, Ambrose Henkel published in 1814 *The Drunkards Emblem or An Enquiry into the effects of Ardent Spirits Upon the Human*

---

agent and a by-product of the political movement of Jeffersonian Democracy." A. R. Newsome, "Twelve North Carolina Counties in 1810-1811," *North Carolina Historical Review*, VI (1929), 89. The practice seems to have been current in Virginia before Jefferson's influence was felt.

44. Jefferson, *Papers*, VII, 569.

45. Norfolk and Portsmouth *Herald*, May 14, 1818; Feb. 26, 1819. Richmond *Enquirer*, Aug. 11, 1820. A thorough reading of newspaper files would doubtless yield many more such items.

46. Cabell Papers, University of Virginia Library. Cabell, best known as the co-worker of Jefferson in establishing the state university, was wealthy, aristocratic, and unusually well educated. His life was devoted to the state's internal improvement. University interests and the James River and Kanawha Canal brought him and Cocke together long and intimately. He lived in Nelson County, not so far from Charlottesville. For his attitude toward liquor in the construction of the canal see below, p. 84.

47. Kellock, *Parson Weems*, p. 165. His *Drunkard's Looking Glass* was about ready in 1812 and had gone into several editions before his death in 1825. He received many appreciative letters.

*Body and Mind* written by Dr. Benjamin Rush.[48] In 1818
*A Treatise on Gardening* by "A Citizen of Virginia"[49] appeared in Georgetown, D. C., in the preface to which the
editor urged our national inebriety as an argument for the
cultivation of grapes. Finally, in the Virginia *Code* of 1819,
cider, wines, and beer were omitted from the usual list of
liquors whose sale was to be regulated by law. All of this
suggests the influence of Dr. Benjamin Rush, friend of Jefferson and medical teacher of many Virginians. There is,
however, no evidence that Dr. Rush's views or any other
temperance propaganda from the North were being read.[50]
On the other hand, Jefferson had insisted since 1776 that the
*Code* be corrected "with a single eye to reason and the good
of those for whose government it was framed"; and the "pas-
sionate social idealism of the French intellectuals had first
entered America by way of the James River."[51]

A spirit of humanitarianism was being manifested in the
current cultural movements.[52] The Colonization Society was
flourishing. Before the Literary and Philosophical Society of
Hampden-Sidney College William Maxwell,[53] lawyer and
writer of Norfolk, set forth his yearning for the "Improvement
of the People"; Lucian Minor followed him there. At Bremo,
not so far from Monticello, General John Hartwell Cocke,

48. A. S. Edmonds, "The Henkels, Early Printers in New Market, Virginia," *William and Mary Quarterly*, 2nd. ser., XVIII (1938), 182. "The
little book was bound in scraps of wall paper."
49. Probably John Randolph, Jr., father of Edmund Randolph. The
significance of this item lies in the preface and the *nom de plume*.
50. Philadelphia students listed in W. B. Blanton, *Medicine in Virginia
in the Seventeenth Century* (Richmond, 1930), include very few known
for temperance interests. Only the Henkel printing of the Rush pamphlet
has been found in Virginia.
51. Allan Nevins, *The American States During and After the Revolution, 1775-1789* (New York, 1924), p. 453; V. L. Parrington, *Main
Currents in American Thought* (New York, 1930), I, 271; II, 6.
52. A. J. Morrison, "Virginia Works and Days, 1814-1819," *South
Atlantic Quarterly*, XVIII (1919), 24-35.
53. John H. Cocke commended Maxwell's pamphlet to Cabell. Maxwell
was a lawyer, speaker, secretary of the Virginia Historical Society, vice-
president of the Virginia Colonization Society, editor and publisher of the
*Virginia Historical Register* (1848-1852), author of a biography of John
Holt Rice, trustee, and later president of Hampden-Sidney College.

after declining political preferment, put his mind to developing a broad program of social as well as economic reform. Upper classes, then, were concerned with saving the citizen from the harms of drink without awakening his resentment at any restriction of his "rights."

More important was similar concern among the middle classes. Principally owing to the decline of the old aristocratic Episcopal church and the emotional pressures of the Great Awakening, ordinary self-respecting folk had for years been forming little local churches, which were usually Baptist, Methodist, or Presbyterian. From the point of view of social reform it was of great importance that all of the denominations believed that people, being rational beings, could be improved. As yet, however, their membership did not number over 75,000,[54] more than three-fourths of which were women and infants.[55]

These groups organized into larger church groups—conferences, associations and conventions, synods, and the like. At their meetings, whether large or small, these people discussed matters of many kinds that they deemed important to the group or to the individual as a member of the group. On matters which came within the group's sphere they gave advice, made rules, exercised discipline. Among the matters covered were drunkenness, fighting, cursing, debts, adultery, Sabbath-breaking, and "all those exercises and entertainments of pastime and merriment commonly termed recreations."[56]

54. Henry S. Stroupe, *The Religious Press in the South Atlantic States, 1802-1865* (Durham, N. C., 1942), p. 71, gives the figures for 1830: Baptists, 39,000; Methodists, 27,000; Presbyterians, 7,000; none are given for Episcopalians, Disciples, Catholics, or the several German churches. Not included in the Methodist total are those Virginians (*ca.* 2,000) in the Holston and Baltimore conferences.

55. An 1826 estimate of John Holt Rice. William Maxwell, *A Memoir of the Rev. John H. Rice, D.D.* (Philadelphia, 1835), p. 312.

56. Gewehr, *Great Awakening in Virginia,* p. 36, quoting David Thomas, *The Virginia Baptist* (1774). See also the early *Disciplines* and Wesley's rules and Parrington, *Main Currents in American Thought,* I, 267. The position of the Baptists was explained in this manner: "Amusements intended *merely* for recreation, and in accordance with our obligations as social, civil, and immortal beings, are *innocent*: but this can not

If the restraints seemed to be unreasonable restrictions of liberties—something to which the revolutionary era had made men peculiarly sensitive—they were self-imposed and they tended to refine the very raw customs of the day. Altogether, the rules suited the middle-class people, who were not strong enough to stand economic losses, social reproach, or legal entanglements.

Baptists proceeded in a very democratic way, each little congregation being the maker and enforcer of its own rules and the larger organizations being only tenderers of advice and agencies of co-operation. Methodists proceeded in quite the opposite way, the rules being made at the top of their hierarchy and passed on down to the lower orders of the clergy for enforcement among the members. Either way the local preacher exerted much influence. Closely associated with him were always certain lay members who were apt to be reflective men and inclined to take the sterner view of life. These leaders—clerical and lay—were referred to as "church people." Because these men led in the church they were expected to be leaders of the communities in matters of reform. Their revolutionary background disposed them to formulate judgments on their own and to base these judgments on reason rather than on tradition.

Of the Methodists in particular, John Marshall is quoted as saying that they were "destined to shape much of the public thought of the country"—a view which R. E. Lee later confirmed.[57] Jefferson and Madison could have given similar testimony to the influence of Baptists in days recently past. Though Presbyterians were not rapidly increasing in numbers, the superior intellectual equipment of their preachers was generally admitted. Thomas Jefferson thought some of them were most arbitrary and ambitious in mapping out the dom-

---

be said of those by which the young and gay are so captivated. These . . . are not pursued for the glory of God. . . ." Jeter, *Clopton*, p. 13.

57. Edward Leigh Pell, *A Hundred Years of Richmond Methodism* (Richmond, 1899), p. 171.

ination of the state's intellectual life, their church's great mission.[58] To equip their leaders Presbyterians had already established adequate schools. Methodists and Baptists were about to attempt the same thing. The Primitive or Hardshell Baptists objected to this just as they did to other kinds of "progress," but the progressive branch agreed with Abner Clopton that "knowledge, not ignorance, is the mother of true piety." These men did not speak for the upper classes, who were apt to be Episcopalians or Deists.

In the matter of drinking it was the plain people who prompted Northampton's petition of 1676.[59] Perhaps there was an occasional preacher to these people who told of "the great Virtue of Temperance" in the same manner that a Virginian innkeeper had while Braddock's soldiers were dining at his tavern.[60] They occasionally were disturbed at their church meetings by drunkenness and the peddling of drink against which the law provided only feeble protection.[61] Drunkenness among church members continued to be a problem. Not until 1783 (except for disciplining church members) were these people stirred in any collective movement.

In the same year that the Revolution ended the Sussex (Virginia) Conference of Methodists adopted the "Wesley rule," which prohibited "Drunkenness, buying, or selling spiritous liquors; or drinking them, unless in case of necessity." The next year they limited their preachers to wine taken medicinally and in 1812 directed that members convicted of

58. Cited in Clement Eaton, *Freedom of Thought in the Old South* (Durham, N. C., 1940), p. 285.

59. Appendix II. For Northampton people see Wise, *Eastern Shore*, p. 138.

60. Fairfax Harrison (ed.), "With Braddock's Army (Diary of Mrs. Browne)," *Virginia Magazine of History and Biography*, XXXII (1924), 312. Mrs. Browne records, "[I had] Milk & Water to Drink, which my friend Thompson said was temperate Liquor."

61. Under the revised *Code* [1819], I, 555, the disturbance must be "on purpose, maliciously or contemptuously" and even then punishment would be "at the discretion of the jury." The *Supplement to the Revised Code* . . . (Richmond, 1833), p. 247, included "preaching" specifically among the public occasions within one mile of which Negroes were not to be permitted to sell or give liquor.

giving treats at elections be disciplined. Following 1783 at least two ministers tried experiments in the Blue Ridge country—one with liquorless harvesting, the other with personal pledging of men not to drink. Many Methodists associated the Wesley rule with the great Bishop Asbury and cherished it though it proved altogether too strong for the brotherhood and they quickly allowed it to fall into disuse.[62]

Some of the Baptists' district associations also were taking action, notably the Dover Association, which embraced the Richmond-Williamsburg district. Through its circular letter of 1801 the association warned that, while liquor might be used in moderation for one's health and in case of exposure, drunkenness was a New Testament sin. The letter then pointed out that the quarreling, fighting, and profanity which followed its use were crimes and brought shame upon the churches.[63]

Five years later Barnaby Nixon, well-known Quaker of Prince George County, brought out *A Serious Address, to the Rulers of America in General, and the State of Virginia in Particular* in which he charged violation of a compact with God in revolutionary days and warned "Woe . . . to the drunkards of Ephraim . . . they also have erred through wine . . . the priests and the prophet . . . through strong drink . . . they err in vision, they stumble in judgment."[64] By 1815 Presby-

62. Methodism has been rather well studied. For Virginia see William Warren Sweet, *Virginia Methodism, A History* (Richmond, 1955). For various aspects of the relationship between Methodists and liquor during this period see the various church *Disciplines* and Daniel Dorchester, *The Liquor Problem in All Ages* (New York, 1884); Henry Wheeler, *Methodism and the Temperance Reformation* (New York, 1882); and John James Tigert, *A Constitutional History of American Episcopal Methodism* (Nashville, Tenn., 1904). Individual pledging had doubtless often occurred before and the early existence of a temperance society seems probable.

63. Dover Association *Minutes*, 1801, 1812. James B. Blanks, "Social Control by Baptists in Virginia and North Carolina, 1775-1928" (Master's thesis, Wake Forest College, 1929), lists illustrations drawn from church record books.

64. Nixon was of an old North Carolina Quaker family. He included Baltimore and Philadelphia in his extensive travels. Ellen Goode Winslow, *History of Perquimans County* (Raleigh, N. C., 1931), p. 397 *et passim*.

terian synods transmitted[65] to the churches under their care the resolutions of their General Assembly of May, 1812, which warned "not only against intemperance but against all the habits and indulgences which have a tendency to produce it" and recommended in addition to disciplinary measures by the churches the formation of "moral associations" for lessening the use of ardent spirits in members' families. Finally, in 1822, the Dover Association distributed another circular letter, drawn by King and Queen's influential Robert Semple,[66] which pictured a "train of most directful and fatal diseases" that followed daily moderate drinking. The drunkard husband and father, it said, "becomes incapable of doing anything to provide for his family; he destroys everything that comes in his way; renders useless every attempt of his wife and children to provide for themselves. . . ." It urged that the bottle be "set out at the accustomed hour" only "for visitors, and not for our own families" and that visitors be not allowed to get drunk, for hospitality and politeness must never be "set in opposition to the great principles of morality, virtue and religion."

Thus for over a period of forty years individuals and groups denounced current drinking customs. The attack was not directed at selling but at the drinking habits which led to drunkenness. Reform efforts were concerned with either individuals or small groups and no legislation was requested. Church bodies, led by their ministers, attacked the customs and had some success. They were strengthened by reports of successful organized activity in the Northern areas.[67] There

65. Raleigh (N. C.) *Star*, Sept. 1, 1815, contains the text of the resolutions. G. G. Johnson, *Ante-bellum North Carolina* (Chapel Hill, N. C., 1937), pp. 169, 455.
66. Dover Baptist Association Circular Letter, 1822; Semple was a leading spirit on the State Mission Board and author of *A History of the Rise & Progress of the Baptists in Virginia* (Richmond, 1810).
67. Krout, *Origins of Prohibition*, pp. 51-100, discusses conditions in New England, New York, and Philadelphia. Greater concentrations of population and extremely large liquor manufacturing and trading businesses created worse conditions and therefore stronger remedial efforts.

may have been unpublicized temperance organizations in Virginia.[68] If so, their impact was minimal and in 1826 a writer in John H. Rice's *Literary and Evangelical Magazine*[69] said concerning intemperance: "I do not see a single effort to check its growth," a finding confirmed by the absence of news or comment on the subject in the Baptist Roanoke *Religious Correspondent* for 1821-1823.

There was no lack of individual opposition to the excessive use of liquor among the citizens of Virginia. From the very beginnings of the settlement influential people concerned themselves with the damage done to citizens of the Old Dominion through habitual drunkenness. Liquor was such a common item of consumption, however, that to regulate its use by means other than the control of its sale seemed impossible. This, combined with the Virginian's hesitance to infringe upon the rights of his neighbor, tended to weaken the effect of those few temperance movements that did occur prior to 1826. It was necessary that conditions change before the temperance ideal could bear more weight in Virginia affairs. This change was to come during the next few years.

68. See chap. 3.                    69. IX (1826), 86.

## Chapter Three

# THE LOCAL TEMPERANCE SOCIETIES

The first rays of an enduring organized revolt against liquor appeared at Ash Camp Meeting-house in Charlotte County, Virginia, on October 27, 1826. For the state of Virginia, as well as for the South as a whole, this was the beginning of temperance societies that would exert influence on the liquor questions from that time onward.[1] Such a movement was in line with the main current of radical thinking of the previous forty years in its support of the view that intoxicating beverages ought not be drunk because of attendant evils. Since the individual might not be able to resist the temptations of drink, those who organized the first society planned to aid individuals by applying moral pressures by fellow sufferers in volunteer groups.

The society as a device for reform was not unique to the temperance movement. In increasing numbers, Americans were looking about themselves and finding that life as they

1. Jeremiah Bell Jeter, *A Memoir of Abner W. Clopton* (Richmond, 1837), p. 173. Henry S. Stroupe, "History of the Biblical Recorder, 1835-1907" (Master's thesis, Wake Forest College, 1937), p. 53, records a North Carolina editorial in 1835 which indicated that "Thirty years ago, a total abstinence society was formed in Virginia . . ." which was still flourishing. The reference may be to the private pledging done before 1800 in Amherst by Micajah Pendleton, "a shrewd Methodist," or to the liquorless harvesting plan in Botecourt promoted by Edward Mitchell, "one of the first and most decided temperance men in the state." Lucian Minor, "The Temperance Reformation in Virginia," *Southern Literary Messenger*, XVI (1850), 427; William W. Bennett, *Memorials of Methodism in Virginia* (Richmond, 1871), p. 336. No organization, however, is known to have been affected by either. Cf. Wade Crawford Barclay, *Early American Methodism, 1769-1844* (New York, 1950), II, 27-31; and H. A. Scomp, *King Alcohol in the Realm of King Cotton* (Blakely Printing Co.: n.p., *ca.* 1887) for brief discussions of the first efforts toward temperance. The *Religious Herald*, March 18, 1841, carried an item from a Northern newspaper asserting that in 1825 an "Anti-Intemperance Society" was formed by the Charleston Baptist Association in imitation of an association in the North. This seems in error since the American Temperance Society was formed only months before the Virginia Temperance Society in 1826.

and their associates knew it could be much improved. Whereas some concentrated, as in earlier times, on improving the material side of life, others sought to improve the social, moral, and intellectual standards of their communities. Individual reformers actively began to gather others who were interested in their particular cause and to enlist them in a program of reform. Working largely through attempts to bring social pressure on those who had control over the social ills which they fought, these agitators attacked slavery, inhumane laws, inhumane treatment of the insane, and the like, as well as the evils of drink. In some areas the principal exponents of social control were the fast-growing evangelical churches. But they moved haltingly and with little effect in dealing with liquor problems. The real activists in the new movement were the temperance societies.

Not theory or imitation but observation and experience led to the first society. Daniel Witt and Jeremiah Bell Jeter were young Missionary Baptist preachers of plain hill-country stock. "Several years" before 1822 Witt was shocked and saddened by the effects of liquor in his own family and among ministers of his acquaintance. He recalled a sermon by Rev. James Turner, a Presbyterian, on "Do thyself no harm" and resolved to abstain from intoxicating liquor as a beverage. Jeter, who first tried total abstinence and then religion as a defense against the intemperance he feared,[2] in 1822 joined Witt, sealing the "pledge" by a "hearty shaking of hands."

Their decision became known later that year when before

2. Jeremiah Bell Jeter, *The Recollections of a Long Life* (Richmond, 1891), pp. 33-35, and *The Life of Rev. Daniel Witt, D.D. of Prince Edward County, Virginia* (Richmond, 1875), pp. 58-61. This is an "autobiography" prepared by Witt in 1871 and published with extensive comment by Jeter. "We were attending a meeting . . . ," says Witt. "In the morning, as the custom was, a decanter of spirits was set before us, with sugar and water, and we were invited to partake of it . . . we were led into a conversation on the subject. We concurred in the opinion that it was not only a useless habit, but that it was fraught with pernicious consequences. We then and there, on a bright and beautiful Sabbath morning, mutually resolved, *to abstain during the remainder of our lives, from the use of intoxicating liquor as a beverage*, and to use it only as a medicine, if used at all."

a "large company of ministers and laymen" in a private home they declined the "inevitable bottle." "I was considered by most persons present as far gone in ultra Pharasaism," wrote Witt. Gentle and inclined to evangelism, he spent his life as pastor of a country church in Prince Edward County. Jeter was pastor of Richmond's First Baptist Church and editor of the *Religious Herald*. He was a broad-minded, temperamental man and no mean orator and stylist. Both were leaders but neither was a fighter or a crank.

Abner W. Clopton[3] supported them. Clopton, the son of a Pittsylvania farmer, left merchandizing in Virginia to study and tutor at the University of North Carolina, where he eventually earned a Master's degree. He later studied and practiced medicine while conducting a preparatory school first at the University of North Carolina and then in aristocratic Caswell County nearby.[4] Gradually he drifted into preaching. At forty he settled in the pastorate of churches in Charlotte County, Virginia. He was "gloomy and ascetic in his piety" and bitter in rebuke of "vice, in all its shades and shapes." He found his churches "much infested by the sin of drunkenness" and "commenced immediately a war of extermination against it."

Even for such a devoted man the move toward abstinence was a difficult one. Constantly in fear of personal excess, though he "used ardent spirits very moderately," Clopton approved the course of Witt, his understudy, but did not easily imitate it. He was a sensitive man. He had been shocked out of successful business by an unfortunate marriage at twenty-six and out of the study of medicine at the University of Pennsyl-

3. Jeter, *Clopton*, pp. 171-173, 242. Clopton's portrait at the University of Richmond brings out a striking chin. Jeter says of him, "Elder Clopton was of commanding appearance: about six feet high; spare; of his visage, remarkably straight; of dark complexion; dark, curly hair, inclining to baldness; with keen hazel eyes; a countenance grave, bordering on melancholy; of a temperament nervous and ardent; and deemed in his youth very handsome."

4. "He was a very efficient teacher and the reputation of his schools was very high under his administration." K. P. Battle, *History of the University of North Carolina* (Raleigh, N. C., 1907-1912), I, 185.

vania into religion by serious illness. While at dinner one evening he heard that a young lady whom he admired had gotten drunk at a still. "Dropping his knife and fork he resolved, instantly and solemnly, to use ardent spirit no more."

"Early in the spring of 1826" Clopton formed a temperance society. "I disclosed my views," he wrote in his journal, "to brethren . . . as we returned from the Baptist general association in Fredericksburg." He had not heard of the formation of the American Temperance Society in Massachusetts earlier in that year. He stated simply that his object was "to arrest the current of intemperance." He does not explain the selection of a society as the device but the choice was natural since public societies to promote specific ends abounded. During the summer he "widely advertised" a meeting of the society to be held at Ash Camp Meeting-house in Charlotte County, October 27. He also drew up a constitution which was later adopted. The membership articles ran this way: "Any sober person, whether a member of a church or not, who will consent to abstain from the habitual use of spiritous liquors, and use them as medicine only, and, provided he be the head of a family, will enforce the same rule upon his children and domestics, may become a member of this society."[5] Very few people in Virginia at that time had "ever heard of the existence of a Temperance Society;—and almost all of these regarded an attempt to form one in *Virginia*, as the offspring of enthusiasm."[6] Consequently, though

5. Abner W. Clopton and Eli Ball, *Wisdom's Voice to the Rising Generation* (Philadelphia, ca. 1828), p. 146. Jeter, *Clopton*, p. 176, contains an incomplete version apparently taken from *Wisdom's Voice*.

6. Minor, "Temperance Reformation," p. 428. According to Jeter and Clopton neither knew that the American Temperance Society had been organized only months before. Jeter thought that "two societies having in view the same object, and adopting the same means to attain it, should have been originated . . . in the same year, with concert, marks the interposition of a beneficent Providence, and shows that the temperance reform originated, not in blind and capricious fanaticism, but in sound deliberation on the best means. . . ." *Clopton*, p. 178. It is possible that some of the individuals involved knew of earlier temperance movements

a large and excited crowd assembled at the appointed time, only eight besides Clopton, Jeter, and Witt signed the pledge.[7] None were prominent except Eli Ball, a New York–New England man of great energy and tact who had recently become pastor of the Deep Run Baptist Church in Henrico County. Five were Baptist preachers, though none of their names appears in Meade's *Old Churches, Ministers and Families of Virginia*. Half lived in Charlotte County. The Virginia Temperance Society was, accordingly, despite its name, both humble and local in its beginnings. In his journal Clopton wrote: "This society I regard, in some degree, as a means of demolishing the kingdom of Satan. O that He [God] . . . may smile upon our attempts to honor Him, in doing good to our fellow men . . . bless this institution! Amen."[8]

Other temperance societies, local in name as well as in character, quickly appeared.[9] With at least 5 societies in 1827 and more than 50 in 1829 Virginia easily led the South and ranked high among all the states. Beginning with a dozen or fewer members, each of the societies was apt to enroll from 40 to 100 people. Richmond city with the addition of 300 members in 1831 passed the 800 mark and in 1834 went to 1,100. A federation of locals into a county society gave Fluvanna nearly as many members as Richmond. By 1835 the number of societies was estimated by good authorities at

---

described by John A. Krout, *The Origins of Prohibition* (New York, 1925), pp. 83-100. Clopton had resided in Philadelphia and had studied in North Carolina under David Caldwell, a friend of temperance advocate Dr. Benjamin Rush. Ball also had Northern connections.

7. Clopton and Ball, *Wisdom's Voice*, p. 156, give the total as nine. Jeter, *Recollections*, p. 35, says ten. Minor, "Temperance Reformation," p. 427, lists the three plus Eli Ball, Elisha Collins, Reuben Chaney, John A. Davidson, John W. Kelley, B. W. Lester, William Sharp, and Daniel Williams.

8. Except as noted the account of the foundation of the organization is taken from Jeter, *Clopton*, p. 171 *et passim*.

9. Information about the early life of the societies comes principally from Virginia Temperance Society, *Reports*, 1827 (in Clopton and Ball, *Wisdom's Voice*, p. 156), 1829-1831; Virginia Baptist General Association, *Minutes*, 1831-1833; Richmond Temperance Society, Executive Committee, *Report*, 1832, 1833.

nearly 100 and the total membership at 35,000; a news item in 1836 mentioned 250 societies.[10]

The temperance organizations were mostly Baptist in their beginnings and until 1831 their spread followed rather strikingly the route of the Missionary Baptist movement from North Carolina under Shubal Stearns fifty years before. The movement spread rapidly—northward through the Piedmont counties of Prince Edward, Fluvanna, Louisa, Powhatan, Henrico, Spotsylvania, and eastward into the Tidewater where they sometimes met opposition from the Primitive Baptists. As temperance workers moved into the Valley and the southwest they met Scotch-Irish Presbyterians and German Lutherans and more Primitive Baptists, none of whom yielded readily to the new idea. In the first expansion Clopton was undoubtedly the mainspring.[11]

Then came the endorsement of the Presbyterian General Assembly, which opened the way into the upper Valley and the southwest. Methodists became interested in 1831, thereby aiding progress in the great Southside and in the Frederick-Loudon region. Northern influences were at work early around Alexandria and were probably responsible for the appearance of Young Men's Temperance Societies in 1833-1834.[12] After the first years church missionaries were often the leaders in the western parts[13] and the Virginia Society smoothed the way for new temperance groups in all regions.

10. Minor, "Temperance Reformation," pp. 432-433. Some locals founded before 1834 were: King and Queen, Deep Run (Henrico County), Richmond city, Northern Neck (Lancaster County), Dover and Webster (Gouchland County), Amelia (eight formed at one time), Fork Union (Fluvanna County), Second King and Queen, Upper King William, North Anna (Spotsylvania-Louisa), Goldmine (Louisa County), Juvenile (Spotsylvania County), Falls Church, Alexandria, Fredericksburg, University, Charlottesville, Lexington, Petersburg, Winchester, Lynchburg (two), Union (Hanover County), Salem, Mechanicksville, Brunswick, Norfolk, Berkeley, and probably others.

11. See memorial address at Charlotte Court House in 1836 by the Presbyterian A. C. Morton, in Jeter, *Clopton*, p. 190.

12. American Temperance Society, Fourth Report, 1831, *Permanent Temperance Documents* (Boston, 1835), I, 30-33.

13. Barclay, *Early American Methodism*, II, 26-27, 36-38; William

New societies were begun with ease. Frequently the leaders of a neighborhood needed only a word or a nearby example. In Louisa "some gentlemen" (in Albemarle there were five, in Amelia eight) met in a private home and no one remembered who made the suggestion.[14] General Cocke found it easy to obtain members in Fluvanna, and in the nearby Charlottesville region two societies appeared almost simultaneously (in 1830) with the name of J. C. Watson prominent in each.

It is true that church people, especially ministers, often suggested the organization of a society. Sometimes the beginning was connected with a local religious revival, as in Lynchburg,[15] or had as its background the bringing of liquor to church for sale or for drinking. In time it came to be quite the thing for a church to have a society as a sort of auxiliary. Despite this no general evangelical campaign accompanied the early spread of societies and church membership was never required for society membership. Connection of the society with any religious association was generally forbidden. The appeal usually went out to "the friends of order and good morals." The village sot, the occasional debauchers in the neighborhood, the local poverty and crime, the wasting of health and estate, the misery and suffering in one's circle of friends, one's own fear of "falling," and the fear that one's children or his neighbor's would grow up to be drunkards were the appeals mentioned in the scanty records of these little bands.[16]

Membership in the societies was strictly confined to sober people, chiefly adults and chiefly of middle-class status.

---

Warren Sweet, *Religion on the American Frontier, 1783-1840* (4 vols.; New York and Chicago, 1931-1946), IV: *The Methodists*, 55, 403.

14. Edgar Woods, *Albemarle County in Virginia* (Charlottesville, Va., 1932), pp. 90, 103; William S. White, *Rev. William S. White, D.D. and His Times (1800-1873): An Autobiography*, ed. Rev. H. M. White, D.D. (Richmond, 1891), pp. 160-161.

15. W. A. Christian, *Lynchburg and Its People* (Lynchburg, Va., 1900), p. 382.

16. Krout, *Origins of Prohibition*, p. 114, plainly attaches most importance to the role of the church in the New England movement.

Though their reformation is sometimes mentioned, the intemperate were of interest chiefly as horrible examples. Only sober persons were fit for inclusion.[17] Some of the early leaders were interested in the heads of the families, carefully counting those who joined and making it obligatory upon each "to enforce upon the members of his family, the rule observed by himself." By this course they expected to make dry many homes, which in those days were the center of social life. They did not wish to antagonize accepted ideas as to woman's place in society or to suggest that respectable women would be tempted to excess. Some societies expressly forbade the enrolment of children without the consent of their parents. The Virginia Society found it wise to explain that the head of the family ended his obligation when he had used "for this end, such means as he may deem rational and expedient."[18] The volunteer principle was extended to children by enrolling them in juvenile societies where practicable. And the women were invited to join them on the ground that they ought to work for temperance since they were the chief sufferers from the intemperance of others.[19] Though their numbers equaled the men they never held office or took conspicuous part in public proceedings.

Lucian Minor stated: "The middle classes . . . were the main adherents. . . . The two extremes of society—the very lowest and those who . . . stood highest, agreed in disdaining the movement."[20] Jeter and others confirm this idea.[21] So-

17. "Temperance Societies are designed for temperate men. Their object is to keep all sober who are so now; till all the drunkards, who will not reform, are dead, and the world is free." American Temperance Society, Fourth Report, 1831, *Permanent Temperance Documents*, I, 56. Jeter, *Recollections*, p. 34, says it was almost impossible to break the habit of drink.

18. Jeter, *Clopton*, pp. 178, 180, 185; extract from *Minutes* and constitution of the Virginia Society in Clopton and Ball, *Wisdom's Voice*, pp. 145, 156.

19. E.g., in the Richmond City Society in 1829 and the Amelia Society a little later.

20. Minor, "Temperance Reformation," p. 430.

21. Jeter, *Clopton*, p. 189.

cieties for Negroes were organized[22] but there are no records of societies for hired men or "poor whites" nor, for the most part, were the more prominent citizens involved with the societies.[23]

The societies were substantially alike in their organization and activities. Each had a constitution to which all members were supposed to subscribe.[24] To each constitution the pledge was the heart and always included the personal abstinence of the signer, the extent of the abstinence varying from place to place and from time to time. Other provisions included the discouraging of drinking by children, of treating at elections or at sales or at funerals, of the making or selling of liquor, and encouraging the use of one's influence against drinking.

Particularly troublesome was the matter of offering liquor to guests or other forms of private treating. The very respectability of this practice made it all the more dangerous in the view of early leaders, but attempts to prohibit it met stub-

22. In the Cocke Papers of the University of Virginia there is a manuscript preamble and constitution for The Fork Union Temperance Society for Colored Persons, dated May 1, 1830, which recited that intemperance leads to idleness, falsehood, stealing, and most murders and that few can use liquor without intemperance. Members joined voluntarily and promised to obey certain rules. The plan contemplated a small medal to be worn on a string around the neck. The names of John H. Cocke's slaves who joined are recorded. Cocke also preserved Thomas S. Clay's pamphlet, *Detail of a Plan for the Moral Improvement of Negroes on Plantations* (1833), which J. C. Baldwin sent him, in which the formation of temperance societies among slaves is advocated because "they have suffered their full share from the vice of intemperance and masters have, by their example, encouraged it." Martin Boyd Coyner, "John Hartwell Cocke of Bremo" (Ph.D. dissertation, University of Virginia, 1961), I, 337-341. A liquorless harvest in Fluvanna was liked by the Negroes, or so the temperance advocates reported, and saved the master 80 gallons of liquor. A society in Henrico and the Richmond African Society are the only other societies among Negroes for which records have been found.

23. At least no such evidence appears in their writings or biographies.

24. Constitutions of the Virginia Temperance Society and the Northern Neck Society are in Clopton and Ball, *Wisdom's Voice*; those of Second King and Queen and Upper King William are in manuscript in the Virginia Baptist Historical Society's library. Others appear in newspapers— e.g., Salem in *Christian Sentinel*, Jan. 4, 1833, and Lynchburg Young Men's in Lynchburg *Virginian*, March 30, 1835. The Virginia Temperance Society *Proceedings*, 1830, 1833, 1834, give essentials of several. Examples of resolutions appear in the same places.

born resistance from genial souls who respected the habits of
their guests and from businessmen who feared that customers
would deem them close or unappreciative.[25] Apparently most
societies followed the example of Clopton's group, which
voted that nothing in its constitution prohibited "the exercise
of the common civilities due to friends and neighbors."[26]

The meetings were held in some church or in several
churches in succession when there were jealousies to be
avoided or a large territory to be covered. The meetings were
open to all. There was usually a sermon or an address by an
invited speaker or, especially in later days, a debate by selected speakers on some topic of interest. On less formal
occasions there might be no more than a relation of personal
observations or a reading. Once a society successfully met the
attractions of a barbecue nearby with an impromptu reading
of "Putnam and the Wolf."[27] Reports of activities between
meetings, committee visits to other societies or to breakers
of the pledge, investigations of local jails or almshouses with
a view to discovering whether liquor had brought the inmates
there, inquiries into the amount of liquor selling or family
drinking in the neighborhood, and always the invitation to
new members made up the meeting. If there were names to
be added or to be dropped for violation of the pledge this
was done also in open meeting. There were no dues attached
to membership. On occasion a collection would be taken to
pay the cost of literature to be distributed. Occasionally a
special meeting would be held on July Fourth. These were the
"quiet methods" which were preferred and which distinguished
these earlier societies.

25. Jeremiah Bell Jeter, *The Mirror; or a Delineation of Different
Classes of Christians* (Charleston, S. C., 1855), p. 223, mentions concern over customer reaction and Cornelius Walker, *Memoirs and Sermons
of the Rev. William Duval, City Missionary, Richmond* (Richmond, 1854),
p. 87, records the objections of a Captain Dimmock of the Richmond
Public Guard on the grounds that he hesitated to offend his friends.
26. This appears in 1829 constitution of the Second King and Queen
also.
27. In Amelia. Virginia Temperance Society *Proceedings*, 1830.

Propagation of their ideas was a duty enjoined by the societies upon their members. For this the circles of one's family, friends, and servants were considered most appropriate but other persons were to be approached privately when opportunity was offered. The amount of work like this is unrecorded but it must have been extensive, especially if the work of mothers is considered.[28] The dissemination of information through public addresses and the distribution of literature by hand or through the local newspaper was another approved device. In 1827 the Virginia Society's *Circular* stated that its purpose was to "enforce and urge upon the community" the society's objectives. To this end ministers were called upon to create the right atmosphere through adequate expositions of the Bible and strict personal example.[29]

In these ways "Sound Argument, mild persuasion, and the influence of a good example"[30] epitomized the societies' ideal of propaganda: "argument" because both members and those whom they sought were deemed rational beings; "persuasion" because men's wills must be won; "good example" because it strengthened both argument and persuasion; and soundness and mildness to prevent wrangling. Data concerning the consequences of drunkenness were sometimes collected locally, in which case the collection was careful and the presentation dispassionate.[31] Much more frequently, however, reliance was placed upon outside publications. Clopton and Ball published *Wisdom's Voice to the Rising Generation*, a compilation of tracts, sermons, rules, and other documents.

28. An illustration of this work is given in Richard McIlwaine, *Memories of Three Score Years and Ten* (New York, 1908), p. 31. The influence of women is discussed below.

29. Clopton and Ball, *Wisdom's Voice*, p. 150; "Progress of Temperance," *Southern Literary Journal*, I (1835), 89.

30. Expression used by the state temperance convention of 1834.

31. Jeter, *Clopton*, pp. 185-186, says that Clopton's addresses "abounded with interesting and striking incidents which he collected in his journeys," specifically relating to the wasting of estates. These addresses, says Jeter, were "pre-eminently adapted to interest and profit assemblies," but he does not say that Clopton's presentation was dispassionate.

In the summer or early fall of 1834 the Young Men's Temperance Society of Frederick County brought out *The Temperance Pioneer*, which may have been the first regular temperance publication in the South.[32] For the most part the leaders preferred to go directly to the Northern societies' reports and newspapers, and the general membership enjoyed Sargent's *Temperance Tales* and the like. These materials were frequently unsound and harsh.

In their argument[33] the societies naturally emphasized the enormity of the evil from which they sought to protect men. Intemperance, they said, was "the most fruitful source of the numerous evils which infest society," "the most deadly evil which afflicts the state," an "absolutely incalculable" evil. To enforce this view they were apt to launch into a savage attack upon the drunkard. His "disposition is changed into that of a tiger," they said, and his family suffers accordingly. The election of drunkards to make or execute the laws was "not only to *legalize* but to honor *crime* . . . to lay the axe at the very root of Liberty." The employment of them as mechanics, physicians, or schoolmasters because they were cheaper was selfish and against the good of the whole community. Fathers were asked to point out to their children examples of physical decay and ruined fortune; matrons were to teach their children "to shrink at the approach of the drunkard . . . he, who with ruthless treachery . . . squanders in taverns and brothels the patrimony he never earned . . . and saith, 'Am I not in sport?' . . . he shall drink the wrath of God—for ever—for ever—for ever." They found the cause of this ancient evil to be, not the laws or the dealers or the climate or even sheer human weakness, but habit, the habit of drinking. Accordingly they attacked the habit as

32. Minor, "Temperance Reformation." For this paper and for other Frederick County activities see below.
33. The following quotations are extracted from the Virginia Temperance Society's "Resolutions" and "Circular" and from documents of the Northern Neck, the Second King and Queen, and the Upper King William societies, all in Clopton and Ball, *Wisdom's Voice, passim.*

being bad in itself. In this they could not make much use of Scriptures for the Scriptures were not altogether clear and some members were not Christians,[34] though one could, and usually did, insist that it was at least unselfish to set an example for a weaker brother. The economic and physiological arguments were stronger. The "*habitual* use of ardent spirits," they contended, was "rather injurious than beneficial to the health of men," quoting Dr. Benjamin Rush of Philadelphia and medical societies of Northern states. Wine also was injurious since it had been shown by modern chemical analysis to be sometimes half as strong as ardent spirits, which were half alcohol. It seemed to follow that occasional drinking also ought to be avoided even though the rules of the societies permitted the "common civilities" to guests and strangers, for this tended to become habitual. From the angle of cost the matter was equally clear. In most families which used liquor the annual cost was from ten to a hundred dollars. To what good purposes these sums could be put! "In how few families can a good library be found! People are too *poor* to procure one." Propaganda such as this was not expected to reach the drunkard—he would not care to gaze into what was often called "the drunkard's looking glass." In evaluating it one must remember that the propaganda was intended principally for good and substantial people, middle-class folk, in whom Providence had "implanted the conservative principle."[35] To these men it would mean that they could not hope to get ahead in the world or even maintain their highly prized standing in church and community if they imitated the thoughtless of lower rank or the profligates of higher rank.

The societies were effective in many neighborhoods for

34. Lucian Minor was long an agnostic. Dr. James Jones of Brunswick County was much influenced by an "infidel club" that met at Painesville, according to William Spottswood White, *The African Preacher* (Philadelphia, 1849), p. 121, but whether Dr. Jones was converted to Christianity before he helped form the local society in 1828 is not clear.
35. Minor, "Temperance Reformation," p. 430.

at least the first dozen years.[36] For example, one county which had annually consumed 65,000 gallons reported in 1830 a decrease of two-thirds. Only two of the almost 800 members of the Richmond group broke the pledge in 1831. Clopton reported to the Appomattox Baptist District Association in 1832 that all but two ministers under its jurisdiction were members. From Charlotte Court House in 1829 came word that all the merchants of the village had agreed to sell no more liquor and the Northern Neck reported in 1833 that only two of the ten merchants in Lancaster County were retailing it. Minor says that "it was now unusual in many neighborhoods to offer the bottle to a guest." A prominent member of the legislature, Archibald Bryce of Goochland, rejoiced that this change of custom had saved him sixty or seventy dollars a year. The *Religious Herald*, never extremist, declared in 1839 that "an entire revolution of opinion . . . in the thinking of the enlightened part of the community" had taken place.

Societies helped many a local church conscious of its duty as an important organization in its community, for the local churches became integral parts of every community's thinking and activity. On the other hand, society leaders often admitted that its obvious influence was severely confined to its "district" or neighborhood. Judging from the frequency with which societies reorganized or ceased to exist after the novelty wore off, their meetings must have been as dull and decorous as a modern prayer meeting and as thinly attended. The executive committee of the Richmond Society, for instance, spoke in 1832 of the "difficulty in giving interest to a subject that has so long attracted a great degree of public

---

36. Jeter, *Clopton*, p. 186; Virginia Baptist General Association, *Minutes*, 1833; *Religious Herald*, cited in American Temperance Union *Journal*, March, 1839; Minor, "Temperance Reformation," p. 429. P. H. Gilmer, who was not a member, admitted the good done in a letter to Cocke in 1832. Cocke Papers, University of Virginia. Dr. William E. Hatcher, who grew up in Jeter's native Bedford County, confirmed this view for that county in his *Life of J. B. Jeter, D.D.* (Baltimore, 1887), p. 34.

attention," yet it felt that reiteration was essential to combat so insidious a foe "which confessedly unable to stand in the field of fair controversy, lurks in hidden recesses. . . ." Nor did the device of county-wide meetings of the societies tried in Buckingham, Charlotte, and elsewhere succeed.

Temperance societies met with apathy and positive antagonism. Liquor dealers were hostile. In the region south of Norfolk, where several anti-temperance societies were formed, temperance societies were condemned as "destructive of communities." These counties had many distilleries "for which they are famous."[37]

Primitive Baptists were forthright in concerted opposition. In Alexandria, Benthal L. Beebe through his *Signs of the Times* year after year denounced all church auxiliaries as "progeny of Arminianism" designed to make churches popular, with resulting loss of distinction between those who have received grace and others.[38] John Clark, widely traveled preacher and rival of Beebe, did likewise through his *Zion's Christian Advocate*, published at Front Royal. At Tarboro, in northeastern North Carolina, the *Primitive Baptist* proclaimed against "trying to cramp the consciences" of their fellow men and advised: "let every man eat and drink to please himself, with liberty of the law to do so."[39] As expounded years later among Virginia mountaineers' southern neighbors the popular idea was: "That God gave the spirit in the fruit of grain, and the ability to extract and decoct it, and then he gave them the inclination to drink; and that it is sinful to oppose the full use of liquor; one of God's rich mercies!"[40] In response some

37. Virginia Temperance Society *Report*, 1834; *Niles Weekly Register*, XLIV (1833), 423. A meeting was held in Elizabeth City County courthouse, July 20, 1833.

38. Benthal L. Beebe, *A Compilation of Editorial Articles from the "Signs of the Times"* (Middletown, N. Y., 1868), p. 5.

39. Jan. 27, 1836, Henry S. Stroupe, *The Religious Press in the South Atlantic States, 1802-1865* (Durham, N. C., 1942), p. 107. Dr. Stroupe has been of great help in dealing with Primitive Baptists and Campbell.

40. Stroupe, *The Religious Press in the South Atlantic States*, p. 107. Letter to *Biblical Recorder*, July 10, 1832.

of their churches even expelled members for joining temperance societies.[41]

In the other religious bodies opposition to the societies came from many ministers. Henry Keeling, previously pastor of Richmond's First Baptist Church, editorially insisted in the *Religious Herald* (of which he was the first editor), October 3, 1828, on the right to drink in moderation[42] and never recanted. The influential Alexander Campbell published his *Millenial Harbinger* in Bethany in Brook County, West Virginia, in September, 1835. Though advocating temperance he took a positive stand "against Temperance Societies, Missionary Societies, and every other human institution opposed to the honor, dignity, and usefulness of the Christian Institution." He asserted that if the societies could "banish vice from the land, [infidels would] sound the triumph of human wisdom over the Christian Institution." There was little criticism by Episcopalian ministers but some of them probably found items to approve in *Reasons for not Joining the Temperance Society, By a Clergyman*, published by the elders of the church in 1836. Clement Read,[43] the author, was sometime board chairman of the Presbyterian Theological Seminary at Hampden-Sidney. In sixty-seven closely printed and devastating pages the author went to the very roots of the matter from the standpoint of a Christian of the old school. Joining a society, he said, was superfluous for a member of the church since this could bring him under no stronger obligation to be sober than he was already. The temperate use of liquor, he continued, could not be bad because it was sanctioned in the Bible notwithstanding contemporaneous abuses; nor could it be deemed a bad example because following it

41. American Temperance Union *Journal*, March, 1839, citing the *Religious Herald*; Roanoke Association *Minutes*, 1839; so also in North Carolina, Kehukee Association *Minutes*, 1822.
42. Stroupe, *The Religious Press in the South Atlantic States*, p. 100.
43. Read at this time was of Charlotte Court House and the Cub Creek Church, West Hanover Presbytery. He was raised an Episcopalian and for a while belonged to the Republican Methodist Church. J. D. Eggleston to Dr. Pearson, Dec. 27, 1938.

would lead to no bad result. Moreover, the total abstinence pledge was positively wrong because it interfered with one's Christian freedom to drink moderately or not to drink, which was the Bible rule and accordingly all-sufficient. It was also "in conflict with reason," for man as a moral agent is "endowed with both reason and appetite—appetite to be gratified, and reason to govern his appetite." All unreasonable restrictions are dangerous because they "tend to reaction, to the throwing off of all that are unreasonable. Drunkenness is a great evil; but if it is to be put down at the expense of any important principle in morality or religion, the injury would be greater than the benefit produced." Similarly, if a law against drinking should be made it would be a wrongful act because "the preservation of civil liberty is of more importance than the restraining of some men from intoxication."

Superfluous and wrong in principle, the societies were also injurious to the churches whose sanction they were continually invoking. For this sanction constituted "an implied admission on the part of the church of the insufficiency of Christianity to preserve the temperance of the members of the church." Finally the societies "injured the peace of the church" because attempts to introduce them led to "warm contests . . . and parties were soon formed" with consequent "alienation of affection . . . , suspension of Christian fellowship. . . ."

There were also "more plausible and popular" objections. On the Virginia Society's list of 1829 were the usefulness of liquor and the inevitableness of drinking. Missionary McIntyre reported the next year that the people were "alarmed" at the attack on their "idol."[44] Both suggest a survival of the old devotion to "drams." With some this took the form of sorrow at disturbance of the old customs of hospitality and good fellowship, especially when wine came under the ban; and it may have been this that led some outstanding faculty

44. Virginia Temperance Society *Proceedings,* 1829.

members of the University of Virginia to exert their great influence against the university society, causing it to decline.[45] Jeter recalled that drinkers thought the societies "an up-righteous combination against their liberties" and Minor, that some who depended for popularity upon their convivial talents inveighed against asking one to sign away his liberties.[46] This objection to group coercion of the individual was to prove one of the hardest to meet to the satisfaction of the ordinary man.

To understand the persistence of the anti-liquor movement one must understand its foundations in these little bands of plain but respectable people bent on "useful virtues." They struck at what did most harm according to their understanding. Doubtless excessive eating hurt some people and possibly tobacco hurt some but these didn't lead to beating wives or starving children or wasting estates. These people were reformers but reformers who began with themselves. By taking the pledge they bucked social custom and exposed themselves to ridicule. Keeping the pledge meant pride in proved self-control. There was much variation in the nuclei of anti-liquor endeavor—in their number, location, organization, methods, immediate aim. The movement which they began so simply and so sincerely took curious turns. But for a hundred years the movement survived.

45. Philip Alexander Bruce, *History of the University of Virginia, 1819-1919; the Lengthened Shadow of One Man* (5 vols.; New York, 1920-1922), II, 276; III, 129.
46. Jeter, *Clopton*, p. 182; Minor, "Temperance Reformation," p. 428.

## Chapter Four

# THE VIRGINIA SOCIETY

The small group gathered at Ash Camp Meeting-house in 1826 ambitiously called the organization founded there the Virginia Society for the Promotion of Temperance. Unpretentious at first, the society grew rapidly under the leadership of such men as Abner Clopton, who believed that the cause it endorsed was "far more important to us as a nation than the American revolution."[1] Soon clergymen of all denominations were joining the movement and the addition of such socially prominent men as General John Hartwell Cooke brought state-wide success. The Virginia Society quickly became the recognized leader of temperance opinion within the state and it remained so until the Sons of Temperance began activity in the middle forties.

Transition from local to state-wide interest and significance came gradually. At its first anniversary, held at Eli Ball's church in Henrico County, 1827, 81 members were recorded. Of these 29 were ministers—all but 2 of them Baptist. These included the able Robert Semple, Robert Ryland, and James B. Taylor, who represented the approving Dover District Association.[2]

The second and third anniversaries were held in Powhatan and Fluvanna counties. Progress in expanding and diversifying membership was being made as from these meetings "many clergymen and gentlemen of respectability went home with zeal to work in the cause."[3] Accessions from churches other than the Baptist came through the efforts of the nation-

1. Jeremiah Bell Jeter, *A Memoir of Abner W. Clopton* (Richmond, 1837), p. 185.
2. Jeter, *Clopton*, pp. 186-187; Ryland was the first president of Richmond College and pastor of the Richmond African Baptist Church. All were deeply interested in missions.
3. Virginia Temperance Society *Report*, 1833; "Extract from the Minutes of the First Annual Meeting of the Virginia Society," in Abner W. Clopton and Eli Ball, *Wisdom's Voice to the Rising Generation* (Philadelphia, *ca.* 1828), p. 156.

wide American Temperance Society. In various ways the national church organizations endorsed the temperance movement as one unselfishly directed at a great evil, thus inciting their ministers to active co-operation.[4]

In Virginia the Methodist church had the most numerous and the best organized of these groups and worked most closely with the people. More prominent socially and more scholarly were the Episcopalian and Presbyterian ministers enlisted in the cause. But according to Lucian Minor[5] they had no adequate conception of the evils of drink since they were apt to be "men of the closet" and without contact either with the lowly or with the "gross dissipations of high life."

Ministers of all denominations shared leadership in the movement. A few laymen of wealth and distinction came to the aid of the clergy. Heretofore few from this class had thought any general temperance reform possible.[6] But the Jeffersonian belief in the improvability of men was strong within some of them and they liked to think of themselves as "philanthropists" or "patriots" or friends of "humanity."

4. John A. Krout, *The Origins of Prohibition* (New York, 1925), p. 112; the Presbyterian General Assembly commended the movement to the presbyteries in 1827; the Virginia Synod carried reports on local societies in its *Minutes*. The Methodist General Conference recommended temperance to its members in 1828; the Baltimore Annual Conference approved the movement in 1830; the Holston Conference also approved early but there seems to have been no approval by the Virginia Conference. The Richmond *Christian Sentinel* was a supporter in 1832 and Lucian Minor, "The Temperance Reformation in Virginia," *Southern Literary Messenger*, XVI (1850), 430, dates Methodist support from 1831. In 1829 the Virginia Episcopal Church, then under the liberal leadership of William Meade, endorsed this movement of "the Christian, the patriot, and the philanthropist" to arrest "one of the most deplorable vices." The Virginia Baptist General Associations of 1831 and 1833 heard reports on societies in six of the ten and eleven of the fourteen constituent district associations respectively; men afterwards recalled that the encouragement of temperance was one of the reasons for the establishment of the General Association.

5. Minor, "Temperance Reformation," p. 430.

6. "We recollect, indeed, only one or two conspicuous for intelligence (out of the pulpit) who, before 1830, dissented from this general opinion" as to the inevitableness of drinking. "The Temperance Reform," *Virginia Historical Register*, April, July, 1850. This article bears a close resemblance to Minor, "Temperance Reformation." Its author, "N. R.," has not been identified.

Among them were General Cocke, who optimistically solicited the co-operation of Joseph C. Cabell for "the moral regeneration of our rising countrymen"; young Lucian Minor, who opened his mind to the factual arguments of the American Temperance Society; and Thomas W. Gilmer, William M. Blackford, General William H. Broadnax, Hugh Nelson, Fleming Saunders, E. C. Carrington, William Maxwell, Thomas A. Holcombe, William Fitzhugh Gordon, and J. B. Minor. Believing that the cause was entitled to the support of all philanthropists and patriots—laymen as well as clergymen, non-Christians only somewhat less than Christians—the older workers welcomed them.[7] With their accession the Virginia Society boasted as well-rounded a leadership as any contemporary organization.[8]

From 1827 on the society was a parent organization with provision for the representation of auxiliaries.[9] Beginning in 1830 its headquarters were in Richmond since it usually chose as its secretaries men residing there and always held its annual meetings there. Its officers and the members of its board of managers, none of whom were ever compensated in any way, always included both prominent clergymen and distinguished laymen of the different denominations.[10]

7. Armstrong to Clopton, 1830, in Jeter, *Clopton*, p. 188; Minor, "Temperance Reformation," pp. 430-431; Cocke to Cabell, April 1, 1829, Cabell Papers, University of Virginia Library. Cabell did not join.

8. Cf. the Connecticut and Massachusetts Societies for the Reformation of Morals as discussed in Krout, *Origins of Prohibition*, pp. 86-91.

9. Any temperance society could become an auxiliary with the approval of its constitution and representatives at the annual meetings. There were 4 auxiliaries in 1827, 30 in 1829, 47 in 1830, but by 1834 only 7 were sending reports. Union with the Richmond Society in 1833 gave the parent society a temporary league membership and two of its best officers, D. I. Burr and James Crane. As headquarters Richmond had the disadvantages of being nearer the Tidewater where temperance sentiment was weak and too far from other parts of the state.

10. Presidents: Rev. A. B. Semple, Rev. Stephen Taylor, General John H. Cocke; recording secretaries: Rev. Abner W. Clopton, Dr. James Blair, D. I. Burr, James W. Douglass; treasurers: Rev. James Fife, William Crane, James A. Crane, Major Jesse Snead; vice-presidents: Rev. William Armstrong, Rev. William S. Plumer, Major Thomas Nelson, Dr. Lewis Marshall, Rev. A. W. Clopton; chairmen of the board of managers (executive committee): Hon. Fleming Saunders, George Woodfin; other members

Article I of the society's constitution clearly defined its work: "it shall be the only business and design of this Society to counteract, lessen, and prevent . . . the *detestable* and ruinous *vice* of Intemperance."[11] True to its own history the society insisted that the best way to accomplish this was to encourage local organizations. The *Proceedings* of its annual meetings always included reports from the locals and such pleas and admonitions to them which it felt to be proper and prudent. Its officers insisted[12] that the "circulatory influence" thus created was essential for the local groups as well as for itself. There was little that the society could do except pass resolutions defining its position and order the distributions of its own *Proceedings* and other literature such as Clopton's and Ball's *Wisdom's Voice to the Coming Generation.*[13] Little more could be undertaken because it had no income other than voluntary contributions from its members and auxiliaries. The society was limited also by Article II of its constitution, which read: "This Society, as a body, shall have no connexion with any church or association." In 1829, however, it joined the American Temperance Society with the condition of "directing its own efforts" and later the American Temperance Union. The relationship, though never organically close, served to stimulate the Virginia leaders and through them, the rank and file. To emphasize the oneness of the great movement, in 1833 the society changed the date of its annual meetings to the anniversary date of the Northern society.[14]

---

of the board: General Edward C. Carrington, Captain Fred K. Lester, Captain Thomas Holcombe, John N. Gordon, William Pope, Fleming Bates, John B. Clopton, Dr. Vohanna.

11. The italics varied in different printings.

12. E.g., *Report*, 1833.

13. Philadelphia, undated but probably 1827 or 1828. It contains the constitution, resolutions, and circular for 1827, the "constitution, etc.," of the Northern Neck Society and the literature current in the North.

14. In 1833—from October to February. Consequently there are no *Proceedings* for 1832. Much of the above information is extracted from the *Proceedings* of other years (1829, 1830, 1833, 1834) and the material in *Wisdom's Voice.*

# LESSON XVIII.

1. Con-ten'tions; *n.* angry contests; quarrels.
2. De-mo'ni-ac; *n.* one possessed by a devil.
4. Gen-er-a'tion; *n.* a race; the people of the same period.
4. De-bauch'ed; *adj.* corrupted in morals.
5. Ten'e-ments; *n.* houses.
5. In-her'it-ance; *n.* an estate received from parents.
6. Des-o-la'tion; *n.* ruin; destruction.
8. Con-so-la'tion; *n.* comfort.
8. Phi-lan'thro-pist; *n.* one who loves his fellow-men.
11. Ben-e-dic'tion; *n.* blessing.
12. Pen-i-ten'tia-ry; *n.* a house where criminals are confined to labor.
12. De-gen'er-a-cy; *n.* the state of growing worse.

---

### TOUCH NOT—TASTE NOT—HANDLE NOT.

Remark.—When there are poetical quotations in prose pieces, they should be read as if they were part of the same line, unless the sense requires a pause.

Pronounce correctly. Do not say *com-par-er-tive-ly* for com-par-*a*-tive-ly; *fre-kwunt* for fre-quent; *tem-per-it-ly* for tem-per-*ate*-ly; *scurce-ly* for scarce-ly; *ut-ter-unce* for ut-ter-ance.

1. "Wine is a mocker, and strong drink is raging. Who hath woe? who hath sorrow? who hath contentions? who hath babbling? who hath wounds without a cause? who hath redness of eyes? They that tarry long at the wine."

2. How often do men meet in good humor, then drink to excess, talk nonsense, fancy themselves insulted, take fire within, ⁺rave, threaten, and then come to blows? A long time ago, Seneca spoke of those who "let in a thief at the mouth to steal away the brains." In such a case, the stupidity of a brute is often united with the fury of a demoniac. Nay, the man among the tombs was ⁺comparatively harmless; he only injured himself. But how often does the drunken revel end in the cry of murder!

3. How often does the hand of the intoxicated man,

---

Lesson XVIII "Touch Not—Taste Not—Handle Not" typical temperance lesson from William Holmes McGuffey, *Fifth Eclectic Reader* (Cincinnati and New York, c. 1866).

The society attempted a broader and more aggressive program during the middle thirties. No doubt this was a reflection of the reinvigorated Northern phase of the movement to which prominent and wealthy men made large contributions.[15] Thomas W. Gilmer said, "That the slow progress of the cause of Temperance in this State, slow even in comparison with its progress in many other parts of the country, calls loudly upon its friends for more efficient measures than have heretofore been employed." The society voted in 1833 to hold quarterly meetings by districts, employ a full-time field agent, send delegates to the coming United States Temperance Convention in Philadelphia, and call upon the auxiliaries for funds.[16] General Cocke was elected to its presidency. The response to this program was not encouraging. The agent was appointed[17] and during a few weeks of service demonstrated in the Norfolk region the value of "circulatory influence." The societies began distribution of 150,000 copies of the *Temperance Recorder* containing the famous "Ox Sermon" which the New York Society sent to them.[18] At the next annual meeting delegates appeared from new territory, including Portsmouth and Norfolk and the western counties of Berkeley and Pendleton.

The auxiliaries sent few reports and no money, so the agent was discontinued. The expense of distributing the *Recorder* was not repaid. District meetings were not held. A rumor was circulated that there was something extraneous, perhaps politics, back of the stirring temperance organization and it was thought necessary to repudiate this idea.[19] Never-

15. Krout, *Origins of Prohibition*, pp. 146-152.
16. A Mr. Hooker, General Broadnax, and Rev. William J. Armstrong sponsored this program. Broadnax was then president of the Virginia Sunday School Union. He was an Episcopalian, a successful lawyer of Petersburg, and member of the House of Delegates.
17. Ruben D. Turner was employed as an agent at a cost of $180.
18. The sermon was probably the "Ox Discourse," between "two and three million [copies]" of which were "gratuitously distributed" in 1833. *Temperance Recorder*, Oct., 1834.
19. Resolutions were introduced by William Maxwell and B. H. Smith, the latter specifically repudiating the idea that "we can ever turn aside from

theless, the executive committee acting by the society's direction proceeded to call a state-wide convention of all the
friends of temperance, making its call coincide with that of
the Young Men's Temperance Society of Frederick County
and so merging the young men's movements with its own.[20]
The convention idea proved to be a capital one and the
society found an interested and able organizer in General
Cocke.

Unlike most Virginia temperance leaders, John Hartwell
Cocke[21] could boast of a background of inherited wealth and
culture; and unlike most Virginians of his class, he cared
nothing for politics. He earned the title of General in the
War of 1812 and for a full half-century thereafter lived the
life of a planter-baron and philanthropist at Bremo in the
Piedmont county of Fluvanna. "In power of foresight . . . the
most remarkable of all his Virginia contemporaries of his
own generation,"[22] he gave heed to all progressive economic
and social movements, attending their meetings, helping liberally in their financing, and preserving their literature.[23]
Had Virginia followed his leadership she would have remained

---

the great moral design before us to meddle with popular elections, or
connect ourselves, in any manner whatsoever, with the party politics of
the day."
20. There was a nation-wide young men's temperance movement in
1832-1833. Krout, *Origins of Prohibition*, p. 145.
21. Cocke Papers; Cabell Papers (University of Virginia Library);
both collections contain extensive and invaluable insights to the upper-class
Virginians of this day. Philip Alexander Bruce, *History of the University
of Virginia, 1819-1919; the Lengthened Shadow of One Man* (5 vols.;
New York, 1920-1922), I, 153 ff.; Armistead C. Gordon, Jr., "John Hartwell Cocke," *Dictionary of American Biography*, ed. Allen Johnson and
Dumas Malone (20 vols., New York, 1928-1936), IV, 253-254; American
Temperance Union, *Journal*, especially Aug., 1837, and *Seventh Report*;
"Letter to Gen. John H. Cocke, of Virginia, from Edward C. Delavan, October 1, 1856" (William and Mary College Library). See especially Martin
Boyd Coyner, "John Hartwell Cocke of Bremo" (Ph.D. dissertation, University of Virginia, 1961), chap. 1.
22. Bruce, *History of the University of Virginia*, I, 163.
23. Matters in which he was actively interested included: Bible societies, Sunday schools, tract societies, agricultural societies, and transportation. He was second on the board of American Foreign Missions and
senior vice-president of the American Colonization Society. He wrote
*Tobacco the Bane of Virginia Husbandry* (Richmond, 1860).

aristocratic in economic structure but with little liquor or tobacco produced or consumed, fewer and better slaves, more convenient and more artistic homes, more literature and more libraries, better farming, and vastly better transportation. Of all reforms he thought temperance was the most important. His contemporaries sometimes assigned his zeal in this to his knowledge of men as soldiers, laborers, fellow-planters; he spoke of "the mighty works of Providence," "the divine principles of our philosophy," "the cause of God, our country, and our firesides." In Fluvanna he organized one of the largest and perhaps the most efficient of the county societies, one branch of which was for slaves and free Negroes. Although busy with his lands in Alabama where he sometimes spent the winter, he became deeply involved as a director in the affairs of the James River and Kanawha Canal Company. Because of the canal project many liberals and reformers came to Bremo, among them Edward C. Delavan of New York, who also was a man of wealth and affairs and with whom Cocke corresponded long and intimately. On the canal's bank he built a "Temperance Temple" where boatmen and travelers could fill their jugs with water running from over Bremo's bluffs.[24] In 1856, at the age of seventy-six, he visited temperance leaders in the North and on the very eve of the Civil War he financed the completion of a temperance hall at the University of Virginia, an institution which he, with much practical counsel, had assisted Jefferson in erecting just before the societies began.[25]

President Cocke evidently planned most carefully for the Charlottesville Convention of 1834. The place selected was

24. "The last of my wild oats in the way of building," he wrote J. C. Cabell. The temple was dedicated to the Sons of Temperance, Sept. 19, 1849. It still stands; the pitcher has been removed to the lawn above. Cabell Papers.

25. In Fork Union was another temperance hall for which he was probably responsible. There too was the Baptist church which he left the Episcopal church to join. Oranie V. Hatcher, *The Sneads of Fluvanna* (Roanoke, Va., 1910), p. 103. On the eve of the Civil War he was a member of one of the Baptist state boards.

well adapted for bringing together men of the Valley and the Piedmont who in turn could reach the more remote regions of east and west. Able men such as Mann Page, Hugh Nelson, T. W. Gilmer, and W. C. Rives, with whom the Jeffersonian tradition of liberalism and progress was strong,[26] lived in or near Charlottesville. From Edward C. Delavan of the New York State Temperance Society Cocke obtained suggestions as to organization and a great batch of literature. Delavan particularly urged that a newspaper similar to his New York *Recorder* be established with which he thought "your state could move the whole South and West." At a preliminary meeting in the Valley, Staunton Bishop William Meade preached a strong sermon in behalf of temperance societies and pledges of total abstinence from distilled spirits, the most practical means of fighting drunkenness. The *Virginian* of Lynchburg published (along with notices of lotteries and choice wines for sale) an encouraging report from that city's society, the conspicuous members of which included R. H. Toler, who later became editor of the *Virginian* and of the Richmond *Whig*, and Captain Thomas A. Holcombe, some-time mayor of the city and state-wide temperance lecturer. It was sending a strong delegation and asking Justin Edwards, Boston pastor who was active in the American Temperance Society, to address them.

In October the convention met for three days. A total of 180 delegates were present from 38 counties. All the cis-Alleghany sections were represented. Among the delegates were 37 ministers and 18 physicians—a notable and perhaps intentional shifting away from the ministerial preponderance of the early days. General Cocke presided; Lucian Minor and Mann Page were secretaries. The vice-presidents were: Hugh Nelson who had been congressman and minister to Spain and who recently had helped in the formation of a society in Clarke (then Frederick) County; T. W. Gilmer who was

26. Armistead C. Gordon, Jr., *William Fitzhugh Gordon* (New York, 1909), pp. 65-66, 71, 113, portrays these men admirably.

to be governor (1840-1841) and secretary of the navy; Jonathan P. Cushing, the Northern-born president of Hampden-Sidney College who, in company with Rives and Maxwell, also Hampden-Sidney men, had fathered the Virginia Historical and Philosophical Society; and the self-made German, Conrad Speece, a Princeton D.D. with Washington College connections, then pastor of a great Presbyterian country church near Staunton.[27] From the national society came E. C. Delavan and Justin Edwards, authors of the American Temperance Society's much admired *Fourth Annual Report*, who were heard with interest and admiration. Many resolutions were presented and there was some "animated debate." Finally twenty of them, asserting principles "more or less important" according to a local newspaper, were adopted. One resolution significantly omitted wine in the list of forbidden drinks. Another declared the making and selling of liquor morally wrong but this was rendered less obnoxious to some by an amendment declaring that opposition to the business should be made only by the familiar "mild persuasion, sound argument, and the influence of example."

Through these resolutions Virginia temperance forces were brought into line with the national organization on the issues of the day.[28] The proceedings were ordered to be published along with an "Address" which was prepared by a committee consisting of Cocke and three coming young men, Lucian Minor, Jeremiah Morton, and William M. Blackford.[29] The Frederick Society's *Temperance Pioneer* was

27. Dr. Mann Page was a grandson of Archibald Cary and progenitor of the University of Virginia Pages. A monument was later erected and a temperance hall named in honor of Holcombe in Lynchburg. Speece was a man of great power and not a few eccentricities, among them an extraordinary capacity for tobacco chewing.

28. Justin Edwards wrote his wife that the meeting was "an intensely interesting one, and closed very happily." William A. Hallock, *"Light and Love," A Sketch of the Life and Labors of the Rev. Justin Edwards* (New York, 1855), p. 391. Cf. *Permanent Temperance Documents*, I, 342.

29. Blackford conducted the Lynchburg *Virginian* and developed a banking business; he married a cousin of Lucian Minor. Morton became distinguished as an orator and rather independent politician in Orange County.

adopted as the organ of the convention, to be published by a committee headed by Bishop Meade. In organization and procedure as well as in personnel the convention was following the recent pattern of the national society. The social elements which were so conspicuous at first were lacking. Some of the discussions reflected that the meeting was the "product" of Clopton's endeavors. And the proceedings seem to be preserved only in the files of the Baptist *Religious Herald*.[30]

Many indications of progress followed this clarifying and inspirational convention. From Bremo Delavan went to see James Madison, learned that Madison did not drink, and obtained his signature to a highly prized testimonial against liquor which President Jackson and John Quincy Adams also signed.[31] To the Baptist General Association came news of encouraging activity among Baptist preachers in the northwest.[32] At the annual meeting of the Virginia Society the next February (1835), "authentic accounts were given of many distilleries and liquor stores discontinued, through the workings of conscience or from the decrease of profits." Soon the society's executive committee concurred in a call for a district meeting at Warrenton and suggested five similar meetings— one at Martinsburg in the northwest and one at Tazewell in the southwest, regions where progress had scarcely begun. All of these, it was reported, were "numerously attended" by auditors and members. Among the members were many able

30. *Religious Herald*, Nov. 4, 1834; Lynchburg *Virginian*, Oct. 20, 1834; Delavan to Cocke, Oct. and Nov., 1834, in Cocke Papers; Jeremiah Bell Jeter, *The Recollections of a Long Life* (Richmond, 1891), p. 36; "Sermon by Bishop William Meade before the Convention in Staunton, May, 1834" (Staunton, 1835).

31. Delavan to Cocke, Nov., 1834, in Cocke Papers. Madison hesitated to sign, saying that "ardent spirit was not yet banished from his house"; but on the explanation that it was his opinion only that was asked and this for the sake of its influence upon young men and that without his signature Delavan could not go with confidence to Jackson and Adams, he signed. An early copy of the document is in Cocke's papers. It was reprinted in the *Christian Federation* in July, 1901, as a "Pledge" signed by Madison, Jackson, and Adams. See Appendix VII.

32. Baptist General Association, *Proceedings*, 1834, report of General Board.

and distinguished men.[33] Publicity and propaganda unusual for the day accompanied this activity and continued for several years. The projected newspaper began to appear under the direction of the Virginia Society's executive committee in Richmond in January, 1835. It was an eight-page monthly bearing the suggestive name of *Southern Temperance Star* and prices were such as to invite an extensive circulation.[34] In it appeared the authorized "Address," signed by Lucian Minor and Mann Page, in which the writer added warmth and color and a bit of his own observation to the arguments already familiar in the North. Delavan wrote that this address was "calculated to arouse the whole nation, and will."[35]

Just before this the Lynchburg *Virginian* published the document signed by Madison and soon afterward the arguments of the newly formed Young Men's Temperance Society of that city appeared in its columns.[36] In the Lexington *Gazette* of 1835 appeared the testimony of five local doctors that "entire abstinence by men in health, from the use of a drink, of all that can intoxicate, is a duty which a rational regard for health, makes universally obligatory"; a Presbyterian pastoral letter on the liquor business followed later that year.[37] In Richmond in December, 1836, Edmund Ruffin's *Farmer's Register* carried an article on the bad physical results of drinking cider[38] and the unprofitableness of using apples for cider and brandy instead of feeding them to man and beast. The

33. Minor, "Temperance Reformation," p. 433; Lynchburg *Virginian*, April 16, 1835. The other places of meeting were: Charlotte Court House, the Brick Church in King and Queen, and Staunton.

34. Lynchburg *Virginian*, Dec. 8, 1834; Minor, "Temperance Reformation," p. 432. It contained "many things of pith," says Minor, but "was edited and printed in so slovenly a manner as to produce little effect."

35. *Religious Herald*, Jan. 16, 1835; Delavan to Cocke, Dec. 3, 1834, Cocke Papers. Delavan read the proof.

36. Lynchburg *Virginian*, Nov., 1834, *passim*; March 30, 1835.

37. Lexington *Gazette*, March 30, 1835.

38. "Cider drinkers are peculiarly subject to rheumatism, to inflamed eyelids, to headaches, bleeding at the nose . . . [and are] the most brutish and cruel of the unhappy tribe of inebriates." Apples made into brandy brought 15 cents a bushel; good eating apples, 25 cents. Also it was pointed out that apples were excellent food for stock. *Farmer's Register*, IV (1836), 508.

Richmond *Enquirer* printed in 1837 a poem, "I've Thrown the Bowl Aside," as well as two letters from General Cocke, in 1838, arguing for higher insurance rates on steamers that sold liquor since under its influence passengers and officers often put the boilers under a pressure which modern machinery could not stand.[39] From Fredericksburg William M. Blackford offered to print pieces from the New York *Recorder* in his paper, the *Arena*.[40]

Perhaps even more significant to thoughtful men was the news published by the *Southern Churchman* and reprinted by the *Religious Herald* in 1837 that for two years the James River and Kanawha Canal Company (the state's largest business concern) had, under the direction of Cabell, enforced stringent rules to keep liquor away from its 3,000 workers.[41] Writing to John Marsh in 1837 Cocke said that his influential political friends, when he could gain their attention, were "lost in astonishment" at the results being effected. That year Henry A. Wise published his denunciation of intemperance in federal circles and the next year Senator W. C. Rives became vice-president of the Congressional Temperance Society.[42] Local activity began to pick up sharply in some quarters. Particularly noteworthy was an invasion of the Staunton distillery region through the establishment of a society at Mt. Crawford among the Rockingham Germans and another in Augusta County at Young's Chapel, where Conrad Speece preached his long-remembered final sermon,

39. Richmond *Enquirer*, April 4, 1837; Sept. 4, Oct. 19, 1838. The letters on marine insurance were written by Cocke as president of the national organization. The Norfolk and Portsmouth *Herald* also printed such items as " 'Confessions of a Drunkard' from the pen of the lamented Charles Lamb," Oct. 7, 1839.

40. Dec. 12, 1837, Cocke Papers.

41. *Religious Herald*, Nov. 3, 1837, quoting *Southern Churchman*. The company's contracts bound contractors to neither give nor sell spiritous liquor to the workmen or permit others to do so and not to employ overseers or laborers dismissed elsewhere for drunkenness or continue to employ the habitually intemperate.

42. American Temperance Union *Journal*, Aug., 1837.

"Is this thy kindness to thy friend?"[43] The number of societies and members is unknown, but the number of both was probably at a peak and far greater than in any other Southern state.[44] In 1836 Cocke became president of the American Temperance Union and Delavan wrote to him that year that the next convention of that body would be held in the South.[45] On May 14, 1840, the *Religious Herald* editorially broached the matter of a state prohibitory law, probably hoping to bring the Virginia Society's goal more in line with recent activities elsewhere in the South.

By 1836 the Virginia Society reached its zenith. Its last recorded meeting came in 1837; thereafter its status was, to use Jeter's description, one of "apathy and inactivity." The local bodies continued, some for a dozen years or more, but the period of their central guidance and cohesion was over. Lucian Minor thought in 1850 that between 1835 and 1841 "as many, probably renounced or violated the pledge, sometimes relapsing into drunkenness, as were added to the ranks. . . ."[46]

For its decline the leaders of the Virginia society were themselves partly responsible because they failed to devise adequate machinery. If they could have maintained a permanent headquarters, staff, and field men charged with continually organizing societies in new territories and reorganizing old ones as suggested by local situations, the society would have continued its usefulness. The effort would have

43. John W. Wayland, *A History of Rockingham County, Virginia* (Dayton, Va., 1912); William Henry Foote, *Sketches of Virginia, Historical and Biographical* (2nd ser.; Philadelphia, 1855), p. 481.

44. The number of societies was put at 250 in a brief report from Charlottesville in the Richmond *Enquirer*, Sept. 27, 1836. The estimate in 1835 was nearly 100 societies with 35,000 members. A fair guess for 1836 is 200 societies and perhaps 40,000 members. Daniel Jay Whitener, *Prohibition in North Carolina, 1715-1945* ("The James Sprunt Studies in History and Political Science," Vol. XXVII [Chapel Hill, N. C., 1946]), p. 62, mentions 51 societies with 4,700 members in North Carolina in 1834.

45. Dec. 7, 1836, Cocke Papers.

46. Minor, "Temperance Reformation," p. 433; Jeter, *Clopton*, p. 189; William M. Blackford to Cocke, Dec. 12, 1837, Cocke Papers.

been more fruitful if the machinery had been adjusted to the level of the great masses.

Since the decline in temperance occurred elsewhere simultaneously[47] there must have been other reasons which brought the society era to an end. Foremost among the reasons for the decline was dissension within temperance ranks brought on by the "total abstinence" question. The Virginia Society originally pledged its members only against immoderate use of ardent spirits. By 1830 total abstinence from ardent spirits was expected by state and local societies alike. The extension was due to the fixed belief that drunkenness came from moderate drinking, reinforced by the argument that total abstinence was really an easier rule to keep than moderation in drinking.

The fight over the use of wine was more long-lived. The Northern Neck Society in 1827[48] and the Falls Church Society (across the Potomac from Washington) in 1829 pledged their members against wine. Other locals quickly followed. This decision was due at first to Brande's *Manual of Chymistry*; before Brande's experiments nobody "was aware, that the various fermented liquors contained so large a quantity of alcohol."[49] To the authority of science was added the observation that some members would "doctor" their wine or pretend that brandy colored with grapefruit juice was wine, in consequence of which they became "fuddled" and brought reproach upon their society.[50] From the principle of republicanism and equal rights some argued that the rich man ought

47. James Benson Sellers, *The Prohibition Movement in Alabama, 1702 to 1943* ("The James Sprunt Studies in History and Political Science," Vol. XXVI [Chapel Hill, N. C., 1943]), pp. 27-28.

48. The constitution printed in Clopton and Ball, *Wisdom's Voice*, p. 158.

49. Clopton and Ball, *Wisdom's Voice*, p. 169, which also reprints tables to show that wines then in common usage contained up to 22.96 per cent alcohol. The tables came from the 1821 first American edition of William Thomas Brande's *A Manual of Chymistry* (New York, 1821, based on the 2nd London edition, 1821).

50. Letter from Greenbrier County in American Temperance Union *Journal*, April, 1837; letter of John C. Harris in *ibid.*, Sept., 1842.

not to have his wine if the poor man could not have his whiskey. Others contended that wine-drinking countries were noted for soberness. Wine entered into the economy of housewives; to bar it was an "invasion of the table." Its use seemed to be expressly sanctioned in the Bible and, in the opinion of some abstaining clergymen, it was by Scriptural injunction as well as by immemorial custom essential to the Communion service.

The Rev. John Kelly, in his effectively humorous style, and Conrad Speece warned against undertaking too much.[51] Bishop Meade protested that since "whiskey, brandy, and rum are the great authors of mischief," an "equal and indiscriminate warfare against things so unequal in their effects" was unwise—a view in which some physicians then and later concurred.[52] Cocke, personally convinced by the Northern leaders of the necessity of a prohibition on wine as well as all other drinks, yet remembering that "the established habits of society require more than the force of reason and the demonstration of argument to remove them at once," played for delay.[53]

One state meeting voted against the inclusion of wine in the pledge; another sidestepped by appointing an investigating committee;[54] and a third—a regular meeting of the Virginia society in 1837—reiterated the position of the first but

51. Jeter, *Recollections*, p. 36. Kelly argued for "one dose [of abstinence medicine] at a time."
52. John Johns, *A Memoir of the Life of the Right Rev. William Bishop Meade* (Baltimore, 1867), p. 249. Meade also hesitated to join the fight against wine on the grounds that it might reflect upon the New Testament use of wine in the Communion service. Speece opposed inclusion at the Charlottesville convention for both reasons. Opposition of physicians is illustrated by R. B. Barton of Rockbridge County in the Lexington *Gazette*, Feb. 12, 1836, and John P. Little, *History of Richmond* (Richmond, 1933), p. 251. Dr. Little was coroner of Richmond and ran his history first in the *Southern Literary Messenger*, 1851-1852.
53. In 1856 Delavan published his "Letter to General John H. Cocke," giving at Cocke's request a history of the wine controversy, then called the Communion question. Cocke replied and indicated his belief that it was due to Delavan's efforts that total abstinence had been adopted by the cause. He added that Christ had used unfermented grape juice. Delavan to Cocke, Dec., 1835; Cocke to Delavan, Nov., 1856. Cocke Papers.
54. The Charlottesville conventions of 1834 and 1836.

with the suggestion that locals which desired could reorganize on a teetotal basis. This suggestion already had been tried by some of the locals and was rapidly adopted by others, but it was much longer before members could "find it in their hearts to renounce cider."[55]

Men still debated the merits of total and moderate abstinence. Contention in Virginia, however, brought unrestrained condemnation on moderate drinkers and societies of the older type. Jeter remembered meetings as "attended with discussions, ineradicable discords and dissatisfactions."[56] This was one reason for the "apathy" among temperance men that brought complaints from those concerned. Leaders and members had quit work and begun to wrangle.

Another disturbing influence was entirely Northern in its origin. In the North in the middle thirties temperance came to be associated with abolition through endorsement of the new radicalism by temperance leaders and, in not a few cases, by formal resolutions identifying liquor and slavery as evils from which men must be set free.[57] Slavery in Virginia had been under suspicion among the elements from which the societies were drawing for some time.[58] Abolition was altogether a different matter and a movement for it came as a distinct shock and harmed the societies coincidentally with the wine controversy. Many a temperance leader was alarmed at

55. Minor, "Temperance Reformation," p. 433. The *Religious Herald*, May 1, 1845, tells of a three-day rally under the auspices of the Albemarle Union at which debate raged over the idea of a total-abstinence society—the heatedness of the debate owing to the fact that this was a cider-making neighborhood.

56. Jeter, *Recollections*, p. 36.

57. Cf. Krout, *Origins of Prohibition*, pp. 176-177; Connecticut Baptists, for example, resolved in 1839 that every man has a duty to be sober and a right to be free. Philip S. Evans, *History of the Connecticutt Baptist State Convention, 1823-1907* (Hartford, Conn., 1909), p. 46.

58. For example: B. Nixon, Margaret Mercer, Mrs. William M. Blackford (Mary Berkeley Minor), C. W. Andrews and wife, and others. At least six vice-presidents of the American Colonization Society before 1840 were known as active temperance men: Cocke, C. F. Mercer, Meade, Rives, and James Garland. Similarly, Dr. Thomas Massey, Rev. Jno. Early, and Rev. Robert Ryland, vice-presidents after 1840.

the company into which he was getting and at suggestions that his ardor and his associations were likely to jeopardize other good causes. Such friends of temperance as the Baptist Roanoke Association and the Methodist *Christian Sentinel* definitely condemned abolition and ceased to work for temperance.[59] Cocke wrote Delavan in 1837 in long and earnest protest against the latter's endorsement of abolition, noting the harm which it could do to their common cause in the South and West where opinion was very sensitive.[60] Connections with the national temperance society continued, but the next national convention was not held in the South as had been planned. Thereafter when leaders came from the North they were under suspicion and often this was justified.

No explanation of this temperance lull is complete without emphasis on the resistance to changing old habits from sheer inertia. The most that the societies' leaders ever claimed was a change of opinion in "many communities" and the support of the middle classes. Two incidents suggest that these claims were sufficiently strong. When Delavan, dining at Montpelier in 1834, told Dolley Madison of his abstinence pledge she "hardly knew how to take it but at last said that 'such an example was worthy of imitation' and then helped herself to some toddy and soon after to some wine." Delavan also feared that "Mrs. Cocke will not have much sympathy for me."[61] A correspondent of the Richmond *Enquirer* in 1836 told of a barbecue dinner in Halifax at which 13 "regular" toasts, 64 impromptu toasts, and "many other toasts" were "proposed and drunk, with truly Democratic zest and applause," each followed by a bit of song, after which "the company broke up in the most perfect harmony and good

59. In 1835 and 1836 respectively. The *Christian Sentinel* had previously carried a column for both slavery amelioration and temperance. Similar changes occurred in other Southern journals.

60. The original draft is in the Cocke Papers. Delavan talked with Cocke on slavery while at Bremo; so apparently had Justin Edwards.

61. Delavan to Cocke, Nov., 1834, Cocke Papers.

feeling, just about dark"; at the ensuing presidential election the Democrats won by 732 to 183![62]

Despite inertia, natural inclination to drink, and internal dissensions the temperance societies accomplished a great deal. The sentiments of the dry element of the middle class were united with the concern of some of the members of the upper class and this union was to produce much labor in the common cause. This was as far as this type of society could go. Any further work for the spread of temperance and abstinence must come from a different sort of organization with a greater stimulus for action.

62. Richmond *Enquirer*, Nov. 11, Dec. 6, 1836. The president for the day was Dr. James Snead; the vice-presidents, appropriately seated, were John C. Michie, Thomas Young, Dr. Henry Easley. The Richmond *Whig*, Sept. 27, 1836, carried an account of a dinner from John Bell in Davidson County, Tennessee, at which 17 toasts were drunk. William S. White says that the day after the election of Taylor in 1848 in Lexington "the streets . . . were filled with drinking men, and about twelve o'clock the fighting began." *Rev. William S. White, D.D. and His Times (1800-1873): An Autobiography*, ed. Rev. H. M. White, D.D. (Richmond, 1891), p. 159.

*Chapter Five*

# OTHER TEMPERANCE SOCIETIES

With internal dissensions and bickering consuming much of their efforts, the temperance societies could hardly expect to make great strides toward reforming the drinking habits of the nation. The "hard cider" presidential campaign of 1840 made obvious the decline of the temperance movement. In the same year that Martin Van Buren's champagne and William Henry Harrison's hard cider were helping unseat one president and elect another, the Washingtonians, a society of reformed drunkards organized in Baltimore, came to the rescue. The Washingtonians created quite a stir in the Northern states in the first year after their organization, but it was not until 1841 that representatives of the movement came quietly into Virginia.[1] The arrival of J. G. Pollard and W. E. Wright, members of the original group, was unheralded. As men who had "been there" they sought out the intemperate, brought them to their meetings, and set them to bringing others of their kind, telling them that they too could reform themselves. This idea was contrary to the preachment of the old societies which principally sought to save the temperate and looked upon the drunkards as quite beyond the pale. The cause of temperance now received a hearing among groups never before reached.[2]

Quite unlike the clerical or classical speakers of the societies, the Washingtonians, themselves rough men, spoke directly and harshly. Pollard's rough, deep voice reminded a contemporary of John Randolph's "kitchen knife, whetted on a brickbat."[3] Altogether the Washingtonians impressed Rich-

1. John A. Krout, *The Origins of Prohibition* (New York, 1925), describes the Washingtonians, pp. 182-222.
2. William George Hawkins (comp.), *Life of John H. W. Hawkins* (Boston, 1859), p. 66.
3. Lucian Minor, "The Temperance Reformation in Virginia," *Southern Literary Messenger*, XVI (1850), 433.

monders as something of a "novelty."[4] But the times were undoubtedly ripe for the success of their democratic procedure.
Men, particularly the working classes, proved in the presidential campaign of 1840 that they would turn out en masse
for a meeting if it had been much talked about and was likely
to be lively and informal.[5]

At the early Richmond meetings "multitudes were pleased,
convinced and fired." Pollard toured the state with Wright
early the next year and with Christian Keener in 1843. Together they covered the principal cities from Norfolk into
the Valley and were received as well in all their stops as they
had been in Richmond. Later some leading citizens sought out
and engaged John B. Gough, notwithstanding his objectionable abolitionist sympathies, for addresses in Norfolk, Richmond, Fredericksburg, Charlottesville, and Lynchburg; at
each he spoke to great audiences.[6]

Deeply impressed, Virginians both new and old in the
temperance movement sought to imitate the techniques of
the Washingtonians. Consequently the "temperance orator"
evolved. His audiences did not require—would not even permit—scientific or judicial discussion. To these men the drunkard was unfortunate, not contemptible, and the reformed
drunkard something of a hero who perhaps should become a
temperance leader. Liquor was "Demon Rum" and the great
business of a temperance speaker was to "castigate"[7] him.
Wherever these men went, on their own or by invitation, they
offered the pledge to their audiences. Believing that drunk-

4. Richmond *Star*, Aug. 26, 1841.
5. Instead of providing drinks for only the leading political elements, in
1840 the politicians distributed liquor for everybody. The crowds came
eagerly.
6. Pollard and Wright went as far as Charlottesville; Keener and Pollard
went to Charlottesville and Winchester. Keener was a Baltimore man of
affairs and philanthropist as well as a temperance lecturer. Gough found his
message on temperance well received but faced threatened attack in
Lynchburg and elsewhere because of his known abolitionism. John B.
Gough, *Autobiography* (Springfield, Mass., 1871), pp. 214-219.
7. This word was often used in reports. T. C. Johnson, associate of
Dr. Pearson at Wake Forest and at the University of Virginia, supplied
the following from the manuscript *Mu Sigma Rho Star* of Richmond Col-

ards could not stand a single drink, their pledge was always to total abstinence. And many took it. In Richmond, according to reports, 800 or 900 took the pledge; in Petersburg, 1,000, including 300 Negroes; in Charlottesville, amid "great excitement," 600 men and 100 students at the university took it. There were no reports of the number who signed privately as a "means of staying their downward career and of reinstating themselves in the confidence of their fellow citizens."[8] Nor were there any reports of the children who received from these meetings impressions that lasted through life.

Under this impulse societies of the old type quickly gave way to total abstinence societies. Actually such a movement was already in progress. As the Virginia Society declined almost to the point of ceasing to function, many of its leaders saw hope only in the direction of a movement similar to that made by the Washingtonians.[9]

Total membership in the new organization was never estimated. For a while it was probably much larger than that of the old societies.[10] In Lynchburg, a town of 6,000, there was a Merchants' Society of 1,200, a Washington Union of

---

lege, March 9, 1860:

> Ah brandy, brandy, bane of life
> Source of tumult and of strife
> Could I but half thy curses tell
> The wise would wish thee safe in hell.

8. Richard McIlwaine, *Memories of Three Score Years and Ten* (New York, 1908), p. 32.

9. *Religious Herald*, July 23, 1843. Washingtonian Temperance societies were formed first in some areas while in others older societies were revived and the name changed. One of the influencing factors in the decline of the Virginia society was Cocke's inactivity. Interested in business ventures in Alabama and suffering from a severe illness, he devoted most of his efforts in 1841 to the university situation.

10. Figures given below come principally from the current American Temperance Union *Journals* as do some of the news items. Also used: *Religious Herald*, 1841-1843, especially July 1, 13, 20, 27, Aug. 17, and Oct. 27, 1843; W. A. Christian, *Lynchburg and Its People* (Lynchburg, Va., 1900), *passim*; Oren F. Morton, *The Story of Winchester in Virginia* (Strasburg, Va., 1925), pp. 126, 217; McIlwaine, *Three Score Years and Ten*; and T. C. Johnson, *The Life and Letters of Robert Lewis Dabney* (Richmond, 1903).

600, a Cold Water Army of 250 children, and a society of 850 for colored people. In the southwest, Abingdon in 1842 had a society of 90 despite its 100 stills producing over 40,-000 gallons annually. Westernmost Lee County had 785 members in a society though the group was but a year old. These figures indicate that not only former drunkards but the numerous lower classes were reached and enrolled. The appearance of societies in the "Rocketts" and Armory sections of Richmond and the enlistment of Negroes in Petersburg and Lynchburg confirms this. Lacking any central direction, these total abstinence societies were looser affairs than the old locals had been. Certainly some had constitutions[11] but policy, in accord with the spirit of the day, was directed toward arousing enthusiasm rather than checking the habits of individual members. In the Lee County region "log-rollings, houseraisings and all public gatherings are unattended with alcoholic drinks." Especially approved were "mass conventions" accompanied by parades and the like. In 1842 and 1843 representatives of 5,000 members in nine Valley counties assembled in Winchester; in Salem a "Temperance Tea Party" with band and choir was held with 1,200 members attending; in Culpeper 1,500 people met at the courthouse and marched to the church to a dinner; in Caroline the Port Royal Guards and the Caroline Dragoons aided in a parade on the Fourth of July, the banners of which proclaimed "Freedom from the Tyranny of Great Britain in 1776. Freedom from the Tyranny of Alcohol in 1843."

Perhaps some leaders hoped that by encouraging decency and dignity on public occasions and relating temperance to the "stability of our freedom" the upper classes might be attracted.[12] Certainly some important people did become interested. An Executive and Legislative Temperance Society

11. See the "Record of the Total Abstinence Society of King William County, Organized 19th June, 1842." The record book contained Sunday School records also. About one-half the 250 members were women.

12. William S. White, "Fourth of July Reminiscences and Reflections: A Sermon."

appeared at the state capital with Robert White as chairman and 41 of the legislators as pledged members. Governor James McDowell banished liquors from the executive mansion as no governor had ever done before and he presided and spoke at a state temperance convention in Richmond in February, 1844. Immensely pleased, Marsh, of the national temperance organization, had a special edition of *Temperance Tales* encased in a rosewood box and sent it to Cocke for presentation to the Governor.[13] Cocke felt that the "upper circles of our society" which had "very generally held themselves aloof" could do so no longer.

From the university, where student rioting was notorious, nationally known Professor William B. Rogers wrote in 1842 on the organization of a student total abstinence society: "This I deem the happiest movement for the University that has ever been made. . . . You will smile at my earnestness, but in truth I know that 99/100ths of all our troubles spring from drink, and that too, generally wine. . . ."[14] For the benefit of drinkers, William Wertenbaker, postmaster, librarian, and perennial temperance "crank," kept posted in his office a pledge signed by the prominent students. Cocke announced in 1845, "The chairs of the two last remaining old wine bibbers will soon be filled by two of the most distinguished Teetotalers of the age."[15] In May, 1847, a committee of the Norfolk Total Abstinence Society established the Virginia *Temperance Advocate* which was devoted to "Temperance, Litera-

13. Marsh to Cocke, 1844. Cocke wrote Secretary John Y. Mason, June 3, 1844, asking that intoxicants be banished from the navy. Cocke Papers.

14. William B. Rogers, *Life and Letters of William B. Rogers* (Boston, 1896), I, 206. Rogers was the founder of the Massachusetts Institute of Technology.

15. William McGuffey and John B. Minor. Philip Alexander Bruce, *History of the University of Virginia, 1819-1919; the Lengthened Shadow of One Man* (5 vols.; New York, 1920-1922), II, 129, attributes the former's selection to a desire to conciliate critics of the school's lack of religious interest. One riot led to the killing of a professor of law, bosom friend of Rogers, and a temperance man. Bruce deems Cocke too severe on the Tuckers. L. C. Helderman, "A Social Scientist of the Old South," *Journal of Southern History*, II (1936), 151-154, severely criticizes Cocke and McGuffey.

ture and General Intelligence." William S. Forrest was editor and "W. Reid, Esq., agent," and judging from its general excellence it obviously was intended to reach homes of wealth and refinement.[16]

Enthusiasm subsided even while it was being aroused. In 1842 Professor Beverley Tucker warned the young men's society of William and Mary College against the temperance orators' "credulous simplicity" and "statements that stagger the imagination." Notable leaders stated flatly that temperance societies did no good. Cocke wrote that "our drinking gentry" boasted that Governor McDowell lost popularity because of his anti-liquor hospitality.[17] At the university students conducted their elections, celebrated the results in thoroughly wet fashion, and rioting again broke out.[18] No great meetings were reported for 1844-1845 and news of the societies was scarce during these years.[19]

Clearly the inertia of old personal habits and social customs did not yield easily to a treatment of enthusiasm and emotion, however generous or energetic. It was evident that some had joined for "love of notoriety to be gained by speaking" and because joining was the fashion of the hour.[20] But the new leadership had affronted many of the clergy and ranking social leaders. Endorsement of the new procedure caused Cocke, Wertenbaker, and William B. Rogers to be labeled as "fanatics" in important social circles. Others saved themselves from similar opprobrium by making their contributions in secret.[21] Among the newly interested masses, extreme

16. It was well received in good circles and was continued by W. W. Davis, Esq., says W. S. Forrest, *Historical and Descriptive Sketches of Norfolk and Vicinity* (Philadelphia, 1853), p. 232. William Reid had been a candidate for mayor and was later an active officer of the Howard Association. He was a shipbroker and a friend of William Maxwell.

17. Beverley Tucker, "Temperance," *Southern Literary Messenger*, VIII (1842), 439-440.

18. University of Virginia Faculty Minute Book, 1844, 1845.

19. The *Religious Herald* obtained no reports in 1844 and carried only five notices of societies in 1845.

20. *Religious Herald*, Jan. 23, 1845.

21. Bruce, *University of Virginia*, III, 129-133, admirably portrays events there. See also Forrest, *Sketches of Norfolk*, p. 228.

stimulation frequently was followed by sudden and violent relapses. The broad-based movement was established at the cost of being deemed extreme and spasmodic rather than solid and enduring.

From the middle forties to the Civil War the Sons of Temperance were the most active in anti-liquor activities. This national fraternal order was organized in 1842 in New York City and apparently came to Norfolk-Portsmouth the following year. In 1844 it entered the Valley from Washington, D. C., at the request of citizens of Harrisonburg.[22] Its original object was to back up the Washingtonian movement, which necessarily caused it to be a rival of the societies and other temperance organizations. The rivalry was limited, for the order did not seek everybody for membership, it did not forbid its members to belong to other organizations, and its program did not include direction of the activities of other organizations or any other sort of temperance monopoly.

According to its contemporary historian[23] the order had many difficulties to encounter and many obstacles to overcome. Men objected to the secrecy of its proceedings, to the incorporation of local units with the right to own property, and to its political potentialities. Consequently they refused to grant charters to the local groups petitioning for them. Its rivalry with the churches in the field of good works was also objected to and some churches forbade their members to join. On the other hand, many thought that the avoidance of "any union of church and work" was good. Others applauded the pledge as "democratic" in that it prohibited drinking among the rich as well as the poor.

Some members were attracted by the cash benefits of becoming temperate, some were attracted to membership by

22. *Record Book of Marshall Division, No. 3, Harrisonburg.* The Staunton Division seems to have originated through the introduction of Pike Powers (below) and others at Harrisonburg.

23. Thomas J. Evans, *A Digest of the Resolutions and Decisions of the National Division of the Sons of Temperance of the United States and of the Grand Division of Virginia* (Richmond, 1847).

the comradeship which it engendered through its secret meetings and intriguing ritual,[24] and some, especially at a later date, by its spectacular parades. Each "division" had a "Temperance Hall" which was sometimes a pretentious building erected and owned by the division[25]—an evidence of substantialness that appealed to local men of the "solid" type. In the setup of offices there was opportunity for those desiring distinction, travel, pleasant social intercourse, or pecuniary reward for active service. Accordingly, the order spread rapidly, absorbing in the process most of the societies. By 1847 there were 62 divisions with 3,000 members; by 1850, 353 divisions with 15,000 members. Each member paid a small weekly fee. In 1850 the total receipts were $48,000 whereas the total expenditures were about one-half of this sum; the accumulated surplus was $34,000. At their height in 1853 the Virginia Sons were the strongest in the South and among the half-dozen strongest in America.

The members, all white adult males,[26] were found in all parts of the state but particularly in the Piedmont and the cities. Not many were distinguished, Edgar Allan Poe being an interesting exception to the rule.[27] Some complained that the order received only the self-supporting, thereby denying the most lowly whites, as it did all the blacks, the benefits of its temperance work. They were mostly middle- and lower-middle-class people: preachers, doctors, small merchants,

24. One of their songs is given in Appendix VI.
25. A notable example was the one erected at the entrance to the university on grounds assigned by the university. William Wertenbaker proposed the building in 1852. Among the broadsides in the Library of Congress is an address (probably written in 1852) begging that contributions for the building be sent to Wertenbaker. John B. Minor was named as chairman of the committee to distribute the address, which was signed by John A. Broaddus, William M. Blackford, A. T. Goodloe, James Southall. For Cocke's share see above. The university division had been established after John B. Gough's visit, with Edmund Broadus, John B. Minor, and William Alexander apparently leading.
26. For boys there were several divisions of Cadets of Temperance, and for women at least one division of Sisters of Temperance, located in Richmond.
27. Harvey Allen, *Israfel, The Life and Times of Edgar Allan Poe* (New York, 1927), I, 169 ff.

farmers, teachers, lawyers.[28] General Cocke saw them as an "array of organized and determined men—made up of the bone and sinew of the Country—the working men with strong hands and clear heads—who will most certainly take their part in the honor of glorifying God and doing good to their fellow men."[29]

The leaders, like the members, were of the middle classes. They were usually professional or businessmen with whom temperance was a side-line, but they also were workers for, rather than patrons of, the order. Among the prominent was A. J. Cunningham, who in the early forties founded, merged, and edited newspapers in Portsmouth and Norfolk; J. M. Conrad, member of a strong Valley family, went with him to the order's national meeting in 1845. A speaker of uncommon ability who became head of the order and lectured in all parts of the state was Thomas E. Galley, businessman and Whig politician of Wheeling. William R. Drinkard, a lawyer from William and Mary, edited the Petersburg *Republican* between 1845-1850 and later became chief clerk for Secretary of War John B. Floyd. A lawyer, a Whig politician, and a great Methodist, Waitman T. Willey of Morgantown represented his section in state legislatures and constitutional conventions. He spoke often and effectively for temperance, was deemed a man of character, and was selected by the Sons to lead in western parts in the crisis of 1853. Major Edmund Broadus and his son John A. (the latter became head of the order in Virginia and a power among Baptist clergymen) were strong in the Charlottesville area. Pike Powers, Episcopalian friend of Cocke, who conducted schools for boys in Staunton and Charlottesville and later became a Richmond rector, was always active. Second only to Cocke

28. This conclusion is based in part on the Virginia Grand Division, Minutes of 1847, listing those expelled, and the Manuscript Record Book of the Harrisonburg Sons and in part on a study of numerous names met with in reports of meetings.

29. Letter to Cabell, Nov. 11, 1847, Cabell Papers.

in length and conspicuousness of services to anti-liquor was Lucian Minor,[30] commonwealth's attorney of his native county of Louisa and after 1855 professor of law in William and Mary College. Detesting the insincerity of jury practice and the rough-and-tumble of current politics, he steeped himself in philosophy and the classics from which he developed a stern personal morality and a social-mindedness that rivaled that of his friend and mentor, General Cocke. From his youth he spoke and wrote—indeed, he was the movement's penman —for organized temperance workers. The Sons of Temperance later erected a monument in Williamsburg to his memory. But these were above the average of the leaders. The capable leaders who worked unselfishly were fewer than the enthusiastic egotists who actively sought the places of influence and profit.

The organizational plan used by the leaders was simple. Each local division annually elected a "Worthy Patriarch" as its chief officer. Four times yearly these local leaders assembled as a "Grand Division," the meeting place being wherever the previous meeting had voted. At the fall session— "annual meeting"—a "Grand Worthy Patriarch," other state officers, and delegates to the "National Division" were chosen and important policies were determined. The weakness involved in annual selection of officers was avoided in the case of "Grand Scribe" and "Grand Treasurer" by a custom of re-election. Year after year Thomas J. Evans, Richmond Baptist, lawyer, and Whig, superintended routine work. He was a versatile man, fond of dabbling in politics. At the same time, H. K. Ellyson, who was even more closely identified with Richmond Baptists and Whigs, was responsible for the treasury and printing. For several years W. W. Green, "Grand Worshipful Potentate" in 1852, was "Grand Lecturer," the

30. John B. Minor, "Sketch of Lucian Minor" (MS, incomplete, undated); C. C. Pearson, "Lucian Minor," *Dictionary of American Biography*, ed. Allen Johnson and Dumas Malone (New York, 1928-1936), XIII, 27.

field man with the duties of organization, verification, and education; he seems to have filled his place well.[31]

The activities of the Sons, like those of their predecessors, centered around the pledge and its enforcement. The pledge ran: "No brother shall make, buy, sell or use any spirituous or malt liquors, wine or cider."[32] The "solemn ceremonies" that accompanied the oath were supposed to increase its binding force. Weekly meetings with their invitations, songs, and gossip probably diminished the pledged man's dependence upon the drinking places for social diversion. Discipline was fairly systematic and prompt but kindly. Yet in 1850, when enthusiasm was near its peak, over 1,500 were expelled for violation of the pledge and less than 200 of these were reclaimed on second trial.

As the societies declined in the face of new and superior attractions, however, several divisions[33] sought and obtained permission to hold public meetings and these soon became a conspicuous feature of the program. Lucian Minor's[34] planning for the Louisa division's "fete" in 1847 was interesting in that he hoped to have General Cocke and John B. Minor present, with Professor William Holmes McGuffey who had come to the university from Ohio in 1845, preaching

31. The Grand Scribe seems to have drawn $900 a year. In 1853 two lecturers were appointed at $1,800 a year, out of which they were to pay their own expenses. For difficulties see letters to W. T. Willey from T. E. Galley, Thomas J. Evans, W. R. Drinkard, dated Jan. 27, 1849, March 9, 1849, and Jan. 4, 1850, respectively; Galley wrote Willey, June 18, 1853, that a lecturer would have to collect his own salary and work harder than in a political campaign; and besides the position would not be a compliment in the common estimate. Waitman T. Willey Papers, West Virginia University Library. In 1853-1854 part of the money was forthcoming from donations; in 1854 the services of even W. W. Green were dispensed with. Grand Division *Minutes*.

32. This was officially interpreted to exclude all alcoholic and intoxicating liquors as beverages.

33. Of course there was a wide variation in the practice of the different divisions. This comes out strikingly in the reports sent in by them in 1851 to Cocke who was then a district supervisor. Cocke Papers.

34. Letter to Cocke, July 1, Cocke Papers. For meetings of the Washingtonians and the total abstinence societies see above. Since these were declining as the Sons were beginning one cannot always tell who was responsible for the public occasions mentioned.

the Sunday before. The culmination came when the National Division met in Richmond in 1852. The city was "thronged with visiting teetotalers" and after addresses in the African Church 80 members of the National Division in carriages and nearly 1,200 others on foot moved to Howard's Grove (William W. Weisinger directing them) where William R. Drinkard presided and Philip S. White spoke amid "rapturous applause" to a crowd that would not disperse even when rain fell until they heard Samuel S. Carey.[36] Similar public exercises which appealed tremendously to the youth were quite frequent after this.

The Sons also sponsored and paid for a good deal of printed matter. Printed minutes of divisions were plentiful and a *Digest of the Proceedings*, both national and state, by a youthful Richmond lawyer, Thomas J. Evans, long Grand Scribe of the Virginia division, was brought out in 1847. For a while prizes were awarded for temperance essays, one of which in 1851 went to Alexander Martin, Presbyterian minister of Hanover, and another in 1852 to Leroy M. Lee, D.D., once editor of the *Christian Sentinel* and from 1841 to 1857 editor of the *Richmond Christian Advocate* and Grand Worthy Patriarch in 1851. A total of 10,000 of these pamphlets were sent out and Lucian Minor's pamphlet of 1853 was copied 30,000 times.

Even these manifold activities did not satisfy many members, though not until later was there any serious attempt at establishing a journal of the order, perhaps because the *Banner of Temperance* which Martin and Lee successively conducted as a private venture was deemed as satisfactory as any temperance paper could be and less expensive.[37] A plan

35. Both came from western Pennsylvania.
36. Richmond *Dispatch*, June 3, 4, 1852. Neal Dow and Judge O'Neal of South Carolina were there also. A city directory of 1852 lists eleven divisions in Richmond. Headquarters of the Grand Division seems to have been transferred from Richmond to Charlottesville in 1847.
37. Martin wrote Cocke, Aug., 1849, of his desire to sell out. Cocke Papers. Circulation was then around 2,500. The Sons several times endorsed the *Omnibus* as the "organ of the order" around 1847.

for a college in the Valley-Piedmont region was projected by the Grand Division in 1847 and approved by several divisions as well as by a special committee consisting of E. J. Willis, John Tyler, Jr., and J. D. Mitchell. This proposal was abandoned the next year on Lucian Minor's insistence that such a scheme would not only injure the standing of the order with other colleges but would also lead the public to regard it "as a mere sect and perhaps an arrogant sect" and not "the catholic, diffusive thing that it ought to be."[38]

From 1846 until 1854 many ardent Sons were bent on wresting a prohibitory law from the legislature.[39] Much of the order's expansion and activity came during these six years. For a short time the order was committed to the principle of legal prohibition. Individual Sons were the leaders of the movement and naturally the public mind made no real distinction between the prohibition movement and the order. At the same time there were elements within the movement which were not happy with the methods of the Sons of Temperance. Although working for the same end they chose different means and often stood in each other's way. Chief among these elements were the churches.

Although church members played a large role in the prohibition movement, churches as such did not work for total abstinence during this period. They all were against drunkenness, although the Episcopalians had no rule on the matter.[40] Certainly the minute books of Baptist churches abound in cases of "excommunication" for the offense, as do the records of Presbyterian and Methodist churches.[41] There

38. Cocke prepared an article on the Sons as "Schools for the People." The MS bears no date. Cocke Papers.

39. This study is continued below. See Evans, *Digest: Journal of the National Division of the Sons of Temperance, 1844-1853*; various minutes of the Virginia Grand Division from 1845 to 1860; Liberty Division Minutes, 1845; University Division, *Constitution and By-Laws*, 1856; Minor, "Temperance Reformation"; Cocke Papers; Willey Papers.

40. It is not included in the list of punishable offenses in 1849-1850 in Dashiel's *Digest of the Proceedings of the Conventions and Councils in the Diocese of Virginia* (Richmond, 1883).

41. The assumption as to Methodists is based on their rule concerning

had been no general change of rules against drinking without excess since Clopton began his societies. Altogether, the working rules of the churches and the standards of the civil law were nearly the same.

There were two reasons for the failure of the churches to do more in the cause despite the temperance enthusiasm of so many church people: mundane things were not their chief interest, and church rules were deemed important according to their helpfulness to the church as an organization. To an evangelical church "conversion" was the principal thing in one's life. Since conversion was mainly a matter of surrender to God for the saving of one's soul in the Hereafter, the religion of simple-minded folk naturally was highly surcharged with "otherworldliness." Kittredge recognized the fact in a temperance address which the Virginia Society reprinted in its first days[42] and it is attested to in the hymns which the plain people loved to sing. Mundane conduct was important but, as the Dover Association said in a report on temperance in 1846: "Make good the tree and the fruit will be good." William Maxwell accordingly argued eloquently that ministers were "almost naturally as it were, and of course, the friends and patrons and inspirers of all that is good and useful in society; and it is a part of their professional duty even to foster all the virtues, and charities, and graces of life. . . ."[43]

The main duty of ministers was "Gospel-preaching" through which conversion most often came and was sustained; and when a congregation assembled it was with no expectation or desire of hearing the preacher's views on drinking or

---

drunkenness and on their similarity to Baptists in social status. Concerning Presbyterians Dr. T. C. Johnson of the Union Theological Seminary, Richmond, stated to Dr. Pearson that though they did not have a fast rule, the church was "doing more that you would think" since they proceeded through church courts which handled each case on its merits.

42. Virginia Society *Report*, 1829.

43. Dover Association Minutes, 1846; William Maxwell, *An Oration on the Improvement of the People Spoken Before the Literary and Philosophical Society of Hampden-Sydney College* (Norfolk, Virginia, 1826), p. 29.

any other temporal matter. For the mundane conduct of the individual members there were many rules to be established and enforced. Although these were deemed a valuable aid to the individual, their primary object was to preserve the internal peace of the church that made them and to enhance its reputation among non-members.[44] The churches were not free to make rules designed to aid every good cause. A regulation opposed to the interests or opinions of important members would divide the church, as current experimenting plainly showed; and one that flaunted neighborhood interests or opinions would be speedily repealed or ignored.[45]

Each denomination approached the matter in its own way. Among Baptists the Scriptures, rather literally interpreted, were an adequate guide. Such competent men as Jeter and Witt could not find modern drinking therein forbidden and when, as a means of combatting drunkenness, total abstinence was proposed as a test for church membership, the answer was apt to come as it did in the Roanoke and Goshen Associations: "Not the Scriptural means."[46] In the Methodist General Conference the restoration of John Wesley's rule against drinking came up several times, with the net result that in 1846 the conference refused even to declare moderate drinking an "inconsistency" in a church member. Rev. W. A. Smith voiced the sentiment of the Virginia Annual Conference that there was no necessity for action: the temperance reformation, said Dr. Smith, achieved its amazing results "without any aid from rules of Methodist Discipline or legislation."[47] Presbyterians preferred to leave the matter to the

44. It also needs to be remembered that the churches—perhaps because they were so young and full of enthusiasm—were spending much of their energies fighting one another through discussions of matters which modern men would call mere dogma.

45. Efforts to adopt a "test" (below) and the fate of the Wesley rule against slaveholding are illustrations.

46. *Religious Herald*, March 4, April 13, 1847; Roanoke Baptist District Association, *Minutes*, 1857; George Braxton Taylor, "W. R. Powell," *Virginia Baptist Ministers* (3rd ser.; Lynchburg, Va., 1912), pp. 12-17.

47. *Report of Debates . . . 1844*, p. 61. Adoption of this rule was apparently prevented only by a technical ruling. Smith was joined by

judgment of local church authorities without adopting a restrictive rule.

The churches were, however, doing a great deal of anti-liquor work. Though they were no longer active they continued their endorsement of both the movement and of temperance as an individual practice. In 1840 the Baptist Dover Association, through a committee of which Jeter was chairman, urged church members to abstain from ardent spirits and requested the churches to "adopt such measures, as to them may seem best, to influence their members, and the community generally . . ."; and this resolution, passed when the temperance cause was low, was followed the next year by the pledging of the delegates at the Portsmouth Association's meeting led by Eli Ball. Sentiment in the Methodist Baltimore and Holston annual conferences was so strong that they favored reviving the Wesley rule. The General Conference in 1844, though about to split into two branches, voted that its ministers give to the temperance reformation their unreserved and proper support; the Southern branch in 1846 recommended that members "unite their efforts" in its promotion. Though little more than gestures, such actions at least held up the temperance ideal.

Most ministers set an example of great moderation if not of abstinence.[48] As pastors their quiet work among members was probably great though subject to the handicap which prevented a church rule. They shone brightest when serving as missionaries. The Episcopal minister, William Duval, was always working where conditions were worst—among the tenant class in Fairfax, especially in the settlement near Alexandria known as "Hades," among the "vicious, ignorant,

---

A. B. Longstreet who said: "I have always feared that you would begin to presume upon your authority and power to operate reforms, not by the simple, Blessed power of the Gospel, but by your ideas of what will best conduce to the general interests of Methodism."

48. The prohibition on Methodist ministers still stood. At the General Conference of 1844 Bishop stated that all its members were temperance men and that he himself had not tasted a toddy for forty years.

and intemperate men and women" who assembled seasonally for packing fish in Alexandria, at the state penitentiary in Richmond, among the Public Guard and in the city's almshouse, jail, and hospital, among the factory workers of Belle-Isle. "Suggested by the immediate wants of the people under his care,"[49] Duval felt temperance and an orphanage to be the chief necessities. Presbyterian Stephen Taylor who, after service in Petersburg, became pastor of the Duval Street Church in Richmond, a missionary field, and came to be known as "Father Taylor," was ever ready to assist the temperance movement. And similarly, John E. Massey,[50] missionary of the Baptists in the Valley region, was to be so long the able representative of the common people.[51]

Relations between church people and the temperance societies were uncertain and unsatisfactory in the forties. Church endorsements were not rescinded and church buildings were available for temperance meetings; also, church leaders were often active temperance leaders. The societies, especially the Sons, were able to point to occasional cases among Primitive Baptists and some among Methodists where members were forbidden to join them or were expelled for doing so,[52] but an official historical sketch of the university

49. Cornelius Walker, *Memoirs and Sermons of the Rev. William Duval, City Missionary, Richmond* (Richmond, 1854), p. 58. Duval joined and helped spread the Sons.

50. See sketch by C. C. Pearson in *Dictionary of American Biography*, XII, 382.

51. Consulted here were the minutes of the Dover (1838, 1841), Portsmouth (1841, 1842), Concord (1842, 1843), Valley (1848, 1849, 1852), and Roanoke Baptist district associations; Virginia Synod, minutes; Richard Nye Price, *Holston Methodism* (Nashville, Tenn., 1903); and Henry Wheeler, *Methodism and the Temperance Reformation* (New York, 1882).

52. *Virginia Historical Register and Literary Adviser*, III, No. 2; the Baptist Valley Association minutes record that it had before it in 1848 and again in 1849 a query from the Cowpasture Church whether membership in the Sons was consistent with church membership; and in 1857 it put on record that the Sons had given up their enterprise as unappreciated by religious people. The Mountain Association which included Virginia counties in 1848 favored prohibiting joining secret orders but without specifically naming the Sons. James F. Fletcher, *A History of the Ashe County, North Carolina and New River Virginia Baptist Associations* (Raleigh, N. C., 1935), p. 31.

division complained of the "occasional neglect . . . by the Religious portion of the community."[53] Lucian Minor in 1845 boldly asserted that the Episcopal ministers and many of the Presbyterians in western parts were standing aloof. "More unanimous," he stated, were the Baptist, Methodist, and Disciples preachers but "in those churches the influence of the ministers for good has been far less potent than in the Episcopal and Presbyterian for evil. Among Baptist and Methodist people," he continued, "there are almost as many as among Episcopalians, and more than among Presbyterians, who turn a cold and jealous glance upon the Temperance Reformation."[54] Such jealousy was manifest in the southwest when missionaries reported to their Home Board that their societies could not stand the "competition" and forecasted a terrible relapse when the "novelty" had worn off.[55]

Further trouble came for the cause in Richmond where "extreme and violent men crowded into the ranks of the reformers and clamored for mastery." Jeter's biographer reports that "Dissension arose among the leaders" and that "Jeter, alarmed . . . came to a pause." He was joined in his doubts about the direction the movement was taking by Daniel Witt in his quiet country parsonage.[56] The contemporary historian[57] of the Norfolk region, a clergyman and an old society man, recorded that some Washingtonians and

53. Sons of Temperance, *Constitution and By-laws of the University Division* (Charlottesville, 1856).

54. In the preface to his edition of Archdeacon Jefferys' *The Religious Objections to Teetotalism*. The book was dedicated to Bishop William Meade. Cocke's copy is in the Duke University Library.

55. For missionary reactions in the South during this entire period see C. Tinsley Thrift, "The Operations of the American Home Missionary Society in the South, 1826-1861" (Ph.D. dissertation, University of Chicago, 1936).

56. William E. Hatcher, *Life of J. B. Jeter, D.D.* (Baltimore, 1887), p. 258; *Religious Herald*, May 13, 1847; William Spottswood White, *Rev. William S. White, D.D. and His Times (1800-1873): An Autobiography*, ed. Rev. H. M. White, D.D. (Richmond, 1891), pp. 158-161.

57. Forrest, *Sketches of Norfolk*, p. 228. Philip S. White, Most Worthy Patriarch of the National Division, denied any attempt of the order to control or substitute for the religious beliefs of their members; Krout, *Origins of Prohibition*, p. 213.

some Sons asserted that temperance organizations were quite adequate without help from religion, whereas "some pious men, have been led by their devotion to its objects, to neglect their religious obligations" and some asserted that the reform "should be conducted entirely by non-professors." The Presbyterian General Assembly at its Richmond meeting in May, 1847, voted in a minute drawn by Moderator Thornwell that the church, because it is a "spiritual body," could not "league itself to any secular institutions for moral ends, nor be subsidiary to associations founded upon human policy"; and that "it is a matter of Christian liberty whether connection shall be had with these or not."[58] In 1850 a large number of the ministers of Richmond held a conference at which it was stated that the temperance movement "had been too much disassociated from religion" so that ministers and other church leaders had neglected it, "thus leaving the control of it measurably in other hands."[59] It was agreed that Presbyterian, Baptist, and Methodist ministers would exchange pulpits for the discussion of temperance and that a new total abstinence society should be sponsored. But these were only indications of the churches' determination to remain part of the temperance movement.

The work of the Washingtonians and the Sons of Temperance in Virginia was the natural response of a strong native anti-liquor sentiment to stimulus from without. The base was broader than when the old societies flourished and was in conformity with the democratic feeling of the times. The real strength of the movement lay as before among middle-class people, mainly of the evangelical churches, who were interested in the practical aspects of liquor drinking. The dissension which arose within the ranks was the inevitable result of new enlistment methods and the existence of a new

58. B. M. Palmer, *Life and Letters of James Henley Thornwell* (Richmond, 1875), p. 203.
59. *Religious Herald*, Feb. 21, 1850.

organization. It involved no temperance principle but for a time it remained a reproach to the entire movement. Of all the lessons learned the most important one was that church and civic forces must unite if success were to come to the cause of temperance.

## Chapter Six

# THE LIQUOR BUSINESS
# ATTACKED, 1846-1855

When the organized anti-liquor movement was twenty years old it began an activity altogether different from the attempt to induce men to quit drinking. Beyond doubt the principal object of the new endeavor was the same as that of the old—the saving of men from the evils of drink. The new attack was against business, not against personal habits. It attempted to obtain legislation to prevent or more rigidly control the sale of liquor rather than to obtain pledges from those who drank it. This was legal coercion and before this, coercion had not seemed to be desirable.

In the late 1820's individual opposition to excessive drinking had given way to sharp temperance agitation. A rising standard of living and the spread of democracy involved hosts of citizens with American society for the first time. Evangelical religious organizations pushed the desire to reform in order that the climate of the world be made more favorable to salvation. And for those looking for something to reform, the problem of drink made an excellent target. For years the temperance movement tried numerous approaches. Individual pledging, the organization of societies, anti-liquor pamphlets of an educational nature, and mass conventions—supported by many of the churches—all had their day. But still the evil persisted.[1]

This was not unique to the temperance movement. Many reform programs were seized upon by Americans in the early part of the nineteenth century and as the century wore on the ills they strove to eradicate persisted. Anti-slavery people, those fighting for more humane laws, kinder treatment of

1. J. C. Furnas, *The Life and Times of the Late Demon Rum* (New York, 1965), has done a delightful, breezy (though of necessity sometimes shallow) coverage of the entire temperance movement.

the insane, and other such reformers, along with the temperance workers, found that the inertia and self-interest of mankind often surpassed the desire for improvement. As a result of political developments during and after the Jacksonian period, more citizens were participating in government to a much greater degree than earlier in the century. In their search for ways to achieve their goals they naturally turned to legislative means to seek laws to curtail the evils which they fought.

The retailing of liquor, a problem with which legislators had long wrestled, was to bear the brunt of the new attack. The sellers of drink ranged from the taverns of the large centers of population which catered to the aristocrats, with perhaps a separate table for the common folk, to the still house of the isolated mountain community where sales, though illegal, were commonly made. In between were the taverns of the highways frequented by an occasional visitor, passing teamsters, and the neighboring idlers and roughs, and the local "groceries" who carried liquor as a part of their stock. Wherever retailing existed there was always the possibility of occasional disturbances and the temperance workers found a ready-made sentiment to support any movement toward more rigid control.

The portion of the business facing the least restrictions and generally enjoying the greatest respect were the taverns. Though discretionary power to license them rested with the county or municipal courts, their number was determined principally by business demands. Usually there was one at the county seat, one in the important villages where roads crossed or the justices of the peace met to try warrants, and one here and there along the highways and several in the larger or more bustling places.[2]

2. In 1859, 14 of the 140 counties and one of the towns reported none. *Biennial Report of the Auditor of Public Accounts, 1858 and 1859* (Richmond, 1859). Abingdon in its beginnings had 4, Alexandria in the day of its greatness, 34. Lewis Preston Summers, *History of Southwest Virginia* (Richmond, 1903), p. 627; Mary G. Powell, *History of Old Alexandria*

Regarded by some as picturesque and romantic, the taverns were technically intended to provide food and lodging for travelers. In reality they were usually small with little room for lodgers and their existence was dependent upon the monopoly of legal selling for on-premise drinking. The tavern bar received more attention from the proprietor and most of his customers than the food and overnight accommodations which by law must be supplied. Indeed few taverns were so one-sided or so frank as one on the Morgantown branch of the Winchester-Clarksburg road whose sign read: "Tavern by William Price; Grain for Horses, Whiskey for Men."[3] "Temperance Taverns" which provided food and lodging for man and horse but no liquor to drink were late in coming and were always rare.[4]

Most taverns served as social meeting places rivaled only by the home and the church; and as a local political meeting place rivaled only by the courthouse. The proprietor, in consequence, was apt to be quite a local figure in politics as well as in business and he was sometimes a pillar of the church. Discerning travelers understood all this and spoke well of these places,[5] whereas those who observed these facts but

---

(Richmond, 1928), chap. 13. Helen Hill, *George Mason, Constitutionalist* (Cambridge, Mass., 1938), pp. 42-43, names and describes taverns. Elise L. Lathrop, *Early American Inns and Taverns* (New York, 1936), gives photographs of ante bellum inns.

3. Oren F. Morton, *History of Preston County West Virginia* (Kingwood, W. Va., 1914), p. 77.

4. William Duval stopped at "Mr. Moore's Temperance Tavern near Campbell Court House" in 1849. Cornelius Walker, *Memoirs and Sermons of the Rev. William Duval, City Missionary, Richmond* (Richmond, 1854), p. 169.

5. John Davis, *Travels of Four Years and a Half in the United States of America* (London, 1803), p. 244; Anne Royall, *Mrs. Royall's Southern Tour* (Washington, 1830), pp. 31, 65. Fairfax Harrison, *Landmarks of Old Prince William* (Richmond, 1924), II, 295, cites Rouchefoucauld-Liancourt, *Travels*, who commended Virginia taverns as "on the whole better than in the other states. Those in the back country . . . are preferable to the inns in many of the most inhabited parts of New England." Francois Jean Chastellux was cautioned by Rochambeau, however, "against sleeping at Louisa Courthouse, as the worst lodging he had found in America"; and Chastellux found Mrs. Teaze's not far away, "one of the worst . . . in all America." *Travels in North America in the Years 1780, 1781 and 1782*, rev., trans., and ed. Howard C. Rice, Jr. (Chapel Hill, 1963), II, 401.

did not understand them found nothing to appreciate.[6] Doubt-less much that was bad besides too much drinking went on in some taverns, but there was little complaint on this score—partly because the proprietor was powerful and partly because he was proud of the quality of his patronage and the good name of his place and guarded both accordingly.[7]

Producers and merchants could legally retail liquor for off-premise drinking only. The *Code* of 1849, following an act of 1822, clearly stated that the right to sell included both the farmer producing the fruit or grain from which the beverage was made and the distiller who produced the actual drink. All restrictions on its sale were removed except for the requirement that no drinking be allowed on the premises.[8] There are no reports of the number of producers who retailed, but it seems safe to assume that the majority of them did so at one time or another.

The economics of production were such that the grower who possessed his own distillery could make handsome profits. When Ruffin's *Farmer's Register* in December, 1836, argued against growing apples for production into brandy the warning was meant only for those who sold to the professional dis-tiller. For the man who made his own whiskey a good side-line profit was possible—especially if he increased his business by allowing discreet drinking behind the still house. Even to the small farmer who produced goods for his own consump-tion, the right to distill was a precious one and any move toward restriction was likely to raise much protest. The sav-

6. Frederick Law Olmsted in Norfolk had to spend most of the time in "the stinking bar-room, where the landlord, all the time, sat with his boon companions, smoking and chewing and talking obscenely." He found a similar place in Petersburg. *A Journey in the Seaboard Slave States* (New York, 1856), pp. 74, 304, 306.

7. Lyon G. Tyler, *Williamsburg, the Old Colonial Capital* (Richmond, 1907), p. 53; Charlottesville *Jeffersonian Republican*, March 3, 1886 (a historical account); for another view, see Lynchburg *Virginian*, March 13, 1851, March 23, 1854, concerning the "Three Jolly Pigeons."

8. E. G. Swem, *A Bibliography of Virginia* (3 vols.; Richmond, 1916-1955), Pt. 2, lists items indicating an attempted taxation of stills in 1795 (item No. 7841), and prohibition on retailing ardent spirits by distillers in the 1841-1842 legislature (item No. 11882).

ings involved in production for self-consumption or the profits for sale were never excessive: the price of whiskey per gallon was only about one dollar, and an average acre of grain, plus considerable labor, could be made to yield only from 20 to 40 gallons of "good merchantable whiskey."[9] Even so there was usually a ready market either in the immediate locale or a nearby town and stills were numerous among the Scotch-Irish and the mountain folk. The eastern southside counties were known as "brandy counties" and in 1814 a license tax was paid on 197 stills and 492 vehicles in the counties of Essex, King and Queen, and King William.[10] Besides the thousands of stills, larger ones producing primarily for the market gradually began to appear until in 1850 the census noted 60 "establishments" with a capital of $100,000, employing 131 men, using 330,000 bushels of materials, and producing 879,000 gallons of whiskey and 5,500 barrels of beer.[11]

More conspicuous in the annals of the day were those licensed as merchants with the liquor retailing privilege. Their number in 1859 was more than 2,000 of a total of 6,634 merchants licensed that year. They were found in all the cities and counties except in mountainous and far-western regions where the still house probably satisfied drinking requirements.[12] These were most often complete mercantile establishments with liquor as only one of the many items carried. Such

9. A Gloucester County contract of 1793 called for six quarts from each bushel of corn and buckwheat and eight from each bushel of rye. The distiller probably kept the rest of the product as his pay. *William and Mary College Quarterly*, 1st ser., V (1896-1897), 175. For varying drinks and prices and an inventory of plantation equipment see Appendixes IV, VIII.

10. Lists of James Garnett, collector, loaned by Dr. Garnett Ryland.

11. William Waller Hening's still near Staunton was the first to be widely known. C. Tinsley Thrift, "The Operations of the American Home Missionary Society in the South, 1826-1861" (Ph.D. dissertation, University of Chicago, 1936), p. 166.

12. See the contemporary tax law and the Auditor's *Report* for 1859, which gives the total revenue derived thereunder. Two or three counties in the Southside had no licensed liquor merchant though they did have ordinaries.

were the big-city and rural merchants as the large Easley store of Halifax County, whose books show occasional charging of liquor. Such also was Courtland Cabiness of Franklin County, who for over thirty years occasionally credited or debited poor neighbors for small quantities as one part of a rural merchant's many-sided business.[13]

Somewhat different were those who catered principally to country people who came to town on Saturdays or special occasions for a good time as well as for their necessities. Moncure D. Conway remembered one such establishment from his childhood and the warnings given to little boys to stay away from its neighborhood.[14]

With others the sale of liquor was the main thing, though perhaps food was stocked as an added attraction—"groceries" they were called. Here, very often, liquor was drunk in violation of the establishment's license:

over the door of the cabin was a sign, done in black, upon a hogshead stave, showing that it was a "grosery," . . . a dramshop. . . . At one end . . . was a range of shelves, on which were two decanters, some dirty tumblers, a box of crackers, a canister, and several packages of paper; under the shelves were a table and a barrel. At the other end of the room was a fire-place; near this, a chest, and another range of shelves, on which stood plates and cooking utensils. Between these and the grocery end were a bed and a spinning-wheel. Near the spinning-wheel sat a tall, bony, sickly, sullen young woman, nursing a languishing infant. . . . In a corner . . . sat a man, smoking a pipe.[15]

Even more objectionable than permitting on-premise drinking was selling to slaves. This was done extensively, as

13. Easley and Cabiness account books, University of Virginia Library. Cabiness is not among those licensed in 1853 (the auditor's report from some of the counties show those licensed in 1853). His personal property as listed was above the average.

14. Moncure D. Conway, *Autobiography, Memories and Experiences* (Boston, 1904), p. 14; Ann Royall found forty-one "groceries" in Lynchburg in 1830. W. A. Christian, *Lynchburg and Its People* (Lynchburg, Va., 1900), p. 103.

15. Olmstead, *Journey in the Seaboard Slave States*, p. 73.

is shown by numerous petitions, laws, newspaper reports, proposals in lodges, and private correspondence[16] which speak against the practice. The first anti-liquor resolution presented to the Sons (1846) concerned selling to slaves.[17] In 1852 William Maxwell suggested to Cocke that petitions to the legislature against the practice would be a good way to arouse interest and secure support for the drive against the business among the planters.[18] There is little evidence that the practice was universal and it was never alarming.[19] A good part of the 2,626 merchants whose annual sales in 1859 were less than a thousand dollars retailed liquor illegally. Such conduct constituted a local nuisance, which gave ground for local hostility. On the other hand, each legal retailer had his own social and political strength. The total pressure was for the status quo.

The use of liquor was so interwoven with the economic and social life of the day that even the churches were unable to maintain a position of antagonism. With Wesley's severe indictment back of them, the Methodist conferences in Baltimore and Sussex, Virginia, boldly voted in 1780 and 1783 to "disown our friends" who would not cease to make or sell liquor.[20] This was too strong an indictment for most Methodists, however, and from 1790 to 1800 there was no

16. Lexington and Richmond incidents and the Strawberry Association's resolutions of 1852-1853 are mentioned below. John H. Russell, *The Free Negro in Virginia, 1619-1865* (Baltimore, 1913), mentions the early petitions, pp. 98, 160, 163; later ones are mentioned in the House *Journals*, 1852-1853, 1854-1855.

17. Presented June, 1846, on instruction of the Barboursville (Orange County) Division.

18. Maxwell to Cocke, July 26, 1852, Cocke Papers.

19. The plantation records of Thomas Massie show no trouble over a period of thirty years. Cocke seems to have mentioned the matter only in reply to Maxwell's suggestion. The Richmond *Enquirer* printed nothing about it in its daily account of criminal cases in Richmond city courts. Though drinking by slaves was a problem, it was regarded as a matter for the individual master to handle as he saw fit.

20. "Poisoners-general" who "murder his majesty's subjects" and "drive them to hell like sheep," Wesley said of liquor dealers. Daniel D. Dorchester, *The Liquor Problem in All Ages* (New York, 1884), p. 105. John James Tigert, *A Constitutional History of American Episcopal Methodism* (2nd. ed.; Nashville, Tenn., 1904), pp. 112, 132.

rule at all. From 1800 to 1840 a person selling was to be disciplined if "anything disorderly be transacted under his roof." This was interpreted as an endorsement of a well-conducted business.[21] Among Baptists the Dover Association in 1822 had called "Public Grog Shops a pest" and in the 1840's certain militant members were about to establish "test churches." The Presbyterian General Assembly bore testimony against the traffic as "a fruitful source of abounding iniquity and misery" and in Lexington James C. Wilson circulated a pastoral letter on the subject in 1835.[22] The Holston and Baltimore Methodist conferences favored restoring the old rule and so did a strong minority of the Virginia Conference.[23] Nothing came of all these rules because church authorities, as a Methodist bishop reportedly explained, did not wish to "intrude upon the proper religious or civil liberty of our people." Important Baptist preachers, among them Henry Keeling and J. B. Jeter, stoutly contended that properly conducted liquor-selling was one of their rights.[24] Such entrenchment was strengthened by political considerations.

In 1846 a report of the Baptist Dover District Association stated that "your committee cannot agree in stigmatizing

21. "Let the Methodist rum-sellers and their apologists hear . . . ." *Christian Herald*, May 30, 1834. Ministers were forbidden to make or sell on pain of losing official standing after 1817; and this rule was extended to elders and deacons in 1850.

22. "Dear friends, will you not suffer us to be earnest and importunate when the dearest interests of individuals, of families, of the church of Christ, and of our country, are so deeply involved? . . . and abandoning this business in all its forms, permit the gratifying intelligence to be circulated . . . that there is not one member . . . who is engaged in the manufacture or sale of ardent spirit." Lexington *Gazette*, Oct. 30, 1835. William Spottswood White, *Rev. William S. White, D.D. and His Times (1800-1873): An Autobiography*, ed. Rev. H. M. White, D.D. (Richmond, 1891), p. 160.

23. Lynchburg *Virginian*, Nov. 3, 1853; *Religious Herald*, Nov. 17, 1853. The Baltimore Conference vote in 1833 was 87 to 2. James Edward Armstrong, *History of the Old Baltimore Conference* (Baltimore, 1907), p. 236. The *Southwestern Christian Advocate* (Nashville) in 1842 was strong against the business; see also Richard Nye Price, *Holston Methodism* (Nashville, Tenn., 1903), *passim*.

24. Henry Wheeler, *Methodism and the Temperance Reformation* (New York, 1882), chap. 3, *passim*; *Religious Herald*, March 4, 1847. Keeling was first editor of the *Religious Herald*.

as infamous, a practice licensed by the laws of the state."[25] To do so would be deemed by many an interference in the political sphere and was forbidden by a principle commonly accepted by the Baptists and the Presbyterians. Virginia Methodists, on the other hand, hesitated to take a strong stand against selling liquor at least in part because their leaders saw a connection between such selling and slaveholding. Wesley laid down a rule against both practices and if one rule was upheld the other must be. In the forties many favored restoring both rules, but when Virginia sentiment toward slavery changed, the majority apparently feared that if a General Conference could forbid liquor-selling to its constituents it might in the same way attack the problem of slavery. This was the view of Rev. W. A. Smith, the able president of Randolph-Macon College (1846-1866) and editor of the Richmond *Christian Advocate*. Smith, supported by Bishop Early, president of Randolph-Macon's board of trustees, opposed any action against making and selling liquor in the same way that he supported slavery and secession— by constitutional and Biblical arguments.[26] Whether for these or for other reasons, the rules of the churches did not hamper their members in making and selling and those engaged in

25. This statement came in an attempt to levy a charge of immoral conduct against a member engaged in making and selling liquor.

26. The influence of the slaveholding Southside may have been reflected in this for Randolph-Macon was then located in Mecklenburg County. Dr. Smith's *Lectures on the Philosophy and Practice of Slavery* (1860) are an example of the Christian justification for slavery in the South. His willingness to abandon worthwhile connections when they countered his beliefs is further indicated by the fact that he was one of the leaders in the movement to divide the Methodist church when the national organization refused to expunge everything in the discipline attacking slavery. Bishop Collins Denny in his introduction to the "Diary of John Early," *Virginia Magazine of History and Biography*, XXXIII (1925), 166-172, shows how influential Bishop Early, a resident of Lynchburg, was in civil affairs and in the building of Randolph-Macon. Rev. L. Rosser, another prominent leader, voted in 1853 to restore the Wesley rule but in the next year was chairman of the General Conference committee which recommended that no change be made in the rules of the M. E. Church, South, although five states asked for a specific rule against selling and using liquor.

the business could point to this as justification of their position.

The business was not immune to attack despite its own strength and the apathy of the churches. The old societies usually did not put either selling or making liquor in their pledge. Cocke in 1832 conformed to current rules of neighborliness so far as to accompany a temperance report with a bottle of homemade brandy[27] and it was half a century later before other good members gave up the exchanging of their fruit for a share of its distillation. Respectable members differentiated sharply between retailers who sold "indiscriminately" and those who were prudent as well as obedient to the law and they refused to condemn the latter.[28] But some old societies worked to redeem men from selling. Their convention of 1834 voted that the business was morally wrong and the Young Men's Temperance Society of Lynchburg, formed in 1835, put selling ahead of drinking in its indictment of the liquor evil and pledged its members not to participate.[29]

Such hostility was not unnatural even if the abuses of the trade be passed over. The temptation of the selling place was usually foremost among the complaints of the workers. Drunkards readily testified to such temptation and temperance workers usually blamed it for the relapsing of the pledged. This temptation became stronger as drinking shifted from the home to the public place along with the shifting of population to towns and villages. Moreover, some dealers put up open and active opposition to the temperance movement: by serving brandy colored with grapejuice when wine was permitted to the pledged, by inveighing against teetotalism as contrary to true temperance, by rejoicing in and perhaps

27. P. R. Gilmer, letter to Cocke acknowledging the gift, Cocke Papers.
28. Clopton had condemned "places of drunkenness," not selling places in general. Jeremiah Bell Jeter, *A Memoir of Abner W. Clopton* (Richmond, 1837), p. 179. The Upper King William Society in 1829 said that "the indiscriminate retailing of ardent spirits is inconsistent with the cause of temperance."
29. Lynchburg *Virginian*, March 30, 1835.

abetting the relapse of drunkards trying to reform, and occasionally by personal attack or threat of attack on temperance workers.[30] For these reasons the Sons of Temperance pledged their members not to participate in the business in any manner. Even so, the idea of legal compulsion beyond reasonable regulation was generally repudiated. The convention of 1834 specifically limited permissible opposition to argument and persuasion. The Lynchburg young men said that "experience has fully proved that it [the liquor evil] cannot be arrested by law." The Washingtonians had not advocated legal action nor had the Sons.

At the Virginia Society's Charlottesville convention of 1834 Justin Edwards unsuccessfully urged legal prohibition. He argued that since scientific studies showed liquor to be seriously injurious to health and of no compensatory advantage the state had a right under its police powers to prevent its manufacture and sale. Referring to the matter six years later, the *Religious Herald* suggested that "the time has now arrived in which it may dispassionately be discussed. Public opinion," it continued, must first be enlightened and "general acquiescence" obtained, for "to pass it against the will of the majority would be useless. It would either be speedily repealed, or be evaded."[31] Subsequent consideration in neither case was more than casual and incidental to happenings elsewhere with which the many subscribers to Delavan's *Recorder* and American Temperance Union's *Journal* were well acquainted.[32] In 1844

30. *Religious Herald*, July 13, 1842; American Temperance Union *Journal*, Sept. 1842; Third National Temperance Convention, July 27, 1841, *Proceedings* (Cocke's address); John B. Gough, *Autobiography* (Springfield, Mass., 1871), pp. 211-222.

31. *Religious Herald*, May 14, 1840; the idea of legal aid to temperance was advanced in 1834 in the *Southern Rosebud* which in turn had borrowed it from the *Christian Examiner*. Christian Keener, "Diary," Nov. 1834. (Prof. F. P. Dunnington, Keener's grandson, made available to Dr. Pearson the seven volume diary. This, along with Prof. Dunnington's other papers, appears not to have survived.)

32. John A. Krout, *The Origins of Prohibition* (New York, 1925), pp. 262-296, conveniently summarizes the movements toward legal prohibition. In 1838 Massachusetts passed the fifteen-gallon law (prohibiting the sale of drinking alcohol in quantities of less than fifteen gallons), Tennessee prohibited selling in taverns and stores, and the "Flournoy

Cocke wrote, "we are not prepared for legislation in any form." But he added, "we shall be prepared for action before long," counting upon stimulus from New York State where the Sons were agitating for a local-option law and the movement, growing broader and managed by Delavan, was to succeed in 1845.[33]

Instigated by the news from New York, widespread and unco-ordinated outbursts of anti-liquor sentiment began in 1845. In January a long petition against local selling was unsuccessfully presented to the Lynchburg city council. In Richmond a local group led by Samuel Reeve and James B. Crane arranged an engagement with John B. Gough in February. To the *Religious Herald* came historical sketches of the societies and reports of their current doings along with the Christmas reflections of a Richmond lawyer on the profitableness of the works of liquor to him.[34] In the Piedmont Lucian Minor imitated Delavan by bringing out at Charlottesville an edition of Archdeacon Jeffreys' *Religious Objections to Teetotalism.* Cocke, who was in Alabama in February, received a note from Jeremiah Morton announcing his intention to speak on temperance. Dr. G. P. Holeman of Spring Garden proposed Gough and William Maxwell to conduct a rally at Fork Union.

In several areas, but especially in the Piedmont, agitation broke out over the selling of liquor by church members. This agitation soon led to the formation of churches among the Baptists which tolerated no seller ("test" churches) and which seriously disturbed the peace of the churches in such Baptist citadels as Richmond, Caroline, and King and Queen.[35] Out in the northwest where societies were few and the Sons hardly

---

movement" against licensing in Georgia failed; in 1839 Mississippi passed a gallon law and a South Carolina movement against licensing failed.

33. American Temperance Union *Journal,* March, 1844, in which Cocke mentions a Virginia Temperance convention (unidentified).

34. *Religious Herald,* April 3, 1845.

35. Cocke Papers, 1845, contain many references to the renewed agitation.

begun, Waitman T. Willey assembled a temperance convention.[36] January 15, 1846, the *Religious Herald* printed "Licensing Dram Shops. Why not Leave It To The People?" The legislature, the author thought, would readily grant, to any village that would ask for it, the privilege of deciding the matter by popular vote. Gough spoke on "The Traffic" at Lynchburg, Richmond, and elsewhere.[37]

In June the Grand Division of the Sons, on motion of Cunningham of Norfolk and Willis of Orange, recommended that the divisions obtain signatures to a memorial for a "law that no license be granted for the sale of ardent spirits." By August the Barboursville correspondent of the *Religious Herald* claimed for Orange County, as against the neighboring Albemarle, the honor of having "weeks ago" started the movement to strike from the code all licensing laws. In October the Baptist Dover Association led by Rev. Scervant Jones[38] of the Williamsburg region denounced license laws as a "violation of the laws of God . . . and discreditable to the age." The association voted that "the axe must be laid at the root of the tree by the strong arm of the law" and appointed a committee to take the matter up with the next legislature.

Concurrently the General Conference of the M. E. Church, South, voted to "recommend to the members of our Church, to unite their efforts in promoting the great Temperance

36. "We would have sent a delegate to your Temperance Convention, but temperance is out of the question here. May the tide of feeling be reversed speedily." J. I. Moore to Willey, from Waynesboro, July 14, 1845, Willey Papers.

37. William M. Blackford, recently named editor of the Lynchburg *Virginian*, reported Gough's Lynchburg visit to Cocke. Blackford to Cocke, June 15, 1846, Cocke Papers.

38. Once lawyer and legislator, now pastor of the feeble Williamsburg Church which he served earnestly and gratuitously from his nearby plantation. His reputation for humor and eccentricity is illustrated by a "grace" which Jones is reputed to have rendered when faced by a scrawny chicken on the dinner table (Dr. Pearson recalled the story from his childhood):

> Lord, bless the Owl that ate the fowl
> And left the bones for Scervant Jones.

Reformation now in successful operation."[39] Early next year (1847) at least four public meetings of Richmonders were held. At these meetings it was formally resolved to petition the legislature for a special poll by towns, to urge other places to endorse this course, and to approve a suggestion from Norfolk for a state temperance convention.[40]

Seeking to give unity and definiteness of objective to the anti-license sentiment so aroused, in December, 1847, and again in 1848 Richmonders assembled two state-wide conventions and organized the Virginia General Association. The group had an impressive list of prominent men participating in its management and seemingly should have made a great impact on the community. Cocke, Governor McDowell, and Lucian Minor served as presidents in successive years and John Tyler, Jr., was the first secretary.[41] McDowell and Tyler did not attend the meeting in 1848 and Minor, who afterwards spoke disparagingly of the management, was incapacitated after a fall from a horse in 1849. The movement was too much an affair of Richmonders and of clergymen, particularly Baptist and Presbyterian clergymen. It did not receive adequate publicity and its work was hindered further by an action of the Sons rescinding their approval of petitioning "in a Divisional capacity." The Sons and apparently many

39. General Conference *Journal* (1846), pp. 59-61. The Presbyterian General Assembly, meeting in Richmond in May, 1847, was cold to the movement but left the individual member free to participate as a matter of Christian liberty. "Minutes" (1847).

40. *Religious Herald*, Jan. 23, May 1, 22, June 19, 26, Aug. 28, Sept. 4, 11, 1845; Jan. 15, Aug. 13, 1846; March 11, 18, April 29, May 7, 1847.

41. Cocke and McDowell were already known for their temperance work. Tyler was sometime secretary to President Tyler and assistant secretary of war and was also a member of the Sons. Additional leaders were William Sands, English-born owner and editor of the *Religious Herald*, who served as chairman of the finance committee; Captain Charles Dimmock, Massachusetts-born West Pointer, commander of the Virginia Public Guard since 1839, superintendent of the State Armory, manufacturer of small arms, who presided at the preliminary meeting; Episcopalian missionary William Duval who had interested Dimmock in temperance and was named corresponding secretary in 1847; Scervant Jones who presided at the two conventions; Rev. Stephen Taylor, Presbyterian, now of Petersburg. Cocke was present and effective at all the meetings. *Religious Herald*, Nov. 4, Dec. 28, 1848; Lynchburg *Republican*, Dec. 20, 1847.

others still felt that non-interference with civil and legislative affairs was the best policy.[42] So, despite the work of Cocke and the support of the *Religious Herald*, the movement died —a casualty of poor direction and lack of unity in public opinion.

The incitement for the next and the greatest pre-war temperance effort came from Maine.[43] A large portion of the Richmond clergy met in early 1850 and voted that temperance was lately "too much dissociated from religion," with the consequent neglect of the subject by ministers, "leaving the control of it measurably in other hands." They then formed an association so that Methodists, Presbyterians, and Baptists could exchange pulpits for temperance sermons.[44] Also in 1850, the character and literary talent of Lucian Minor, who was recovering from a serious illness, opened the columns of the *Southern Literary Messenger* to his informed historical sketch of the "Temperance Reformation in Virginia." Concurrently William Maxwell ran a similar article in his new *Virginia Historical Register*. With over a hundred new divisions in 1850-1851 the Sons were definitely prospering. They were awarding prizes for temperance essays, two of which went (in 1851 and 1852) to Presbyterian and Methodist ministers. In early 1851 discussion of licensing broke out in Lexington and other places.[45] Such happenings indicated an abiding interest in temperance rather than any likelihood that the great public participation of 1846-1848 would be repeated. In May, 1851, came the Maine legislature's state-wide prohibitory law. Lucian Minor wrote Cocke that the news "fired" him and soon he was busy in Fluvanna against licensing as well as illegal selling.[46] Virginia's neighbors, Maryland and North Carolina, organized strong anti-

42. *Proceedings*, 1847; *Southern Churchman*, March 17, 1848, a reprint from the *Banner of Temperance*.
43. Krout, *Origins of Prohibition*, pp. 291-294.
44. *Religious Herald*, Feb. 21, 1850.
45. Lexington *Gazette*, Feb. 13, 1851.
46. Minor to Cocke, Aug. 18, Dec. 7, Dec. 11, 1851, Cocke Papers.

license movements.[47] But Virginians were slow to move. The Richmond clergy made no move for a law. The Sons were still committed against one and Evans wrote privately[48] of the order's coming to a halt.

Things began to move early in 1852. In Lynchburg, where there had been agitation over licensing before, the *Virginian* of March 13 spoke editorially of the "almost unrestricted traffic" and suggested enforcement of the already existing laws as an answer to the problem. In Lexington public meetings considered petitioning the legislature for more stringent laws with most of the leaders, including outstanding figures at the Virginia Military Institute and Washington College, favoring such a course.[49] The National Division met in Richmond in June. From his contacts there Cocke received new inspiration.[50] Whether by design or fate, the succeeding happenings were rapid, unifying, and aggressive. First in Winchester, in the northern Valley where Lutherans, Presbyterians, Episcopalians, and Northern Methodists lived together in comfort and the roads still gave easy access to men and movements of Pennsylvania, Maryland, and northern Virginia, A. J. Smith and other Sons promoted a Temperance Mass Convention (July 1 and 2, 1852).

Neal Dow and P. S. White, national leaders in the cause, could not come, but able local men participated, especially C. W. Andrews, the liberal rector in nearby Shepherdstown.

47. *Religious Herald*, Feb. 26, 1852; Daniel Jay Whitener, *Prohibition in North Carolina, 1715-1945* ("The James Sprunt Studies in History and Political Science," Vol. XXVII [Chapel Hill, N. C., 1946]), pp. 20, 34.

48. Thomas J. Evans to Willey, Oct. 9, 1852, Willey Papers.

49. Lexington *Gazette*, March 18, 1852. Among those mentioned in the *Gazette* as active in the movement are: George Junkin, J. T. L. Preston, John L. Campbell, William S. White, Jacob Fuller (principal, Lexington Classical School), J. P. Jordan (iron manufacturer and Lexington postmaster under Fillmore), McDonald Reid, and J. B. Dorman. Others probably included Francis H. Smith (founder of V.M.I.) and T. J. (Stonewall) Jackson. Jackson and Preston were sons-in-law of Junkin, who had come from Maine by way of Ohio.

50. Cocke to Cabell, June 21, 1852; Delavan to Cocke, Feb. 12, 28, 1852; Peyton Harrison to Cocke, May 31, 1852; Mrs. William Maxwell to Cocke, July 26, 1852. Cocke Papers.

The convention listened to a notable address by Andrews, roundly condemned the existing liquor laws as a failure, and voted participation in a forthcoming state temperance convention.[51] The latter followed quickly in Staunton, further up the Valley.[52] Over a hundred delegates from 36 counties attended and some of them were from the northwest where the Sons had recently made great progress especially around Morgantown and Clarksburg. For four nights and two days large crowds were attracted.

Even yet the participants in the movement had not settled on the best plan of attack to follow. They heeded neither the suggestion of the Lynchburg *Virginian* concerning stricter enforcement of existing laws nor the call of the Strawberry Baptist District Association that trade with the Negroes be the primary target. Despite the impact which the adoption of prohibition in Maine made on the movement in Virginia and the fact that the Lexington meetings called for such a program, the convention simply asked that local popular approval be required before licenses were issued.

Lucian Minor was appropriately chosen as leader.[53] Back in 1849 Cocke had written Cabell that the "High Church" clergy disdained "the auxiliary efforts of Common Christian Moralists" and in June, 1852, that "the Bishop [Johns?] is cold" though an abstainer from strong drink. Perhaps influenced by the views of Bishop Alonzo Potter of Pennsylvania (well and favorably known in Virginia as a friend and correspondent of Bishop Meade), the *Southern Churchman* edi-

---

51. Smith to Willey, June 11, 1852, Willey Papers; *Proceedings* of Temperance Mass Convention . . . Winchester, Virginia, July 1 and 2, 1852. Cornelius Walker, *Memoir of Rev. C. W. Andrews* (New York, 1877); Andrews came from Vermont to tutor, became a protégé of Bishop Meade (whose niece he married), and assumed a position of great local influence. He was opposed to slavery and favored public education. Important also were R. W. Barton, Rev. A. H. H. Boyd (Presbyterian), and Robert Y. Conrad (Methodist).

52. Strawberry District Association *Minutes*, 1852.

53. Minor had proposed a popular referendum in 1846.

torially announced its approval.[54] C. W. Andrews followed by engaging in joint debate with opponents in the Winchester region.[55] Only Catholics and Primitive Baptists among the church bodies could be called positively antagonistic. Though the Sons at their October meeting in Lynchburg did not line up as insiders had expected,[56] work went on during the winter and spring of 1853 through the press, preachers, and local ratification meetings.[57]

In August, 1853, came the decisive state temperance convention at Charlottesville. The highly respected John B. Minor presided. Led by a well-balanced Committee on Business[58] this body set its seal of approval on the stand of the Staunton convention and laid plans for an advance on the next legislature. All the members[59] of the strong central committee then named were Sons. This order already was publishing Lucian Minor's *Reasons for Abolishing the Liquor Traffic*. In October, at Winchester, came its formal repeal of Galley's "Norfolk resolution" of 1851 (D. J. Woodfin of New Canton leading) and its formal commitment of the order to "a Prohibitory Law." R. G. Staples of the Norfolk region

54. See *Southern Churchman*, Aug. 19, Sept. 2, 1852, and Feb. 16, 1854. Cocke to Cabell, Nov. 7, 1849, June 21, 1852, Cabell Papers. Alonzo Potter, *Drinking Usages of Society, Being the Substance of a Lecture Delivered in the Masonic Hall, Pittsburg, April 5, 1852* (Boston, 1852). E. C. Delavan, *Temperance Essays* (New York, 1869), p. 130, quotes Potter as saying that the future abatement of the drinking evil depends on whether "the educated, the wealthy, the respectable, persist in sustaining the usages which sustain it?"

55. Walker, *C. W. Andrews*; one opponent was Dudley Tyng, an able politician who "retreated," p. 104.

56. Evans to Willey, Oct. 9, 1852, Willey Papers. The North Carolina Sons at about the same time approved such a law. Whitener, *Prohibition in North Carolina*, p. 88.

57. Activity existed in Caroline, Fluvanna, Powhatan, Monongalia, and Hanover counties. The last had organized with Nathaniel Earnshaw and Dr. George W. Pollard, president and secretary, and named delegates to the Charlottesville meeting. Richmond *Enquirer*, July 8, 1853. For Reilley's address in Winchester see below.

58. Rev. I. S. Tinsley (Baptist, once pastor in Danville), John A. Paine of Lexington, Rev. B. M. Smith of Staunton (Presbyterian), A. S. Lee of Richmond (Methodist), Rev. P. Fletcher of Jefferson, Colonel C. Martin of Prince William, and Daniel Dobson of Petersburg.

59. For names, see below.

protested, fearing politics; and Galley in Wheeling, peeved and sulking, said, "Let the people drink and go to Hell."[60] The action at Winchester was popular for a time and helpful to anti-license. On the surface at least, all the forces of anti-liquor throughout the state were at last united and organized. The management was in the hands of Sons of Temperance, which included ministers as well as laymen and local workers as well as theorizers.

From these various conventions came resolutions which in 1847, 1848, and 1853 were worked into memorials to the legislature.[61] As set forth by Lucian Minor in 1853-1854, the objective was a law prohibiting the sale of liquor within the state but effective only in such counties and cities as should declare for it by a popular vote.[62] After a fashion this coincided with the view of many that the code of the commonwealth should not give countenance to "the Traffic" and also the more general view that popular approval should be obtained before licensing was prohibited. The argument for such a course was based on the economic and social damage done by liquor. This was stated in various ways at different

60. Silas Burns of South Wheeling to Willey, June 11, 1852, Willey Papers; *Proceedings* of Temperance Mass Convention; Staunton *Spectator*, Aug. 11, 1852; *Proceedings* of State Temperance Convention, Aug., 1853.

61. Lucian Minor, "The Temperance Reformation in Virginia," *Southern Literary Messenger*, XVI (1850), 435-437, gives in part the memorials of 1847 and 1848. The former, which Captain Charles Dimmock probably drew, asked only for a popular vote; it was presented to the House and is recorded in the *Journals*, p. 135, as asking for a local-option law. The latter, drawn by Lucian Minor, asked for such consequent action "as would become . . . the Legislature."

62. As printed and preserved in the Virginia State Library this petition asked the legislature "to enact a law, prohibiting within this Commonwealth, the sale or barter of any intoxicating liquor, except for sacramental, medicinal and mechanical uses, under such penalties, and with such provisions as will make the law effectual; especially providing, that all intoxicating liquors found to be kept for sale . . . shall be destroyed; and with further provision that the law shall not take effect until it shall have been submitted to the voters of Virginia, at the polls; when, if a majority of them in every county or city shall approve the law, it shall be in force throughout the State; but if approved by majorities in some of the counties and cities, it shall be in force in those counties and cities only." The manufacture as well as the sale of liquor was covered by the Charlottesville resolution on which this petition was based. It appears from the memorial that only one election was anticipated.

times: once as a grievance greater than all the persecutions of the past, including the tyrannies of George III, and once in 1848 as the cost of one-third of the lunatics, one-half of the crime, and nine-tenths of the poverty; in 1853-1854 as "an amount of pecuniary waste and loss, of destruction of property, injury to health and morals, of domestic misery, and of violence, pauperism and crime greater than any one, or all of them put together, of many practices forbidden by present laws." "The *making and selling* of liquor," the memorialists of 1853-1854 insisted, "being the manifest and *easily removable* cause . . . should no more be permitted than the many other practices which are sternly prohibited. . . . A State . . . is bound . . . when practicable, to protect her people."

The law which the leaders asked for in 1853-1854 affected neither manufacturing for one's own use nor importation from without the state and so could scarcely be called a prohibition act. It was based on the New York law of 1845 and did not at all embody the Maine idea of legislative determination for the whole state. Even so, both friends and foes habitually spoke of it as the "Maine Law."[63]

In addition to the memorials, argument for the proposed law took a wider range, but the dominant note was still that of social statesmanship. Abstract questions such as the state's ethical right to license or the philosophy underlying a prohibition of drink by statute were avoided.[64] Propositions such as the damage done by drink to church efficiency or to immortal souls were rarely emphasized. Little was said of law violation under the regulatory system lest men should rise to make the point that they would be satisfied if only "indis-

63. The Richmond *Whig*, Feb. 12, 1852, printed a letter of Delavan to Cocke stating that neither New York nor Virginia was ready for the Maine Law. For the precise details of the Maine Law see Krout, *Origins of Prohibition*, pp. 291-294.

64. "Mind you, it [the proposed law] interferes with no man furnishing himself and getting drunk in his own House. This would be invading a privilege held sacred with us at present." Cocke to Cabell, June, 1852, Cocke Papers.

criminate selling" were prevented.[65] Nor was there much mention of concern to save the lower classes from exploitation or from their own heedlessness and ignorance.

Above all, the selfish interests of the opposition were exposed. Cocke published a letter from Delavan showing excessive retailers' profits which must have enraged thrifty customers. W. Timberlake questioned the right of the brandy-making counties to dictate policy for the whole state.[66] Lucian Minor turned with bitter scorn upon the upper classes, the people of wealth, intellect and character, because on pretext of defending personal liberty they opposed a measure beneficial to the masses. C. W. Andrews, claiming that the middle classes were the "bone and sinew" of the state, boldly asserted their right to have a law which they wanted, implying a lack of interest or concern in the privileged classes.[67] There were always estimates of the cost of liquor to all the taxpayers, accounts of fortunes squandered and health and efficiency impaired.[68]

Concerning the prices charged by the retailers, Cocke warned all Virginians that if the middle states adopted a policy of prohibition, prices would increase to the point that

65. An execption is a resolution of the Temperance Convention in Winchester in 1852: "That if the laws of Virginia were intended (as they undoubtedly were) by forbidding promiscuous sale and confining it to a few by special license to confine the sale thus, then the laws have utterly failed."

66. Delavan's statement was reprinted from the *Whig* by the *Religious Herald*, March 11, 1852. It was apparently made in reply to an inquiry as to the wisdom of restricting selling to wholesaling to heads of families. He estimated the profits on beer at 200 per cent, on whiskey at 400, and on wine at 500. Timberlake was a Methodist minister of Carter's Bridge Post Office, Albemarle County. *Southern Planter*, March, 1854.

67. Minor, *Reasons for Abolishing the Liquor Traffic* (pamphlet, n.p., 1853); Rev. C. W. Andrews in *Proceedings* of the Temperance Mass Convention.

68. Minor put the yearly cost at 1,500 deaths, direct expenditure of five million dollars, and the indirect loss of as much more through loss of time, bad management, and so forth, more than 2,000 declared paupers and a countless number of other impoverished people, four-fifths of the murders and misdemeanors, 20,000 habitual or occasional drunkards and their brutality to their families and the consequent break-up of homes. *Reasons, passim.* Occasional pieces in the Richmond *Enquirer* and the Norfolk and Portsmouth *Herald* were along the same lines.

Virginians would not be able to maintain themselves "under our present drinking habits."[69] He wrote to Cabell: "There is no man who would not go heart and hand in keeping the Negroes and the overseers sober." Lucian Minor listed a "throng of sorrows," adding, "far the most numerous and most torturing of those pangs have wrung female hearts. . . ." With a belief in the natural goodness and sense of men so characteristic of his group Minor asked, "Search your memories . . . and say if a vast majority [of sorrows] . . . are not directly traceable to the Liquor Traffic." With the curious belief that if the voters approved a law it would certainly accomplish its object, he concluded: "You, People of Virginia, by one word, can put an end to the annual repetition [of such troubles]. . . ."[70]

Along with the debating went plans for pressure on the legislature of 1853-1854. The state temperance conventions entrusted this work to a central committee[71] of which Minor was chairman in 1852 and Cocke in 1853 and 1854. The committee, imbued with the idea that the voters were really on its side, relied principally upon an extensive signing of a printed petition. Preparatory to this in 1853 the convention's request that county committees be set up was sent by Thomas J. Evans to every active temperance man in every county;[72] 30,000 copies of Minor's *Reasons for Abolishing the Liquor Traffic* were also distributed that year. Owners of secular newspapers contributed some space, though Cocke complained severely of the "political press" of the capital city. Temperance

69. Letter to the Editor, Richmond *Whig*, Jan. 18, 1852.
70. Minor, *Reasons*; for the connection of women with the movement, see below.
71. In 1852: L. Minor, S. K. Taylor, R. H. Gambill, P. Powers, and J. Cross; in 1853: Cocke, Samuel Reeve (Richmond), Dr. R. A. Ree (Henry), A. S. Lee (Richmond), L. Minor, John A. Paine (Lexington), Rev. B. M. Smith (Staunton), Daniel Dodson (Petersburg), Thomas J. Evans, Rev. P. Fletcher (Jefferson), C. Dimmock (Richmond).
72. Evans to Cocke, 1853, Cocke Papers. Members of several local committees are named in Richmond *Enquirer*, July 8, 1853, and the *Religious Herald*, Jan. 13, 1853.

and church journals did more since their fields of special interest demanded it.[73]

Both Minor and Evans thought it essential to have agents through whose "domiciliary visits" access might be had to the minds of the adverse or the lukewarm. As Minor wrote Cocke in May, 1853, "What with the 80,000 men and women in Virginia who cannot read, and the twice 80,000 who will not read or cannot understand and appreciate, it is very few after all, who can be approached by the Press." A great deal of work of this sort was done by W. W. Green as he went about the state lecturing and organizing divisions for the Sons of Temperance[74] and some, no doubt, by Minor and Evans.

The cost of this work was borne by the Sons through their regular payroll.[75] The labor of obtaining signatures to the petitions fell to the plain people, mostly Sons, who could expect no material reward. They worked as much as weather and health and, especially, time would permit.[76] Voters signed in astonishing numbers—15,000 of them in 1853, in 92 counties and towns. Richmond's list numbered over 1,500 with the names of Revs. George Woodbridge, R. B. Howell, and J. B. Jeter foremost; H. K. Ellyson presented it to the legislature. Petersburg sent in a petition of 800 signatures. The longest

73. The temperance newspapers (which apparently were not widely read) included: the *Teetoller* of Richmond in 1843, the Richmond *Star* in 1844, the *Virginia Temperance Advocate* in 1847, and the longer-lived *Banner of Temperance* and Richmond *Omnibus*.

74. Minor to Cocke, Cocke Papers; in the year 1853-1854 Green delivered 195 addresses and secured 1,323 signatures to total abstinence pledges. *Minutes*, Oct., 1854. Willey was chosen for similar work in the west but did not accept.

75. The conventions did almost nothing financially. Apparently $182 was collected at the first convention. In 1853 the delegates to the convention promised that their counties would contribute more than $2,000 of which only $545 materialized. Duval was appointed General Agent in Aug., 1848, but seems never to have served. He was, however, helpful as agent of the Tract Society. Walker, *Duval*, pp. 106-154. An experiment with agents was reported to the convention of 1854.

76. This account is made up principally from the petitions of 1853 preserved in the State Archives Room in Richmond and occasional notes accompanying them.

and best lists came from Fredericksburg, Lynchburg, Winchester, and from Hanover, Campbell, Frederick, Smyth, Dinwiddie, Augusta, and Wythe. Clark and Warren were poorest among the counties, the Tidewater and the Southside among the sections; the Kanawha region did well. The "Macs" were few but German names were frequent. On the whole the signatures were those of good, steady men who wrote their own names without the blurs and blots of the lowest classes or the marked individuality of the distinguished.

A careful check of the Richmond list discloses that not over one-fifth of the "substantial business men" signed and lawyers, doctors, and city officials were also quite shy.[77] There were exceptions, of course; many names on the Rockingham list are in the same handwriting. In Richmond B. W. Leigh and J. Hampden Pleasants signed. Astonishing as the lists were, fewer than half of the voters of Richmond, Petersburg, and other places wanted prohibition. Some signed to be with a mainspring which was good and unselfish and some signed so that they might not injure their business and some from mere carelessness. Besides, the petition was only for an election.

Although there was much front porch and tavern talk[78] and the lists reflected the sentiment of many, the opponents of prohibition did not trouble themselves. In Frederick County the Winchester *Virginian* presented its position by representing a Negro, in the droll fashion of his race, who argued that to keep liquor away was wrong, for liquor was innocent— it was the abusers of liquor that ought to be "lawed."[79] Others applauded Jesse Hargrave, well-to-do farmer of Sussex County, who argued irately that "this crusade . . . gotten up

77. A total of 200 names of business and professional men (eliminating known liquor dealers and ministers) were checked against over 1,000 signatures on the petitions. Helpful here was H. K. Ellyson's *Richmond Business Directory, 1845* (Richmond, 1845) and *Richmond Advertisements* (Richmond, 1851).

78. Cocke recorded in his diary, Jan. 22, 1854, that a neighbor was declaring his intention of moving from Virginia if prohibition was enacted.

79. Lexington *Gazette*, April 1, 1852.

by certain fanatics" would destroy private property which in five counties of the southside annually produced as much income as tobacco did in the five best tobacco counties.[80]

The thought of others went deeper. In 1842 Professor Beverley Tucker told the young men of William and Mary College that the acquisition of self-control should be their great objective. In February, 1848, Henry Washington, son-in-law to Tucker and successor to Thomas Dew at William and Mary, wrote in the *Southern Literary Messenger* without any mention of prohibition that Virginia was not adapted to "social progress" or "social amelioration" because the principles on which her institutions were based required individual activity and pursuit and forbade "all limitations upon this which were not essential to the great ends of social organization."[81]

Five years later "Layman"[82] in an able pamphlet protested against prohibition by either church or state. The proposed law, he thought, was really intended to prevent drinking even though some of its proponents were willing to permit importation or the use of homemade liquor. It was, therefore, contrary to the Bible, to the influence of which English people owed so much of their superiority, and was also a gross invasion of personal rights.[83] The "reform," he continued, was, like abolition, women's rights, anti-Bible societies, and Latter Day Saints, a product of the "prurient philanthropy

80. Sussex County tax returns, 1853, 1854. The estimated income from brandy in a good year was between $3,000 and $4,000 in the five counties. Southampton led. *Southern Planter*, Nov., 1853, March, 1854.

81. The article is signed "H. A. W., Westmoreland County." "The Social System of Virginia," *Southern Literary Messenger*, XIV (1848), 65-81.

82. *The Layman's Argument Against the Interdiction of Intoxicating Liquors by Church or State* (n.p., 1853). The author is unknown.

83. In North Carolina it was argued: "morally and physically man is a free agent, and any law which seeks to control his volition is an insult to his dignity and understanding. . . . Man's right to the use of the gifts of God is a fundamental doctrine"; surrender of this right would "change him into a mere automatic machine. . . ." N. C. Legislature, 1854-1855, Committee on Propositions and Grievances on Temperance Memorials, *Report*.

of the present day." Sharing the same view, R. M. Garnett tersely described the proposed law as "a bantling of Northern Yankees and Slavery agitators—an insolent intermeddling with private rights and privileges."[84]

Concerning enforcement, "Layman" argued that the proposed law would be "wholly insufficient to lessen the evils of intemperance" because nothing would be easier than to manufacture liquor in small quantities secretly and the most orderly of citizens would wink at such violation of so unreasonable and unpopular a law. Repeal would come, though perhaps not until bitter efforts at enforcement failed. This was the serious view also of the Richmond *Enquirer* which in January, 1854, declared: "The law would be evaded, or its enforcement attended by such outrageous invasion of private rights as to make it intolerable."[85] Less dictatorial in tone but even more dangerous because it tended to divide and confuse temperance forces was the Lynchburg *Virginian*'s argument[86] that the legislature should assume entire responsibility for a law and that none should be enacted until the "force of public opinion is so strongly and so permanently in its favor, that a legislature may expect to be supported in such action, and thus some guarantee afforded that it may be carried out."

The outcome of the appeals to the legislature and the people was not to be determined on the merits of the discussion alone. "Politics" also came to be one of the major considerations. In earlier days the support of leaders in this field had not been overlooked. Cocke had written Cabell in 1838 of his hope that "our despised Cause has risen to the rank of claiming attention with our big-wig worthies of the South" and much had been made of Governor McDowell's stand.[87] Still it was not desirable that the cause should be combined

84. *Religious Herald*, March, 1854. Reported by J. E. Massey.
85. Quoted in the Richmond *Whig*, Feb. 7, 1854.
86. Lynchburg *Virginian*, April 6, 1854.
87. June 13, 1838, Cabell Papers. The letter was sent to Albany in care of Delavan.

with "the party politics of the day."[88] The principal leaders had not abandoned this policy now that legislation was being sought. Some of them were not interested in politics and those who were kept the two interests separate. Their thought was that the politicians would accede to the demands of "such an array of organized men," bent only upon good in this as in other matters of ordinary legislation.[89]

In this spirit Cocke solicited the aid of the Whig Cabell and rejoiced at the adhesion of Democrat William H. Cook. Cocke apparently believed the editors of both the *Whig* and *Enquirer* "not unfriendly."[90] And in 1851 the Sons' Grand Division, on motion of the Whig Galley, formally reprobated "making total abstinence a test in the qualifications of candidates for office, thereby perverting the pursuit of its objects, and virtually making it the basis for a political party. . . ."[91]

Such altruism was beyond most politicians even in ordinary times and these years were not ordinary. Badly shattered by defeat in 1851 and 1852, the Whigs were in need of a new organization and a revised program. Many of them, along with some Democrats, were drifting into secret Know Nothing societies for purposes which no one precisely stated.[92] Democratic leaders knew that leading Whigs liked progressive and reforming measures and had effectively accused them of thinking poorly of ordinary people. They reflected that temperance leaders were more often Whigs than Democrats.[93]

88. Resolution of Rev. B. W. Smith, Virginia Temperance Society *Reports*, 1834.
89. Cocke to Cabell, Nov. 7, 1849, Cabell Papers; C. W. Andrews address in the Winchester Convention *Proceedings*.
90. Undated MS in Cocke Papers; "Sobriety" in the Richmond *Whig*, Feb. 7, 1854.
91. No Virginia attempt to require such a test has been found.
92. Henry T. Shanks, *Succession Movement in Virginia* (Richmond, 1934), p. 48; J. P. Hambleton, *A Biographical Sketch of Henry A. Wise* (Richmond, 1856), p. 86; Constance Gay, "The Campaign of 1855 in Virginia," *Richmond College Historical Papers*, I, No. 1 (1916), 7-8.
93. Henry H. Sims, *The Rise of the Whig Party in Virginia, 1824-1840* (Richmond, 1929), p. 144. Dr. Sims finds no temperance influence in the rise of the Whigs. Dr. Henry Shanks notes no temperance cross-current in his *Secession Movement in Virginia*. During the period of their chief interest in temperance the following were probably Whigs: Cocke, the

Clearly some Democrats believed the issue to be taking on party overtones. On July 8, 1853, the Richmond *Enquirer* observed that, "In many parts of the union, even in some counties of Virginia, the Maine Liquor Law is becoming a prominent Whig principle." The idea seemed to unite discordant elements "upon the broad cold water platform" in the hope that cold water would do for the party what hard cider had done in 1840. The *Enquirer* implied that the movement was also associated with reforming radicals and agitators.[94] In commenting on the call for a world temperance convention it remarked, "It is supposed and hoped that Virginia will not be present on that occasion" because of the connection of Horace Greeley, Joshua Reed Giddings, and Lucy Stone. Cocke and N. A. Sturdevant protested against the *Enquirer's* snap judgment and explained that the radicals were not the ones responsible for the meeting.[95] Cocke privately expressed relief that the cause had shaken off the "bold intruders" who tried to make it the "stepping stone of a new political party."[96]

The Whigs for their part did not seem anxious to take up the cause under the name of the party. Whig editors though more cautious were hardly more favorable than the Democrats. Good local leaders in the temperance movement who were also good party men could not but pause, and defections from the cause were numerous.

In the legislature the procedure adopted with respect to the memorials foreshadowed the course of many years to come. The first of them were referred to regular committees

Minors, Maxwell, Rives, the Broaduses, T. W. Gilmer, S. M. Price, Lewis Marshall, H. K. Ellyson, Thomas J. Evans, W. T. Willey, J. T. L. Preston, and Landon C. Berkeley. Probably Democrats were: Broadnax, Governor McDowell, John Tyler, Jr., E. F. Paxton, D. C. De Jarnette, William H. Cook, and T. J. Jackson. Wise changed from Whig and temperance to Democrat and anti-license law. Mentioned most often as opponents by Cocke were T. J. Randolph and the Tuckers. Cf. Percy Scott Flippin, *Herschel V. Johnson of Georgia* (Richmond, 1931), p. 55.

94. Richmond *Enquirer*, July 26, 1853. Similar charges were made in 1853 in North Carolina. Here the gubernatorial candidates agreed to a hands-off policy. Whitener, *Prohibition in North Carolina*, pp. 95 ff.

95. Richmond *Enquirer*, Aug. 23, 1853.

96. Undated MS, Cocke Papers.

and they reported in routine fashion that it was "inexpedient to grant the request." In 1853-1854, with the petitions pouring in, at the instance of D. C. De Jarnette of Caroline[97] and H. K. Ellyson of Richmond, the House voted by a slender majority to turn the matter over to a special committee.[98] On this committee those who favored permitting a popular vote had a distinct majority but action was delayed so that the committee was unable to report. In refusing to permit a popular vote on licensing most legislators probably were expressing their preference for the existing system. "The chief reason assigned," wrote "Sobriety," was "that it is deemed inexpedient to legislate on the subject in any form, lest it should lead to making a political, or test question in elections."[99] Whigs and Democrats agreed on this point at least.

At Lynchburg, August 17, 1854, the ante bellum no-license convention movement made its "last great expiring effort."[100] With the general elections near, the leaders of the Sons indignant and threatening, and the Know-Nothing societies increasingly active,[101] the secular press gave unwonted

97. Here the Washingtonians still had organizations and the Sons were flourishing. *Religious Herald*, Jan. 13, 1853. The De Jarnette family stood high in Caroline and intermarried with the Reids of Norfolk. D. C. De Jarnette served the House of Delegates until 1858 when he was elected to Congress as an anti-administration Democrat. He later served in the Confederate Congress. Marshall Wingfield, *History of Caroline County, Virginia* (Richmond, 1924), p. 424. He was something of a political philosopher; W. G. Bean, "Anti-Jeffersonians in the *Ante Bellum* South," *North Carolina Historical Review*, XII (1935), 103-124.

98. House *Journal*, 1847-1848, 263; 1853-1854, 181, 308, 316; Senate *Journal*, 1853-1854, 237; Richmond *Whig*, Jan. 24, 1854. The western counties were the strongest for it. Speaker Crutchfield of Spotsylvania favored it. Of the committee members only two (from Norfolk and Alleghany) opposed it.

99. In Richmond *Whig*, Feb. 7, 1854.

100. Petersburg *New Kaleidoscope*, cited in American Temperance Union *Journal*, Feb., 1855; Virginia *Sentinel* (Alexandria), *passim*; Richmond *Dispatch*, Aug. 21, 1854; Abingdon *Virginian*, Sept. 2, 1854 (reprinting the Lynchburg *Virginian's* account). J. B. L. Logan of Roanoke presided. George W. Purkins of Halifax was chosen president and George W. Phillips of Petersburg, William H. Cook of Carroll, Major Preston of Lexington, and George W. Mathey of Alleghany, vice-presidents.

101. At the April, 1854, meeting A. J. Smith spoke of the "outrage sought to be committed by the legislature" against the signers of the petitions. He said that "the great battle of *Legal Prohibition*, at no very distant

attention. Knowing the strong sentiment against radical action within[102] as well as without temperance ranks, the Committee on Business proposed the development of anti-license law leagues in all the counties, whose object for the time would be mainly educational. Led by the Methodist minister George E. Neff of Washington County and the recently converted William H. Cook of Carroll County, the western representatives were for making a prohibitory law a test in the coming elections. Neff's motion to this effect, debated morning, afternoon, and night, once actually passed. Eventually it was recommended that temperance men organize their counties with a view to electing members of the General Assembly and members of the county courts (but not state-wide officials) favorable to a prohibitory law. Back in their home counties temperance men soon took the sense of the voters at the polls in five western counties with very favorable results and the same thing happened a little later in some of the towns.[103]

At the Democratic state convention of 1855 temperance societies were rated along with Know-Nothings as a "damnableness" which had to be fought; and the Democrats won. Accordingly in the legislature of 1855-1856 a resolution for a popular referendum, introduced by Landon C. Berkeley of Westmoreland and Richmond counties, was summarily disposed of. With a show of impatience the legislature also turned down resolutions both for easing and for tightening the licensing process.[104] The temperance advocates' movement to obtain legislation to control the selling of liquor failed. Such radical action was not acceptable to a majority of Virginians either within or without the temperance cause.

---

period, is to be fought on the soil of this Commonwealth" and advised preparation to use the ballot box if necessary.

102. In King and Queen at an organizational meeting Elder R. F. Stubbs spoke for a prohibitory law and committees, county and district, were set up. Colonel Alexander Fleet, the county's most important man, was made president and Fleet, "unlike most temperance men, is opposed to further legislation upon the subject." *Religious Herald*, July, 1854.

103. Abingdon *Virginian*, Sept. 2, 1854.

104. House *Journal*, 1855-1856, 73, 169, 265.

*Chapter Seven*

# ON THE EVE OF THE
# CIVIL WAR

After years of temperance agitation liquor was still easily obtained over the entire state. Certainly some parts were wetter than others, but the evidence is meager in most other matters. Unlicensed selling with the sellers hard to convict and escaping with light or no penalties, less care in the selection of licensees especially in such places as Richmond and Norfolk, the requirement of an oath from retailers to abide by the law with respect to Negroes and the speedy repeal of this enactment—such things indicated something of a breakdown in the old regulatory system. Yet this was not new but newly recognized because there were at hand sentiment and leadership to uncover it and attempt remedial measures. The *New Kaleidoscope* of Petersburg emphasized that in many parts it was the "settled belief still, that to good fellowship, good living and good society liquor is indispensable."[1] General Cocke admitted that the custom of offering it to guests still prevailed "in the upper tendon and the lower sinks of vulgarism."[2] A "great, fine Virginian practioner" prescribed for visiting English journalist W. H. Russell "a powder every two hours, with a mint julep"—a prescription which Russell followed for a month.[3]

From Goochland, "X" wrote to the Richmond *Enquirer*[4] that, whereas a few years before drinking's "destruction seemed almost inevitable," now the temperance societies had been "annihilated" and the drinkers were "daily increasing." It was a matter of record too that neither the state's highest

1. In American Temperance Union *Journal*, Feb., 1855.
2. Cocke's Diary, Cocke Papers. He also recorded in 1854 that in Washington "a cant phrase is common here when a drunken party is proposed—is to close the doors and go into executive session."
3. William Howard Russell, *My Diary North and South* (London, 1863), II, 267.
4. Feb. 2, 1858.

court nor some Sons of Temperance saw harm in one's taking a social drink while serving as a juror.[5] George W. Bagby humorously confirms these views.[6]

Yet Cocke insisted that the custom of offering liquor to guests had vanished from "the best society" and the *Virginia Conductor* thought that "a very wholesome temperance sentiment prevails in the state."[7] Certainly there were many personal abstainers who daily radiated, in the language of the old societies, "the influence of a good example." Among them, according to the Richmond *Enquirer*,[8] were one-third of the members of the legislature of 1857-1858 and joining them were the coming great soldiers, Lee, Jackson, and Stuart.[9] Daily men entered the ranks of abstainers; some had never tasted liquor because they had taken the pledge as children. One learned to read from McGuffey's *Readers* and in "Mc-Guffey" one learned about intemperance.[10]

Editor Roger A. Pryor of the Richmond *Enquirer* sought to insult and damn his rival of the *Whig* by calling him a "drunken bully," a "scribbler under the habitual inspiration of refuse whiskey."[11] At the university "the chairs of the last remaining old wine bibbers" were filled by "two of the most distinguished Teetotalers of the age."[12] There Cocke was

5. *Reports of Cases Decided in the Supreme Court of Appeals of Virginia*, rep. Peachy R. Grattan (33 vols.; Richmond, 1845-1881), VIII (1856), 675.
6. George W. Bagby, *John M. Daniels Latch-Key* (Lynchburg, Va., 1868), *passim*.
7. Sept., 1858.                    8. Oct. 1, 1858.
9. Jeb Stuart at twelve promised his mother (an Episcopalian) never to drink. He became a Methodist as a result of evangelical services while a student at Emory and Henry College. John W. Thomason, *Jeb Stuart* (New York, 1930), p. 18. Robert E. Lee "carried a bottle of the fine old whiskey" through the Mexican War and then "sent it back to my good friend that she might be convinced that I could get on without liquor." He did the same in the Civil War. J. W. Jones, *Life and Letters of R. E. Lee* (New York, 1906), p. 442; and Douglas Southall Freeman, *R. E. Lee, A Biography* (4 vols.; New York, 1934-1935), IV, 281.
10. See the *Third* and *Fifth Readers* of 1853. Mark Sullivan, *Our Times; The United States, 1900-1925* (6 vols.; New York, 1927-1935), II, 12, 41-42, discusses the influence of McGuffey.
11. Richmond *Enquirer*, Aug. 1, 1856.
12. Cocke to Cabell, Aug. 11, Sept. 29, 1845, Cabell Papers. Cocke ex-

# THE WONDERFUL ADVANTAGES

## OF

# DRUNKENNESS.

---

IF you wish to be always thirsty, be a *Drunkard;* for the oftener and more you drink, the oftener and more thirsty you will be.

If you seek to prevent your friends raising you in the world, be a *Drunkard;* for that will defeat all their efforts.

If you would effectually counteract your own attempts to do well, be a *Drunkard;* and you will not be disappointed.

If you wish to repel the endeavours of the whole human race to raise you to character, credit, and prosperity, be a *Drunkard;* and you will most assuredly triumph.

If you are determined to be poor, be a *Drunkard;* and you will soon be ragged and penniless.

If you would wish to starve your family, be a *Drunkard;* for that will consume the means of their support.

If you would be imposed on by knaves, be a *Drunkard;* for that will make their task easy.

If you would wish to be robbed, be a *Drunkard;* which will enable the thief to do it with more safety.

If you would wish to blunt your senses, be a *Drunkard;* and you will soon be more stupid than an ass.

If you would become a fool, be a *Drunkard;* and you will soon lose your understanding.

If you wish to unfit yourself for rational intercourse, be a *Drunkard;* for that will render you wholly unfit for it.

If you are resolved to kill yourself, be a *Drunkard;* that being a sure mode of destruction.

If you would expose both your folly and secrets, be a *Drunkard;* and they will soon run out as the liquor runs in.

12

"The Wonderful Advantages of Drunkenness" a page from Abner W. Clopton and Eli Ball, *Wisdom's Voice to the Rising Generation* (Philadelphia, c. 1828).

building Temperance Hall, aided in this as in other temperance matters by W. C. Rives, later ambassador to France.[13] At William and Mary students could hardly fail to see the new monument erected by the Sons to Lucian Minor, late professor of law. At Richmond College doggerel verse against brandy was deemed fit stuff for an embryo magazine and the secular press seemed much more willing than before to talk about the abuses of liquor and print the doings of anti-liquor leaders.[14]

Despite indications that temperance was still favored by some groups, there was little prospect for any immediate legislation to advance the cause. In Virginia as well as in the rest of the country a revulsion set in against any form of prohibition law.[15] Prior to 1860 Bishop Meade published a copy of a petition drawn by Edmund Pendleton calling for a law against treating at elections and added: "If such a paper were now drawn up and signed by a number of people, no matter how conscientiously, there are those who would regard it as fanatical or as an assault on individual rights and liberty. . . ."[16] Governor Henry A. Wise, in the year that he was elected, showed his awareness of current trends when he demanded in a letter published in the Richmond *Enquirer:* "Where is the principle of liquor laws to stop? Nowhere short of invading every inalienable right of the individual person. . . . If they may prohibit a man from buying and selling whiskey, may they not prohibit his planting and selling his

aggerated the drinking habits of the Tuckers. Philip Alexander Bruce, *History of the University of Virginia, 1819-1919; the Lengthened Shadow of One Man* (5 vols.; New York, 1920-1922), III, 187. William H. McGuffey and John B. Minor are the two dry professors referred to here.

13. Rives to Cocke, May 25, 1855, Cocke Papers. Rives is said to have cast the decisive vote for McGuffey's election.

14. E.g., Richmond *Enquirer* of Dec. 15, 1858, on a woman in court for being drunk on the streets; Nov. 19, 1858, for a change of editorship of the *Virginia Conductor*; April 9, 20, Oct. 1, Nov. 5, 1858, for parades of the Sons in Richmond and Petersburg and other activities.

15. John B. McMaster, *History of the People of the United States* (8 vols.; New York, 1888-1919), VIII, 126-132.

16. William Meade, *Old Churches, Ministers and Families of Virginia* (Philadelphia, 1885), I, 416.

corn and rye from which the whiskey is distilled?"[17] The Sons who had committed themselves to a prohibition law saw their members falling away. For a time they had nearly monopolized temperance activity but by 1860 they numbered only 7,000 and their receipts were scarcely $1,500.

But other methods of advancing temperance were not forgotten. Retreat, rest, and probably reorganization were necessary before the stigma could be dissipated. The work of the Sons of Temperance illustrated the paths which were followed. Their work went on, but slowly. They began in late 1856 to publish in Richmond the monthly *Virginia Conductor* with Thomas J. Evans as editor and W. T. Willey, Rev. John A. Broadus, and Lucian Minor, as supervising committee. This paper was still being published in 1860 in Petersburg with J. R. Lewellen[18] as editor and was deemed by the head of the order as "a fixed institution." They continued their spectacular parades but the fire had been taken out of them. A tendency toward greater exclusiveness, stricter discipline, and a greater emphasis upon the social side of their meetings together with a disposition to aid in enforcing the laws evidenced a desire for rest and respectability. And as yet no other leaders had appeared.

In the west the possibility for aggressive temperance action was stronger than elsewhere in the state. Strong wet forces prevented the rise of a native temperance movement of any appreciable strength, but with inspiration from all sides the movement showed promise. The wet traditions were still a hindrance. Wherever the Tidewater aristocracy had settled and was still dominant—as in Clarke County of the Valley and the Abingdon region of the southwest—the tendency was to oppose any temperance action. In the lower (northern) Valley the German Lutherans also were drinkers and in Shenandoah County the petitioners against prohibition were

17. Nov. 6, 1855.
18. Also editor of *The Southern Farmer* in 1858 and *The Constitution* in 1859. See Lester J. Cappon, *Virginia Newspapers, 1821-1935* (New York, 1936), p. 79.

more numerous in 1853 than those for it. In the northwest the society stage was virtually skipped, with a consequently greater ignorance of the matter than in other parts even among those intuitively against liquor. Here some Methodist congregations behaved like the Primitive Baptists of the south.

The Scotch-Irish dominated the upper Valley and the southwest. Their reputation for making and drinking hard liquor is better known than their contrition after getting drunk. Organized temperance activity entered this region rather late and progressed slowly because there were few Baptists except Primitive or Hardshell groups, who did not easily give up their belief in the goodness of liquor or their hostility to societies and "progress" in general.[19]

The southwest was greatly influenced by Tennessee where from 1831 to 1860 the management of the retailing of liquor was a recurring party issue and where Methodist "Parson" Brownlow once ran independently for governor on an anti-liquor platform. Methodists from eastern Tennessee displaced Primitive Baptists as the dominant denomination and their ideas as expressed by the Holston District Conference were far different from those of the recalcitrant Hardshells. The newcomers favored restoration of Wesley's rule to the discipline, a sermon on temperance by the circuit rider at each place that he preached, and definite approval of Tennessee's prohibitory law of 1838.[20] Also from the upper Valley came

19. In the Virginia State Library's transcript of the *Minutes* of the Washington District Primitive Baptist Association from 1811 to the Civil War there is no reference to liquor. Art. III of this association's constitution reads: "the members thus chosen and convened, shall have no power to lord it over God's heritage; nor shall they have any classical power over the churches. . . ."

20. T. P. Abernethy, *From Frontier to Plantation in Tennessee* (Chapel Hill, N. C., 1932), pp. 307, 321; James Phelan, *History of Tennessee* (Boston, ca. 1888), p. 424; Richard Nye Price, *Holston Methodism* (Nashville, Tenn., 1903), II, *passim*, and III, 355. Both students and faculty of the East Tennessee University at Knoxville were influenced by a division of the Sons there, according to the university *Magazine* of 1842 and the university catalogue of 1848. The *Southwestern Christian Advocate*, April 5, 1838, speaking of the Tennessee law of that year declared that Tennessee had taken the lead "in the work of *true reform* . . . destined to work its way throughout . . . the United States, as the only

members of important German sects whose traditions too were against drinking.

Thriving temperance movements elsewhere permeated the entire Valley. When some of the citizens of Harrisonburg in the upper Valley heard of the Sons of Temperance in Washington they sent a letter to the order there asking for information. In the same neighborhood, at Bridgewater, the Sons staged an elaborate parade on Christmas Day, 1860, with the Mt. Crawford cavalry participating.[21] In the lower Valley Baltimore temperance influences had weight, especially among the Methodists around Winchester who were members of the Baltimore Conference. In the north and northwest the influence of Pennsylvania added to that dry element already present in some of the German sects and aided the development of leaders like Galley and W. T. Willey. The late start which the region had was largely overcome and by 1853, if the votes in the legislature and the Lynchburg convention are tests, the west was more anxious for political action than the east.

But the full strength of anti-liquor sentiment was still not behind the main movement, for the southwest on the one hand and the northwest and lower Valley on the other were drawn to other states and the German sects in between were not fully vocal owing to their tenacious clinging to their own dialects and customs and to their desire to remain a "peculiar people."[22] Refining forces already at work would modify the drinking habits of the mountainous parts of all this region. Whether the forces of sectionalism were strong

efficient means of 'effectually protecting the property, lives and reputation' of their constituents." From this it is seen that the motive behind the temperance movement in Tennessee was the same as that behind the early movement in Virginia.

21. John W. Wayland, *History of Rockingham County, Virginia* (Dayton, Va., 1912), p. 281.

22. Much of this description is drawn from talks between Dr. Pearson and Dr. J. P. McConnell of East Radford who knew the southwest intimately and with Dr. J. W. Wayland of Harrisonburg who was fully acquainted with the Valley and is the author of histories of Rockingham and Shenandoah counties.

enough to block a united forward movement of the whole state remained an open question.[23]

In the state as a whole great possibilities were open for more positive action by the middle-class churches. Methodists, Baptists, and Presbyterians were increasing rapidly both in numbers and in wealth during the fifties.[24] With 2,500 congregations and church property valued at nearly four million dollars, with their own colleges and their own press, and with some of their leading members writing for the state press and teaching in state institutions, they could be expected to wield greater influence as organizations than ever before.[25]

Among Baptists there was much agitation and much confusion. In 1857 the Valley Association (in which John E. Massey had been a missionary), claiming that the Sons of Temperance had failed both in work among the people and in seeking a prohibition law, resolved that making, selling, and using liquor should be discountenanced by its constituent churches. Strong resolutions against the business passed the northwest and the Judson associations in 1852[26] and the Strawberry[27] and the Dover associations in 1857—the last condemning "in the strongest terms the practice of many professing Christians of trafficking in this soul destroying element" and calling upon ministers to "speak, in tones deep,

23. The northwest is not fully discussed because this region soon became West Virginia.

24. U. S. Department of Commerce, Bureau of the Census, *Historical Statistics of the United States, Colonial Times to 1957* (Washington, 1960), Series H 526-543, pp. 228-229; *Seventh Census of the United States,* 1850 (Washington, 1853), Appendix, pp. 285-292; *Eighth Census of the United States, 1860* (Washington, 1866), Mortality and Miscellaneous Statistics, pp. 477-488. The rate of increase in congregations varied from 20 to 50 per cent. Methodist congregations numbered 1,403; Baptists, 787; Presbyterians, 300.

25. In all cases cited below the church organizations' minutes were used unless otherwise indicated.

26. *Religious Herald,* Oct. 22, Nov. 25, 1852.

27. This association was grandmother to the United Baptist Association formed in Wilkes County, N. C., in 1859 which was the "first in our mountain country" to declare for temperance. It voted to withdraw fellowship from any church which granted membership to those who "distill, vend or use spiritous liquors as a beverage." James F. Fletcher, *A History of the Ashe County, North Carolina and New River Baptist Associations* (Raleigh, N. C., 1935), p. 37.

and solemn and constant, and reverberating throughout the land."

Meanwhile individual churches in King and Queen, Richmond, the Spotsylvania region, and probably elsewhere applied to members the "test" of total abstinence and sometimes of no participation in the liquor business. In 1857 there appeared in the Spotsylvania region the Hebron Association composed entirely of "test" churches. Such earnestness principally appealed to the humbler folk. Jeter, for instance, tolerated liquor sellers in the Richmond First Baptist Church and later persuaded the Richmond Grace Street Church to admit a dealer to membership.

Certainly the great Baptist leaders deprecated radicalism and the Roanoke Association, which in 1856 voted for the test, rescinded its action in 1857. More pleasing to the leaders was the course of the Mattaponi in King and Queen which in 1859 gravely and fully argued the matter of selling liquor on scriptural grounds. They concluded that the practice was "pernicious in its tendency especially in a church member and inconsistent with the spirit and teachings of the New Testament" since it contributed to stumbling and the encouragement of evil. They warned and in 1865 finally expelled Brother W. Martin, who would not give up his tavern at the courthouse because he felt his obligation to support his family to be his first duty.

Nevertheless the Hebron Association continued on its way until past the Civil War. The leader of the test movement, Rev. William Rufus Powell, assisted by John Churchill Willis, another layman turned preacher, established in Fredericksburg in May, 1858, the *Virginia Baptist*, which "like John the Baptist, the great founder of the sect, comes: 'neither drinking wine nor strong drink.' "[28] Under pressure of this

28. W. T. Hundley, *History of Mattoponi Baptist Church, King and Queen County Virginia* (Richmond, n.d.), *passim*, especially pp. 371, 405; George Braxton Taylor, "W. R. Powell," *Virginia Baptist Ministers* (3rd ser.; Lynchburg, Va., 1912), pp. 13-17; "J. C. Willis," in *ibid.* (4th ser.), pp. 222-226. Both Powell and Willis were substantial middle-class

sort the General Association of Virginia in revising its constitution in 1854 broke a twenty-year silence on a matter of liquor. It asserted that the encouragement of temperance societies was one of the objects for which it was founded and in 1860 it voted that either drinking or selling liquor was "an inconsistency in a Christian."

Two years earlier the General Conference of Southern Methodists, after a bit of educational work,[29] declared that the existing church rule on drinking ought to be interpreted as a "total abstinence pledge" and that members who sold liquor ought to be dealt with as in the case of "other immoralities." This great organization now stood against liquor since the danger from Northern abolitionists passed with the formation of a Southern Methodist conference and since the state failed to take action.[30]

As for the Presbyterians, neither the minutes of their synod nor their General Assembly disclosed any likelihood of early aggressive action. Their influence would have been small, however, because they were fewer than the Methodists and Baptists and were usually the most conservative. There are no records of the other churches' position.[31]

---

men. Test churches were sometimes formed by secession—Salem in King and Queen and Clay Street in Richmond, for example. *Religious Herald,* 1847, *passim,* especially March 4, Jan. 22; William E. Hatcher, *Life of J. B. Jeter, D.D.* (Baltimore, 1887), pp. 254-260. Jeter said in the *Religious Herald,* March 4, 1847, that if a member "keeps a groggery—gives the countenance to intemperance . . . let him be dealt with. He is a most ungodly wretch." But if he gave no encouragement to drunkenness and was otherwise a Christian, "he should . . . be borne with." The African Church, Richmond, early adopted the test. Dover Association, *Minutes,* 1844. The Kentuck Church of Pittsylvania voted to exclude sellers in 1857. The Grace Street Church, Richmond, became practically a test church under the influence of Rev. Edward Kingsford (1846-1852), Hatcher, *Jeter,* p. 255.

29. *Methodist Pamphlets for the People,* IV (1857), contains addresses on temperance "to the members of the M. E. Church," "to Fathers," etc., and other similar material, all of which could be had "in a neat package" for "gratuitous distribution."

30. M. E. Church, South, General Conference *Journal* (1860), p. 468. The Holston Conference in 1858 voted that the use of ardent spirits is "a capital offense against the laws of God." Price, *Holston Methodism,* IV, 224. The Virginia Conference was silent.

31. The *Christian Sun,* organ of the Christian (Disciples) Church, was regularly carrying a temperance column in Aug., 1861.

Although the churches were not willing to declare the drinking and selling of liquor as definitely immoral, the attacks against the retailing business went on. At the temperance convention of 1854 Lucian Minor reported from the executive committee that in at least 57 of the 140 counties opposition to licensing had been made the previous May before the local courts. He gave no details beyond a list of 36 counties and one town in which no merchant was licensed to sell liquor, in 12 of which (including the town) there was also no tavern.[32] Evidence to support his general statement can be shown. As a result of dissatisfaction over the conduct in selling places, public meetings designed to win control of the government were held in Lynchburg in 1854. No licenses were issued for Lexington that year apparently for the same reason. After a regular campaign in Winchester dry officials were elected in 1855 and they at once refused licenses.[33] Cocke wrote in 1854 that the court had granted one license and refused one for the town of Palmyra and Rives said in 1855 that there would be no selling place in his home district and the university districts. Both indicated that public sentiment had forced these decisions. "Thus we get on slowly," recorded Cocke.[34] Since such local activity soon subsided it may have been somewhat dependent upon state-wide agitation.[35] Its strong point was that it had existing law and old recognition of

32. The counties named in the minutes were: without taverns, Barbour, Braxton, Danville (town), Giles, Highland, Mason, Nicholas, Ohio, Pocahontas, Roanoke, Tazwell, and Tyler. Those without merchants licensed to retail: the above and Alleghany, Amelia, Carroll, Craig, Dinwiddie, Fluvanna, Gilmer, Halifax, Houston, Hardy, Henry, Madison, Montgomery, Page, Pendleton, Pennsylvania, Putnam, Rockbridge, Russell, Scott, Shenandoah, Warren, Wirt, and Wythe. Others "refusing license": Boone, Cabell, Grayson, Pulaski, and Warren.

33. Lynchburg *Virginian*, March 13, 1851, March 23, 1854; Alexandria *Gazette*, April 10, May 3, 1855; A. J. Smith of Winchester to Willey, July 17, 1855, Willey Papers.

34. Rives to Cocke, May 25, 1855; Cocke's diary, July 30, 1854. Cocke Papers.

35. *Biennial Report of the Auditor of Public Accounts, 1858 and 1859* (Richmond, 1859). The convention of 1848 had asked the courts to bear in mind the convention's objections when passing on licenses but no other formal reference to the matter had been noted.

right behind it. The future was to show how powerful it could become in building opinion and carrying elections.

Anti-liquor people were forced to admit that the antagonism of politicians to reform by legal means was deeper and their ability to block it greater than had been expected. They were beginning to understand how complex the adjustments of interests and prejudices that must be worked out to hold men together as a party could be. They also admitted the strength of the pull of the party loyalty call which leaders exerted all the way down from the newspaper owner to the local worker. How clever were the devices which the party men used to block the will of the unsophisticated and single-minded!

General Cocke held the opinion that the grip of the "master vice" was broken. Proof existed in the host of men in all walks of life who found that they could do very well with little or no drinking and with little or no treating. The list included nearly all the clergymen, many doctors, prominent members of all college faculties, some officers in both national and state military forces, literary men (including some editors), national and local statesmen and politicians, planters and farmers, lawyers, and businessmen. "King Alcohol" no longer tyrannized society as a whole nor was the country in danger of becoming a "nation of drunkards." The anti-liquor movement had made some headway among many individuals. Organized agitation, however, remained largely a movement of the middle and lower-middle classes and found indifference or opposition from the majority of political, social, and economic leaders. Presently the movement was at an ebb, but recurring evidence of abuses and attempts by isolated members of the upper class to renew the fight indicated that the temperance cause was far from dead. Whatever the prospects for the immediate future, the temperance forces would be heard from again and again.

## Chapter Eight

# LAISSEZ FAIRE,
# 1861-1879

The Civil War played havoc with temperance and temperance work. Despite the examples of Lee, Jackson, and Stuart, drinking and drunkenness increased alarmingly, especially in the army. The liquor problem became the subject of serious discussion in the daily press and in the legislative halls of Richmond—something that had never happened before. The causes were the lessening of accustomed restraints and the excitement of victory. Counteracting influences soon got under way. Laws were passed in 1862 and 1863 to prohibit the making of liquor from foodstuffs and in 1865 to prevent the licensing of ordinaries to sell in or near towns or at railroad depots. The heavy hand of commanding generals fell on nefarious retailers and brawling soldiers alike in the cities where troops were quartered.[1] There was even some undisguised temperance propaganda based on patriotic themes.[2]

1. The Confederate Congress regulated imports of liquors after 1864 to save space on the few blockade runners but did not move in the direction of a national prohibition law even for the sake of conserving foodstuff. Most of the states, however, acted early in the war to pass some sort of law prohibiting the manufacture of liquor from wheat, etc. Apparently many of these were ineffective. William M. Robinson, "Prohibition in the Confederacy," *American Historical Review*, XXXVII (1931-1932), 50-58. W. B. Yearns, *The Confederate Congress* (Athens, Ga., 1960), records no national laws of a prohibitory nature. For drinking among the soldiers see J. William Jones, *Christ in the Camp* (Richmond, 1887), pp. 267-272; *Army and Navy Messenger*, numerous issues; *The American Union*, July 11, 1861; The Richmond *Enquirer*, Dec. 2, 1862. For the attitude of the church organizations see *Religious Herald*, Dec. 14, 1865, Jan. 18, Feb. 8, 1866; Baptist General Association *Minutes*, 1866, p. 22; Richard Nye Price, *Holston Methodism* (Nashville, Tenn., 1903), V, 364. Life from the soldier's point of view in Bell I. Wiley, *The Life of Johnny Reb* (New York, 1943), pp. 40-43. For Virginia laws establishing and enforcing prohibition and restrictions see *Acts and Joint Resolutions Passed by the General Assembly of the State of Virginia* (Richmond, 1820-1919) (hereinafter cited as *Acts*), March 11, 12, 1863, March 10, 1864.

2. "Physician's" *Lincoln and Liquor* (a four-page tract, 1,500 copies for $1.00) alleged a conspiracy between the head of the oppressor government and the liquor interests and pictured the terrific costs to the Confederate states of drunken soldiers, drunken officers, and drunken legislators.

The churches, with the hearty approval of many high officers, conducted a series of remarkable evangelical services in the armies and distributed millions of pages of tracts among the soldiers.[3] Soon the excitement of victory ebbed. Liquor like everything else became scarce. But heavy and general drinking continued and temperance societies virtually ceased to exist.

War's "awful demoralization" did not end with the coming of peace. "Intemperance," said the *Episcopal Methodist*, August 23, 1865, "has spread like the plague." "The alarming prevalence of intemperance . . . assuredly on the increase" was the topic for the Baptist General Association in 1866. When men stated the reasons for intemperance they named war habits, despondency over failure (public or private), the wounds and diseases of war for which liquor was a ready and acceptable remedy, and sometimes reaction from the extremes of pre-war teetotalism. There was seldom excessive drinking by preachers or by women. But laymen, veterans, and the leaders of politics and of business usually drank and the younger men followed.[4] There is no recorded reversal and but little let-up in these tendencies before 1877.

Reconstruction led to changes in the state's regulatory laws which emasculated the old system and marked the death of the old aristocratic idea on which it largely was built. First came the immediate and complete repeal of restrictions relating to Negroes.[5] This paved the way for a great enlargement of that lower class of drinkers who in the past

3. J. William Jones led in this work. Cf. his *Christ in Camp, passim*. On the other hand, an address of Rev. J. C. Stiles, *National Rectitude the Only True Basis of National Prosperity: An Appeal to the Confederate States* (Petersburg, 1863), printed by the Evangelical Tract Society for similar distribution, had nothing to say about drinking although it attacked the speculator, the extortioner, and the political demagogue.

4. *Religious Herald*, Dec. 14, 1865, Jan. 18, Feb. 8, 1866; Baptist General Association, *Minutes*, 1866, p. 22; Oren F. Morton, *Rockbridge County Virginia* (Staunton, Va., 1910), p. 181.

5. *Acts*, 1865-1866, p. 84. See also John P. McConnell, *Negroes and Their Treatment in Virginia from 1865 to 1867* (Richmond, 1910), p. 59.

had been so hard to control. A second change gave first to "eating houses" and then to "any other person" who was duly licensed the privilege, enjoyed previously only by taverns, of retailing for on-premise drinking. For the first time in a century and a half tippling houses—"barrooms" they were now called—were legal. Furthermore, under an act of 1871-1872, the old discretionary power of the local courts disappeared: any "other person" was eligible for licensing to retail.[6]

This wide-open policy was inevitable. The old trouble with merchants indicated a trend toward democracy in drinking; the removal of restrictions was the consummation of this trend. Nonetheless, the change was important. The keepers of barrooms, having nothing to sell but liquor, would tempt men to drink as they never had before and they were unrestrained by fear of losing a license which was so easy to obtain.[7] Thus the law came to regard private profits rather than general public needs as an adequate reason for licensing. Democracy involved exploitation of the drinkers.[8]

A third change concerned the administration of the liquor laws, which under the Reconstruction Constitution were administered by a single judge elected by the legislature instead of by the old court of county magistrates. This change lessened the effectiveness of neighborhood opinion. The judge, no longer necessarily a local and respected citizen, tended to look only to the legal technicalities and in some instances was the attorney for liquor interests outside the county. Since the legislature elected the judge, for the first time the liquor interests could make their voices heard in places where the power rested. Liquor interests inevitably became power-

6. *Acts*, 1865-1866, pp. 33, 35, 351, 831; 1871-1872, p. 179.
7. Charlottesville *Jeffersonian Republican*, March 3, 1886, an historical account. Court records in half a dozen counties and towns show the lack of care in issuing licenses.
8. For an able prohibitionist's views on the similar effect of a high federal tax see D. Leigh Colvin, *Prohibition in the United States* (New York, 1926), pp. 52-55.

ful in the legislature and whatever the will of the people was, there was no chance for its expression.[9]

The wretched fiscal situation of the state was the most pressing and urgent problem of democracy. To increase the state's revenue the legislature of 1865-1867 required of ordinaries and eating houses a "liquor dealer's" license (which was similar to the old merchant's license) in addition to the ordinary license if they would sell for off-premise drinking. The legislature of 1877 began the taxation of small stills.

The state had to make a choice between repudiating its debt or abandoning public schools for lack of revenue. Accordingly, in 1877 the Moffett bill, along with other taxes designed to reach the masses, was presented by the committee on finance and enacted.[10] It sought to tax not only the seller but also the buyer on each drink or half-pint bought, increased penalties for unauthorized selling, revived "informers," made licenses easier to obtain by lessening safeguards and permitting appeals from adverse decisions of county courts. The theory was that men would pay taxes on their luxuries and vices when they would not on anything else and there were many who wanted to see public education profit from such taxes. When this taxing experiment proved unenforceable the legislature promptly substituted a tax on gross sales or rental value of the selling premises.[11] By such devices the liquor revenue was brought up to the $300,000 mark and over. This was two-and-one-half times the income from this

9. C. C. Pearson, *The Readjuster Movement in Virginia* (New Haven, 1917), pp. 1-16, 47-67, *et passim.*
10. *Acts,* 1867-1877, pp. 245, 301.
11. For a discussion of the fiscal merits, see Richmond *Dispatch,* June 17, 1879. The Washington *Sentinel* thought the Moffett bill was not based on "prohibition principles" but opposed it as imposing an unfair handicap on retailers of beer and unlikely to be productive of revenue. See the March issues. It suggested that Samuel H. Moffett, inventor of the "bell-punch" for recording sales, was making money out of his invention. Louisiana also tried this plan but it was rejected after much consideration by Maryland and South Carolina. *Ibid.,* May 4, 1878. It does not appear that the retailers tried to collect the tax from customers. Another source of revenue for the schools favored at this time was a tax on dogs— another "luxury" tax.

source in 1857 and it constituted 40 per cent of the total derived from licenses, which was twice the percentage of 1857. Liquor revenue remained around this figure ($300,000) for twenty years. Liquor regulations were now reflected by tax laws. The state was directly profiting by the exploitation of drinkers, which gave the exploiters a great reason for interest in the government.[12]

To offset all this a few restrictions appeared in the laws. The giving or selling of liquor in election districts on election days was forbidden for the first time and later the closing of saloons on election days was required.[13] Sale within three miles of religious services[14] or to minors[15] was forbidden. The omission of a Sunday selling provision in the code of 1873 was not corrected until 1879 and then with special provisions for towns, which suggests the influence of dealers.[16] Not until a strong anti-liquor movement had gotten under way were there adequate restrictions on selling to idiots or to habitual drunkards or to students of colleges or even of high schools, or on employing women in saloons or keeping open all night, or any penalty except the old dollar fine for getting beastly drunk.[17] As if in acceptance of fate a group of the state's best citizens in 1871-1872 sought and obtained from the legislature that first legalized barrooms a charter for a "Virginia Inebriates' Home," to which "an habitual drunkard and lost to self-control" might under certain conditions be committed by the magistrates.[18] Neither contemporary court

12. *Acts,* 1876-1877, p. 245; 1878-1879, p. 310; and amendment of 1879-1880, p. 147. The minimum taxes were $62.50 for the barroom license plus 15 per cent of the rental value of the place. "Informers" were not rewarded under the act until 1918, but imprisonment at the discretion of the court was added to the penalty.

13. *Acts,* 1866-1867, 1869-1870.

14. *Acts,* 1870-1871. In 1893 sale within three miles of a temperance meeting was forbidden.

15. *Acts,* 1874. Sale to students of the Hampton Institute was also forbidden this year.

16. *Acts,* March 14, 1879, March 8, 1880.

17. Cf. Byrd Law of 1908, below.

18. *Acts,* 1871-1872. Six clergymen were among the incorporators, who included Peterfield Trent, William W. Parker, W. C. Mayo, Thomas J.

records nor secular or religious newspapers disclose in the enforcement of the laws anything compensatory.[19]

Until about 1879 opposition to liquor was made chiefly on the basis of personal abstinence and by temperance societies.[20] First to move were old Sons of Temperance of the Richmond-Petersburg region, including Thomas J. Evans, now "Colonel" Evans. Most striking was their statement that "Legal enactments on the subject have proven a mistake." To accomplish anything permanent "the Christian and the social influence of society must be combined." Jeter, now editor of the *Religious Herald*, urged them to take broad grounds only—the inexpedience and injury of intoxicants and the wrong of tempting men by offering them for sale—and to rely upon continuous pressure from press, preachers, women, and schools. John A. Broadus entreated that extremists be avoided.

At a Petersburg meeting in December, 1865, a new order was founded which combined features of the old societies and the old Sons. It was called "The Friends of Temperance."[21] It was welcomed by important church bodies, received the approbation of R. E. Lee, president of Washington College, and developed some strength in the Valley-Piedmont region. Despite the old apathy and the new turmoil of Reconstruction it did not die, though it faded into insignifi-

Evans, R. G. Staples, and John W. Daniel. Some of them were old Sons whose similar plan is mentioned before the Civil War.

19. The Abingdon *Virginian*, April 28, 1876, called the inquiry into fitness of keeper and place "A Farce" and proposed abandonment of it.

20. Not mentioned below are two Catholic societies, one appearing in Lynchburg in 1873 and another in Norfolk in 1876. The Rechabites also were established in Norfolk during this period. W. A. Christian, *Lynchburg and Its People* (Lynchburg, Va., 1900), p. 295; H. W. Burton, *History of Norfolk, Virginia* (Norfolk, 1877), p. 280.

21. *Religious Herald*, Nov. 23, 30, Dec. 14, 1865; Jan. 18, Feb. 8, 22, 29, 1866; Friends of Temperance, *Minutes*, 1865 and constitution, 1866. Others who backed the movement from its early days were D'Arcy Paul, Abner Clopton, R. G. Morris, John W. Ferguson, and J. William Jones. There were to be active members who must be fourteen years old and pay weekly dues, and associate members of any age or sex who had only to sign the pledge and attend open meetings once a month.

cance.[22] It is important as another recrudescence of old ideas, an effort of native white forces to disentangle themselves from Northern affiliations and set their own house in order.

Next came a foreign influence, more radical and not adverse to politics. Serving the same cause which the old Sons of Temperance served years before, the Independent Order of Good Templars came to Virginia.[23] Its members, who might be Negroes as well as whites, were pledged to abstinence and the reform of drunkards. Its national platform envisioned prohibition and politics with "third party" interests.[24] It came in with the carpetbaggers from Washington and set up Pioneer Lodge No. I in the Baptist Church of Falls Church, Fairfax County, April 18, 1867. Two years later a

22. Lee approved the establishment of a chapter at his college saying that "while moderation and temperance in all things are commendable, abstinence from spirituous liquors is the best safeguard to morals and health." He was strongly opposed to "the grogshops which are luring our young men to destruction." J. W. Jones, *Life and Letters of R. E. Lee* (New York, 1906), p. 442; and Douglas Southall Freeman, *R. E. Lee; A Biography* (4 vols.; New York, 1934-1935), IV, 280-282. General John E. Roller and J. E. Pennybacker were active in the Valley. Morton, *Rockbridge County*, p. 217; and John W. Wayland, *History of Rockingham County, Virginia* (Dayton, Va., 1912), p. 381. Pennybacker was president of the State Council in 1869. The Friends at the university kept their minutes in the record book of the old Sons, used and apparently held title to the Temperance Hall. They tried to sustain interest through debates and scholarships for students and were allowed a part in commencement exercises in 1869. Led by John B. Minor they took part in local licensing issues in 1869 and again in 1882-1883. In 1883 they disbanded.

23. Mr. George Washington Hawxhurst, who in a letter to Dr. Pearson in 1926 signed himself "77 year old Prohibitionist," very kindly loaned the minutes of this order and also a brief manuscript history of it. Alvin LeRoy Hall, "The Prohibition Movement in Virginia, 1826-1916" (Master's thesis, University of Virginia, 1964), p. 49, debates the relative importance of those involved in the coming of the Good Templars. He refers to the "apparently lost" manuscript history by G. W. Hawxhurst which has fortunately survived and is in the Pearson Papers, Wake Forest College. The minutes seem to have disappeared. Mr. Hall deserves credit for unearthing *Liquor and Anti-Liquor in Virginia* through an obscure reference in E. H. Cherrington *et al.* (eds.), *Standard Encyclopedia of the Alcohol Problem* (6 vols.; Westerville, Ohio, 1925-1930). His thesis is largely a look at the legislative actions in Virginia from 1890 to 1916 and much of the early portion was drawn from the unedited Pearson manuscript.

24. Simeon B. Chase, *A Digest of Laws, Decisions, Rules and Usages of the Independent Order of Good Templars* (10th ed.; Philadelphia, 1874), pp. 274-275.

state Grand Lodge was constituted. The order "progressed very slowly the first few years" according to G. W. Hawxhurst, grand secretary from 1872 to 1887, "owing to the strong antagonism on the part of native Virginians who considered it an invasion of their rights." The antagonism was not unreasonable, for the Northern members included prominent abolitionists who were still connecting liquor with slavery in their public orations.[25] The Hawxhursts, among the Virginia leaders, were openly active in the recent detested doings of Radicals[26] and Pioneer Lodge showed its colors in 1869 by petitioning for prohibition in the District of Columbia. The order shed its radicalism quickly and helped with the nationwide revival of interest in temperance. It grew rapidly after 1874—from 3,500 in 1875 to 8,000 in 1878 and to 13,000 by 1887.

Excepting that women entered on equal terms and in about equal numbers with men, the Good Templars' membership was similar to that of the old Sons.[27] Like the Sons they spent much of their energies in admitting and dropping members, in organizing and reorganizing lodges. Thus in 1878, 4,430 members were received and 2,445 were lost; in 1886, when the order was at its height, of the 600 lodges formed 356 no longer existed. From dues and fees it received as much as $7,000 annually.

Most interesting were the "lecturers" who, going out from headquarters, not only made addresses which very large crowds attended but also in preparation for a new lodge did just the kind of house-to-house work which ante bellum leaders had desired so much. By these means, supplemented by the newspapers[28] that it established or inspired, the Grand

25. Colvin, *Prohibition Party*, pp. 61-62, 119.
26. Job Hawxhurst was a member of the Alexandria legislature. John Hawxhurst was a member of the constitutional conventions of 1864 and 1867 and presided at a mass meeting of Negroes in Capitol Square, Richmond, April 17, 1867. Hamilton J. Eckenrode, *The Political History of Virginia During the Reconstruction* (Baltimore, 1904), pp. 18, 25.
27. Three-sevenths of the members were reckoned to be voters.
28. The following seems to be the chronological succession of principal

Lodge made itself the principal anti-liquor agency in the state until the early eighties.

The increase in membership around 1875 coincided with an attempt on the part of some leaders to commit this order to a program of local option elections. This inspired some agitation in Norfolk. Other societies[29] were established in this rather "wide-open" city so much frequented by sailors. A sermon preached on April 4 in the Union Station M. E. Church by Rev. Owen Hicks was published as *Intemperance: Report of the Last Annual Conclave of the Pit . . . Addresses by Generals Avarice, Lust . . . and King Alcohol.* The author's figures showed the significance of liquor. In Norfolk there were 2,200 white and 1,900 Negro voters and 212 selling places—almost 1 for every 20 voters; in Portsmouth (across the river), there were 76 selling places or one for every 30 voters. The attempt was abandoned after politically minded members of the Grand Lodge objected, as was a proposal to recommend that temperance men vote for temperance candidates only. But the locals continued to inform and train ordinary men, nuclei for the future in many communities. There were a number of able men affiliated with order; its leaders, however, never rose above mediocrity in ability or unselfishness.

In 1874 the United Order of True Reformers was established under the auspices of the Good Templars.[30] This was for Negroes only. The Virginia Good Templars thus sought to settle the problem of admitting Negroes to their own lodges. But Good Templars from the outside—principally English-

ones: *The Temperance Advocate* (1882-1887, a Good Templar publication); *Temperance Worker* (1887); *Good Templar Sentinel* (1888-1891); *Anti-Liquor* (1890-1892); *Virginia Bugle* (1893); *Daily Pilot* (1894-1895). The Augusta County *Argus* (1887-1915) was independent prohibitionist. Anti-liquor papers numbered approximately two in the seventies, seven in the eighties, and five in the nineties.

29. Burton, *Norfolk*, pp. 250-253.

30. D. Webster Davis, *Life and Public Services of Rev. William Washington Brown* ([Richmond], 1910), is useful for activities in Richmond.

men—admitted Negroes. In consequence the Virginia Good Templars worked out a system of dual lodges under which Negro locals were controlled by a Grand Lodge representing them as well as the white Grand Lodge. Though aided with money and lecturers and highly praised by their white contemporaries, Negro Good Templars were more tolerated than welcomed.

The Negro elements like their white counterparts were troubled with dissension but came to include some leading Negro citizens—among them Giles Jackson, a Richmond lawyer, and probably Rev. John Jasper, the noted preacher. There was need for temperance work among the Negroes. As a race they were no more addicted to drinking than the whites, if as much, and they usually did not have money with which to buy. Now, however, they were free from the old restraints imposed by masters or by laws and needed time and experience to develop new ones. Sometimes there were whites to exploit them and few to protest or to intercede when drink brought on misconduct. Their societies were seemingly no more popular than those of the whites and even little Negro children yelled "Reformer" at the members. Since the conditions under which these orders labored were so difficult they exerted little influence upon the anti-liquor movement as conducted by the whites.[31]

In May, 1878, a chapter of the Woman's Christian Temperance Union (WCTU) with seven members was established at Lincoln, Loudon County. In its outside origin, its national scope, and the radical views of its national leaders this society resembled the Good Templars.[32]

31. "If there were no barrooms in the city, we would get along without any trouble," John Jasper is reported as saying in an interview. Richmond *Dispatch*, April 14, 1889. William E. Hatcher, *John Jasper, the Unmatched Philosopher and Preacher* (New York, 1908), p. 106, portrays the experience of Jasper.
32. Colvin, *Prohibition Party*, pp. 276 ff. Elizabeth Hogg Ironmonger and Pauline L. Phillips, *History of the Woman's Christian Temperance Union of Virginia* (Richmond, 1958), p. 24.

Those who called the Petersburg meeting of 1865 said that although the teachings of Virginia's churches were admittedly adequate, their "practical inefficiency, so far as intemperance is concerned" was "for some reason . . . glaring." The churches did not dispute this statement of friendly critics. Indeed the state organizations of Baptists and Methodists, in 1866 and 1869 respectively, lamented that great damage was being done them by the drinking and selling activities of their own members. The Baptists heartily endorsed "the energetic steps being taken by temperance reformers" and urged both "earnest persuasion, denunciation from their pulpits of this great besetting sin [intemperance]" and the personal cooperation and assistance of "them that love the Lord." The Methodists resolved that a "direct and positive prohibition of manufacture and sale" by members was "necessary."

Activity ceased rather suddenly and without having advanced beyond pre-war days. In their state organizations Baptists had no more to say. The Virginia Annual Conference would not support in its Southside body the recommendation to uphold the Wesley rule which it had made in 1869.[33] The Virginia Synod declined in 1878 the suggestion of the Lexington Presbytery for aggressive action and the Virginia Episcopalians moved in 1876 and 1878 only against intemperance. Echoing and inspiring the prevailing attitude the *Religious Herald* in 1874 warned against extreme action and in 1881 carried in its "Farmers' Column" an approving report of Albemarle experiments in grape and wine production.[34] In the Richmond *Christian Advocate* editor J. J. Lafferty had scarcely a word about liquor though he found space for attacking lotteries, gambling, Episcopalians, and politicians.

33. See *Journal*, 1886, p. 195, and report of F. M. Edwards to Virginia Annual Conference in *Minutes*, 1880. The *Journals* of 1874, 1878, show the unsuccessful effort to restore the Wesley rule.
34. See March 26, June 25, 1874; Jan. 13, 1881.

The churches were not neglecting their all-time tasks of evangelizing, building, and disciplining. Against drunkards and especially dancing and Sabbath-breaking they were more active than ever before.[35] Their leaders thought seriously about and were intimately involved with conservative politicians, the matter of white rule, and the debt controversy. There was also the danger of being linked with former abolitionists and carpetbaggers. There were memories (buttressed by words of warning from their elders) of how the ante bellum temperance cause produced a reaction that effectively ended its work for years. As usual there were some good and able ministers and laymen who questioned the efficiency of any human devices in this matter.[36]

To the liquor interests the situation in Virginia was eminently satisfactory in 1879. The federal government granted over 1,000 licenses to distilleries and 2,500 to retailers. The only Southern states having larger numbers involved in the business were Kentucky and Tennessee.[37] Especially pleasing to retail trade were the 1,266 places licensed by the state to

35. In 1865 the Mattaponi Baptist Church expelled ladies for dancing by a unanimous vote, a liquor dealer by a divided vote. Baptist church minute-books abound in cases of discipline for drunkenness and dancing. The minutes of five Baptist District Associations examined show the Concord receiving a temperance report in 1867 and recommending in 1871 that the churches be stricter as to drinking and selling. The Roanoke Association resolved in 1866 that members be persuaded not to sell and in 1877 that the churches get rid of sellers and drunkards. North Carolina Baptists went further than Virginia Baptists in liquor matters. Blanks, "Social Control by the Baptist Churches in North Carolina and Virginia, 1775-1928," pp. 44-48. For Sabbath-breaking see Virginia Baptist General Association, *Proceedings*, 1879, citing action of the Presbyterians.

36. Dr. Charles Minnegerode in *Temperance and Intemperance: A Sermon Preached in St. Paul's Church, Richmond, on the 21st. January, 1877* (Richmond, 1877), which a group of prominent Richmonders had published, declared that there was: *"no remedy by external means.* Legislation vainly attempts it. If I could stop all the distilleries in the world (and no power can do that) it would not cure the evil. *Mere rules will not do it.* . . . Mere palliatives won't do. Nothing of man's devices, I have tried it in a hundred cases. *Nothing but God's grace . . . Nothing but a new heart and a Christian spirit can do it."*

37. Commissioner of Internal Revenue *Report*, 1880. Some took out retail licenses as technical protection from federal "revenuers" when they probably did little more than distribute small quantities to friends and neighbors.

sell for on-premise drinking.[38] Nine-tenths of these were no more than barrooms. Through these most of the liquor was channeled directly to the consumer. Profits were very good even with high taxes, which was agreeable to the legislative committee and temperance cranks alike. In the barroom one usually bought by the drink instead of by the quart as in the old days and in the joy of talking and treating there was rarely more than a "finger" or two to a drink.[39]

As social centers the barrooms democratized the good and the bad of the old taverns.[40] Any man could drop in, even those who had no other place to go. The location was convenient and the keeper who was also often proprietor was there at all hours and usually full of local news and gossip. Old men could hold long sessions of reminiscences and spin "tales" while sitting by the fire or on a shady porch. The more vigorous loved the footrail and the high counter which was so easy on the elbow. Here "setting 'em up" was a custom often disastrous to the hospitable. There was always sawdust on the floor. Between drinks there would be talk of business, politics, and sports followed perhaps by argument, wagers, quarrels, and sometimes fisticuffs.

In the cities one's opportunity to select resulted in Negro barrooms. But in the country, where three-fourths of these institutions were, the Negro came in perhaps by a separate door but drank from an end of the same counter as the whites. If he was impolite or failed to "know his place" the bartender threw him out. Whether from lack of inclination or of time

38. Auditor's *Report*, 1879. There were 400 licensed for off-premise drinking and 408 to manufacture and to sell as little as a gallon. Many barrooms had licenses for off-premise selling.

39. The *Southern Churchman*, July 13, 1889, reprinted this estimate: for one bushel of corn made into liquor the farmer received 40 cents, the government $3, the manufacturer $4, the vender $7. George Ade, *The Old Time Saloon* (New York, 1931), presents an interesting and neither wet nor dry picture of the saloon and quotes an old time bartender's estimate of 20 to 25 drinks per gallon and a distiller's estimate of three gallons of whiskey per bushel of corn. An estimate of 1793 was one half this.

40. James J. McDonald, *Life in Old Virginia* (Norfolk, Va., 1907), pp. 299-309, describes taverns and "sto' Keepin' " nostalgically.

or of money the numerous plantation Negroes were apt to come only on Saturdays when they would loll around and perhaps take home a bottle. Negroes of the towns and villages and those from the sawmills, the waterfront, and the industrial areas and others who controlled their own time and had money in their pockets tended to congregate around "the barrooms and stores where liquor was sold . . . drinking and idling, to the great loss of their money and character and to the disgust of the community, for frequent quarrels and fights scandalized the neighbors and passers-by."[41] Ladies sometimes complained that the stores and the streets were unpleasant for them and later there was widespread terror of drunken Negroes in rural areas. These things were incidental—the customers did not object. The barroom was a man's institution in a man's world.

Liquor dealers needed political influence to protect their businesses and this they undoubtedly possessed. Locally the barroom often supported several who had votes but little else. It kept in close touch with the constable or the policeman who in the name of the law quieted the quarrelers and fighters and helped the drunk home with understanding and sympathy. Directly or indirectly it contributed much business to local lawyers who were conspicuous in politics and on good terms with the local judge—sometimes even members of the same social club. There was a state association of liquor dealers which through counsel had connection with railroad and bondholding interests and with the management of political parties.[42] It could count on the support of the powerful national liquor organizations which, conscious of their con-

41. W. T. Thorn, "The Negroes of Litwalton, Virginia: A Social Study of the 'Oyster Negro,'" *Bureau of Labor Bulletin*, No. 37 (Washington, 1901), p. 1167.

42. Among the important lawyers and agents were Judge A. B. Cochran, who represented the Pennsylvania railroad interests in 1871; General Bradley T. Johnson, agent of the bondholders' funding syndicate and friend of W. L. Royal who represented both liquor interests and bondholders. C. V. Meredith became counsel of the dealers' association in 1886.

tributions to the national treasury through federal taxes instituted and maintained by the Republican party, were demanding and receiving from both the government and the party that controlled its activities a share in the councils of each.

The national Democratic party opposed the tax and wrote in its platform of 1876: "In . . . the liberty of individual conduct, unvexed by sumptuary laws . . . we behold the noblest products of a hundred years of changeful history." "Noble" said Louis Schade, editor of the Washington *Sentinel*, which was published by the brewing industry.[43] When the objectionable Moffett Law was passed Schade denounced it as prohibitory and threatened that its promoters would find that they had dug their political graves. The state dealers' association, meeting in Richmond, voted approval of a substitute which Colonel A. Fulkerson introduced and the legislature passed.[44]

After a break of about ten years anti-liquor activities were resumed in the middle sixties under severe handicaps. The experiences of the later pre-war effort, the legacy of the war, the great increase in the number of free lower-class people with votes, the emasculation of the old selective licensing system, and the stronger economic and political position of liquor interests were all hindrances. As before there was a native agency relying on moral suasion and a foreign agency which contemplated resorting to prohibitory laws. There was nothing new in the motivation or arguments of either. For a dozen years the cause of temperance made scarcely perceptible progress.

43. Washington *Sentinel*, July 1, 1876; Colvin, *Prohibition Party*, pp. 108-114.
44. Pearson, *Readjuster Movement in Virginia*, pp. 76, 144. Colonel A. Fulkerson introduced the law which repealed and replaced the Moffett Law at the request of the liquor dealers. Washington *Sentinel*, April 7, 1877; Richmond *Whig*, Jan. 16, 1880; Richmond *Dispatch*, June 17, 1879.

## Chapter Nine

# LOCAL OPTION:
# GENESIS AND OPERATION,
# 1877-1902

When the Reconstruction period was over the attention of Virginians turned first to state-wide matters of debt, schools, and party control. Following this came long years of localism, reminiscence, and political frustration.[1] During this period— from about 1877 to 1902—anti-liquor interest and activity centered around the General Local Option Act of 1886. This law permitted each local unit to decide by popular vote whether licenses should be issued for the selling of liquor within it. A "local optionist" or "dry" was one who voted against licensing. Support of local option did not require personal abstinence or any objection to the sale of liquor except when it was against the will of the community. The development of this policy and the manner in which it operated after adoption marked a further step in Virginia's anti-liquor movement.

There were two ways during the post-war days by which a community might seek to prevent the sale of liquor. As before the war individual citizens could appear in court, with counsel if they wished, and present evidence and argument against the issuance of a license. Judges no longer had wide discretionary authority in the matter but they could still invoke the old requirement that the proposed place of sale be suitable, interpret it rigidly, and take a chance of reversal on appeal to a higher court. And occasionally a judge would do this. Judge William Hodges Mann of Nottoway often declared that no place was suitable for a barroom. This method was practicable only if the judge was quite friendly and community sentiment quite strong and the opposed business was unwilling

---

1. These matters are discussed in the following chapters.

to stand the expense of appeal to the higher courts.[2] The other way liquor selling could be prevented was through special act of the legislature. In 1870-1871 a petition on licensing came from Fairfax and two years later one asking for prohibition came from nearby Loudon.[3] The policy of the legislature was to refuse special action. In almost two hundred years only the town of Marion in 1872 and certain small places in Bland and Giles counties in 1874 received exceptional treatment from the legislature.[4]

In 1877-1878 a change occurred in the legislature's policy. On petition from Blacksburg, the home of Virginia Polytechnic Institute, the county judge was given full legal authority to refuse license to retail in or near that little town, which practically amounted to legislative prohibition for a special district. Next year the faculty and students of the nearby Emory and Henry College asked similar treatment. In 1878-1879 petitions for permission to hold local elections on licensing came from Loudon, Alexandria County, Dranesville, Quaker settlement in Fairfax, and other places in the north and from Wytheville, Pulaski, and Fincastle in Botecourt County in the southwest. The former group was successful and on May 25, 1879, five of the six districts of Fairfax, including the courthouse districts where liquor had been sold since time immemorial, voted "dry."[5] Custom was broken and petitions for special elections poured in to the legislature

2. Use of this method in Charlotte and Culpeper is indicated in the *Christian Federation*, June, 1902. The Baptist Concord Association approved Judge Mann's course in 1876 and also commended Judge Treadway; perhaps in reply, a petition for a law compelling judges to grant a license when the legal requirements were met was filed with the legislature the same year.

3. General in character were a resolution introduced in 1870-1871 by D. B. White of the Warwick district that the House inquire into the expediency of prohibition and a petition in 1872-1873 from Loudon that the seller of liquor be held responsible for damages arising from its drinking.

4. These laws only required that the town council must approve before the license could be granted by the court. Jeffersonville district in Tazwell County made the same request as Marion and in the same year.

5. *Acts*, 1877-1878, p. 187; Hawxhurst, "Virginia Good Templars," in C. C. Pearson Papers.

of 1879-1881, some of them from such scattered territories as Accomac, King George, and James City in the east and Waynesboro on the pass to the Valley. Some of them were granted, notably those of Waynesboro and Botecourt and Roanoke. Thus, through legislative willingness, local option came to Virginia.[6]

The available data indicates that for each of these sporadic outbursts the primary reason was the same: the petitioners decided that the local retail place was a community nuisance which they were unwilling to tolerate longer. Marion was getting ready for a woman's college, which seemed sufficient reason for abolishing or very strictly regulating barrooms. In Blacksburg a notorious saloon-keeper was corrupting the young men of the state A. & M. College, a fact which helped win the support of level-headed conservative Judge Phlegar, the legislative patron of the Blacksburg bill, for the local-option cause. In Tazewell Robert Sheffey, best known of Methodist ministers in that region, found stillhouses his greatest enemy[7] and received hearty support from J. N. Harman, a minister of the Christian denomination and a Republican politician.

The region around Alexandria had long been noted for liquor drinking but was now the home of Good Templar headquarters, a Quaker settlement, numerous Methodists, and the homes of commuters to government jobs in Washington. In Accomac the seasonal workers in packing fish and oysters thronged the barrooms as they once did in Alexandria. In Hampton the barkeepers lay in wait for the incoming Indian students.[8] In Richmond, though no petition for a special election was circulated, a mass meeting directed by leading citizens of all denominations disclosed unmistakably the in-

6. *Acts* and *Journals*, 1879-1881, *passim*.
7. John Newton Harman, *Annals of Tazewell County, Virginia* (2 vols.; Richmond, 1922-1925), II, 296.
8. An act of March 3, 1880, was to forbid sale to any student of the Hampton Normal and Agricultural Institute.

dignation of many at the saloons' law-breaking and insolence.[9] Charlottesville, which like Richmond did not move for local option, soon heard careful testimony concerning "their [the saloons'] demoralizing effects upon the community."[10]

Local attitudes were reinforced by the anti-wine attitude of President Hayes and his wife and the nation-wide contention by the women and by the recent authorization of local-option elections in West Virginia, Maryland, Alabama, and Georgia.[11] Some were moved by their temperance society connections and some by the political situation, which gave an independent the opportunity to win local office if he could find a good issue to exploit. In these first stirrings it was the objectionable aspects of the liquor business as they knew it, and not general hostility to liquor, that incited men to action.[12]

This general outbreak of sentiment for local-option elections suggested a universal local-option law similar to those of several Southern states.[13] Such a law would save communities the burden of having to ask the legislature for the privilege of voting and also spare legislators the distraction and sometimes the embarrassment which petitions for special treatment were apt to entail. Realizing that public sentiment offered them the opportunity for leadership, some Good Templars sought to have their Grand Lodge take the lead in 1878, but their political members objected and they lapsed into inac-

9. Taylor Ellyson in Richmond *Virginian*, March 18, 1915. Lyon G. Tyler found a similar situation in and around Williamsburg when he became president of William and Mary College in 1888.

10. "Y" in *Jeffersonian Republican*, March 3, 1886.

11. Leonard Stott Blakey, *The Sale of Liquor in the South* ("Studies in History, Economics and Public Law, Edited by the Faculty of Political Science of Columbia University," Vol. LI, whole No. 127 [New York, 1912]), Table I, pp. 39-40.

12. Letters to Dr. Pearson from President Julian A. Burruss of V.P.I., Dec. 17, 1928, and Jan. 1, 1929; President James A. Gregg of Hampton Normal and Agricultural Institute, Dec. 5, 1928, and Jan. 8, 1929; and a conversation between Dr. Pearson and President J. P. McConnell of Radford at East Radford, Virginia, in Aug., 1931. A letter from President James N. Hillman of Emory and Henry College leads one to believe that the action there was a result of the traditional policy of the college.

13. Blakey, *Sale of Liquor in the South*, p. 39, indicated that by the time the Virginia law was passed in 1886 six other Southern states had similar laws.

tivity.[14] In and around Randolph-Macon College[15] clustered a small but strong, cultured group who saw the same opportunity and were able to give the anti-liquor movement in its latest phase a Christian college leadership. The initiative came from President W. W. Bennett, who from 1868 to 1877 had owned and edited the Richmond *Christian Advocate*. Dr. Bennett began to publish the bi-monthly *Southern Crusader*[16] in 1881. Soon he was lending the prestige of his name as well as his energies to the creation of a Local Option Alliance like those other states had. Professor W. W. Smith, who like his father[17] had once been a newspaper man, came to his aid. He was full of energy and gifted with ability to organize on the practical level. In 1881 he secured the financial support of the proprietor of the Buffalo Lithia Springs, Thomas F. Goode, and sent the *Crusader* to everyone he considered to be worth while. Though neither the other colleges nor the religious press gave noticeable encouragement,[18] the Virginia Baptist General Association assisted Bennett and Smith.

14. Hawxhurst, "Virginia Good Templars"; the National Prohibition Party and the Readjuster movement in Virginia were the principal matters of concern to the politically minded during this period.

15. The college was located at Ashland, just north of Richmond.

16. Perhaps Dr. Bennett was influenced by the anti-saloon movement in North Carolina in 1880-1881, perhaps by a pamphlet, *Abolish the Saloon*, which Atticus Haygood, president of Emory College in Georgia, published in 1880. Dr. Haygood was in the Holston Conference in the seventies.

17. His father, R. M. Smith, was editor of the Alexandria *Evening Sentinel* before the Civil War and served as printer to the Confederate Congress and printed the Richmond *Enquirer* during the war. W. B. Yearns, *The Confederate Congress* (Athens, Ga., 1960), pp. 33-34. After the war father and son attempted to revive the *Enquirer*. W. W. Smith was a veteran of the Civil War and later became president of Randolph-Macon, founder of the Randolph-Macon Woman's College, and chancellor of the Randolph-Macon system of schools and colleges. He previously had been interested in Sabbath traffic laws, desiring to have them made practicable and enforced. Others of the group were Colonel Thomas Whitehead and Richard Irby, Civil War veterans like Smith, and men of affairs and politicians. Co-operating, though like his father opposed to the extreme views of Dr. Bennett, was young R. E. Blackwell, son-in-law of Bennett's predecessor and future president of the college.

18. Rev. C. H. Ryland, long identified with Richmond College and Richmond Baptists, reported favorably in the *Religious Herald* the ensuing temperance convention.

Led by A. E. Owen, a self-made but eloquent pastor in the very wet Portsmouth region, the Baptist body broke its quarter-century silence with resolutions that recalled its old-time interest and cautiously invoked the active support of the brethren for "every judicious measure" for suppressing the use and sale of intoxicants "in an indiscriminate manner." The Holston Annual Conference, meeting in Wytheville, voted that its members use their rights as citizens for local-option laws.[19] Militantly the Baptist Roanoke District Association declared: "Moral suasion will not do for the liquor dealer, legal suasion is the best remedy for him." Then the Good Templars skeptically yielded to Dr. Smith's personal solicitation and agreed to co-operate.

On December 20, 1881, the first post bellum state temperance convention met at Charlottesville. A total of 100 representatives from 50 counties and cities and all the churches, societies, and races testified to the strength of the old cause. Enthusiastically they voted to organize a Local Option Alliance, borrowing the name of a Maryland group which had operated successfully for some years. Ex-Governor William Smith was named president and Bennett became executive chairman. Its sole object was to crusade for a general local-option law. Conspicuously the *Crusader* published "Our Creed: (1) We believe that the sale of intoxicating liquors as a beverage is an injury to any community. (2) We believe that each community should protect itself against this injury by refusing to allow such sale." The objective was strictly limited. Neither the wholesaling of liquor nor its retailing by mail was included. The matter at issue was community selling, which was to be handled by the individual community. The organization was state-wide in order to "bring all sympathizing agencies into accord for the above purpose."[20]

19. "Or such other legislation as may aid in suppressing intemperance." Richard Nye Price, *Holston Methodism* (Nashville, Tenn., 1903), V, 246.
20. *Religious Herald*, Dec. 29, 1881; *Southern Crusader*, March 1.

In the legislative session of 1881-1882 Representative James Stubbs[21] of Gloucester, citing the many requests for special elections as a reason, moved that the Committee of Finance bring in a general local-option bill. This was quickly done by the committee's chairman, R. R. Farr of Fairfax. The alliance backed the bill with the signed endorsement of 35,000 voters, including "104 feet of names" from Accomac and 36 feet from Rockingham, and 1,500 individual signatures from Shenandoah, the home county of United States Senator R. R. Riddleberger, an ardent wet.[22] At Manassas Court-house ex-Governor Smith, whom everyone knew to be honest and beyond further political ambition, explained that the alliance was only a union of all the forces favoring a general law. The *Crusader* continued its amazing activity.[23] So great was the support that the House passed the bill despite the opposition of Speaker I. C. Fowler, by a vote of 59 to 23. But the Senate, as House members anticipated, did not find time to vote before adjournment.[24]

The defeat served only to evoke and consolidate local-

---

1882; *Randolph-Macon Monthly*, April, 1882; minutes of church bodies and Good Templars. The meeting and organizational efforts were accomplished with remarkably little effort. Much of the above information came from conversations between Dr. Pearson and R. E. Blackwell and others associated with the period.

21. A man of good family and not inclined to an austere life in a neighborhood where the better people were noted for clinging to the old-time hospitality, he was also a great friend of the oysterman.

22. Stubbs and Farr were Good Templars. For political aspects, see below.

23. Since March, 1881, 415,000 *Crusaders*, 9,000 letters, 36,000 circulars had been mailed. *Randolph-Macon Monthly*, April, 1882. Among those folding and addressing the *Crusaders* was young James Cannon, Jr., student at the college and within a few years to become the leader of the prohibition movement in Virginia. Virginius Dabney, *Dry Messiah, The Life of Bishop Cannon* (New York, 1949), p. 9. Apparently the workers were entirely unpaid and the *Crusader* was forced to suspend publication for "several months" in 1883 for lack of funds.

24. On Feb. 9, 1882, this organ protested the "flippant style" of some legislators in dealing with the issue. On Feb. 16 it asserted that a religious paper had "no right to ignore those moral questions which may enter into politics," of which local option was one. Rev. William E. Hatcher was now succeeding H. H. Harrison in the editorship. Also in 1882 it published the letter of a doctor who questioned the wisdom of the movement, thinking it intended to prohibit the use of liquor.

option sentiment. In the Baptist General Association, Rev. John Pollard, vice-president of the alliance, encouraged by the changing attitude of the Baptist *Religious Herald*, put through a resolution that it was time for the government to consider "the propriety and practicability of preventing by law" "the common traffic" in liquor, so wasteful of national resources, so demoralizing to society, and so antagonistic to the Christian spirit. Less cautiously the Baptist Roanoke General Association the next year voted "that the state must combine with the church for the suppression of the evils that threaten our ruin." In the Richmond *Christian Advocate*, December 20, 1883, Dr. Bennett explained that the plan was to bring on elections only as individual counties were ready and to hold the counties when carried as was being done in Maryland and Georgia. He begged for funds for literature and speakers to offset the charge that local option had failed where it had been tried.

The Good Templars appointed a special legislative committee and the alliance prepared a new petition which 60,000 signed. The legislature of 1883-1884 gave the curt response that it was not desirable for the matter of license or no license to be debated in the counties. As they had thirty years before, the legislative and political thinkers regarded this simply as an attempt of small men and cranks to modify the state's traditional policy. In the face of such legislative recalcitrance some local optionists forgot the earlier experiment and in 1884 favored independent political action under the banner of the Prohibition party, which that year set up a state committee in Virginia. They were few in number. Certainly stung by their rejection, temperance men were acting with greater confidence in themselves and less respect for the old parties than ever before.

In May, 1884, the Baptist General Association listened to some radical proposals and agreed to definite endorsement of local option. It then chose as president H. R. Pollard, brother of John Pollard and a dry in principle and practice, a lawyer of ability, and a man of great political ambition. Meeting in Bristol, the ever-militant Holston Methodists recommended: "Act as you think and vote as you pray." In the east the Richmond *Christian Advocate* severely condemned liquor sellers and Bennett brought out his pamphlet, *The Great Red Dragon, An Appeal to Plain People on the Evils of the Liquor Traffic.* The conservative Virginia Methodist Conference on motion of Rev. F. M. Edwards asked support for "all enterprises" against the saloon.[25] Then the Good Templars voted that the two state political parties be invited to endorse the desired law next year and, in case of refusal, a state convention be called to determine what should be done next. To the Good Templar's proposal General William Mahone, boss of the Republican-Readjuster coalition, readily agreed, telling Hawxhurst to "write out what you want and give it to Col. Elam" for the platform, adding, however, that he himself would probably vote for license.[26] Thereupon the Democratic Richmond *Dispatch* warned of so strong a sentiment for local option in the southwest that the organization of a third party was a certainty if the relief asked for was not granted.

In the state Democratic platform of 1885 Major John W. Daniel easily reconciled opportunity for local decision in the matter with the national party's hostility to "sumptuary legislation." After the elections both Baptist and Methodist state bodies tactfully reminded the victorious Democrats of these platform pronouncements. The Good Templars framed another bill, again entrusting it to James Stubbs, who was now a senator. In the House Henry Pollard became floor leader. Even so, liquor interests felt no great alarm, believing their financial contributions, the national Democratic platform, and the known wet proclivities of the state party leaders

25. For the attitude of the churches and the activity of the Prohibition party in Virginia, see the next chapter.
26. Hawxhurst in *Civic Sentinel*, April, 1905.

would protect them against this absurd effort of "temperance topers" to "yankeeize the Old Dominion." Editor Louis Schade in the liquor dealers' Washington *Sentinel* deemed the movement "prohibition" and promised that its opponents in the legislature "will not be without their reward."

Clerical backers of the bill offered to except cities from its operation, hoping, the Richmond *Dispatch* explained, to divide the opposition and perhaps keep these men "with all their money" out of the prospective local contests. City dealers repulsed this strategic move. In the end both houses passed the bill by majorities of about 2 to 1.[27] Belatedly, Schade asked for an appointment with Governor Fitzhugh Lee. But the Governor had already signed the measure, although he wrote Schade that "personally I agree that temperance is not produced by law makers but by the influence of education, morality and religion." Whether this was true remained to be seen, but for now local option was part of the laws of the state. The plain people by their efforts—for few of the upper class and none of the rabble were helpful—had brought along the reluctant management of both religious and political organizations.[28]

Under this local-option law of February 26, 1886, elections could be held for any county, magisterial district, or town (but not oftener than once in two years) upon petition

27. *Acts*, 1885-1886, pp. 258-260. Robert A. Hohner, "The Anti-Saloon League in Virginia, 1901-1910: Prelude to Prohibition" (Master's thesis, Duke University, 1963), p. 6, says that passage of the law was "largely through the efforts of the Good Templars. . . ." He depends primarily upon the Templars' *Minutes* and perhaps a misreading of the article "Virginia" in E. H. Cherrington *et al.* (eds.), *Standard Encyclopedia of the Alcohol Problem* (Westerville, Ohio, 1925-1930), VI, 2768-2773. The article was drawn from Dr. Pearson's then unfinished manuscript (see note, VI, 2773). Hawxhurst, "Virginia Good Templars," supports the idea that other elements were probably just as influential in the movement.

28. House and Senate *Journals*, 1881-1882, 1883-1884, 1885-1886, *passim*; Grand Lodge of Good Templars, *Minutes*, 1881-1885; Baptist General Association *Minutes*, 1882-1884, 1885; Roanoke District Association *Minutes*, 1881, 1883; Methodist Virginia Annual Conference *Minutes*, 1884, 1885; Hawxhurst, "Virginia Good Templars" and in *Civic Sentinel*, April, 1905; Price, *Holston Methodism*, V, 291; Richmond *Dispatch*, July 16, 31, 1885, Feb. 3, 7, 23, 1886; Washington *Sentinel*, Jan. 30, March 6, 1886, the latter containing Governor Lee's views.

signed by one-fourth of the voters at the last November election; and, if the majority in any district or in any city[29] voted against license, no license to sell alcoholic or malt liquors or wines by anyone, including the maker, would be issued therein. It was the old plan of local decision as to licensing completely democratized.

To give inspiration and general direction to local contests under the new law a Local Option Convention was assembled in Lynchburg, April 21, 1886.[30] It was the second general temperance convention since 1854. Men from 75 counties and 20 cities, representing "every section of the state, all parties, creeds and colors," were present. If any came expecting either some endorsement of the Prohibition party or a platform of general reform they were disappointed. Though in the discussion there was talk of the "corruption of public life" and the "cause of the home and fireside against those who would seek to profit by the destruction of both," it was specifically voted that tobacco was not being attacked and that "this is not a political question." The object was "simply and solely to close the saloons." Dr. W. W. Smith was named head of the state-wide organization then set up. But public sentiment was against state-wide crusading. Dr. Smith, chancellor of Randolph-Macon, felt impelled to resign his place as leader and no successor was named. Good Templar leaders were soon busy throughout the state but were described as "small men" and "cranks." The convention and its machinery ceased to be noteworthy and only one more convention, and that abortive, met before 1902.[31]

29. If the city constituted a separate election district. In 1903 all cities of 1,000 were made self-determining in the matter.

30. W. C. Dutton, George Mayo, W. J. Kidd, and Mrs. E. J. Pleasants spoke for the Good Templars, the Sons of the Temperance, the Friends of Temperance, and the WCTU respectively. Richmond *Dispatch*, March 28, 1886.

31. *Religious Herald*, March 4, 1886; Richmond *Dispatch*, March 28, April 22, 23, 1886. Hawxhurst and other Good Templars moved over to Richmond and practically took charge, calling to their aid Edgar ("Yankee") Allen. Grand Worshipful Commander Dutton visited many places to give aid; and in the summer "bush meetings" were held in Fauquier

The local-option contests of 1886 set the pattern for most others of ensuing years. The dries started work first and at the Lynchburg convention were able to announce two victories. The first was in the little shipping town of West Point, despite its twelve saloons and its proximity to Richmond's wet resources; the success was the result of the work of Rev. E. M. Pilcher and Mrs. T. B. Bagby. The next came in Smyth County in the southwest, where A. T. Lincoln and Rev. John Hannon worked. The wets shrewdly countered by initiating contests in some of the larger cities, thus "outflanking the enemy." The dries did not want to attack these "citadels" until their movement had gained momentum, knowing that defeat would discourage their local forces.

Among dries the usual guiding organization was a "league" which would include local ministers and representatives of temperance societies. In Charlottesville the ministers of the Methodist and Christian churches were joined with the veteran temperance workers Ormond Stone, John B. Minor, and F. P. Dunnington, all university professors. In Richmond most Protestant clergymen aided leaders Joseph Mayo and Job Hawxhurst, who represented respectively the old Sons of Temperance and the Good Templars. Outstanding politicians and men of wealth did not often assist. Funds were always small.[32] Liquor dealers were the mainspring of the opposition. They hired leaders, often under the guise of "attorneys." "Workers" were supplied with ready money and drinks, and delivered the votes of their employees and hangers-on. The local political rings, lawyers, newspapers, and most of the businessmen, notably hotel men and those interested in "downtown" real estate in the towns and cities, supported them.

Strategy varied. Sometimes the opposition tried to divide and confuse. In Richmond an important element sponsored a

---

and Loudon at which Lecturer J. R. Miller is reported to have addressed crowds of 5,000 or 6,000.

32. The principal known expense was for thousands of copies of the *Temperance Recorder* which apparently was a combination of the *Crusader* and the Good Templars' paper.

Law and Order League, carried the city elections in May, and in October brought out the *Times* to support their reform position.[33] Here too word was spread among the Negro workers that tobacco would be attacked[34] next—a device employed also in the tobacco-growing counties. In Charlottesville much was made of the certain ruin that prohibition would bring to the fruit-growing enterprises in that section.[35] In some strongly Democratic parts it was insinuated that Democratic party endorsement of local option was only a device to thwart Mahone. Everywhere Democrats were warned that the whole movement might turn out to be a Republican trick aimed at breaking the Solid South through the development of a third party. Dries, pointing to the Lynchburg statement, concentrated on closing the local saloons. A new feature in their otherwise familiar tactics was the active participation of women and children working from the church. Stimulus came from a local WCTU unit,[36] which could tell of doings else-

33. Herbert T. Ezekiel, *Recollections of a Virginia Newspaperman* (Richmond, 1920). The *Times* was established Oct. 22, 1866, by Lewis Ginter, an important tobacconist. This suggests that the tobacco alarm was genuine. Once established, however, Ginter's interest declined and he turned control over to Joseph Bryan. John S. Bryan, *Joseph Bryan* (Richmond, 1935), pp. 249-250.

34. Tobacco and alcohol had long been connected by reformers. Cocke's hostility has been noted. In the southwest the Nashville *Christian Advocate*, Feb. 12, 1873, admitted that some might chew "to the glory of God"; the report on temperance to the Holston Association in 1883 attacked tobacco. In 1885 the Pleasant Hill Society resolved, "The general use of tobacco is not only injurious to health, but is an incentive that leads to excess in the use of intoxicating liquors also. . . ." The hatred of Dr. John Pollard for the weed was well known in Richmond. And the Methodists were soon to forbid its use by their young ministers. Altogether, tobacconists like Major Ginter of Richmond might well be alarmed—especially if they were also promoting hotels as Major Ginter later did. But probably the injection of tobacco into the fray was intended to discredit the leaders of the movement.

35. The Monticello Grape and Fruit Growers' Association had recently invested half a million dollars here, principally in vineyards and wineries. B. P. Chamberlain of Charlottesville reported that in 1878 Virginia received a medal at the Paris exposition for the "best American wine" and that Charlottesville was the principal wine center. Virginia Chamber of Commerce, *Commonwealth*, July 18, 1934.

36. In Charlottesville a unit had been established at the home of Mrs. J. L. Cochran of which Mrs. Noah K. Davis was an original member. This unit was remembered for opening the unsuccessful White Ribbon House, a place to eat without a bar, in opposition to the Redland House,

where and supply leadership and social sponsorship. It had been asserted that women were the "chief sufferers" of drink and that it was the duty of ministers to lead in all good community causes. The combination of women and ministers meant "the church in action against the saloon." Inevitably religious fervor "was transferred to the campaign"[37] and dries did not disdain to utilize the atmosphere created by a great religious revival. In Lynchburg a Moody and Sankey meeting was followed by the importation of dry orators, mostly ministers; and here, "on street corners, at the hotels, in stores, everywhere that men met, there were long and hot discussions."[38] Both sides made their bid for the Negro vote. The dries relied principally upon the Negro preachers who spoke from the platform with them to whites as well as blacks. The more experienced wets applauded the suggestion of a Negro worker that poor men needed to be informed *"personally"* (usually a drink or two was included with the information).

Arguments varied. The dries emphasized the temptations of the barrooms, their disorderliness and crime-breeding tendencies, foretold the growth of towns through the influx of people seeking a decent place in which to live and educate their children, and especially, the decrease in taxes as crimes lessened. The opposition insisted that the liquor business was necessary and legitimate and that its conduct had improved within the last ten years and could be further improved by regulations. They pointed to the local divisions sure to arise out of the attempt of dries to choose local officials with a primary view to enforcement of the no-license laws and the danger to party and white control arising out of such divisions. They made a great parade of the big men and big names on their side in answer to the dries' displays of men such as Lee,

---

a sporting hang-out of lawyers and judges. Charlottesville *Daily Progress,* June 1, 1895.

37. Cornelius Walker, *Memoir of Rev. C. W. Andrews* (New York, 1877), p. 574.

38. W. A. Christian, *Lynchburg and Its People* (Lynchburg, Va., 1900), pp. 360 ff.

Randolph, Wise, and Rives.[39] Through the local newspapers the wets protested "the use of the agencies and the ministers of the Church to control the ballot" and the dragging of the churches "through the mire of a political contest." They insisted that prohibition was the ultimate aim. They maintained this would be an invasion of men's households and consciences and utterly futile in its operation. "I never had any use for local option," wrote an old lady of a substantial Orange County family:

. . . every man should carry it in his heart. God gave us the ten commandments. They will never make those stop drinking that will drink. They must stop making it and then all these hot-headed prohibitionists will have several baskets stored away and drink their dram in between. When I see things working as they are it makes me feel sad. It seems that man has taken more on himself than he can accomplish.[40]

The dries were especially quick to deny any prohibitionist tendencies. Many feared this infringement on man's right to choose as a "free moral agent." Young R. E. Blackwell repudiated the prohibitionist label with a vigorous assertion that he had rather see America drunk and free than sober and in chains. More subtly one of the Rylands of King and Queen County frequently stated that the enticements of the saloon robbed men of their freedom not to drink.[41]

The contests, according to the press, were waged fairly and for the most part in good temper.[42] Yet resentments appeared and some of them lingered. In Richmond, for instance,

39. Among the influential wets: Micajah Woods, R. T. W. Duke, General James G. Field, and the coming Thomas S. Martin of Charlottesville; General Peyton Wise, Major N. V. Randolph, Charles M. Wallace, C. H. Harvey, B. M. Quarles, and C. V. Meredith, counsel for the Liquor Dealers Association in Richmond; L. S. Marye, Jr., J. H. Flood, and J. H. Rives in Lynchburg.

40. This letter, written to a grandson, was copied by D. M. Davidson of Orange, Virginia. It is dated June 17, 1888.

41. Garnet Ryland and President R. E. Blackwell of Randolph-Macon helped with this. It seems logical that farmers would have weighed the economic advantages of keeping liquor from their laborers but this argument does not appear in print.

42. *The Shenandoah Valley* (New Market), April 30, 1886.

dries long remembered the complete indifference of the Catholic clergy and the preoccupation of Episcopal ministers. Many conservative folk resented the activity of the women and the preachers and shuddered at the screaming of women and children who were worked into frenzy by the dry orators. On the other hand, good men and women came to entertain a cold, hard, relentless hate for the liquor-seller—no longer a "genial host" nor even a mistaken man trying to feed his family but a "leather-neck bar-tender," a "bloated bar-tender."

At the polls, by the end of the year, the dries had won 9 counties, 4 towns, and 18 magisterial districts. Their greatest victories were in the southwest in Washington, Smyth, and Pulaski counties and the town of Wytheville and in the Valley town of Winchester. The wets' great victories were in the cities of the east, in Charlottesville, Lynchburg, Fredericksburg, Richmond, Manchester, and in the Valley counties of Botecourt and Rockbridge. Nothing had been attempted by either side in all the extensive southside.

The only surprise of the elections was that Negroes, voting with the highest and lowest whites, voted wet with great unanimity.[43] That the Negro vote was bought was the convenient explanation. Another factor may have been that the Negroes were more attached to the barrooms, their amusement centers, than to the churches or that an agent of the wets had whispered that they must vote against the Democrats, explaining that General Mahone, their party leader, wanted them to.

The local-option program found itself losing supporters in two directions almost as soon as it was adopted. The coming of the Prohibition party to the national and state scene meant that many church bodies and the major political parties

43. Richmond *Dispatch*; Charlottesville *Jeffersonian Republican* (especially "extras"), March and April, 1886; Good Templars *Proceedings*, 1886; Christian, *Lynchburg*, pp. 360 ff. The Washington *Sentinel*, May 29, 1886, quoted the Alexandria *Gazette* as thinking the Negroes would vote for anything that would weaken the Democratic party. This may have been mere propaganda.

and their newspapers turned their support or opposition to this organization. Reformers had never been popular in Virginia. Even moderate temperance men were tired of temperance lectures, especially the women speakers, with their assumption of superior intelligence and virtue and their imputation of bad motives to the drinkers. People were generally out of patience with temperance agitation.

Yet much was done. Where licensing was continued opponents could and did oppose each individual application to the court.[44] Special prohibitory laws were sought by some areas and at times these were won.[45] Local-option elections were held in perhaps half the towns and counties and in some of them more than once,[46] whereas in others the overwhelming dominance of dry sentiment rendered elections unnecessary.[47] Since most of this activity left little or no record it would be futile to attempt a detailed discussion. But it is possible to determine what parts of the state went dry and to examine their characteristics. From this the effectiveness of local option as an anti-liquor device as well as its impact on local opinion will be evident.

In 1902 there were no licensed barrooms in 23 of the 100 counties and in 11 other counties the license fees paid

44. In Williamsburg the dries succeeded in having all licenses "taken away or refused." A successful local-option election in town and county followed. Harman, *Annals of Tazewell*, pp. 91-94, chronicles the opposition to licensing made in the courts there for 1884-1891. J. N. Harman was a chief leader in it. The *Temperance Advocate*, March 18, 1887, records a fifteen-year court contest in Chincoteague on the Eastern Shore. One place in Charlottesville was refused a license three times. *Daily Progress*, April 27, 1893.

45. The following areas received special prohibitory acts after 1886: Buena Vista, 1898; Palmyra, 1899; White Hall, 1900; Stony Creek (Sussex County), 1902; Carson (Dinwiddie County), 1903; Tazewell, Giles, Buchanan, and Dickinson counties, March 25, 1902. In the Franklin and Jerusalem districts of Southampton County and the Farmville district of Prince Edward County by acts of 1900 and 1901 dispensaries were established.

46. E.g., Charlottesville, Harrisonburg, Roanoke, and Norfolk voted dry but declined enforcement.

47. Replies to a questionnaire printed in the *Christian Federation*, June, 1902, indicate that 34 counties out of 84 reporting had no territory dry by local election; at least 9 of the 84 were dry in whole or part through public sentiment's operation.

were so small as to suggest the existence of only one or two in the county.[48] Altogether probably three-fourths of the magisterial districts were dry. Undoubtedly much territory had been won under local option and supplementary processes since 1886. Since this implies that many communities now had no barrooms the immediate objective was being attained,[49] but the success was rural and not urban. The cities were prospering. Property there was assessed for taxes in 1890 at 64 per cent of the state's total as compared with 16 per cent in 1860. The factories of Richmond, Norfolk, Danville, Petersburg, and Lynchburg were in all respects more valuable than all the others of the state; the merchants of Richmond alone were selling three-fourths as much as those of all the state in 1860. The property which the barrooms occupied in Richmond was worth nearly a million and a half dollars, in Norfolk, nearly a million dollars. Their employees were 714 in Richmond and 318 in Norfolk, which meant livelihood for several times as many people. Municipal governments derived $200,000 yearly from their licensing.[50] People had more money to spend here than in the country and they felt the tensions of modern business life more. The barrooms were conveniently located. Besides, the barroom, "saloon" it was now being called, was apt to be a more attractive place with its mirrors and pictures and appetizing free lunches or a restaurant, poolroom, or bath. So the barroom was popular to the disadvantage of the old demijohn. Politically the business was strong with its ready cash, its

48. To obtain a broader basis for the discussion following, both groups are counted as dry.

49. Estimates of John S. Barbour and William A. Anderson in *Proceedings and Debates of the Constitutional Convention, 1901-1902* (Richmond, 1906). Cf. also "Document X," *Journals and Documents of the Constitutional Convention, 1901-1902* (Richmond, 1902), which indicates 27 of 100 counties dry and dry districts in 28 additional counties. The Annual Reports of Boards, Officers and Institutions: *Reports of the Auditor, 1902* (Richmond, 1903), *passim*, gives revenue from the licenses sold in the counties.

50. U. S. Commissioner of Labor, "Economic Aspects of the Liquor Question," *Twelfth Annual Report, 1897* (Washington, 1897).

tie-up with the underworld, the hotels, the clubs, and municipal officials and employees and newspapers. Most businessmen felt that "agitation" would be bad for business. They preferred that the city itself work out the practical reforms needed and execute them through their more efficient police and courts. From this feeling came demands for and experiments with higher local license charges, fewer saloons, a more frequent closing of disorderly places, and efforts at enforcing Sunday-closing laws, excise boards and other administrative devices, and occasionally an experiment with dispensaries. The churches were by no means aggressively favorable to local-option elections. Catholics and Episcopalians were strong in the cities, and though they were supposed to favor reforms they rarely took forceful action.[51] The others favored reform but feared division in their churches and remembered the experiment of 1886. Besides, it seemed to be the policy of state leaders to wait until the situation became ripe before attacking the "citadels." And so of the cities only tiny Buena Vista and Williamsburg had no saloons.

The successful dry movement in the rural areas assumed interesting characteristics. The predominately white areas were drier than those with heavy Negro populations. The prosperous rural sections, the ones with free and militant churches and relatively free and open elections, all tended to be dry. Of the 40 counties with less than one-third Negro population in 1890, 25 were dry or near-dry; of the 60 counties with more than one-third Negro population, only 11 were dry or nearly so.

The driest region was the southwest, with 15 of its 22 counties dry. It was growing in population and property value more than any other section owing primarily to mining and railroad developments and the activities of real estate promoters.[52] The barrooms which normally accompanied

51. See *Southern Churchman*, June 6, July 27, 1889; *Christian Sentinel*, Nov., 1901, quoting *Richmond Clericus*.
52. Allen W. Moger, *The Rebuilding of the Old Dominion* (Ann Arbor, Mich., 1940). Chap. 3 is very good.

such progress were discouraged by the managers of the new concerns.[53] Catholics and Episcopalians were few and Primitive Baptists were less influential than in earlier times. Militant Methodists and Christians were taking the lead in most affairs.[54] Here politics as well as religion was practiced with fervor.[55] The sparse Negro population meant no race problem and the people tended toward individualism in politics. Republicans and Democrats were about equal in number, with the Republicans being generally associated with the new industrialism and not as friendly to liquor as the Democrats.

In the Valley four of the nine counties were dry or near-dry. Without much boom or bustle it had been steadily growing in wealth. It had no Negro problem but did have strong temperance elements in its population (though some of the isolated religious groups still did not participate in politics). Republicans and Independents abounded but the area was normally Democratic.

The 69 eastern counties were very different from those in the west. In 60 of them Negroes constituted one-third of the population; in 39 they were a majority which ran as high as 3 to 1. While farming was better in some and almost hopelessly bad in other counties, the Piedmont as a whole showed a decrease in 1860 to 1890 from 116 to 85 million dollars in cash value of farms, and the Tidewater, from 84 to 69 million dollars. In church policy Episcopalians were inclined to be exclusive, Presbyterians were cautious, while the all-important Methodists would scarcely have been recognized as such by their vigorous and social-minded brethren of the southwest. Negroes were decidedly church-minded. Long organized into Baptist and Methodist church bodies and

53. See for example the Iron and Steelworkers Association of America, Ltd., and property owners in Rockbridge County opposing the granting of a license due to the unsuitability of the location. William A. Anderson Papers, University of Virginia Library.

54. U. S. Census Office, *Twelfth Census of the United States* [1900], "Religious Bodies" (Washington, 1906), Table 4.

55. William C. Pendleton, *Political History of Appalachian Virginia* (Dayton, Va., 1927), p. 429.

housed with comparative spaciousness, they could be seen wending their way to and from services almost any time on Sunday or during the protracted meeting season. Their preachers were potent in arousing emotions in meetings and sometimes in political seasons.[56] Between whites and blacks contacts were mainly on a personal basis, far from unfriendly, and with frank recognition of race distinction and of white supremacy. In politics there was no amity. For most whites, politics meant control in such a way that there might be no Negro office-holders. For Negroes to vote was to vote against the Democratic party. Everywhere barrooms were plentiful. Of the nine counties with less than one-third Negroes, three were dry.[57] Of the 60 remaining, only 12 were dry.[58] The greater the proportion of Negroes the less the likelihood of successful movements against licensing. Since the private interests of the Negroes would have inclined many to oppose the sale of alcohol it seems a certainty that Democratic control over election machinery was responsible for the tendency to vote wet year after year.

Even though the rural areas were going dry the number of selling places did not decrease. Not only did entirely legitimate saloons increase in and near the cities but selling places appeared just across the dry boundaries. Sympathetic judges in the wet districts could completely destroy the effectiveness of an area's desire to remain dry. Within the dry areas illegal selling began to appear. A field study of Tidewater Lancaster four years after it had gone dry disclosed that 75 speak-easies had appeared in place of the former

56. Philip Alexander Bruce, *The Plantation Negro as a Freeman* (New York, 1889), discusses the Negro and his religious life at length. W. E. B. DuBois, *Negro Church* (Atlanta, Ga., 1903), pp. 35-37, presents statements from friendly observers supporting the idea that most Negro ministers were making significant contributions to their congregations and communities.

57. Green, Mathews, Patrick.

58. Appomattox, Charlotte, King George, Lancaster, Madison, Middlesex, Northumberland, Amelia, Amherst, Brunswick, Henry, Spotsylvania.

25 or 30 barrooms. A seeming advance was made in that there was less drinking among the Negroes and less noise and disturbance, since the drunks were kept inside instead of being kicked out. But the flimsy excuses which the keepers made the Negroes put forward to avoid the law were teaching them to lie and to lose respect for all laws. State authorities were ignored and the places were protected against federal officers by federal licenses. Even the jury box had been invaded by personal and political hostilities and a general air of subterfuge and legal abuse was present.[59] All these were hardly arguments which could be used to further the cause of local option.

To these findings should be added purported arrangements among the speak-easies whereby all would bear the court expenses of any one of them and apparent collusion between shrewd lawyers and negligent or technically inclined magistrates for the defeat of the law's plain intent. Not unlike Lancaster were the four counties of the Northern Neck and Mathews across the Rappahannock.[60] In the Piedmont when Amherst Court House, with its 600 people and its nine bars, went dry in 1898 one of the barrooms immediately changed to a drugstore which dispensed in one year 25 barrels of "medicated whiskey" without violating the law in the opinion of the county judge.[61] In Roanoke County, to the astonishment of the county's commonwealth attorney and the mildly expressed indignation of the Roanoke *Times*, 100 persons were indicted at one sitting in 1890 for "blind tiger" operations. A skilful lawyer got most if not all of them free.[62] In the far southwest in 1902, 40 were indicted at one time in Wise County and stores there were closed by injunction.[63]

59. W. T. Thorn, "The Negroes of Litwalton, Virginia: A Social Study of the 'Oyster Negro,'" *Bureau of Labor Bulletin*, No. 37 (Washington, 1901), pp. 1168-1170.
60. See act of April 2, 1902, for these counties.
61. *Christian Federation*, March, 1902.
62. Roanoke *Times*, July, 1890, *passim*.
63. *Christian Federation*, Feb., 1902.

The problem by no means was unexpected.[64] Illegal selling always came with a change of policy. It had been predicted by the wets and feared by the dries from the days when the abolishing of licenses was first suggested. Nor were the cities, for all their claims that they would reform themselves, accomplishing much. Retailers in Manchester and Alexandria fought any increase in license charges—in Alexandria even though the money was to go to the public schools. In Richmond, which the *Dispatch* each January 1 proclaimed to be statistically a city of churches, reforms had been pledged.[65] Yet three years after 1886 Judge S. B. Witt officially stated that in one place "every crime from murder down had been committed" and a police officer testified that at or near another place 500 arrests had been made within his recollection.[66] From the Baptist college in the far west of the city to the First Baptist Church in the heart of the business section one side of the principal thoroughfare and shopping street was given over to barrooms and the businesses that thrived in their atmosphere. It was the "wrong side of Broad Street." Not all of Richmond's 300 saloons were questionable places, however. The bar of the palatial Jefferson Hotel shared plaudits with its lobby. With equal elegance the Westmoreland Club catered to the older gentry, the Commonwealth to the younger, Reuger's to the lover of seafood, and Murphy's to state officialdom.

In meeting this situation the legislature, often instigated by the dries, acted with wisdom. It avoided antagonizing distilleries by striking from the act of 1886 a provision against sale for delivery in territory not dry. Later it required brandy-makers to obtain licenses as other distillers had done since

64. When the General Local Option Bill had just passed the Senate in 1886, Colonel A. Fulkerson moved that its title be changed to read, "A bill to multiply still houses, increase drunkenness in the state, and diminish the revenues." The motion is recorded in the Senate *Journal* as "Rejected."

65. Richmond *Dispatch*, March 25, 1886.

66. Richmond *Dispatch*, May 18, June 5, 1889, April 8, 17, 23, 1892.

1877, thereby obtaining a better check on their operations. As something of a safety valve it removed cider and wine from the category of liquor as far as regulating the manufacture and sale by the makers was concerned. More important still, it left importation unhampered, thereby saving the well-to-do from any excuse for patronizing and supporting the lower classes who violated the law. It made new regulations for druggists, steamboats, sample merchants, and social clubs. For local situations deemed particularly bad it passed special enforcement laws.[67] It carefully avoided "informers" or new and terrifying penalties or procedures that might provoke sympathy with law-breakers. Though the process was long, this policy was supported by the sentiment of the majority in the regions where it was operative and won by wearing out those who fought it.[68]

Out of the local contests over licensing and law enforcement emerged local opinions, local interests, and local political factions. Faced with the necessity of taking a stand for or against the property interests or even the freedom of a neighbor, not for or against some abstract or remote proposition, men's opinions clarified and became fixed. Experience in co-operation and in leadership was gained. Pride of position which was underestimated by political analysts appeared to hold men steady. If the community remained dry, "interests" developed which were petty in character but powerful in sustaining sentiment. The merchant noticed that trade

67. See revenue acts of 1890-1900; *Acts* of Feb. 29, 1892 (for Lee, Pulaski, Scott, Wise, Dickinson, Buchanan, Bland, and Russell), April 2, 1902 (for Richmond, Lancaster, Westmoreland, and Mathews). The act of 1892 declared any structure where liquor was illegally sold a common nuisance and provided for its abatement, gave a broad interpretation of what constituted selling and removed technical difficulties in proving sale, made possession of federal license to sell evidence and required the commonwealth's attorney to represent them. The act was declared to be in assistance of the revenue laws. The act of 1902 was similar except that it took cognizance of liquor disguised as preserved fruits and similar devices and declared that it was in aid of the local-option laws adopted by these counties.

68. But in some places a dry policy was abandoned because the law was not enforced, e.g., in Accomac. *Civic Sentinel*, June, 1902.

picked up when liquor no longer drew business to a com-
petitor. The employer of low-grade labor on fishing-steamers
and in mills, packing plants, fertilizer factories, mines, farms,
and around the home found fewer scraps to settle and greater
punctuality among his hands or servants. These all backed
the temperance cause. But there were many who did not,
among whom was the railroad employee who toward the end
of the period found himself continually in danger of losing
his job if found with a foaming glass at the wayside station.
Frequently there were attempts to replace the constables and
the sheriff who did the arresting of offenders and the county
attorney who prosecuted them; and change in these positions
often meant change in the other local officers and in legislators. Mixed with politics on the local scene, the temperance
movement was weakened by those who forgot their dry leanings when it was convenient.

In taking stock around 1895 Virginia temperance leaders
read Washington Gladden and Charles W. Elliot. Both minimized the effectiveness of laws but preferred those of the
local-option type. Most Virginians held the same opinion.[69]
This democratization of the ante bellum licensing process
called local option must be set down as a valuable gain for
communities. Some good men deemed it an unworthy compromise with evil and some objected to the practical difficulties involved in its use, especially the enforcement difficulties.
On the other hand, through it many moderate men were enabled to express their dislike of the saloon and the stillhouse
without relinquishing their hostility to prohibitory laws and
the ideas behind them. Despite the severe handicap of poor
enforcement, public opinion continued to veer to its side

69. Washington Gladden, *Moral Gains and Losses of the Temperance
Reformation* (Boston, 1895), delivered in Temperance Hall, University of
Virginia, May 14, 1895. Committee of Fifty, Charles W. Elliot, chairman,
"Report of Sub-Committee," University Society Minutes (1895), Gallus
Thomann, *Real and Imaginary Effects of Intemperance* (New York, 1884),
and Thomann, *Colonial Liquor Laws* (New York, 1887), were easily
available and were read by some.

until public leaders agreed that sentiment was definitely dry in rural areas. A general law making all rural areas dry would be democratic in origin and would make enforcement easier. For such a law there was available the same slowly developing strength that had brought about a law in 1900 requiring the public schools to teach the effects of alcohol upon the human body.[70] The chief weakness of a policy so local in its application lay in the lack of enthusiasm, drive, and broad-gauged leadership that seem to go along with large-scale organization and endeavor. The Anti-Saloon League showed in its early days that those defects could be remedied.

70. *Acts*, 1899-1900, p. 134.

## Chapter Ten

# THE BACKGROUND OF
# THE VIRGINIA ANTI-SALOON
# LEAGUE

After 1902 the anti-liquor movement gained momentum rapidly and soon assumed forms far beyond that of personal pledging and local option, which had brought prior success. Certainly the foundation of the movement in its later aspects lay principally in the work just chronicled, and in years to come recourse was frequently made to the vitalizing force of local elections. Developments not primarily connected with temperance societies or local-option elections also made contributions to the twentieth-century anti-liquor movement. They can best be studied first as they operated through the churches and then in their political aspects.

The forty years after the Civil War witnessed, despite depressions and agitation, a thorough setting-in-order of Virginia's fiscal house. Economic conditions for the state as a whole improved and steadied.[1] The improvement was not uniform, for the cities all fared significantly better than the rural areas. The many small places commonly called "towns" prospered almost as much as their larger counterparts. Farmlands showed a return to pre-war levels of production in some areas and presented a remarkable lack of advancement in others. This was particularly evident along the sandy roads of the Southside or the almost impassable route from Richmond north to the Rappahannock.

1. C. C. Pearson, *The Readjuster Movement in Virginia* (New Haven, 1917), pp. 91-94, 110-111, 173; William DuBose Sheldon, *Populism in the Old Dominion: Virginia Farm Politics, 1885-1900* (Princeton, N. J., 1935), pp. 1-21. Census figures of 1900 are used throughout the chapter unless otherwise stated. Also used to add meaning and interpretation are the observations of Dr. Pearson after conversations with many of the major figures and extensive work in contemporary newspapers. Notes on many of the interviews conducted by Dr. Pearson are in the Pearson Papers, Wake Forest College Library.

At the same time a change was taking place in the number and size of rural land-holdings as well as in the class alignment of the owners. The number of large farms declined and those which remained were unable to maintain pre-war levels of life. This meant either an exodus or a significant decline in importance for the old community leaders.[2] In contrast, middle-sized farms were growing more steadily and quickly than any other group. They constituted about one-half of the total number of farms and placed their owners in positions of community responsibility.[3] They were home owners of status and though the economy which developed rarely made use of hired help they were able to acquire the necessities and even the comforts of the rural life of that day.

The more than 14,000 persons engaged in the retail mercantile business were of more importance than in ante bellum days. Even subtracting from this figure those in the cities and towns and the influential clerks, there were—certainly in many regions—more store proprietors than lawyers, doctors, and preachers altogether. Some had sunk to this position, some had climbed. All had more money and more neighborhood influence than the burgeoning class of farmers and, though most of them "tended store" and served as their own principal clerk, for the most part they were of the upper middle class.

The churches of the whites (those of the Negroes were not important to liquor sentiments at this time) were undergoing significant development. Their members in 1890 numbered approximately 333,000 and in 1906, 491,000—an increase of nearly 50 per cent in a population that grew scarcely 25 per cent in twenty years. The ability and the willingness of members to support their churches grew even

2. One reason for this phenomenon was suggested by the *Religious Herald*, Jan. 27, 1881, in editorially describing a community "in which the sons of well-to-do families have almost without exception, for a long series of years, become worthless."

3. This estimate is obtained by adding to the number of farms of 20 to 100 acres a small portion of those of 100 to 500 acres.

faster. From 1890 to 1906 the gain in value of church property was from 50 to 200 per cent in each of the more important denominations, which was much greater than that for all property within the state. This came on top of a gain of well over 100 per cent for each of them in 1890 over 1860, with the church buildings of West Virginia included in the figures of the latter year. Nearly all of the Catholics and Jews, half of the Episcopalians, and a third of the Presbyterians lived in cities and perhaps most of the rest of them in good-sized towns. The smaller bodies along with the German sects had fairly narrow habitats. The middle-class and evangelical Methodists and Baptists were to be found everywhere in varying proportions. Speaking broadly, the Episcopalians and Presbyterians wielded the greatest influence politically, socially, and intellectually.[4] But in both totals and ratios of increase in numbers and church property Methodists led,[5] followed by Baptists. These two combined with the socially akin Christians (and Disciples) constituted two-thirds of the church people. The significance of all this was not entirely religious, for in a total white population of voting age and sex of 301,000, Protestant church members numbered about 92,000, or nearly one-third. Furthermore, the proportionate strength of the Protestant women members was very much greater than this.[6] Nowhere other than in the saloons and at the courthouse on monthly court days was

4. This, of course, would not be true in particular communities, and there were wide variations between churches of the same denomination in the same city or section.

5. Baptists led in value of property in 1906 according to the census; but this was probably an error since their figure was lower in 1916 than in 1906 and lower than that of Methodists then also.

6. The following figures, derived directly or indirectly from census reports, may be serviceable: Church membership for 1906 in thousands was: Methodists, 175; Baptists (including Primitives), 145; Presbyterians, 38; Episcopalians, 28; Christians (including Disciples), 34; German sects, 30 (Lutherans, 14, Dunkers, 10, United Brethren, 6); Roman Catholics, 28; Jews, 2. Value of church property in 1906 in thousands: Methodists, 4,504; Baptists (see preceding note), 5,912; Presbyterians, 2,100; Episcopalians, 2,435; Christians, 700; Lutherans, 344. About 61 per cent of Protestant members were female; about 52 per cent were twenty-one years old or above.

opportunity for molding public opinion so good as at the churches' meetings.

Middle-class education was increasing and here temperance information was readily available.[7] After the Readjuster movement it was not until 1905 that there was sufficient stir about public schools to make politicians take much notice. There were, however, fewer adults and near-adults who could not read, the Sunday schools were improving, and the local newspaper was having its great day. Temperance lessons which had been given occasionally in the Sunday schools began to appear at regularly recurring intervals in the 1890's. Similarly, young folk had learned of the bad effects of alcohol through textbooks, lectures, or debates in the schools of some communities. Now, in 1900, there was a state law requiring that the public schools all teach systematically as a part of physiology and hygiene "the effects of alcohol and other narcotics on the human system."[8]

Whatever the quality of the instruction, many, outside the schools as well as in them, were introduced to the "teachings of science" on the subject at a time when the sciences were beginning to attract popular attention. Temperance pieces were again appearing in McGuffey's *Readers*, from which they had disappeared since the Civil War. And the list of workers and devices grew: Atticus Haygood, Methodist Sunday school secretary; Josephus Hopgood and his Milligan (Christian) College in Tennessee; the Demarest speaking contests for medals; Children's Bands of Hope, promoted by the WCTU; and the crudely illustrated *Ram's Horn*. Voters bore all of these with amused tolerance, but the lasting impression made on the children involved is in part responsible for the rapid growth of the prohibition cause which was to triumph in less than a generation.[9]

7. Taunting the *Religious Herald* over its alleged admission that Baptists were unfit for high public office, Lafferty said, "Time and Free Schools will do much for them." Richmond *Christian Advocate*, March 29, 1877.
8. The law was a result of WCTU agitation. *Acts*, 1899-1900, p. 134.
9. The same idea is expressed and emphasized in Mark Sullivan, *Our*

The increasing importance of women was difficult to evaluate. Recognized almost from the beginning as the chief sufferers from the excesses of others and unhampered by any extensive habit of personal indulgence or fashion of public treating, women were expected to play a leading part in the war on liquor. They were sympathetic and helpful, particularly those of the middle classes. "The ladies are with us, and warmly so. . . . They are training, and will train, the rising generation to be sober," Scervant Jones told the Dover Baptist Association in 1849. The *Religious Herald* in 1874 assumed a continuation of their support.[10] But according to the accepted creed of all the ante bellum period the man was head of the household and sole director of affairs outside. Even in the churches women were expected to listen and acquiesce.[11] So the war on liquor was a man's war with the women only as auxiliaries.[12]

The day for so subordinate a woman's role was passing. Women were beginning to take over most of the jobs in the great new industry of public education and many of them were feeling the sense of independence that comes from earning one's own livelihood. In the churches it was the women who got the children to Sunday school, furnished the dinners so essential to all-day meetings, and, through their "aid-societies" of one sort or another, built the parsonages and bought the carpets. In the Southern Methodist church the publications of the Woman's Foreign Missionary Society date from 1878; those of the Woman's Home Missionary Society date from 1886. In 1889 the contribution of the Women's Southern Baptist Missionary Union was $30,000; in 1918,

---

*Times; The United States, 1900-1925* (6 vols.; New York, 1927-1935), II, 113-115, 192.

10. Editorial of March 26 on "The Grand Temperance Revival." For Scervant Jones see above, p. 123n.

11. This idea is emphasized in the writings of Jesse Mercer among Baptists and of W. A. Smith among Methodists. Smith was sorry to observe a lessening in man's dominance.

12. Mary Minor Blackford (Mrs. William M. Blackford), Margaret Mercer, and Mrs. William McDowell are the only ones prominently identified.

$515,000.[13] Whether it came promptly as in the Upper King
and Queen Baptist Church or was delayed on Biblical grounds
as in the Southern Baptist Convention,[14] recognition of
women's right to participate in the determination of church
policy was surely coming. And with the increasing importance
and influence of women came increasing hostility to liquor.
For as drinking shifted from the home to the barroom the
husband was more often away from home and spent more
money, and the boy was in greater danger owing to the
saloon's glamour and the custom of treating at the bar. While
the drinking was done in the home, which was a man's
"castle," there was little that a woman could do but plead,
pray, and endure.[15] No one could deny her right to invoke
the aid of her relatives and her pastor against the barroom
that made her men drunk or the neighborhood unsafe for her.
The women took an active part against the saloon in the
local-option campaigns and almost always with the church as
a base. The war, once started, came to involve a social pro-
scription which the liquor dealer and his family found hard
to withstand.[16]

In the WCTU[17] women governed and men were the auxiliaries, a plan which very naturally had its appeal for some

13. Southern Baptist Convention, *Proceedings*, 1918, p. 30.
14. See *Proceedings*, 1885, p. 30. The manuscript minute-book of the
King and Queen church shows that in revising the constitution of the
church in 1882 women were permitted to share in the selection of the
pastor.
15. Margaret Mercer so stated.
16. "The families of liquor men are cut socially"; Portsmouth Baptist
District Association *Minutes*, 1909. Judge Martin Williams and others
made valuable suggestions for this section.
17. Early presidents of the WCTU were: Mrs. Rebecca D. Wilson of
Lincoln, 1883-1886; Mrs. William H. Pleasants of Richmond, 1886-1888;
Mrs. R. H. Jones of Norfolk, 1888-1889; Mrs. H. H. Hoge, 1898-1938.
WCTU records in Virginia are housed in the University of Virginia
Library where manuscript minutes of the state organization, the printed
reports of most of the years, as well as most of the organization's publications, are preserved. Many county records and minutes are also located
there. An account of the founding of the Virginia WCTU along with
accounts of the various county chapters is given in Elizabeth Hogg Ironmonger and Pauline L. Phillips, *History of the Woman's Christian Temperance Union of Virginia* (Richmond, 1958).

of the ladies. Though this organization was never so prominent in Virginia as elsewhere, its activities and its influence were apparent. Circles welcomed the temperance workers and helped in the local contests, and its state leaders co-operated in state temperance conventions. In its early days it undoubtedly frightened conservative temperance leaders. In the *Religious Herald* of March 26, 1874, an observer of its beginnings in another state noted that the women invested their fight with religious fervor and would not be discouraged like men, that "when it becomes fashionable the crusade runs through society as easily as new style in bonnets." Undoubtedly the activities of some of its women leaders prejudiced some prominent people against the cause and gave opportunity for jibes that emphasized the sexual or the social note with great effectiveness. Offsetting all this was the influence of the organization through its important leaders in the great middle-class churches. Presbyterians held back but Southern Methodists in 1882 and again in 1890 welcomed the organization as a co-worker in the "Cause." Among Baptists in 1890 Mr. B. F. Jacobs promised Miss Frances Willard that the Sunday school Lesson Committee would give four temperance lessons per year—a rule which was adhered to well into the twentieth century.[18] Finally, it was at the insistence of the state WCTU, backed by the principal evangelical churches, that the legislature in 1900 passed a bill which young John Garland Pollard drew and sponsored for them. This bill read: "In the teaching of physiology and hygiene approved textbooks shall be used, plainly setting forth the effects of alcohol and other narcotics on the human system, and such

18. "For many years occasional temperance lessons were inserted in the International Uniform Lessons. At first there was no rule as to the number of temperance lessons in a given year. In 1890 Mr. B. F. Jacobs promised Miss Frances Willard, in the presence of the International Sunday School Convention in Pittsburg, that the Lesson Committee would give four temperance lessons per year. This rule has been adhered to down to the present time. . . . When graded lessons were introduced into many Sunday Schools in 1909 and the years immediately following, those who framed the lessons sought to put similar emphasis upon temperance instruction. . . ." John R. Sampey to Dr. Pearson, June 16, 1930.

effects shall be as fully and thoroughly taught as other branches of said last named subjects."[19] It is said that J. Hoge Tyler thought this measure gave distinction to his term as governor.

In many sections anti-liquor sentiment was built up principally by evangelists. Few pastors were seriously handicapped by personal fondness for liquor as they once had been. But neither their education in the classics and theology nor any positive command from their church organizations incited them to leadership in anti-liquor reforms. The way to professional advancement was known to be through harmonizing discords, not through arousing them. Local pastors even when moved to action by local influences did not present a picture of heroic and effective crusaders. Describing a Richmond scene of 1900, Mrs. Thomas P. Bagby wrote: "There in the foreground were the handsome, well-clothed, portly representatives of the liquor interests wondering what mischief the women were up to; yonder in the background sat the dignified, solemn ministers . . . the weight of empires on their shoulders."[20]

Quite different was the evangelist who in those days was appearing everywhere, especially in the rural regions.[21] Like

19. *Acts*, 1899-1900, p. 134. Ten other Southern states had adopted similar legislation. Leonard Stott Blakey, *The Sale of Liquor in the South* ("Studies in History, Economics and Public Law, Edited by the Faculty of Political Science of Columbia University," Vol. LI, whole No. 127 [New York, 1912]), p. 40.

20. *Christian Federation*, Jan., 1902.

21. Definite recognition of the technique of evangelists as well their qualities is to be found in George R. Stuart, *Methodist Evangelism* (Nashville, Tenn., 1923), a series of lectures memorializing Sam Jones delivered at Emory University, Georgia. Rev. Samuel P. Jones, Methodist evangelist from Georgia, transferred the informality of the camp meeting to the city auditorium. A widely read man, he consciously avoided the rules of grammar and offered a deliberate change from the formality of the regular clergy. Converted after a wild and liquorous youth he attacked alcohol along with other social evils. From the pulpit he said of drinkers: "I would rather associate with a hog." Bernard A. Weisberger, *They Gathered at the River* (Boston, 1958), pp. 233-235, 241-242. Some preachers combined pastoral work with evangelical work elsewhere. A notable example was H. M. Wharton of Baltimore; see also Richmond *Christian Advocate*, Sept. 1, 1898, for Lewis P. Bransford of Danville

the old circuit-rider and the missionary, he came into a community only occasionally and so was not subject to the pressure of powerful local opinions. Since his object was to arouse people he used emotional stories. He specialized in attacking sins—the everyday, practical sins that, as Sam Jones had taught him, ordinary good church members could be safely accused of. In the matter of liquor he said plainly, "Making, selling or drinking liquor is sin, and you know it." Men's reactions varied, of course. But few forgot. One competent observer said: "When the corn was laid by and the sweet potatoes were ripe, the mountainmen went to the revivals and got religion; but when the corn was gathered and the fruit had ripened and been made into brandy, they got drunk again, day after day; they did not, however, boast of their relapse but wept and pled human weakness, begetting sin." Reported another observer:

The big distillers had always kept their places in good order, were known as good citizens, contributed liberally to all good causes, tolerated no criticism; but the stories of the evangelists "got under their skin" and they quit selling, leaving the small fry retailers to haul grain or fruit on their backs up into the mountain hollows and there make such liquor as they could.

Often the church leaders did not like the evangelist. A careful reading of the Richmond *Christian Advocate* for August and September, 1898, when camp meetings and protracted meetings were in full swing, discloses no interest of this powerful Methodist organ in them. But the ordinary pastor could not afford to dissent with the evangelist's attack on liquor without appearing to take the other side.

Meantime, a broader conception of the duty of Christians and the function of churches was appearing in the evangelical world and gaining acceptance. In the old days emphasis was laid primarily upon the individual's duty to save his soul

who was then appearing his third successive year in Buckingham and preaching to congregations of 3,000 in the Tabernacle at White Hall.

through faith and self-denial—"other-worldiness" was deemed the highest manifestation of true religion.[22] The churches had not neglected to prescribe temperance, morality, and the like, but their interest in this direction had been subordinate. More recently religious activities were directed to "the up-lifting of the whole man . . . , and to the salvation of society as well as that of the individual."[23] This change of emphasis involved both a socializing and a secularizing of Christianity which was mirrored by the writings of Josiah Strong and Lyman Abbot and by the increasing share of laymen and young people in church work[24] and the teachings of a few college men to eager and responsive youths.

The most important reason for this change was the revelation of science as to the "interdependence of body and mind, and the influence of physical conditions on spiritual life,"[25] for along with it came the idea that the state is a proper agency for the realization of social ends and not principally a defender of property rights. Putting the two ideas together, many felt that Christians could have no higher duty than to use the state's machinery for the removing of obstacles and the providing of opportunities so that the indi-vidual might develop as Christ would have him in His King-dom on Earth. Some declared that for the guidance and

22. Far in advance of his time was W. C. Rives, *Discourse before the Young Men's Christian Association of Richmond on the Ethics of Christianity* (Richmond, 1855), in which he referred to this tendency and mentioned the emphasis of the Bible upon "works."

23. Josiah Strong, *Religious Movements for Social Betterment* (New York, 1900), covers this subject thoroughly; Dr. W. L. Poteat, president of Wake Forest College, 1905-1927, and a leader in the new movement, also made many helpful suggestions.

24. Lay representation in Methodist conferences, the layman's move-ment, the Young Men's Christian Association, the Young Women's Christian Association, the Baptist Young People's Union, to cite only a few illustrations.

25. Strong, *Religious Movements for Social Betterment*, summarizes the causes essentially thus: the change in civilization from an individual-istic to a social type, which awakened a consciousness that religion deals with man in his relations to other men as well as with God, the revelation of science as to the "interdependence of body and mind and the influence of physical conditions on spiritual life," and the re-discovery of "Christ's social ideal, as something possible of realization on this earth."

stimulation of Christians in this work churches ought to make pronouncements and set up agencies.[26]

Acceptance of the broad concept in so radical a form was not easy or rapid. Even the many thoughtful leaders of the plainer people's churches, disturbed as they were over the increasing inability of the old preaching and the old church rules to keep the younger generations in order,[27] were slow to lighten their burden by invoking the aid of the state, which they had understood ought to keep out of this realm. Acceptance might have been delayed indefinitely but for the "Liquor Power." Starting out with attempts along old lines to secure and enforce laws against violation of the Sabbath, church leaders found themselves persistently thwarted in their own states and cities by the political influence of the liquor sellers. They heard dealers say that they would obey the Sunday laws only because they wanted to, heard them boast of their influence in the Democratic party because of their campaign contributions, saw them acting as if they owned the government, and felt keenly their jibes at clergymen.[28] From Prohibition party writers church leaders learned that the liquor interests of the whole country acted in concert to dictate party platforms, choose officials, and block laws, thus making themselves an aggressive enemy of the churches and a demoralizer of public life in the whole nation. Some of them

26. Bishop Francis McConnell's address at the University of Virginia Institute of Public Affairs, Aug. 3, 1930, contains an able statement of this position.

27. The Minute Book of the Upper King and Queen Baptist Church records in 1882 that the "church finds it specially difficult" to fix the limits of the indulgence of its members in worldly amusements. It wished to "carefully guard against giving religion a gloomy or forbidding aspect" and to encourage indulgence "within reasonable limits." Methodists were unable to control dancing; a threat to enforce the rules was met by a demand that the rules against patronizing barrooms be enforced also. The tendency was not new. Cf. James B. Blanks, "Social Control by Baptists in Virginia and North Carolina, 1775-1928" (Master's thesis, Wake Forest College, 1929), pp. 10-11.

28. Atticus Greene Haygood, *Close the Saloons, A Plea for Prohibition* (Macon, Ga., 1880); Richmond *Christian Advocate*, April 15, 1880; Richmond *Virginian*, March 18, 1915; Richmond *Dispatch*, March 25, 1886.

felt compelled to tell their people that, working along the old lines, "We've made good bricks, but the devil's made the building." To some the conclusion seemed inescapable that "The Whiskey power must be put under, or it will put us under."[29] This meant that Christians must enter politics in self-defense, which was a long step away from the old idea and a most important step toward full acceptance of the newer.

Such a broad conception might turn the many separate religious bodies from the rivalry and hostility over dogma and techniques of salvation and unite them under a common banner in the face of a common foe. The relative influence of these various forces in building anti-liquor sentiment down to about 1900 can in no way be determined. Their cumulative effect can only be gauged from the acts of church bodies and the final outcome in legislation.[30] The acts of church bodies are significant enough to merit careful attention.

In the South-wide church organizations, interest and activity were greatest from 1886 to 1896. In 1886 and frequently thereafter both the Southern Baptist Convention and the Methodist General Conference (the former for the first time in its history) appointed committees and adopted resolutions on the liquor issue. As to drinking Methodists would only plead that their church members mind the "solemn vow that rests upon them" and abstain altogether. Then in 1886 they ordered that manufacture and sale be dealt with "as in case of immorality" and not as merely "imprudent or improper conduct."[31] The Baptist organization, unable to make rules, declared in 1896 as the "sense of this body" that no one engaged directly or indirectly in the business should be

29. Bishop McTyeire, cited in M. E. Church South, General Conference *Journal*, 1890.
30. Hunter D. Farish, *The Circuit Rider Dismounts, A Social History of Southern Methodism, 1865-1900* (Richmond, 1938), chap. 9, gives a summary for the Methodist Episcopal Church, South, with very helpful evaluations from church newspapers. The account, however, is laudatory rather than critical.
31. The clergy had previously been ordered to keep out of the business.

a church member; with respect to drinking their declaration was not so strong.

From the standpoint of public policy as contrasted with church policy both bodies spoke vigorously. The business was "opposed to the best interests of society and government and the progress of our holy religion" and "a most powerful hindrance to the gospel of Christ, and an aggressive enemy to social progress." The license system was "a sin against society." By 1889 Baptists favored "the speedy and entire prohibition of the liquor traffic" and Methodists by 1890 approved "the extreme measure of prohibition." In 1890 Methodists also ordered a standing committee on temperance. Such resolutions were often expressions of opinions felt only by a radical minority and acquiesced in by the rest for the sake of harmony.[32]

Sometimes a contrary view prevailed, as in the Southern Baptist Convention of 1888 when temperate anti-liquor resolutions presented by Dr. John Pollard and by "Parson" Massey were successfully ruled out of order.[33] After the early 1890's Methodists and Baptists became increasingly cautious and less active out of fear of entanglement with the Prohibition party. Neither accepted membership on the national Anti-Saloon League's board of directors. Methodists in 1894 declared, "Ours is a prohibition church, but not a party church. . . . We seek not to disturb political affiliations, or to dictate party politics." Baptists from 1897 to 1908 took no official action whatever.

There were militant temperance men among Southern Presbyterians also but, as with the other bodies, movement toward an official temperance position was slow. The records of their General Assembly show that they made no

---

32. The Methodist resolutions of 1886, for example, were on motion of W. A. Chandler of Georgia, where local option was progressing. D. Leigh Colvin, *Prohibition in the United States* (New York, 1926), p. 358. The resolutions carried by a divided vote (107 to 65).

33. Dr. J. B. Hutson and Dr. J. William Jones also favored action by the Southern Baptist Convention.

changes in their ante bellum rules for membership and that they declined the WCTU's request to set apart a special Sabbath as a temperance day. While testifying "against the liquor power and the evils of intemperance"[34] and urging "all people to use all means which may be approved by their Christian Conscience and judgment to remedy this evil throughout the land," they refused to commit themselves "for or against any political question of prohibition or so-called moral reform."[35]

These actions represent the most advanced positions to which the radical elements were able to commit the churches. It must be remembered that actions of some of the important individual churches could frequently nullify or at least stalemate the practical effect of such pronouncements. The actions of individual church members spoke far louder than any official action of an impersonal organization. Dr. Gordon Moore did not exaggerate in 1903 when he said that the churches had been giving "only a transient patronage of active temperance effort."[36]

In Virginia, Catholics, Episcopalians, Presbyterians, and Primitive Baptists made no important change in either their rules for members or their enforcement. Among Methodists the Holston Conference heartily approved the General Conference changes in the *Discipline* (it would have liked them earlier and stronger) and its ministers probably enforced the rules. In the Virginia Conference a ten years' silence on the subject was broken in 1880 by the committee on discipline, Rev. F. M. Edwards, chairman. From 1884 on there was a committee on temperance except for the years 1891-1893. The records of this conference indicate that real interest

34. Resolutions of a sweeping and aggressive character were read to the convention in 1900 but the committee on order of business allowed no time for discussion or voting on them. There was no standing committee on the subject as yet.

35. Thomas Cary Johnson, Sr., librarian of the Spence Library, Union Theological Seminary, Richmond, Virginia, to Dr. Pearson, Oct. 15, 1928.

36. Virginia Baptist General Association *Minutes*, 1903, p. 81.

in the matter was pretty nearly confined to Mr. Edwards, who almost invariably headed the committee and made the report. For this pressing of the matter he is said to have received no thanks from either his superiors in the hierarchy or the general members, including some good temperance men who thought him a crank. Under his prodding the record of the Virginia Conference was kept straight until the amending of the *Discipline*[37] and after that resolutions were passed urging presiding elders to see that the new rule was enforced and interpreting this rule to mean that one could not aid the business in any way without being un-Christian and a bad citizen. This put a ban on such common practices as selling fruit and renting buildings for liquor purposes or testifying to the good name of a would-be licensee. The "solemn vow" of Methodist laymen, however, did not prevent many of them from drinking at least temperately and one sometimes heard of preachers who took a little liquor "for their stomach's sake."

Among Baptist churches, each of which made its own rules in such matters, there was no new outburst in behalf of total abstinence. Apparently all, or nearly all, continued to discipline severely for drunkenness but with a tendency to excuse the offender after he made an apology and promised to sin no more, though here and there one found disciplining for patronizing barrooms.[38] Like Methodists they found the liquor seller a harder problem. A wholesaler, a hotel owner, a large grocer, or a distiller was apt to be a leading citizen and a liberal contributor to church and charity. Besides, other members bought liquor from him. Such a member gave the friends of liquor a chance to scoff and made it hard for the church to present a united front in local-option elections. Since the large majority of the churches who had no dealer members felt that their good name was compromised

37. In 1886. See above.
38. The Liberty Church in the Goshen Association in 1891 and Mattaponi in the Dover Association in 1896.

and their good work was blocked by the minority, the district associations sometimes intervened.

The practice varied greatly. The Roanoke Association (including Danville and Southside counties) was recording resolutions against sellers from 1877 on but with the qualification that the drinkers were the ones to be controlled first.[39] When Dr. John Pollard prodded the Dover Association into asserting that it would non-fellowship a church that did not get rid of sellers and an investigation disclosed that 13 sellers were being retained in 8 of its 69 churches with Deep Run and the Richmond First Baptist not reporting, this one-time temperance pioneer rescinded its threat, alleging that the ground was too technical.[40] The *Religious Herald*, going back to Jeter's position, contended that the matter was one of sentiment only and spoke favorably of the private character of some sellers. Thereupon the Valley Association (composed of the hitherto silent southwest), on motion of Rev. F. H. Martin, condemned the *Herald* for both utterances, insisting that the matter was one of Christian principle. The state association refused to touch the matter out of deference to Dr. J. B. Hawthorne, who was an ardent prohibitionist and pastor of the Richmond First Baptist Church, wealthiest of all the churches and the most conspicuous offender.[41] Chronic silence—no doubt intended to prevent divisive flare-ups—marked the pages of Lafferty's Richmond *Christian Advocate* and the *Religious Herald* of Dickinson and R. H. Pitt.

39. This association in 1888 reported that its churches retained no sellers and were moving to get rid of drinkers—a record, however, that it was apparently not able to maintain. The Portsmouth Association was also active in this matter.

40. The committee of investigation (Walter Syndor, John Pollard, and R. H. Pitt of the *Religious Herald*) added to this recommendation that the association was not thereby committed to a change in its opinion. An essentially similar compromise seems to have been reached in the Portsmouth Association.

41. In 1901 Dr. Pollard was permitted to move that the liquor traffic was inconsistent with church membership and that churches and the district associations, as bodies nearer to the churches, were advised to get rid of such members; then the resolution was tabled on motion of Dr. Hawthorne.

The state organizations of the Episcopalians, Catholics, Negro Baptists, and most of the smaller denominations, though they exerted much control over their members, made no attempt to influence public policy. The Presbyterians inclined toward the dry side if their General Assembly's recommendations and the general reputation of their members as voters are to be credited.[42] But the Virginia synod was particularly careful in guarding the church's traditional policy of avoiding commitment on other than spiritual matters.

The Baptists and Methodists, in their state bodies, passed judgment on the liquor business and the government's relation to it for the first time in their history. They committed themselves to undertake actively the formulation of public policy in the matter. In the middle eighties they worked zealously for a general local-option law. In the early nineties they sponsored a temperance convention[43] designed to procure specific anti-liquor legislation and in this they were joined by the Christians.[44] Because the effort in the nineties became involved with party politics, both church bodies avoided appointing a committee on temperance. Though some district associations preferred a more aggressive course,[45] the Baptist General Association contented itself with firm support of local

42. One with first-hand knowledge of Virginia Presbyterians during this period writes: "the membership of the Presbyterian Church has voted more solidly against the liquor traffic than that of any other Church"; Dr. R. F. Campbell, Asheville, N. C., to Dr. Pearson, Oct. 9, 1928. Bishop L. J. Heatwole to Dr. Pearson, Sept. 10, 1931, wrote with respect to the Mennonites of the Valley: "The Conference never failed to take a definite vote in favor of Local Option. . . . Long years ago members were forbidden to haul apples to distilleries."

43. The Tazewell District Convention, meeting in Tazewell County, Oct. 23, 1889, adopted a resolution pledging members of the convention "not to support any political party which does not emphatically pledge itself to the absolute prohibition" of the liquor business. The Valley Convention at Strasburg the next year was vehement but less clear.

44. John A. Tate to Dr. Pearson, Sept. 24, 1931, citing minutes of Nov. 11-13, 1891. The resolutions of the state convention the next year were general and sweeping. The Missionary Society in 1899 endorsed the measure for teaching the effects of alcohol in the schools.

45. The Portsmouth Association in 1898 and the Roanoke Association in 1900 declared willingness to fight liquor in every way, including politically.

option and occasional pressure on the legislature. They even refused representation at the national Anti-Saloon League.[46] The Methodist Conference, again on the initiative of F. M. Edwards, voted to participate in the councils of the league, thereby committing itself in principle to a policy of political action.[47]

At the beginning of the twentieth century the great middle-class churches of Virginia, both absolutely and relatively stronger than before, were subjected to the pressure of many new forces: local-option elections, women and evangelists, broader concepts of Christian duty and opportunity, and pronouncements of their South-wide organizations which reinforced all these. The churches responded with attempts at stricter regulation of their members' conduct, particularly with respect to the business aspects of liquor and by assertions of a right to determine, at least in part, public policy as to liquor. Even in these churches complete unity was lacking since some were for aggressive action whereas others preferred the slower processes of education and general reform. Church organizations representative of the highest and the lowest classes showed little or no response.

The Democratic party of Virginia, the Conservative party before 1884,[48] was intimately related to the progress of temperance both before and after 1902. It regarded itself as the voice of the white people and was so regarded by most of them. Through it they saved their state and its traditions, including its Confederate traditions. Through it they effectually asserted their rights as the superior race in the state. This assertion was far more than platform or policy; it was

46. See resolutions of 1897, 1902, 1903.
47. F. M. Irby and W. W. Lear were joined with Edwards in 1895 and 1896 respectively as the conference's representatives.
48. Studies of this complex subject can be found in Hamilton J. Eckenrode, *The Political History of Virginia During the Reconstruction* (Baltimore, 1904); Pearson, *Readjuster Movement*; Sheldon, *Populism in the Old Dominion*; Nelson M. Blake, *William Mahone of Virginia* (Richmond, 1935); Allen W. Moger, *Rebuilding of the Old Dominion, 1880-1902* (Ann Arbor, Mich., 1940); all *passim*.

instinct, fortified by experience and fundamental to the preservation of their social order. "I am a Democrat," once said popular John W. Daniel, "because I am a white man,"[49] from which it followed that the Democratic party must continue in political control and that whites must remain—if necessary, be compelled to remain—united in its support. It was developing such a lofty status between 1867 and 1876.

The Democratic party seldom supported reform movements. This it indicated in the 1850's and it had not changed after the war while taking the name "Conservative." It contributed little more than lip service even to public schools and charities. Moreover, business, large as well as small, enjoyed a disproportionate share in its management. This was evidenced during the early seventies in its handling of the huge state debt and the very considerable investments of the state, both of ante bellum origin. It continued to be shown in a certain tenderness toward railroads and liquor interests. This meant management by city people in an overwhelmingly rural community, a fact that could also be explained by the comparative progressiveness of the cities and their contributions to the state's expense bill.[50] Accordingly, the choice elective positions usually went to Confederate soldiers known and popular in western parts, the others to men of proved party loyalty and conservatism and good social standing.[51] But the shibboleth of white man's party led continually to victory.

It was apparent in 1877 that the party's position was not impregnable. Farmers everywhere found times very hard and blamed city people. In the southwest there were very few Negroes and the maintenance of the status quo was not an admired policy. Unsuccessful politicians complained of local "rings"; the Republican party was disorganized, discouraged,

49. C. C. Pearson, "John Warrwick Daniel," *Dictionary of American Biography*, ed. Allen Johnson and Dumas Malone (New York, 1928-1936), V, 68-69; "William Mahone," *ibid.*, XII, 211-212.
50. Sheldon, *Populism in the Old Dominion*, pp. 18, 68.
51. *Christian Advocate*, Jan. 29, 1876.

impotent; and numerous Independents began to take advantage of the opportunity. Soon the elements of discontent became organized as "Readjusters," a name referring to their attitude toward the state debt. Read out of the party by the Democratic management, they were soon joined with Republicans and led to victory by General William Mahone, who had recently lost first his railroad and then the Democratic gubernatorial nomination. Between 1879 and 1882 the combination put through important economic and social legislation. In the earlier days of the upheaval, while party lines were loose, came the beginning of special legislation for particular communities.[52] The combination permitted Negro office-holding and it developed a highly centralized political machine. Together these constituted the essence of "Mahoneism."

For a decade Virginia was a doubtful state. The west was divided. In the east the color line was in abeyance in many places. The Negroes once more displayed something of their political fervor of Reconstruction days—sometimes excited by their preachers, once even to the point of nominating and electing a Negro to Congress in opposition to the will of Mahone.[53] In 39 counties they constituted a majority; in 21 other counties and in most of the cities support by 15 to 20 per cent of the whites would give them a majority.

Alarmed, the Democrats reorganized. John S. Barbour, a railroad man, became chairman. Readjuster Democrats were invited back, some of them to office. The leading Readjuster economic and social legislation was accepted. To this was added conciliation of the anti-liquor elements. Prior to this time no official party cognizance of liquor issues had been taken in the state. If liquor interests looked upon the

52. Sheldon, *Populism in the Old Dominion,* contains a good discussion of the economic and political discontent and the restraining influence of the fear of Negro voters. See Pearson, *Readjuster Movement,* pp. 68-74, for a good brief study of Mahoneism.
53. James H. Johnston, "Negroes in the Government of Virginia from 1877 to 1888," *Journal of Negro History,* XIV (1929), 251-271.

Democratic organization as particularly friendly it was due in part to the national party's alignment and in part to most lawyers' being Democrats.[54] Under pressure the party gave the local optionists' platform approval and after that the desired legislation was passed. To this legislation was added the necessary enforcement laws. License or no license became a matter of local decision, to the great satisfaction of thousands.

The new party management was pre-eminently realistic. With the Negro counties particularly in mind, the Anderson-McCormick election law was passed which, through county electoral boards named by the legislature,[55] enabled Democratic election officials in black counties to control the vital local offices and also permitted the county's vote to be counted for the Democrats in state elections. For the compensation of "workers," funds were obtained from without as well as within the state. This tardy acceptance of reform and reformers, fortified by the increased power of local "rings," was successful for the Democrats. Though Democrats thereafter controlled the state government, beginning with 1885, apathy and division in the ranks had to be watched continually. In 1886, 1887, and 1888, principally because of agrarianism, Republicans polled a majority of the popular vote.[56] Though

54. In Reconstruction legislation there is no mention of party by the press. Samuel H. Moffett, who introduced the bill to tax liquor consumption in the 1870's became a Readjuster; the repeal of his bill was led by A. Fulkerson, Readjuster. On the General Local Option Law "honors" are about even. Readjusters Farr and Stubbs favored but Riddleberger and Fulkerson opposed; Fitshugh opposed but signed the bill. In local elections the local party machine was most often wet. Liquor men seem to have abandoned the rural areas as dry tendencies appeared and increased their interest in the cities.

55. House *Journal*, 1883-1884, p. 556; *Acts*, 1884, *passim*; Pearson, *Readjuster Movement*, p. 167. This feature continued under the Walton Law of 1893-1894, which provided for a form of Australian balloting. See William C. Pendleton, *Political History of Appalachian Virginia* (Dayton, Va., 1927), pp. 345 ff., for operation.

56. Richmond *Dispatch*, Nov. 4, 5, and 6, 1886; Nov. 22, 1887; Pearrisburg *Virginian* (Giles County), June 7, 8, 1888. The sweeping Republican victory in 1886 is ascribed principally to indignation over Cleveland's failure to reward Democratic workers and after that to Democratic failure to remove the excise tax on whiskey and tobacco. Local option is not

the Democrats appeased the farmers by giving them most of what they wanted, they responded handsomely to the cry of "Mahoneism" when Mahone ran for governor in 1889. In 1891, when the Populist danger was greatest, the new Democratic chairman felt compelled to plead the danger of white division.[57]

The coming of the Prohibition party in the middle eighties was observed closely by politicians as well as by temperance people.[58] The interest of this national organization was primarily not in individuals or communities but in abolishing the licensing system completely and without substitute. While this system existed, it argued, the "liquor power" inevitably would try to control and corrupt government. Since the great political parties had become puppets of the "liquor power," the new party called upon temperance men to forsake them and follow it, offering also a wide and varying assortment of more specific reforms.[59]

This party brought attention to the strength of liquor in state politics; it also put Virginians in touch with outsiders of fine ability and idealism. Quite a number joined it. Its program ran squarely counter to the program of immediate and limited objectives and avoidance of politics which had just been agreed upon and was proving successful. There resulted the old curse of division and confusion within the ranks. Moreover, another familiar trouble was accentuated, namely, the tendency of the movement to get into the hands of extremists. Already people were frowning at temperance lectures. The temperance crank became a by-word with wets

mentioned. For an interesting explanation of Cleveland's majority (1888) from the Republican angle, see Pendleton, *Appalachian Virginia*, p. 369.

57. Basil B. Gordon, Aug. 9, 1892, "To the Democratic members of the Third Party," in Sheldon, *Populism in the Old Dominion*, Appendix D, pp. 170-171.

58. Sheldon, *Populism in the Old Dominion*, chap. 3, and Moger, *Rebuilding of the Old Dominion*, chaps. 4, 5 render full accounts of the Farmer-Populist movement and its reforms.

59. Colvin, *Prohibition in the United States*, pp. 83 ff. The state party platform is in Richmond *Dispatch*, Sept. 7, 1893.

and a pest to more moderate dries. Soon the press deemed temperance a "threadbare" subject.

By 1887-1888 some were saying that the dries would flock to the Prohibition party if local option was not given a fair chance[60] and others, that it would play an increasingly important part in politics as the "third party."[61] However, it was not able to attract native leaders of ability, idealism, and social standing as had the old Virginia Temperance Society. These seemed to be going into farmers' organizations.[62] In its competition for votes with the People's party it found that the farmers were certain of their economic grievances but were not positive about denying themselves drinks. It attacked principally the Democratic party, which lent credence to the suspicion that it was just a Republican device for dividing white men. Consequently, it never polled over 2,500 votes in a state-wide election.

In December, 1891, a temperance convention assembled in Richmond, the first since 1886. It met on call of the Baptist General Association for the general purpose of finding a basis for united action by temperance men in these days of temperance lag and party confusion.[63] It hoped to impress the legislature then in session with the strength of temperance sentiment and obtain from it remedial enactments—the more so since it contained many Farmers Alliance men bent upon popular reforms. Present were some 250 delegates represent-

60. *Temperance Advocate*, March 18, 1887 (communication datelined Chincoteague).

61. Sheldon, *Populism in the Old Dominion*, p. 126, citing Petersburg *Index-Appeal*, in 1888. ". . . but there is one thing I don't like," wrote a lady from Orange county, "that is this prohibition it is going into politics. You see now there is three parties. Three parties elected old Abe Lincoln."

62. From 1884 to 1888 Thomas E. Taylor and Ramsey Smithson were national committeemen, James O. Newton and R. H. Rawlins succeeding them. Captain A. H. Fultz was party chairman at first, W. W. Gibbs of Staunton in 1893.

63. The conservative character of the previous management of the religious bodies is indicated by refusal the previous year of a similar request since "existing excellent legislation" indicated "the recent crystallizing of temperance sentiment." Association *Minutes*, 1890, 1891; Richmond *Dispatch*, April 9, 1891; Richmond *Times* and Richmond *Dispatch*, Dec. 15, 16, 31, 1891; *Religious Herald*, Dec. 17, 1891, and *passim*.

ing all the temperance and religious bodies except the Catholic, whose bishop sent regrets. The presiding officer was John E. Massey, Baptist minister and ante bellum temperance man, "Father of the Readjuster Movement" and now Superintendent of Public Instruction. Good Templar Hawxhurst was secretary.

On the eve of the meeting Rev. A. E. Dickinson said in an interview with the Richmond *Times*: "There's going to be a ground swell," explaining that convention members had back of them the church people who wanted no "third party" but were tired of hearing politicians recount the horrors of twenty-five years before while they neglected the "far greater calamities" caused by liquor. The "threat of Negro domination," he continued, "has been handled for all it is worth; we are no longer called upon to pray one way and vote the other way." Coming from the senior editor and field man of the conservative *Religious Herald*, such talk seemed portentous, especially since the managers of Virginia Democracy, alarmed over the prospect of facing a People's party, were planning a tight campaign against the Republican "Force Bill" and for David B. Hill, machine man and friend of liquor.[64] In the meeting next day some delegates proposed radical action but were voted down. Convention members, guided by the veteran Massey, left the work of better organizing the state to a committee and asked the legislature only for specific and reasonable changes in existing laws. The legislature refused peremptorily.[65] The explanation privately given was that the liquor dealers of Richmond alone would contribute more to the campaign funds than all the country and village voters. At the ensuing election the Prohibition candidate received less than 1 per cent of the vote cast.

64. Allan Nevins, *American Press Opinion, Washington to Coolidge* (Boston, 1928); "The Saloon in Politics" from the New York *Evening Post*, pp. 294-396.
65. S. H. Thompson, *The Life of John R. Moffett* (Salem, Va., 1895), pp. 93-94.

Stark tragedy followed the temperance convention of 1891. In north Danville, where an important race riot had occurred in 1883,[66] John R. Moffett was pastor of a Baptist church. A temperance advocate since his childhood in Culpeper, he was Grand Lecturer of the Good Templars. He would "follow the poor weak young man into the saloon and persuade him to desist from taking the glass of grog for which he went. He has taken his own means and bought food for the drunkard's family."[67] Vigorously he personally fought "blind tigers" in the Roanoke region, saloons in and around Norfolk, and liquor in politics all over the state through *Anti-Liquor*. To this small sheet, whose circulation ran to 5,000, W. W. Smith and John E. Massey contributed successively, each retiring in the face of outside criticism. When, following evangelistic services in the city conducted by Sam Jones, there was talk of a local-option election in Danville early in 1889, the Richmond *Dispatch* deemed the report worthy of adverse comment.[68] Later that year a Democratic newspaper warned, "Woe to you, Mr. Moffett, if Mckinney be defeated by votes taken from the white ranks and thrown away on Taylor," referring to Thomas E. Taylor, the Prohibitionist candidate for governor. The next year in the Danville district Congressman P. G. Lester faced an Independent Republican candidate supported by *Anti-Liquor* and its friends in the churches.[69]

Moffett led in initiating the temperance convention of 1891 and was charged by it with the organization work sponsored by that body. Next year he came out flatly for the Prohibition party's presidential candidate. He even preached a sermon in his church in which he condemned the regular parties and declared that the plan used before "for controlling the colored man has been contrary to God's plan. It has been founded on hate and, in too many cases, on corruption and dishonesty at the ballot box." Prudent men deprecated such

66. Pearson, *Readjustor Movement*, p. 163.
67. Thompson, *Moffett*, p. 113.    68. May 26, 1889.
69. Thompson, *Moffett*, p. 113.

talk. Hot-headed local politicians declared that he ought to be hanged. At the elections the Democrats were enraged at Moffett's attempts to insure a truly secret ballot. Soon afterwards he was shot dead on the streets by an ex-bartender of low character. Though the act was generally condemned and there were those who thought the affair was little less than a political murder, no reaction followed.[70]

On September 6, 1893, over one hundred Virginia Prohibitionists convened in Staunton's YMCA building, formulated a platform, and named a full ticket for the coming statewide elections. Its gubernatorial candidate was J. R. Miller, sometime state lecturer for the Good Templars and described as a good "narrator" and mimic. The politicians' interest lay in the tactics of Republicans, which turned out to be support of Populist or Prohibitionist candidates, whichever was strongest in a particular district. Most important was the Valley county of Augusta where, inspired perhaps by doings in the city of Roanoke, dry men had carefully organized the city of Staunton. Prohibitionists nominated a full ticket, which received the support of Populists and Republicans. Heading the ticket was Bodley, a Union soldier from West Virginia and a man of wealth, who was opposed by Edward Echols, regular Democrat. To the aid of Bodley came Sam Jones, evangelist, and Sam Small, both fresh from Georgia liquor fights, who bitterly attacked the state Democratic party.

The Prohibitionist party intended to inaugurate local-option elections in the larger cities, one by one, and to bring

70. Thompson, *Moffett*, pp. 113, 117-166. George Braxton Taylor, *Virginia Baptist Ministers* (4th ser.; Lynchburg, Va., 1912); Virginia Baptist General Association *Minutes*; Richmond *Dispatch*, Jan. 22, Feb. 6, 1892, Feb. 2, 1894; Richmond *Times* and *Times-Dispatch*, Nov. 12, 13, 1892; *Religious Herald*, Dec. 17, 1891, *et passim*; Rockingham *Register*, 1892, *passim*; W. W. Moffett, *Correspondence Between W. W. Moffett and Joseph Bryan, J. S. Bryan, W. S. Copeland, of the Times-Dispatch, concerning Moffett and the Editorial of the Times-Dispatch, amending its first editorial* (Richmond, n.d.). The second editorial appeared May 26, 1903. There was no admission that Moffett was shot as a Prohibitionist but J. S. Bryan declared the shooting an "outrageous murder." W. W. Moffett was a member of the State Democratic Committee, a county and circuit judge, and was considered a machine man.

to bear on each of these "citadels" its outside as well as its local forces and allies. Contrary to its custom, the Democratic party management intervened in local liquor fights. To the aid of Echols went Parson Massey, who for the first time met his match as a rough-and-tumble stump speaker, the "clerical Mountebank," Sam Jones. In the end the Prohibitionists lost.[71] Deceived by this outcome the Senate at its next session passed at the request of Lynchburg citizens a bill to exempt cities of 5,000 from local-option elections. But when Massey and J. Taylor Ellyson, the Democratic party chairman and thrice president of the Baptist General Convention, made clear the probable political consequences, the House promptly killed the bill.[72]

At the Staunton convention a delegate from Norfolk spoke of the perjured testimony of policemen in behalf of liquor dealers in the courts of his city. The local Democratic organization had fallen into bad hands and many citizens long had been tired of its corrupt rule. In the spring of 1894 Sam Small moved in and spoke to overflowing meetings. A citizen's reform organization soon joined the Prohibitionists, who were estimated to have 600 or 700 voters in support of a Prohibition-Reform municipal ticket. Again Massey entered the arena. With the aid of Republicans and Independents the Reform ticket won handsomely. Soon reaction set in. Negroes in official public places were not liked. The Norfolk

71. Richmond *Dispatch*, Sept. 7, Nov. 8, 9, 1893; Staunton *Yost's Weekly* (Republican), Sept. 14, Oct. 19, 26, 1893; Rockingham *Register*, Nov. 9, 1893; Charlottesville *Daily Progress*, April 27, 1901. The platform declared that all moral, economic, and political issues of the day were inseparably connected with the license issue, and it declared licenses unconstitutional.

72. Richmond *Dispatch*, May 27, 28, 1894. Massey in a letter to the Richmond *Dispatch*, Jan. 22, 1894, said: "a party, composed of Republicans, Populists, Third partyites, a few true and honest Democrats, and disappointed aspirants, with no defined political principles or affiliations, sought office under the name of 'Prohibitionists.' They dragged the cause of temperance into the arena of politics . . . . They charged that the Democratic party was run and controlled by the liquor interests." John Edward Massey, *Autobiography of John E. Massey*, ed. Elizabeth H. Hancock (New York and Washington, 1909), p. 301.

*Virginian,* which had supported the movement, called the new regime a "piratical crew." Despite the establishment by Sam Small of the Norfolk *Pilot,* the first daily Prohibition paper in the South, in October, 1894, the old crowd soon regained control.[73] And "fusion" versus "anti-fusion" continued to distinguish Norfolk politics, though there was no improvement in either the liquor situation or the city's government.

Meanwhile the state Prohibition party was in session during August, 1894, with the state populists, themselves a fading group, in an attempt to unite the two on a common platform. The Prohibitionists demanded inclusion of a stand for prohibition but the Populists refused this.[74] Two years later Prohibitionists from towns and cities met to take a stand for gold, thereby supporting the Republicans and certain business elements of towns and cities.[75] At most it had been a sort of agency for arousing support in local attempts at reform in which hostility to Democratic "rings" had been at least as large a factor as hostility to liquor. In Massey's opinion it failed to excite revolt among Democrats against their leadership. Passage and support of the local-option law proved "in a most practical way that they believed in the right of self-government and that they were the friends of temperance and good morals."[76] To this should be added the ever-present feeling that the Democratic party was the white man's party and ought not to be divided.

As the century turned some thoughtful Democrats of the older generation became weary of "management" in elections and in the interest of their sons hoped for an ending to it. Some of the rising generation felt that reform and progress were retarded as long as self-preservation required political

73. Richmond *Dispatch,* May 2, 25, 26, 1894; Rockingham *Register,* June 1, July 13, 1894. A similar contest occurred at this time in the city of Roanoke which had voted dry the previous year; here the coalition lost.
74. Richmond *Dispatch,* Aug. 24, 1894; Sheldon, *Populism in the Old Dominion,* pp. 108-109.
75. Sheldon, *Populism in the Old Dominion,* p. 126, citing Pittsburg *Dispatch,* May 27-29, 1896.
76. Massey, *Autobiography,* p. 301; Richmond *Dispatch,* Jan. 22, 1894.

solidarity of white people. Other Southern states found a way out in the constitutional disfranchisement of the most unfit and the Negroes. Reluctantly, Democratic leaders agreed that a constitutional convention be called to consider this along with other important matters in late 1901.

## Chapter Eleven

# VIRGINIA ANTI-SALOON
# LEAGUE, 1901-1908

The Prohibition party had scarcely been dispelled when a new organization appeared in Virginia. The Anti-Saloon League of America, like the Washingtonians, the Sons of Temperance, the Good Templars, and the WCTU, was a foreigner and its coming was something of an invasion. It originated in Ohio and moved upon Richmond from its national headquarters in Washington. This organization differed from each of its predecessors and yet drew heavily from the lessons they had taught. Concentrating against the business side of liquor and relying primarily upon legislation to gain its goals, it used the slogan, "The Saloon Must Go." Its program was "agitation, legislation, and law enforcement." This policy represented a last stage in the gradual departure of the anti-liquor movement from the original program of personal temperance and moral suasion.[1]

Over the entire nation in the early twentieth century there occurred a massive increase in anti-saloon feeling which was to culminate in the triumph of the temperance (soon to be prohibitionist) forces. On a national level this was often related to the anxieties brought about by urbanization, immigration, and rural depopulation. In Virginia, however, these population movements were not so prominent as in other states. They had their effect on the anti-liquor cause in Virginia both from a native impact and from an influx of stimulating agitation from outside the state. Even though urbanism was not a major factor in the life of Virginia during this period, city populations were growing and the attendant evils

1. Ernest Hurst Cherrington, *The History of the Anti-Saloon League* (Westerville, Ohio, 1913), especially chap. 1; William H. Anderson, *The Church in Action against the Saloon* (Westerville, Ohio, 1910); the Anti-Saloon League of America *Proceedings*, and its constitutions of 1905, 1908, and 1913.

were becoming more noticeable. The very real evils of the saloon and its accompanying invitation to treat one's friends (a dual threat of excessive cost to the overly friendly who could not afford to treat and of the obligation to accept "just one more" as another in the group took his turn to buy) came to Virginia as it had elsewhere. In rural areas as well as in the cities the Populist and Progressive movements were stressing the idea that overseeing the welfare of the citizen was a duty of the state, at least in certain rather limited aspects of life. The temperance drives of earlier years left a definite sentiment that the evils of alcohol could only be corrected by drastic action. The Anti-Saloon League proved to be the organization that tied all these feelings into an irresistible drive.

In form the league was a federation of state Anti-Saloon leagues and other organized societies affiliated for a single purpose. To form a state league the only requirements were "an active executive officer" and "adequate financial support." This plan would at once promote unity of temperance people for a limited objective and supply a much-needed central bureau of information, advice, and leadership. The league proposed to use political methods, something that many temperance men still thought unsuitable, with the explanation that it would work in and through existing parties rather than form a third party. The establishment of such an organization in Virginia followed precedents set in the anti-license movement of 1846-1854 and so was subject to suspicion, but the events of the past few years helped to allay such doubts.

Since 1895 leaders of the Anti-Saloon League of America had been in contact with Virginia anti-liquor forces through delegates sent from Virginia to the national conventions. The new organization had made some effort at getting established in the Piedmont-Valley region but with no success. Nothing of importance developed until at the national convention of 1900 Superintendent Russell pointed to the abundance and disunity of temperance sentiment in the South and added that "the next year should see a rapid growth of our work in the South."[2] Virginia churches took little notice of the convention and the secular newspapers, none. Therefore there was no public mention of the Reverend C. H. Crawford's going to Richmond in December, 1900, and no mention of his activities until February 7 the following year when the *Religious Herald* mentioned that he had moved among the ministers, that he had experience elsewhere, and that his plan seemed practicable. By this time a few earnest and important men meeting in the home of Dr. W. W. Lear, pastor of the Centenary Methodist Church, definitely agreed to sponsor the plan. Notices went out and on March 12, 1901, in the cold basement of Richmond's Second Baptist Church, a "convention" assembled and the Virginia Anti-Saloon League was born. Dr. S. C. Mitchell was named president and Crawford, superintendent.[3]

From the standpoint of the national leaders Superintendent Crawford was a model "active executive officer." Very soon he was sending into 5,000 homes the *Christian Federation*, a creditable eight-page monthly which proclaimed itself the "Official Organ of the Virginia Anti-Saloon League" and

2. American Anti-Saloon League *Proceedings,* 1900; Virginia Anti-Saloon League *Proceedings, 1902* ff. Concerning the situation in Virginia at the turn of the century, Robert A. Hohner, "The Anti-Saloon League in Virginia, 1901-1910; Prelude to Prohibition" (Master's thesis, Duke University, 1963), says, "Some fresh temperance cause was needed to renew old vitality" (p. 11).

3. Dr. Pearson records many conversations with Dr. S. C. Mitchell of the University of Richmond and Dr. M. Ashby Jones, prominent Baptist of the city. Drs. Lear, Mitchell, and Jones, probably B. F. Johnson (publisher and friend of John R. Moffett and member of Jones' church), and possibly one other were at the meeting at Lear's house. Others of all denominations and occupations assisted in launching the movement. Prominent among the Methodist clergy and already regarded as a radical in the temperance drive, was James Cannon, Jr. Appointed by the Methodists in 1898 as representative on the national board of directors of the Anti-Saloon League of America, he was therefore especially active in bringing the organization to the state. James Cannon, Jr., *Bishop Cannon's Own Story: Life as I Have Seen It,* ed. R. L. Watson, Jr. (Durham, N. C., 1955), pp. 117-119; Virginius Dabney, *Dry Messiah, The Life of Bishop Cannon* (New York, 1949), p. 35.

carried the national officers' names above those of the state organization.[4] Rev. J. W. West, once an oiler on a coastal steamer but now a minister of the Christian denomination in the southwest county of Lee, joined him in the enlistment of many anti-liquor people and he carried on the work after Crawford had gone. They spoke wherever they could, chiefly in the smaller or the plainer churches. For the most part they were well received, especially by the women, who asked only what they could do to help the cause. They arranged with local newspapers for a little space. They handed out or printed in the newspapers league membership cards which carried a pledge of financial support though not of personal temperance. They organized local leagues or secured committees which would do so, utilizing the existing nuclei of temperance people. They stimulated and plunged into local fights for no license or for law enforcement.[5] It was through such activities that native John R. Moffett had gotten into trouble. Now so did Dr. Crawford. He was publicly whipped by a county judge in the spring of 1902 and had to leave—taking with him, it is said, the pledge records of the league as security for his unpaid salary.[6] By January, 1903, sixty counties were "organized" and Crawford's whipping was "headlined not only in Virginia papers, but throughout the country and overnight

4. The non-paying *Good Templar News*, edited by Hawxhurst and Rev. J. W. Guy, was merged into this. Good Templars numbered scarcely 700 at this time.

5. The *Christian Federation* abounds in news of this sort of activity. Note, for example, an interdenominational committee formed in Manchester under the leadership of Rev. E. B. Hatcher and W. H. Owens. By Jan., 1904, nine more counties were organized as one of the results of West's 12,000 miles of travel and 226 speeches the preceding year.

6. *Christian Federation*, March, June, 1902, April, May, 1903. The affair grew out of the case of an Amherst druggist who had sold 30 barrels of "medicated whiskey" in a year. As a result of Judge C. F. Campbell's pro-liquor charge to the jury the druggist was not convicted of violation of the liquor laws. Crawford said in print that it wasn't clear which was doctored the more, the whiskey or the Judge. Cited for contempt, Crawford was defended by dry Judge William Hodges Mann and Campbell was forced to drop the charge of contempt. After court was adjourned the Judge sought Crawford out, drew his whip, and administered a lashing. He was impeached by the legislature and dismissed for his actions.

. . . the Anti-Saloon League of Virginia sprang into unusual prominence."[7]

Meanwhile the work of S. C. Mitchell was giving prominence to the league in such a manner as to stress the idea that it was more than an organization of cranks and fanatics.[8] Like the league, he had recently come to Virginia. He came from Mississippi and Kentucky, married into the well-known Broadus family, taught in conservative Richmond College, and occasionally wrote for the conservative *Religious Herald*. He was something of a social seer with a gift for fresh and striking phrases that charmed young men and stimulated the older ones even when it shocked them. He believed the great current need to be a revival of genuine public discussion, a focusing of the minds of all the people upon the really important matters that concerned them all, upon crime and education as well as upon liquor. He felt that education must precede legislation so that the league might be made to serve the larger purpose. In a series of incisive addresses and signed articles he stated the case for the league. The saloon though "legal" was not "legitimate" because it had no moral defense and, indeed, found few sincere advocates. Since in the past defeat had come to anti-liquor forces because of "isolation and fanaticism," the new slogan should be "Unity and Sanity." The league was "excellent in method as well as in aim" because it sought to "solidify and evoke the sentiment of all Christian and civic forces in a righteous cause," a union which "will make itself felt in many other directions." The league would proceed slowly, cultivating "anterior sentiments" in advance of legislation, knowing that its reserve power would

7. Cannon, *Own Story*, p. 119.
8. Dr. Pearson knew Dr. Mitchell well and in his original draft of this section stated, "The writer in this sketch has drawn heavily upon his long acquaintance with Dr. Mitchell and upon Dr. Mitchell's recollections of these days." The flamboyant later career of Bishop Cannon makes it easy to push his dominance on the Virginia scene even further back in time than it properly belongs. Neither Cannon in his autobiography nor critical biographer Virginius Dabney, in *Dry Messiah*, makes mention of Dr. Mitchell even though he was Cannon's immediate predecessor in the office of president of the Virginia league.

give it "the ability to wait."[9] Dr. Mitchell was also a constructive statesman. He knew that with the party leaders'[10] frowning upon "agitation" and the columns of the great newspapers closed to discussion of the liquor question, something at once concrete and dramatic must be done to reach the great masses, so apathetic and so localized in point of view. Fortunately the voters, with unusual disregard of ordinary political considerations, were selecting their best men to meet in constitutional convention. This body would discuss whatever it considered important and its proceedings would find the front page of all the newspapers.[11] Accordingly, it was determined to thrust the liquor question upon the convention by asking for a provision in the Bill of Rights that no license to make or to sell liquor be granted except upon the written request of a majority of the voters of the precinct concerned. Leaders thought that such a provision would not be regarded as radical since it was in line with the generally accepted policy of local option; the Baptist General Association concurred in this opinion at its meetings in the fall of 1901.[12]

9. *Religious Herald*, Feb. 14, 1901; *Christian Federation*, 1901, 1902, *passim*.

10. As Dr. Mitchell afterward described his view at that time, liquor was hedged about by the three-fold barrier of wealth, prestige, and respectability, and the Democratic party was thought by some to be "preserved in alcohol."

11. The task of greatest public interest before the constitutional convention was the legal disfranchisement of the Negroes. Years of preventing the Negro from voting by force or of manipulating the Negro vote to secure the dominance of the Democratic party had created a situation in which no true discussion or division over any matter could be held. The smallest split in the ranks of the party might mean the end of white control. To permit the discussion and division so essential to democracy and progress and to bring an end to the necessity for fraud many leaders of the Democratic party in Virginia as elsewhere in the South decided that disfranchisement of the Negro was necessary. Thus the convention, in opening the way for internal division, enlarged the opportunity for temperance reform through political procedure. Cf. James H. Timberlake, *Prohibition and the Progressive Movement, 1900-1920* (Cambridge, Mass., 1963), p. 123; and R. C. McDaniel, *The Virginia Constitutional Convention of 1901-1902* (Baltimore, 1928), pp. 11-12.

12. Episcopal ministers, through Rev. E. L. Godwin, also approved on the ground of difficulties and objections connected with local-option elections. *Christian Federation*, Nov., 1901.

The strategy proved eminently successful. The Quarles-Barbour Resolution[13] embodying the proposal of the league leaders came before the constitutional convention in January, 1902. There were petitions signed by 20,000 voters to support it, an inflowing of temperance sentiment that surprised everybody. The league assembled in convention in Richmond, January 16, 1902. Some noted the absence of Lafferty of the Richmond *Christian Advocate* and Pastor Cooper of the Richmond First Baptist Church. But warriors from the local fields and donators "in cash" as well as orators and organizers came and a dozen or more members of the constitutional convention dropped in. The proceedings were dignified and redolent of "Unity and Sanity." President Mitchell's ruling that any church member present could participate because "the church is the greatest temperance society on earth" greatly comforted some who feared too narrow a basis for the movement or some kind of political trickery. On motion of W. W. Smith it was voted that if the constitutional convention should think that acceptance of the Quarles-Barbour Resolution would endanger ratification of the new constitution, the league would be content with a separate referendum on the resolution.

The Richmond newspapers, which had begun their brief reporting with sarcastic headlines,[14] changed their tone in the face of such a co-operative spirit and such a quiet confidence in the strength of anti-liquor sentiment. Back at the Capitol the committee on the Bill of Rights, after hearing S. C. Mitchell and James Cannon, Jr., on the right of homes to be protected against an unwelcomed saloon, reported the Quarles-Barbour Resolution favorably.[15] On the floor Robert Trumbull of Brunswick and Judge G. T. Garnett of Mathews favored its passage because they thought that it would save

13. Drawn by W. N. Fishburn of Waynesboro, introduced by J. M. Quarles of Staunton and J. S. Barbour of Culpeper, neither of whom favored the proposal.
14. "Down with the Saloon"; "Sensation Today . . . Minister Claims He was Falsely Imprisoned."
15. William L. Royall and Judge Robertson represented the opposition.

their dry counties from the turmoil of a local-option election. Barbour, co-introducer of the resolution, in an effective speech announced that he had been converted to its support by Dr. Mitchell in committee. Others argued the wisdom of letting well enough alone and the folly of exposing voters to the pressure of petitioners with their jugs, against whom the local women were sure to be arrayed. Some dry members, among them John Garland Pollard, felt that a provision of this sort had no proper place in the constitution and some felt that public sentiment was not ready for the proposed plan.

Strong delegations to argue pro and con came from the cities, notably from Norfolk. Political considerations weighed heavy in the deliberations. The liquor dealers were aroused and threatening to defeat both the new constitution and the controlling party if the resolution was passed.[16] Rumor had it that the Republican members were quite willing to help create trouble for their opponents by voting to include the Quarles-Barbour plan, which would require a vote of the community before a license could be issued. Because of this a moderate dry member, Rev. W. F. Dunaway of Lancaster, (recalling the league's suggestion) proposed a substitute ordinance requiring a state-wide election in 1905 on whether the state should license to sell liquor for on-premise drinking. This proposal actually carried, 32 to 31, amid "wild confusion," only to be reconsidered after a hasty adjournment. Most of the leaders, especially among the dries, considered it imperative that prohibitory legislation not be adopted until the great majority of public sentiment favored it. In the end the Quarles-Barbour Resolution was defeated, 24 to 36, with 16 other members favoring the idea but abstaining from the vote. The great party leaders—Daniel, Flood, Glass, Moore, Anderson, and others—all opposed the plan and its showing simply indicated the strength of the still-developing anti-

16. An extensive amplification of the hostility of the liquor dealers to the movement is in the original autobiography in the Cannon Papers, Duke University Library. Cf. Cannon, *Own Story*, p. 116n.

liquor movement. President Mitchell's first objective was achieved—the state was now quite aware of the league and the work it proposed to do.[17]

The work of the league not only brought it to the public's attention but also accomplished one definite advance in the anti-liquor cause. The new constitution included a specific provision that the legislature might either regulate or prohibit the sale of liquor.[18] This was hailed by anti-saloon leaders as state recognition of the peculiarly evil character of the liquor business and was viewed as a basis for future action by the league. Apparently neither friend nor foe of liquor evaluated the meaning of the constitutional convention's most significant action. The legal elimination of the Negro voter opened the door to discussion and decision on a multiplicity of problems, including liquor, without danger of party disunity or the threat of an end to white domination.

Elated but still unwilling to move beyond what the people would approve, league leaders turned to the legislature in the fall of 1902 with a request to make the rural areas dry. The strategy was as before: approval by Methodist and Baptist state bodies, petitions signed by thousands of voters, especially in the regions deeply concerned, and a state convention in Richmond while the legislature was in session. Liquor people planned shrewdly to counter their actions. Beginning in the fall of 1902 President Lazarus of the State Dealers' Association moved among his peers and soon the national organizations inquired about the price of newspaper editorial space and reminded the retailers of their political power. As some-

17. Conversations between Dr. Pearson and Dr. Mitchell; Richmond *Dispatch*, Jan. 17, 18, Feb. 28, 1902; *Christian Federation*, Jan., Feb., March, 1902; Virginia Anti-Saloon League *Proceedings*, 1901, 1902; *Proceedings and Debates of the Constitutional Convention, 1901-1902* (Richmond, 1906), especially p. 2749. Anti-saloon leaders afterward rejoiced that the desired provision was not inserted because they thought that it would have made the coming of state-wide prohibition more difficult.

18. Art. IV, sec. 62: "The General Assembly shall have full power to enact local option or dispensary laws, or any other laws controlling regulating, or prohibiting the manufacture or sale of intoxicating liquors."

thing of a flank movement a bill was introduced permitting local governments to establish dispensaries even in territories that had voted dry. From resorts, breweries, and distilleries came cries of ruin and the dispensary proposal apparently found little favor in high political circles.[19] Moderate men felt that the country districts were differentiated from the urban through their lack of policing and the decided preponderance of dry sentiment. The larger dealers, seeing that only the "small fry" were in danger, did not seriously exert themselves and some wavering legislators received reports from meetings back home favoring rural prohibition.

The result was the Mann Law of 1903, named for Senator William Hodges Mann of Nottoway who prepared and introduced the bill at the request of the league's executive committee.[20] The bill was intended to make the rural areas completely dry and it did this by exceedingly complex provisions. The manufacture or sale of liquor without a license was first prohibited. Licenses were obtained by application to the county, circuit, or corporation court of the area involved. If the application was for a city of more than 500 inhabitants the court might grant the license if satisfied that the applicant was a fit person and the place of business suitable. If for a place of less than 500 inhabitants, not only must the applicant and place be fit and suitable but the judge must make certain other decisions before granting a license. In the words of the framer of the bill: ". . . the Judge must be satisfied before granting the license that a majority of the qualified voters of the district or town in which it was located should be in favor of the license; that it shall be at a place where police protection is afforded, that the granting of a license at that

19. For dispensaries, see below.
20. A member of the league's executive committee and in 1904 to become its president, James Cannon, Jr., relates in his autobiography that he and Judge Mann "worked together for some time" in framing the law. Cannon, *Own Story*, p. 120; Dabney, *Dry Messiah*, p. 49. No substantiating evidence has been found and Dabney cites no sources. Cf. Hohner, "Anti-Saloon League in Virginia," p. 34.

place shall not be contrary to the moral and material interests of the community."[21] The requirements for license to manufacture liquor were left unchanged. The local still could continue selling its own produce for off-premise drinking.[22]

Mann said of the fate of the bill:

> The introduction of the bill caused a great howl from all of the liquor people; the papers undertook to rule me out of the Democratic Party and there was a perfect storm of criticism. The bill was introduced in December, 1902, well advertised throughout the state, after which I waited to see what public sentiment would have to say in reference to it. The bill was endorsed by the general associations of the Methodist, Baptist and Christian churches; by the Anti-Saloon League and Women's Christian Temperance Union. Besides, petitions commenced to pour in asking for its passage. I think these petitions were signed by some 50,000 people. Strange to say, there was only one adverse petition.
>
> After a hard fight the bill was passed by a considerable majority, both in the Senate and House and becoming a law closed up between 700 and 800 saloons in the rural districts.[23]

Leaders rejoiced that the law of Virginia at last recognized protection of moral welfare as a duty of the state and looked to the future for further control of liquor.[24]

Through special act or local election over 200 other bars closed and the state auditor's report in July, 1904, showed that there remained only about 1,100 retail licenses issued. Among those voting dry in 1903 were Charlottesville and Danville. From Charlottesville came word of President Edwin A. Alderman's decision that wines and liquors would no

21. William Hodges Mann to Dr. Pearson, Feb. 20, 1926.
22. Health resorts, situated on salt water or having natural mineral springs, and territory contiguous to cities having 500 inhabitants and public police protection and a saloon in 1903, were exempted.
23. Mann to Pearson, Feb. 20, 1926. Dabney says "the barrooms were well-nigh eliminated from the rural districts." *Dry Messiah*, p. 50. *Acts*, April 16, 1903—repassed to correct printer's errors Jan. 6, 1904. In North Carolina the same year the Watt Law was passed permitting retailing only in incorporated towns.
24. An unplanned result of this law was the gradual linking of the league with the Democratic party, the so-called machine which controlled Virginia politics. Mann was later elected governor with the support of both elements.

longer be served at public functions of the university. In Richmond Carlton McCarthy won the mayoralty over the saloons' candidate and he plainly told liquor men assembled in state convention that they and their business were under surveillance. In Fluvanna a judge from Campbell County refused to grant license in the village of Columbia although most of the citizens desired it.[25] Watching the ever-widening scope of the movement the *Religious Herald* commented ". . . the doom of the saloon is written in the suffrage clause of the new constitution."[26]

In January, 1904, Dr. Mitchell retired from the presidency of the league because his prominence in anti-liquor work was embarrassing to some of his colleagues in the Association for the Improvement of Public Schools, of which he was also president.[27] He eschewed politics, minimized organization and finance without neglecting them entirely, and relied principally upon evoking and solidifying moral sentiment through broad educational processes. He was succeeded by Rev. James Cannon, Jr.,[28] principal of Blackstone Female Institute and son-in-law of Dr. W. W. Bennett whose son, R. H. Bennett,

25. Report of J. W. West in Virginia Anti-Saloon League *Proceedings,* 1904; *Christian Sentinel,* Oct., 1904, March, June, 1905.
26. March 5, 1904.
27. Recollections of Dr. Mitchell.
28. Cannon was born and raised in a temperance family and often accompanied his mother on her missionary efforts in the saloon districts. He was known as a non-drinker at Randolph-Macon during his student days though his work with Dr. W. W. Bennett's *Crusader* may have been doubly attractive since the first Mrs. Cannon, Dr. Bennett's daughter, was among the others folding and addressing the temperance journal. Mr. and Mrs. Cannon went to Farmville, Va., in 1891 where he became editor of the monthly Farmville *District Methodist* in 1893 and merged this with the *Methodist Recorder* in 1894. These monthlies had limited circulation, however, and Cannon and J. Sidney Peters acquired control of the Baltimore and Richmond *Christian Advocate* in 1904. This weekly journal "reached preachers and leading laymen in every community of the state . . ." said Cannon (*Own Story,* p. 122), and served as a strong voice of prohibition in the state until Cannon began the Richmond *Virginian,* a daily paper in support of the cause, in 1910. A good synthesis of Cannon's methods is found in Floyd V. Spence, "Outstanding Policies Sponsored by James Cannon, Jr. as Editor of the Baltimore and Richmond *Christian Advocate,* 1904-1918" (B.D. thesis. Divinity School, Duke University, 1935).

soon became superintendent of the league.[29] Bennett studied at Princeton and served as pastor in important Virginia cities and was on the faculty of Randolph-Macon College. Leadership of the anti-liquor movement was now back with the Methodist Randolph-Macon group.

The league's convention of 1905 in Lynchburg was attended by many delegates and characterized by a diversified program.[30] The veteran Smith spoke on the saloon and young men, Superintendent S. I. Roberts of the Riverside Cotton Mills (largest of the South) on the saloon and liquor, and Mitchell on the league and politics. The field secretary presented a report featuring law enforcement to the committee on legislation and Judge Mann outlined specific laws from the lawyer-politician's viewpoint. There was a school of methods for local-option workers. Able and popular Methodist minister W. W. Beauchamp presented a plan for financing. President Cannon reviewed the league's success and failures in closing saloons and suggested league intervention in forthcoming elections, from all of which it appeared that the new leadership was headed toward more vigorous action in terms of money and workers and politics. This became evident in its next attempts at law enforcement and at making dry the towns and cities, which all league backers favored and heartily supported.

At the same time the league attempted to apply the third part of its program of agitation, legislation, and enforcement.

29. The superintendency was filled in the interval between Dr. Crawford and Dr. Bennett by Dr. Gordon Moore, brought from Furman University in South Carolina. Dr. Moore emphasized education in moral ideas generally and the cultivation of a more respectful attitude toward the state as the best agency for giving such ideas effect. He told the Baptist General Association that anti-liquor work was just as much their business as missions. Under his editorship the *Christian Federation* became the *Civic Sentinel*; in this paper the names of the national officers of the league did not precede those of the Virginia organization; and it carried the names of representatives of four denominations as corresponding editors.

30. Lynchburg *News*, Richmond *Times-Dispatch*, Roanoke *News*, Jan. 18, 19, 20, 1905.

While there were many evidences of the popularity of both local option and the Mann Law, complaints by Baptist and Methodist state bodies in 1902 and 1903 and a survey by the *Christian Sentinel* in March and April, 1905, clearly indicated that dry laws were not being enforced as well as other laws. Part of the trouble came from speak-easies of the type so familiar during national prohibition. Unauthorized selling by the small stills in rural regions was difficult to prevent. "We impose one of our small fines," said Field Secretary West to the Lynchburg convention, "and then turn them loose to continue in the same business."

Equally serious were violations of the spirit of the dry laws in ways that were within the law—"flank attacks," Dr. Cannon called them. There were the legal dispensaries against which Superintendent Bennett read a paper and which Cannon denounced at league conventions of 1906 and 1907 as "worse than saloons." Particularly objectionable was the new phenomenon known as the "social club." These were often known as "fake" clubs since their sole purpose was the dispensing of liquor, or "Kelley" clubs after the Richmond lawyer who showed the legal opportunity for them. In 1904 they numbered 46 and in 1905 they had grown to 85. Appearing in wet as well as dry territory they were described[31] in 1907 as "bar rooms of the worst type, doing business on Sunday and all night, harboring male and female, adult and child, black and white, breeding lawlessness, arson, murder and all crime." Little was said or could be said in their defense and they were repulsive to a great many who were against the anti-liquor movement as well as the dries. Yet the law-drafting and the parliamentary talents of the league were so poor that in 1906 remedial legislation was blocked in a house which was clearly sympathetic.[32]

31. Circular issued by John R. Doyle, candidate for the Senate from the Petersburg district in 1907. See also letter of J. W. West in Richmond *News-Leader*, July 23, 1907.
32. *Civic Sentinel*, 1906.

This threw upon the league the odium of having created a situation that it could not handle. The *Times-Dispatch* said editorially in 1906:

In a land where liquor is made and sold by citizens who pay their legal taxes and are under the restraints and supervision of authority, the illicit distiller and the blind tiger has to fight not only the revenue officers, but the licensed dealers and distillers also. But where the taste for stimulants is not yet lost or the craving for alcohol not yet satisfied, men will arise to supply the demand, even though the whiskey has to be illicitly manufactured and illegally sold.[33]

The next year Armistead Gordon of Staunton, in articles sponsored by local businessmen, asserted that law and order prevailed in his city under the high license plan while the courts of nearby Lexington were filled with dry law violators and that dry Covington was infested with dives.[34]

With the licensed saloon eliminated from nearly all rural areas by the Mann Law, the Lynchburg convention directed its attention to the thousand or more licensed places in cities, towns, suburbs, and resorts which escaped both local option and the Mann Law.[35] Meanwhile the Virginia Liquor Dealers' Association, under the active leadership of John A. Lesner, a wealthy brewer of Norfolk, let it be known that it had a "defense reserve fund" of $30,000 with which to fight local option.[36] 1905 was an important year politically and the league had little money and few trained workers. No big drive could be undertaken until June, 1907, but within eighteen months from that date elections were held with striking

33. "Moonshine Prohibition," Dec. 6, 1906.
34. In the *Flag*, a small paper put out in the local-option fight of 1907.
35. These remained despite a concentrated campaign by President Cannon and the league forces to turn these areas dry through local-option elections. Cannon, *Own Story*, p. 127. Of 1,106 retail liquor licenses issued in 1904, according to the state auditor's report quoted at the Lynchburg convention, 747 were in the cities, 173 in the suburbs, 159 in 19 towns and summer resorts.
36. *Civic Sentinel*, Oct., 1904.

success in Charlottesville, Bristol, Danville, Winchester, Fredericksburg, Lynchburg, South Boston, and Roanoke.[37]

In Charlottesville Professors Stone, Minor, and Dunnington spoke for the old temperance men. The ministers solicited votes all day in the rain while the church bells tolled and the railway workers joined them to decide the issue. In Bristol Judge William F. Rhea, a prominent and astute leader of the "machine," was confronted by the women of the town who signed and printed in the Bristol *Herald-Courier* a memorial for an election. On election day they brought out the children at daybreak and after an hour's prayer on the streets marshalled them into a mile-long parade led by the Bristol Military Band. In Roanoke a Citizens' Anti-Local Option League, with the support of the mayor and the Roanoke *Times*, urged a policy of fewer saloons, shorter opening hours, higher licenses, and stricter regulation, all influenced by the fear of higher taxes and by the prospect of ruin to the great brewing industry which some of the city's best citizens fostered through many hard years. The dries, organized under James D. Johnston, called in the oratorical services of Seaborn Wright of Georgia and the organizing skill of Secretary McAlister of the league, who showed up the blind tigers existing under the license system and the connection of the saloons with prostitution. On the eve of the election the local league promised a fund of $10,000 to enforce the law if the city went dry and held a night parade with 1,300 men and boys, no women, with the bands of the Red Men and the Roanoke Machine Works at their head. Though local people were doing the bulk of the work, league leaders were contributing much in the way of literature, astute advice, and organizing skill. League leaders did not hesitate when the election went the wrong way in Orange and in Staunton to

37. Superintendent Bennett reported to the Anti-Saloon League of America meeting in Norfolk Sept. 16-19, 1907, that within a year five cities had entered the dry list, six had remained dry, and two had gone wet in local elections.

attribute the results to the vote of purchased Negroes in the former and downright fraud at the polls in the latter.[38] Alarmed, the *Times-Dispatch* of Richmond began to demand that the city clean up its saloons and reduce their number, warning that otherwise "there will be a prohibition movement that will shake up the community, even if it does not succeed."[39]

It was now evident to all that the prohibition movement again was wielding a powerful influence in Virginia. The Anti-Saloon League was the director and spokesman for this influence and as such could make its weight felt in the councils of the state government. From the dry rural areas to the still wet but alarmed cities came rumblings of further action to come and few believed that the issue could rest in its present situation. Wherever the movement went the league would be in the lead.

38. *Civic Sentinel*, 1904-1906, *passim*, June, 1907; *American Issue, Virginia Edition*, March 28, May 9, 23, June 27, Oct. 31, 1908, Jan. 9, 1909; Roanoke *Times*, April 24, June 11, 1907, Dec. 15-31, 1908, Jan. 1, 3, 1909; Virginia Anti-Saloon League *Proceedings*, 1908, 1909.
39. Aug. 2, 1907.

## Chapter Twelve

# THE TWO "MACHINES" AND THE BYRD LAW, 1905-1908

The league, in accordance with the program suggested in 1905, developed itself as an organization and established political contacts. The latter were principally with the so-called machine element of the Democratic party. These matters matured fully by 1908 and immediately became greatly prominent in the Virginia anti-liquor movement. The union of the two machines was so remarkable that many observers wondered whether the end of anti-liquor work was lost sight of in the development of devices to attain it.

## THE LEAGUE

The strongest men behind the league, taught by the past, emphasized the "all-inclusive" nature of their organization.[1] Membership requirements were never rigid. Some belonged because they had signed the enrolment card with its pledge to contribute. Most of these members were loosely organized into local leagues[2] which met most frequently when some local election was approaching or to welcome some representative from headquarters at a rally. Next there were "affiliated" societies. Never did the WCTU fail to send greeting through Mrs. Howard H. Hoge and the Good Templars through George W. Hawxhurst, gestures of good will and co-operation in a common enterprise. Under the early ruling of President S. C. Mitchell and in accordance with the trend of the national league, local religious bodies were considered temperance societies and as such were entitled to membership. At the

1. The following description is based principally upon the manuscript records of the league in Richmond, to which Dr. Pearson was given full access. His notes (Pearson Papers, Wake Forest College) are comprehensive. This is fortunate since the records seem since to have disappeared.
2. Provision was made in the league's constitution for such groups.

league's convention in 1913 there were altogether eighteen different kinds of organizations represented, but at all times it was principally the local churches that organizers turned to. Superintendent C. H. Crawford in 1903 reported a favorable reception "in nearly all the churches"; Field Secretary J. W. West in 1908 stated that the churches of practically all Methodists, Baptists, Disciples, United Brethren, and a large majority of the Presbyterians "are open to us." "The Episcopalians," he optimistically added, "are falling into line more and more, and the Roman Catholics to some extent." In the league's conventions the delegates of these local churches, especially Methodists and Baptists, increasingly predominated.[3]

Because of its composition the league, like all its predecessors, was distinctly an affair of the middle and lower-middle classes. The thousands of whites who did not go to church were usually too poor and too lacking in influence to be sought for membership. Despite the well-founded belief that liquor was a chief cause of crime among them, Negroes were almost never sought and they were not particularly welcomed when they volunteered co-operation.[4] "First Churches" were the slowest to respond among Baptists and Methodists and rarely ever responded among Episcopalians. When league meetings were held in churches of lower rating leading members were usually absent. Among league leaders, scarcely half a dozen rose above the commonplace in the professions (except in the ministry), in business, or in society. Most of them began

3. Of the 114 delegates present in 1904, 21 were from local leagues, 28 from the WCTU, 19 from Baptist, 20 from Methodist, and 3 from Christian churches. Of the 422 delegates in 1913, 22 were from local leagues, 17 from the WCTU, 60 from Sunday schools, and 119 from Methodist, 61 from Baptist, 3 from Presbyterian, and 2 from Episcopalian churches. Summaries usually appear in current newspapers and are incomplete in most cases.

4. The reasons were, first, a fixed belief that Negroes were not dependable politically and, second, a fear that their inclusion would offend many whites and give the opposition a new argument. At times the Negro support of the wets was played up at league meetings as another threat to white supremacy. Similar attitudes were present in the Farmers' Alliance movement. William DuBose Sheldon, *Populism in the Old Dominion: Virginia Farm Politics, 1885-1900* (Princeton, N. J., 1935), p. 35.

life humbly and remained dependent for livelihood upon daily personal exertion. They were a virile crowd, contemptuous of the older men's "mush" and craving to "mix it" with the lawyers whom they feared for their shrewdness, the "leather-necked" bar-tenders whom they hated, and the politicians whom they envied. As the league's efficiency and power became evident it was able to command assistance from the ablest though it was the rallies of the opposition that brought out the elite of Richmond and Norfolk. League leaders were conscious of their social inferiority. They showed it by their eagerness for praise from "great" minds and "great" newspapers and by their inability to understand opposition except as it sprang from love of liquor or love of money. To remind them of their inferiority members of the higher class did not hesitate to jest about their women, ridicule their books (especially their physiologies), and ask why their churches had forsaken evangelism for political tactics, which may have solidified the following.[5]

Each year the league assembled in convention, usually in January or February, always in the larger towns, and always in a church building (strictly alternating between Baptist and Methodist Churches until 1911).[6] State temperance workers, orators from without, aspiring state politicians, representatives of the national league—anyone whom the leaders desired to honor, conciliate, or utilize—appeared before the convention. Here information was spread, enthusiasm generated, policy agreed upon, and machinery set up to carry on until the next convention. Business was conducted very much after the order of political parties except the league did not formally nominate candidates for public office. The conventions were

5. The alignment presented was not so clear in the western counties.
6. The sixth convention met Dec. 4, 1906. The first three met in Richmond, the others successively in Lynchburg, Petersburg, Charlottesville, Richmond, Norfolk, Newport News, Richmond, Roanoke, and Richmond. After 1901 the Presbyterian and Christian churches were occasionally added.

always managed well. They elected as president[7] the man selected by the leaders. He was never a figurehead and he was always re-elected once. They put the leaders, including ex-presidents, on the executive committee, gave this committee wide powers, including selection and control of employees, and backed up its actions. The headquarters committee which developed with the executive committee reported to it, as did the legislative committee, whose chairman was almost continuously either a member or an employee of the executive committee. Continuity of policy was maintained without denying to cranks and dissenters an opportunity to express themselves before the sovereign body. More than one critical situation was faced frankly and met expeditiously.[8] There was danger of bad judgment but the executive committee was usually saved by its knowledge of public sentiment obtained from the reports of its field men and its members' own constant contacts with the constituency. "Results" were gained and the basis for charges of "practicing bossism" and "management by a few," to which President R. S. Barbour officially referred in 1913, was laid.

The employed workers were never numerous nor well paid. Most important was the superintendent,[9] who cared for

7. The presidents were S. C. Mitchell (1901-1904), James Cannon, Jr. (1904-1906), J. W. Mitchell (1906-1907), W. C. Taylor (1907-1909), Henry P. Atkins (1909-1911), E. T. Wellford (1911, resigned), R. S. Barbour (1911-1913), J. W. Hough (1913-1915), R. H. Pitts (1915-1917).

8. Such were the discharging of Superintendent Crawford, the selection of Gordon Moore as superintendent (an act very pleasing to the *Religious Herald*, March 5, 1903), the filling of vacancies in the presidency and the executive committee in 1911, and permitting Cannon to return for a while in the interest of harmony. Such also was the work of "quizzing" candidates for office and determining the satisfactoriness of the answers, and covering up indiscretions of individual members or employees, and such was the making of contacts with newspapers (including the *Virginian* affair) and the determination of legislation through the selection of sponsors for bills and accepting or rejecting specific provisions in them. The above listing is in no way comprehensive.

9. Anti-Saloon League *Proceedings*, 1913. Crawford began at $1,200, part of which he agreed to remit. S. P. Jones and Walter Syndor served without pay as treasurer and attorney respectively for virtually the entire period and so, apparently, did Cannon. The following were superintendents: C. H. Crawford (1901-1903), Gordon Moore (1903-1904), R. H. Bennett (1905-1909), and James Cannon, Jr. (1909-1911, 1912———).

correspondence and edited the league's newspaper and other literature in the intervals between conferences and field work. He was also chief contact man with the national league, whose approval of his selection was necessary in the later days. There were at times district superintendents, West in the southwest and Ed. J. Richardson in northern Virginia, secretaries, field men, and lectures. These men formed the vital connecting link between headquarters and the unpaid and untrained local workers. It was they who went into the by-ways to do educational and organizing work, they who conducted "field days," put "pep" into local campaigns, won the confidence of ministers and other local leaders. In 1913 Secretary J. D. McAlister reported that three and a half regular men had in the past year traveled 56,628 miles, delivered 561 addresses, and brought back $12,734 in subscriptions and $3,559 in cash, while fourteen special men brought back $2,110 in subscriptions and $626 in cash after 89 addresses. That year the total salary budget was about $8,000 and the highest-paid man received $2,000. Few of these men could be called professional, for most of them slipped into the league's employ (usually from the ministry) and out of it again without particular shock. Headquarters in Richmond were very simply equipped, giving an impression of transience, but they were well located for contacts.

"Adequate financial support," the bugaboo of ante bellum days, was a requirement imposed by the national league. It was the state leaders' chief worry. The pioneers, starting with nothing, set up headquarters in a three-dollar room, did the rather heavy clerical work themselves, held organizational meetings in cold church basements. Depending principally at first upon public collections, they were unable to extinguish a debt of $1,300 despite the liberality of Dr. Crawford and the true Methodist boosting of Mr. Bellows of Lancaster. When they shifted to private "donations" and the pledge cards, the income was forced up to around $4,000 in 1904 and from

$6,000 to $16,000 between 1906 and 1908. This was the work largely of the Methodist ministers (Cannon being particularly urgent). They received strong backing from R. S. Barbour, banker of South Boston, under whose insistence debts were paid off and a balanced budget was fairly well maintained until 1914. Adequate financing by the rank and file, principally through the pledge cards, was an important factor in the league's success. Only once before 1914 was it necessary to obtain a "special fund" through larger gifts and this only to the extent of $5,000. No contributions were made to or by the national league.[10]

In the work of "agitation" which the national league set as a first and continuing task, the press played the chief role. Undoubtedly much was accomplished by printing and distributing in pamphlet form addresses and reports made before the conventions, much by the physiology textbooks used in the schools, even more by temperance lessons in Sunday schools, and something by periodicals such as *Ram's Horn* and *Voice* sent in from other states. More important was the league's own newspaper, which appeared monthly or semi-monthly as the *Christian Federation*, the *Civic Sentinel*, and the *American Issue, Virginia Edition*, successively, from 1901 on. Through their constant and copious streams of news about temperance activities and policies the faithful were heartened and co-ordinated. Their great disadvantage lay in their being recognized as organs of a special cause and so avoided by the general reader. Many more people subscribed to and read as "Sunday reading" the denominational weeklies.[11] Though the small-town and country newspapers were rarely completely hostile and sometimes were actively friendly,

10. Virginia Anti-Saloon League *Proceedings*, especially the treasurer's annual report. The treasurer's books appear never to have been formally audited but their correctness was usually attested by a committee of the convention. Dr. Cannon stated that there were no large contributions before 1914. The special fund mentioned above was secured by Ed. J. Richardson in small sums and was used chiefly for the *Virginian*.

11. For the weeklies and the *Virginian* see below.

only three city newspapers, one each in Staunton, Bristol, and Roanoke, were distinctly friendly to the league in 1908.[12] The establishment of the Richmond *Virginian* in 1910 did much to correct this situation.

The propaganda of the league was always aggressive in contrast with that of the opposition. It was directed not so much at the use of liquor as at the liquor business. In a highly applauded address at the Lynchburg convention W. W. Smith emphasized the danger to youth of the saloon because of the treating custom rather than because of the wrong of drink.[13] No opportunity to play up the activities of the "liquor power" was lost. That the daily press was subsidized by this power was suggested over and over and "liquor lawyer" was a frequent term of reproach. That prohibition lowered the cost of local government and taxes was constantly asserted with statistics to back up the claim, particularly in 1907.[14] Maps showing the steady increase of dry territory were often used. Richardson even had one which he had prepared printed in the *Times-Dispatch* in 1906.[15] These were intended at once to hearten the faithful and to convince the doubtful of the inevitableness of prohibition. Behind it, said the *Herald*,[16] was a "robust civic conscience."

Any discussion of the league as an organization or "machine" must include the relationship between it and the state-

12. *Religious Herald*, Feb. 13, 1908.
13. Lynchburg *News*, Jan. 19, 1905. "It was the keeper's business," said Dr. Smith, "to get all the drinkers to drink more and get others to start drinking. For the last he found an easy victim in the young. The hot blood of youth, with its fiery passions, bravado, inexperience and judgment held in abeyance, afforded an easy target. Freedom tingling in his veins, wanting to see for himself, to cut loose from his mother's apron strings, posing as a 'hail, fellow, well met,' he invites five companions in to take a drink, not because he wants the drink but because he wants to be sociable and thought an openhearted, generous fellow. He sets 'em up; then one after the other follows suit . . . . That boy is marked by business men, railroads and great corporations . . . . His prospects blighted, a marked man, he loses ambition . . . to license a man to take a boy's money and give him in return something harmful is worse than robbery. . . ."
14. *Civic Sentinel*, June, 1907.      15. Dec. 5, 1907.
16. Feb. 13, 1908.

wide church organizations. Even before the league came to Virginia the Methodist Annual Conference and the Baptist General Association formally sought to influence legislation concerning the liquor business.[17] As the league proved itself worthy and suitable each of the church organizations became its advocate. Their views found expression in resolutions which informed the league of the denominations' desires and created sentiment favorable for the merging of their work toward common goals. A sort of interlocking leadership between league and denominations reduced disagreement to a minimum. In this matter the Methodists were more forward and effective than the Baptists. From the first the Virginia Annual Conference, a member of the national league before the Virginia league was established, supplied a forum from which Methodist leaders could plead for assistance from the churches in building their organization. Soon it was dealing with specific legislation, advising members how to vote, telling legislators what they were expected to do.[18] Members back home read the story in the Richmond *Christian Advocate* just as Cannon wished them to understand it. The ordinary preachers whose biennial location depended upon the will of the hierarchy naturally took heed.[19] The Baptist General As-

17. Also the Christians. John A. Tate to Dr. Pearson, Sept. 24, 1931.
18. See *Minutes*, 1902-1914. Leaders in this work from 1902 on were W. A. Christian and Cannon. F. M. Edwards no longer appeared. In 1902 voting against the saloon was recommended; in 1903 the legislature was petitioned in the name of 94,000 Methodists; in 1906 it was voted to seek only temperance men for office; in 1907 specific federal legislation was recommended; in 1909 state legislation in great detail was recommended and the attitude of some newspapers was deplored; in 1911 the representation of the U. S. government at a brewers' convention was deplored and congressmen were informed that they were expected to work for desired favorable laws; in 1912 the people were called on to elect legislators favorable to an enabling act. These actions are illustrative of the trend only.
19. Many of the "lower" clergy did not like the organizing and manipulating which were so characteristic of the league. They co-operated because it seemed the only thing to do. They preferred inspiring speakers who set forth the evils of drinking and exhorted the poor unfortunates to reform. They felt that the league's work was artificial and unsound and perhaps unbecoming to ministers.

sociation[20] at first intended only to co-operate occasionally. In 1903 it recognized the league as a suitable agency with which to co-operate and gave attention to legislative matters which the league was pressing. After 1906, however, it was giving temperance equal place with other subjects in its standing program and hearing reports read by its league members. From 1909 on it commended and reprimanded legislators and newspapers much as the conference was doing and in 1913 it admitted league representatives in their official capacity to the privileges of the floor. Their district associations rapidly fell into line with, and sometimes anticipated, league policies.[21] The Southern Baptist Convention in 1908, after a dozen years of silence, voted that a new day had come in politics and began to undertake a practical program of anti-liquor work.[22]

The official attitude of the other large church bodies was quite different. There could be no doubt that the Presbyterian organizations were well-wishers of the league. But their General Assembly declined in 1903 to be represented at the national league's convention, refused in 1907 to appoint a

20. See *Minutes*, 1901-1914. Very active were: Ed. J. Richardson, J. M. Pilcher, J. W. Mitchell, Ryland Knight, J. W. Cammack. Mitchell and Cammack were on the *Religious Herald* staff.

21. E.g., actions of the Valley in 1902, the Roanoke in 1906, the Concord in 1909, and the Portsmouth District association in 1913.

22. The temperance report that year said: "The politicians of today are in increasing numbers consulting with the religious people of the communities rather than with the saloon aggregation. Strong men with statesmen principles have proven that the masses of the people will eagerly support righteous leaders for noble purposes. This is a great gain, and may be called a great discovery—a discovery of incalculable value. . . . Civic righteousness and the Kingdom of God are bound up in each other. We are learning to increase the census of heaven, but to make down here a righteous community. . . ."
Members of the Convention voted that they would "preach temperance, pray for temperance, and vote for temperance" and appointed a committee of fifteen to promote it in every way. In 1914 a report drawn by W. L. Poteat of North Carolina asserted that the church is "directly responsible for the right solution of social problems," among which the liquor traffic was specified. This report, however, carefully set limits to the permissible activities of the church with reference to the state. And it insisted that Christian regeneration of the individual was the prime necessity.

permanent committee on temperance, and failed in 1913 to endorse a petition for state prohibition. When in 1914 it endorsed "National Constitutional Prohibition" the Virginia Synod led in solemn protest against "so serious a departure from the position of the Church on civil questions."[23] In the Episcopal church one of its two councils was reported to have endorsed the league in 1907.[24] No action by the Catholic organization was reported. Though these actions, or the lack of action, did not control members in the exercise of their civic rights, they undoubtedly did greatly affect both the quality of the league and the weight which it had with the general public. More to the point, most of the ministers belonged to the league and could be counted to co-operate through influence, work, and votes in their individual communities.

There were many individuals who generally co-operated with the league's anti-liquor work without giving up the right to independent judgment and expression on procedure. Among them was Carter Glass of Lynchburg, owner of the Lynchburg *News*, who early became suspicious of league leaders and once threatened to disrupt the organization through independent political action, yet he was later found addressing league conventions. There was also Rev. R. H. Pitt, editor of the Richmond *Religious Herald*, who thought that Baptist organizations ought to confine themselves to expressions on the principles of the matter and leave the approving of men and methods to the league as a sort of political agent.[25] But when his church determined otherwise no one wrote more effectively for the league's plans and eventually he became the league's president. There was also Rev. E. L. Goodwin who, with little concealment of disgust for the methods being used, brought the *Southern Churchman*[26] to support state-wide

23. Letter of Rev. T. C. Johnson to Dr. Pearson, Oct. 15, 1928.
24. *Civic Sentinel*, July, 1907.
25. For example see the editorial of Jan. 20, 1910.
26. Aug. 29, 1914.

prohibition, as Rev. W. S. Campbell did the *Presbyterian of the South*—each without denominational authorization.


## THE PARTY

When Virginians in those days spoke of the "machine" they referred to the prominent Democratic politicians who ordinarily collaborated with Senator Thomas S. Martin. Among them would be named J. Taylor Ellyson, chairman of the state Democratic committee, Congressman Henry D. ("Hal") Flood and Claude Swanson (both lawyers of the Southside who acknowledged respectively a Methodist and a Presbyterian connection), Judge William F. Rhea of Bristol and the Williamses, Samuel and Martin, also of the southwest. All were lawyers and not great churchmen though the Williamses professed Methodism.[27] Mr. Martin was known somewhat vaguely as a hard-working railroad attorney of Albemarle and a useful member of the state committee when, in 1893, he surprised the state by getting the legislature to elect him senator instead of the well-known and popular General Fitzhugh Lee. Various explanations of the election followed—a triumph for the younger democracy, a worker instead of a fighter, a Hill man instead of a Cleveland man, and above all, the use of money by the railroads in Martin's behalf back in the legislative districts.[28] By 1905 Mr. Martin

27. Less conspicuous but still important machine men included Edward Echols of Staunton, S. L. Kelley of Richmond, A. P. Thom of Norfolk, all members of the party's executive committee and all friends of liquor. Senator John W. Daniels never opposed the machine but was not a member of it. Henry Stuart of the southwest was considered independent with anti-machine leanings.

28. The Richmond *Times* declared that Martin's election was "inexplicable upon any grounds to which the public . . . have been accustomed to hear in such matters" and the Richmond *Dispatch* cautiously suspected "some extraneous influence at work." Legislators undertook an investigation which disclosed the use of railroad money in the legislative districts and condemned the practice as reprehensible but rather customary. Lee's friends never quite forgave Martin. Richmond *Times* and *Dispatch*, Dec. 16-20, 1893. John F. Ryan (later member of the party executive committee) headed the investigation.

was established in the esteem of most businessmen, won re-election from the legislature, and sought the Democratic nomination by direct primary for a third term.

The basis of the machine was the local officers.[29] By standing together in their counties and towns they were able not only to keep themselves in office but to determine who should represent their people in the legislature. The legislature in turn chose the county or circuit judges and a large number of more-or-less important state officials and employees who, current belief had it, were carefully allocated according to districts by the machine. The number of these local officers was estimated in 1911 at between 7,000 and 10,000 and the number of votes which they could control in conjunction with the state officers and employees at 35,000.[30] Most of them were paid by the fees they collected. When the constitutional convention of 1901-1902 was about to assemble, Mr. Martin made as his sole request of his friends that they "make the fee officers constitutional officers."[31] Supplementing these were the old election boards and their appointees.[32] It was one of this group who argued against suffrage restriction at the convention on the grounds that he knew how to vote an absent Negro and a dead Negro but "damned if I know how to vote a disfranchised negro!" This machinery does not seem to differ radically from that used by the party leadership in the days of John S. Barbour, but it had more systematic management and more money. Since white su-

29. Complaints of local rings had cropped out notably in 1877 and 1886; they were a favorite target of prohibitionists. Taylor Ellyson and his predecessor, John S. Barbour, practiced co-operation with them, but the tardiness of their reward by the party suggests that they did not have control. The use of funds for Martin's benefit seems to have been independent of the party committee.

30. Speech of A. J. Montague, *Times-Dispatch*, Aug. 12, 1911.

31. The extent to which this was done for the counties may be seen in the Constitution of 1902, Arts. VII and IX, secs. 132, 133. The cities and towns had separate officials.

32. For a detailed criticism from the Republican viewpoint see William C. Pendleton, *Political History of Appalachian Virginia* (Dayton, Va., 1927), chaps. 22, 24, pp. 274-289, 369-380.

premacy was no longer in danger the only real justification for its existence was gone. As a rule, the machine was opposed to reforms. Movements for railroad regulation and taxation, for direct primary,[33] for fairer and more honest elections, and for public school progress all met with their disapproval.

There was another, much looser, group who were supposed to favor reform and who were apt to attract support from the old ruling set, those who could not forgive the defeat of Fitzhugh Lee, and those who disliked "management" and "bossism" in political affairs. They were termed "antimachine." Among them were Harry St. George Tucker, William A. Jones, A. J. Montague, Carter Glass, Joseph Willard, the Pollards, and the Richmond Bryans with their newspapers.

The machine was not counted among the moral and religious forces of the state.[34] A clever opportunism was the very essence of its philosophy: Bourbonism cost the old organization its leadership and wrecked the party. If new pressures should become so strong as to threaten Democratic control or their leadership they would know how to fall in line, always in such a manner as to minimize the damage to old friends and to gain strength from the gratitude of the new.[35] Though they probably never read what Pitt had to say in the *Religious Herald* about the new suffrage laws' bringing reform elements into office, one may be sure that Martin was noticing the disappearance of old friends from the local offices and the appearance of new men and was quite prepared to assess, in his own way, the strength of the cause behind the changes.

33. V. Dabney, "History of the Primary" in the Richmond *Times-Dispatch*, Nov. 25, 1928.
34. Governor Mann was an exception. His work in social legislation and reform has never seriously been questioned.
35. The machine opposed the choice of both Cleveland and Wilson as Democratic candidates but was very helpful in the presidential campaigns which followed. They benefited greatly by the patronage and the like thereby obtained.

THE LEAGUE PREPARES TO JOIN THE PARTY

Early backers of the league were very much afraid of politics. Borrowing from the league's policy in states where there were two strong parties, their organization proclaimed itself "omni-party" or "inter-party." They had no clear idea of what this meant in Virginia in the way of program except that there was not to be a third party. President Mitchell hoped that the anti-saloon sentiment evoked by the league's work of education and organization would cause the Democratic party to rid itself of saloon connections for the sake of its own strength. Superintendent Crawford began the creation of a Home Defense Army by getting voters to sign a pledge to vote and use their influence "both in the primary elections of my party and in the general elections" for "staunch temperance men to all offices that have to do with the liquor traffic" and he said this plan favorably impressed the officers of the national league.

Then at the Lynchburg convention of 1905 in his presidential address Dr. Cannon stated that the league must not only formulate and declare what laws it wanted but also ask candidates to state their views and publish the replies. He argued that this was not an unusual procedure, for even then similar inquiries were being made in the matters of oyster laws and taxes on dogs. He did not intend that the inquiries should be reserved until nominations were made but would direct them to aspirants for nomination. He thought that the league would be strong enough to prevent the nomination of any man who would not pledge himself in advance, even to the smallest offices. At the same time it was proposed to create a headquarters' committee which would handle the "quizzing," as it came to be called, and the publication of the replies. The convention endorsed both proposals without recorded discussion, depending upon the good judgment of the executive committee, Cannon, Dr. Mitchell, and Rev. H. P. Atkins, secretary of the league. The secular press took no note of the plan in either news or editorial column except that Carter Glass's Lynchburg *News* mentioned Dr. Cannon's proposing a plan "which he said" would be useful. It was the development of the plan that brought the league into practical cooperation with the Democratic machine and skyrocketed the reputation of Dr. Cannon.

James Cannon, Jr.,[36] was a Marylander by birth, the son of a Methodist minister of little prominence. Though pledged to abstinence in childhood by his mother, when a student at Randolph-Macon he had not shared the college community's excitement over the beginnings of local option. After some years of study at Princeton and some as a Virginia pastor in 1894 he became principal of Blackstone Female Academy which belonged to the Randolph-Macon system of schools and colleges and was located in the Southside not very far from Richmond. He retained this position from 1894-1911 and from 1914-1918 without abandoning the ministry, though he held no further pastorates. Simultaneously through the editorship of a local religious newspaper[37] he trained for the editorship of the Richmond *Christian Advocate*, which he assumed in 1904. His school work took him to many church gatherings where he became well acquainted with the bone and sinew of Methodism. He showed a fondness for getting resolutions passed which he deemed important because those who voted for them thereby became committed. He was quick to grasp the possibilities of the Anti-Saloon League of America and regularly attended both the national and the state conventions. He prepared careful and vigorous papers on

36. The following sketch of Bishop Cannon is as Dr. Pearson wrote it. It presents the views of a scholarly analysis of a controversial man by one who knew his work and corresponded and talked at length with him and his contemporaries. The picture presented captures the essence of a most fascinating individual and is supported rather than altered by Dabney's *Dry Messiah* and Cannon's *Own Story* and the multitude of items in the Cannon Papers at Duke University which have been opened to the public since Dr. Pearson did his research.
37. The Farmville *Methodist,* 1893-1904.

many subjects, beginning with publicity and finance for the state meetings. It was noteworthy that these papers related principally to organized war on liquor as a business, which he always distinguished from other aspects. In this work Dr. Cannon was lengthy and dull, as he was in his sermons, but it was usually found that he chose his ground very carefully and could not be driven from it. In 1903 when the National Anti-Saloon League was still uncertain as to how it might enter the South effectively, the president of that organization —like Cannon a Marylander and a future bishop of the Methodist church—appointed him chairman of a committee to study the matter. The recommendation which he finally made was that the basis of organization there be the churches[38] and in giving effect to this recommendation among Virginia Methodists he was most assiduous. No doubt he was made president of the league in 1904 largely because of his Randolph-Macon connections and because he was a Democrat, and the secular press predicted for his leadership "all sorts of fanaticisms and folly."[39] Unclerical looking, he incarnated the small preacher's hatred of liquor people. He loved argument like a lawyer but without the lawyer's sense of humor and good fellowship. He never sought public office, would perhaps have scorned it, yet no politician seemed to love political intrigue more or succeed better at it. None of this explains why he was perhaps the least loved and most hated man of his day nor why he was willingly followed by a host of good people.

## THE TWO MACHINES

Test of the league's capacity in a first-rate political contest under Dr. Cannon's leadership soon appeared. A query on the enforcement of the Mann Law was addressed to the candidates for governor in the Democratic primary of 1905. Joseph

38. Anti-Saloon League of America *Proceedings*, 1903, 1904.
39. *Religious Herald*, editorial, Feb. 18, 1909.

Willard, anti-machine, answered defiantly; Claude Swanson, machine, rather curtly; Judge Mann, enthusiastically. The guns of the league were turned upon Willard who, despite the high hopes which he had recently aroused, made a poor showing at the polls. Mann received 20,000 votes, which was "a Mann Law vote." Obviously the league could punish and reward. Less noticed but undoubtedly significant was Dr. Cannon's course in the senatorial primary which was fought out simultaneously. Even before the Lynchburg convention he obtained from Senator Martin written assurance of hearty support for the Hepburn-Doliver Bill, then before Congress.[40] Governor Montague, Martin's opponent, also favored this bill because, he said, it was in support of the state's police powers and the policy of local option. During the contest Dr. Cannon asserted that the league was not favoring Martin, which was true, for Montague was favored by many good league men, especially among Baptists. But the Richmond *Christian Advocate*[41] carried a number of items favorable to Martin, including one from the dry-Methodist-machine *Virginia Citizen* of Lancaster which affirmed league support for Martin. Mr. Martin won handsomely. At the Republican state convention, for Republicans did not use the primary system either then or later, no intervention of the league appeared. When L. L. Lewis, their candidate for governor, was quizzed a little later, he replied by quoting his party's declaration for the "traditional Republican doctrine" of local option.[42] No resentment at the league's policy was reflected at the regular elections and the Democratic machine candidates won handsomely. Some noticed that the league could intervene with power and yet without danger to the Democratic party. At any rate, the

40. The bill was an attempt to control interstate shipments of liquor into a dry state for purposes of resale. It died in committee. *Civic Sentinel,* Jan., 1905.

41. Richmond *Christian Advocate*, especially July, Aug., 1905. This weekly, now edited by Dr. Cannon, carried replies to the questionnaire fully.

42. Roanoke *Times*, Aug. 10, 1905.

league's "inter-party" policy became an intra-Democratic party policy.[43]

Two years later, in 1907-1908, came the league's second political test. It was striving for control of the legislature. In Petersburg Senator Lassiter, a lawyer of prominence, was standing for re-election chiefly because of his interest in a sadly needed good-roads bill which bore his name. He was thought to be a "liquor man" by the league and by the local organization through which it operated. Though he answered its many questions courteously and quite sympathetically and had back of him the professional and business elite of his city, he had to fight for his place and was almost beaten by a man of inferior abilities who had no record of past liquor affiliations and who made no reservation of private judgment in the matters of detail on which the league quizzed him.[44]

Of great future importance to the league and its program was Richard Evelyn Byrd, lawyer and editor of the Winchester *Star*. Once personally and politically a thoroughgoing wet he became a supporter of Willard with whose progressive ideas and social standards he was in sympathy. Mr. Byrd and his paper had ignored the doings of the league until now. He was, however, the brother-in-law of Congressman Henry D. Flood[45] and in 1905 had supported Mr. Martin for the federal Senate. In 1907 the *Star* remarked editorially in connection with the Staunton local-option election that temperance sentiment "is organized and militant and is directed with energy and intelligence." It added that liquor men would have to obey the laws in letter and in spirit and, further, that with league help under certain conditions a state-wide prohibitory

43. Many Republicans, especially in the southwest, supported the league in other respects.
44. Dr. J. M. Pilcher's papers (Virginia Baptist Historical Society, University of Richmond) include many items on this contest, among them a circular of John R. Doyle, Lassiter's opponent, a card of Lassiter's, a circular of the league, and clippings from the Richmond newspapers and the Petersburg *Index-Appeal*, May-Aug., 1907.
45. Mr. Flood (sometimes accurately called the "brains" of the machine) was Dr. Cannon's contact man with the machine. Mr. Byrd was the father of Admiral R. E. Byrd and Senator Harry Flood Byrd.

law might be "a great success."[46] Notwithstanding his about-face on liquor Mr. Byrd returned to the House and when the legislature assembled he was elected speaker by vote of both league and machine men. Speaker Byrd's offer to put in one bill the scattered and confusing liquor laws and to add whatever the league leaders desired was gratefully accepted.[47] Thereafter the league enjoyed his complete co-operation.

## THE BYRD LAW

The league, strengthened by political as well as local-option successes, was ready for enforcement legislation. Speaker Byrd and Dr. Cannon drew up and easily guided through the House the Byrd bill, which was the next step forward in Virginia's anti-liquor movement. Mann had a more difficult time in the Senate but on February 20, 1908, the bill became law.[48] It was comprehensive and well drawn. It defined liquor as "all mixtures, preparations and liquids which will produce intoxication" and allowed a "Malt beverage" of not over 2.25 per cent alcoholic content to be legally sold anywhere. It eliminated the possibility that a judge might license a saloon in a town or district of less than 500 inhabitants if he decided it was not injurious to the county by not providing for applications for licenses for such areas. It gave a death sentence to "fake" clubs in dry territory, prohibited any sale for local consumption by any still in dry territory (thus eliminating the small stills in such areas), and limited drinking on passenger trains. There were stricter regulations for drug store liquor sales and for the distributing of liquor samples. Even the makers of cider (intoxicating or otherwise), wine, malt liquor, and malt beverage faced new restrictions. Finally, the expe-

46. Winchester *Star*, especially July 13, 23, Aug. 12, 1907.

47. *American Issue*, March 28, 1908. His opponent for speaker was Withers, an anti-machine man, who was patron of good-road laws along with Lassiter. When Winchester went dry Mr. Byrd refused liquor advertisements for his paper and promised practical co-operation in enforcing the law. *American Issue*, May 8, 1908.

48. *Acts*, 1908, pp. 275 ff.

rience of law enforcement officials in attempting to enforce the Mann Law resulted in new provisions for detecting, bringing to trial, and convicting violators of the law.[49] It was "the most advanced anti-blind tiger legislation ever enacted in any Southern State," said the *American Issue*. Soon judges from over the state were praising its effectiveness in improving conditions.[50]

The Byrd Law did not intimidate the citadels of liquor. It increased the state's revenue from licenses by more than a quarter and crafty liquor men thought that this in itself was a safeguard for the business.[51] Highly respectable clubs continued in the cities. The big manufacturer did not lose the advantage of locating his business outside the cities. Many cities chose to continue their saloons under much stricter state regulation and higher license fees—all tending to bring order and respectability. Shipping liquor into dry territory continued but resale was prohibited. This gave the city distributors a monopoly in many areas.

Liquor interests also saw hope in the dispensaries allowed by the new legislation. From the angle of social policy much could be said for this device, for it eliminated drinking on the premises and private profits and the evils consequent upon these features. From the very first the dispensary met intense opposition from the dries who had witnessed its operation in South Carolina and in some Virginia localities. In 1906 Superintendent Bennett read *Dispensaries Worse than Saloons* be-

49. I.e., sec. 25: "In all prosecutions for the violation of this act, when evidence has been introduced . . . proving that the defendant sold a certain liquor or mixture, by whatever name it may be called, to be drunk as a beverage, and that the drinking of such liquid or mixture produced intoxication, the burden shall be on the defendant to show that such liquid or mixture was not intoxicating within the meaning of this act. . . ."

50. *American Issue*, Jan. 9, 1909. Dean Page of the university and Justice John Crutchfield of the Richmond Police Court are among those who praised the act. Charlottesville *Daily Progress*, Oct. 1, 1909.

51. Receipts were $403,000 for 1908 and $534,000 for 1910-1911. Retailers now paid the state from $550 to $1,000 depending upon the size of the city; distillers from $60 to $600 according to the amount distilled; and brewers, $500.

fore the league convention, arguing not only the immorality of selling by any one but also the danger rising from their very respectability. The next year Dr. Cannon spoke against them. The Richmond *Times-Dispatch* also opposed them, arguing that the dispensary "adds to the liquor evil political corruption."[52] Nevertheless, whether because of pressure from leaders in the machine element of the Democratic party or because of local sentiment, dispensaries set up by local governments after popular votes existed in a dozen communities a year after the Byrd Law went into effect.[53] Nor was any limit put on local governments' taxes on saloons or profits from dispensaries, with the results that some of them could have streets paved or policemen hired or schools kept open at the expense of liquor. League leaders contended that concessions such as these were only tactical and only temporary.

The league's development of its organization, its attack on the larger cities, and its political contacts resulted in blasts of unfriendly criticism from newspapers in Richmond and other cities.[54] For the most part the criticism was directed at Dr. Cannon, whom the writers regarded as the contriver

52. *Christian Federation*, March, 1902, Jan., 1903; *Civic Sentinel*, Jan., June, 1904, Aug., 1906. Rev. C. S. Gardner, who observed dispensaries in South Carolina and was converted from favoring them by what he saw, was one of the foremost opponents at the league convention of 1902 and in the *Times-Dispatch*. Dr. Gardner was pastor of Richmond's Grace Street Church. The Portsmouth Baptist District Association made consistent opposition from 1901 on. The Richmond *News-Leader* was also opposed. For the South Carolina experience see Francis B. Simkins, *The Tillman Movement in South Carolina* (Durham, N. C., 1926), chap. 8; and Simkins, *Pitchfork Ben Tillman* (Baton Rouge, La., 1944), pp. 234-261 *et passim*. See also Ellen Alexander, "The South Carolina Dispensary System" (Master's thesis, Duke University, 1940).

53. Abingdon, Farmville, and Scottsville had dispensaries in the districts of Rhea, Flood, and Martin. Other areas with dispensaries in 1909 were Boydston, Courtland, Emporia, Leigh District, Franklin, Martinsville, Pulaski, Ridgeway, Virgilina, Waverly, and Bedford City.

54. The *Religious Herald*, Feb. 13, 1908, said that only the three dailies in Bristol, Roanoke, and Staunton were fully and outspokenly for the league. The others, it said, maintained a "colorless and weak neutrality." The Bryans, operators of the *Times-Dispatch*, obtained control of the *News-Leader* in 1908 and placed both papers in opposition to "legislation that would deprive men of . . . convivial beverages." John S. Bryan, *Joseph Bryan* (Richmond, 1935), p. 281.

of the activities which they most disliked and whose methods and manners irritated and incensed them almost beyond restraint. Why, they asked, did temperance leaders always attribute bad motives to those who disagreed with them? Did temperance necessarily promote "ferocity and verbosity?"[55] But the criticism went far beyond superficialities. Very seriously they questioned the right of the league to inject the issue in a Democratic primary through its quizzing. They branded as reprehensible condemnation of a candidate, however competent and honorable, because he did not see eye to eye with the league on a single issue. With peculiar bitterness the Richmond *Journal*,[56] while the legislature was in session in 1908, noted the "docile obedience" of the legislature to Dr. Cannon in temperance matters and the "unholy alliance" between prohibitionists and practical politicians. The *Journal* wondered whether Mann and Cannon would co-operate with the machine to elect as Corporation Commissioner the very wet Judge William F. Rhea who was so objectionable to dries of the southwest and to others whose political consciences were not robust.[57] Later the same year the *News-Leader*, in a statistical study, claimed that prohibition had in no respect benefited the counties then dry. The *News-Leader*,[58] it asserted, would not make a single dry county wet. But it was against state-wide prohibition on political principle and because through a lack of sentiment to compel enforcement it "does more harm than good and develops much more hypocrisy and sneakiness than it prevents intemperance." Prohibitionists, the paper continued, seemed to be "trying more for a nominal extension of prohibition and the widening of

55. Richmond *News-Leader*, July 24, 1907. John W. Daniel and the Petersburg *Index-Appeal* held similar views with respect to primary participation. Cf. *Civic Sentinel*, Jan., 1905.
56. Feb. 20, March 4, 1906. Founder Charles B. Cooke is said to have blamed Cannon for his expulsion from the Methodist church after publishing a story on Cannon's relations with the machine.
57. Pendleton, *Appalachian Virginia*, pp. 532-537, contains much on this. The *Religious Herald* in Jan., 1908, opposed Rhea for political support of the liquor interests. Mann and Byrd voted for Rhea.
58. Nov. 28, 30, 1908.

what they call 'dry territory' and to injure the liquor dealer than they are to increase sobriety and morality or to cause real prohibition." The Anti-Saloon League, it explained, "to live must keep going, must always be doing something or pretending to be doing something." Its agents would go to the preachers who must act or lose caste and standing. Therefore many church members, including the emotional women, felt that they must go into a fight whatever their personal convictions. The "Anti-Saloon agent goes on his way to attack another stronghold of Satan, and leaves Satan in his rear to do as he will. The *News-Leader* is against this fussy farce." To which league leaders replied that the *News-Leader* was generally understood to be very close to the liquor dealers.[59]

These opinions were by no means novel. Many other people still adhered to the old belief that orderly dispensation of liquor was an entirely respectable business. They desired neither saloon-less nor wide-open towns. They wanted free competition in politics. On any roster of leading citizens their representatives would have been conspicuous for both number and quality. Unfortunately there was no place for them in either of the two "machines."

59. So said Cannon who at this time was publishing principally in the Richmond *Christian Advocate*.

## Chapter Thirteen

# THE ENABLING ACT AND
# THE REFERENDUM, 1909-1914

State-wide prohibition as opposed to local option was first advocated extensively in Virginia in 1908. Six years elapsed before it became the law and two more before it became operative. During these years there was no new restrictive legislation to mark another "step" toward prohibition, nor was there any notable crusade against drinking to strengthen the foundation for the new policy. Many local optionists became convinced through experience that their plan was inadequate under existing circumstances, among which was a supposedly strong intervention of national interests.

Sentiment for state-wide prohibition in 1908 was due in part to the example of other Southern states, six of whom in 1907 or 1908 undertook the experiment by act of legislature or popular referendum. Throughout the land the press was chronicling this renaissance and wondering what could be the meaning of such a phenomenon as a serious anti-liquor movement proceeding out of the South.[1] When Governor Glenn came up from North Carolina and told the league convention in February, 1908, "Get on the Prohibition bandwagon, Gentlemen, it's going to win,"[2] both his eloquence and his example had weight. To the rank and file of anti-liquor men the idea was attractive because of defects, disclosed by experience, in the local-option policy they had successfully supported. The *Religious Herald* summarized these defects as follows: (1) The constant threat of another

---

1. The state-wide prohibition law of Georgia was the first passed since 1889. Three states had repealed such laws since 1889 and only three had such laws in 1907; D. Leigh Colvin, *Prohibition in the United States* (New York, 1926), pp. 334, 344. For discussion see *Outlook*, Aug. 31, Nov. 30, 1907, June 6, 1908; *American Review of Reviews*, Sept., 1907, April, 1908; *South Atlantic Quarterly*, April, 1907, April, 1908; *Cosmopolitan Magazine*, April, May, June, 1908.
2. *Religious Herald*, Feb. 13, 1908.

election in territory that had voted dry; (2) frequent appeals to the courts to upset dry victories; (3) the constant and increasing flow of liquor into dry territory from wet cities.[3] For one or all of these reasons the Baptist Big Stone Gap Association wanted to try for state-wide prohibition and sentiment within the Holston Conference was preponderantly for it.

From league headquarters in midsummer came the wary announcement that the league would not go ahead of public sentiment and that if there should come a change of policy blame would lie with the liquorites who were forever trying to upset dry victories and violating dry territory.[4] In the fall neither the Virginia Conference nor the Baptist General Association declared for state-wide prohibition. In February, 1909, the *Religious Herald*[5] argued pleasantly but at length against prohibition in Virginia "at this juncture." It indicated that there were many who "think persons should have an opportunity to obtain liquor without the accompaniment of the saloon" and supported the superiority of the local-option process from the angle of law enforcement. It questioned the existence of a majority of voters in favor of prohibition and feared that if pressed the matter would become entangled with the politics of the coming gubernatorial campaign. To these weighty considerations the *Herald* added a defense of Dr. Cannon against recent secular newspaper attacks. The Baptist paper suggested that these attacks were nothing more than attempts by the wets to prod the league into premature action by their jibes that "the Anti-Saloon League and the city interests now stand on common ground. . . ." These and other suggestions implied that Cannon's interests lay much more in the field of political power than in the area of prohibition. Such accusations increased as the years passed.

3. Feb. 18, 1909. A few months after the time under consideration but an excellent summary of the situation.
4. *American Issue, Virginia Edition*, Aug. 8, 1908; statement of McAlister in Richmond *Christian Advocate*, Nov. 26, 1908.
5. Feb. 18, 1909.

Meanwhile Dr. Cannon, on the advice of national league officials, carefully surveyed the Virginia sentiment and concluded that it was not yet time for a change of policy.[6]

A temporary decision in the matter of prohibition as opposed to local option was made early the next year. In Norfolk in February, 1909, the Virginia league assembled in one of its most well attended and widely reported conventions. The usual addresses to the delegates concerned various aspects of the liquor problem, but many of the delegates and most of the state's political leaders recognized that these speeches were of less importance than the political alignments which were developing. The machine decided to run the league's own Judge Mann as its candidate for governor on a local-option platform; but if the league endorsed state-wide prohibition Carter Glass would make the logical dry candidate and Glass was anti-machine and not a good leaguer.[7] Moved by the opportunity for closer association with "a high class Machine"[8] as well as by his pre-convention studies, Dr. Cannon recommended that the policy of local option be given further trial. It was clearly stated that if dry territory was not properly protected by law and proper legal restrictions put upon selling liquor or if it became apparent that the league had gone as far as it could "with profit to our cause" under local option, then the league would move for state-wide prohibition. The convention, though both "state-widers" and politicians tried to stampede it in other directions,[9] adopted this

6. Statement of Dr. Cannon to Dr. Pearson. The national leadership was more interested in the election of dry U. S. congressmen in order to secure an effective interstate commerce law controlling the distribution of liquor than in securing another nominally dry state.

7. Glass, who had been consistently dry, turned against local option because Lynchburg's frequent elections on the matter kept the city in an uproar. Glass intended to enter the Democratic primary on a platform of broad reform, including state-wide prohibition. He withdrew from the race to prevent a splitting of the dry vote but violently opposed what he deemed Cannon's manipulation of the league in its decision not to support state-wide prohibition.

8. Statement of Dr. Cannon to Dr. Pearson.

9. Some anti-liquor workers protested against leaving the cities, which could never be made dry through local action, to flood the state.

recommendation by an overwhelming vote. Once a joke, the league was now "a colossal factor in Old Dominion politics."[10]

There were bitter exchanges between Cannon and anti-machine men—especially Glass.[11] Soon there was talk of a "deal" under which Norfolk wets would vote for Mann in return for a promise from Mann and the dries that no additional liquor legislation would be adopted during Mann's four-year administration. Also in the exchange of accusations were the dry men of anti-machine proclivities. Harry St. George Tucker, Mann's opponent in the primary, projected no great program with which to dignify his obvious bid for the wet vote though he, too, claimed to be for local option.[12] It was quite confusing. Mann won in the primary by the majority which the wets of Norfolk turned in. There were reports of Martin's personally carrying a satchel of money to Norfolk and of Mann's being bound by some promise that would protect liquor men while he was in office.[13]

10. Roanoke *Times*, Feb. 9, 1909.

11. Glass expressed hot indignation at Cannon's monopolizing the temperance sentiment of the state and Cannon replied that the league would not yield to the political dictation of recent adherents. The *Times-Dispatch* pictured Cannon as a runner for Martin and the machine. The exchange between Glass and Cannon continued for some time and is chronicled in the Glass Papers, University of Virginia; Cannon Papers, Duke University; and the contemporary Virginia press.

12. See the league pamphlet concerning the position and record of Mann and Tucker on the liquor traffic and including the league's reply "to Mr. Tucker's insulting charges" which were published in the secular press.

13. The charge of a deal with liquor was denied by Cannon, Martin, and Mann, each for himself. Yet Virginius Dabney, *Dry Messiah, The Life of Bishop Cannon* (New York, 1949), pp. 54-55, says "there is reason to believe that Cannon and Martin made a deal, where Martin threw the support of his friends to Mann in return for a promise from Cannon that statewide prohibition would not be made effective until after the expiration of Mann's term." Dabney records the statement of Colonel Joseph Burton, then clerk of the state Senate and a close friend of Martin, that at a meeting between Cannon and Martin, Cannon soothed the machine's fears of radical liquor legislation by stating: "the temperance people" had gotten about all they could ask for until the people could catch up with the advanced position they had already attained; that it was not their intention to ask for more legislation during Governor Mann's term, in the event of his election. Cannon later denied any deal for himself and said, "I know that Judge Mann himself positively asserted that he was not a party to any agreement of that kind. . . ." James

In January, 1910, the league convention voted to seek state-wide prohibition immediately. Some dubbed this a Cannon double-cross and others pointed to the fact that the policy was not adopted until after Mann left office and said that the league was merely putting up a smoke screen to cover the deal.[14] Cannon did recommend the action as chairman of the committee on legislation. As he made the proposal he argued that this was entirely in accordance with the Norfolk convention's pronouncement since the liquor interests were manifestly increasing their activities. Doubtlessly there were other considerations. Some temperance men chafed at Cannon's czar-like leadership and the widespread talk of politics and deals. Some were moved by Governor Mann's statement that he would not veto a state-wide bill and interpreted this as a promise of his official help. Some were encouraged by prospect of a federal law protecting dry states and some felt that it would be well to catch the anti-liquor tide before it began to ebb in the Southern states. Both Methodist and Baptist state bodies unanimously endorsed state-wide prohibition in November, 1909.[15] Harmony within the ranks and a regaining of the initiative, rather than any improvement in temperance sentiment[16] or any serious hope of early success, motivated the legislative committee's recommenda-

---

Cannon, Jr., *Bishop Cannon's Own Story: Life as I Have Seen It*, ed. R. L. Watson, Jr. (Durham, N. C., 1955), p. 131. Robert A. Hohner, "Prohibition and Virginia Politics: William Hodges Mann Versus Henry St. George Tucker, 1909," *Virginia Magazine of History and Biography*, LXXIV (1966), 88-107, calls "the alleged bargain . . . one of the myths of recent history" (p. 107) and indicates that there was a temporary union of the two factions due largely to the personal beliefs of Mann. Allen W. Moger shows further insight in his review of Dabney's book (*Virginia Magazine*, LXIII [1955], 482) when he states that it is specious to argue whether Cannon did or did not convert the Virginia machine to opposition to the liquor traffic. "He knew that argument without compelling pressure would not convert the leaders. What he did was to so organize public opinion in favor first of local option and then of state prohibition that the political leaders deemed it hopeless to oppose his purposes."

14. Dabney, *Dry Messiah*, p. 56.
15. Charlottesville *Daily Progress*, Nov. 17, 1909; Portsmouth *Star*, Nov. 23, 1909.
16. In fact convention members noted a decline. Lynchburg *News*, Jan. 21, 1910.

tion. The convention's members were pleased and rival factions clashed only over the time to choose for an election.[17] All believed that a law backed by a popular vote would command more respect and be more difficult to repeal than a legislative act. Accordingly, the objective of the league became a state-wide prohibition law effective after a popular referendum. "Now for hard work," headlined the *Religious Herald*.[18]

The decision proved to be premature and four years of disappointment lay ahead. The machine-controlled legislature of 1909-1910 had no intention of abandoning the Democratic party's policy of local option.[19] Indeed it could hardly have been expected to do so with the names of its governor and its House leader so recently and so conspicuously attached to this policy. It was also fairly certain that whatever arrangements made at Norfolk were made with an eye to the selection of federal senators in 1911. Co-operating liquor interests with renewed confidence began a campaign to wear down the league by means short of a state-wide election on the liquor question. Using various devices to add the names of purchasable Negro and white voters[20] to the poll books, they forced local-option elections in dry territory and compelled the dries to exhaust their efforts on local fights rather than building strength for a state-wide battle.

What efforts the league could muster came to nothing. Petitioners numbering about 45,000 were ignored and Senator Aubrey Strode's state-wide prohibition bill was killed. National liquor interests now joined forces with the state elements. With neighboring states going dry it seemed advisable for them to have supply places in Virginia. Dr. Cannon reported that five million dollars was to be spent by a company

17. Anti-Cannon men were adverse to leaving the decision to Cannon as he desired.
18. *Religious Herald*, Jan. 27, 1910.
19. Charlottesville *Daily Progress*, Nov. 17, 1908.
20. Lynchburg *News*, Jan., 1910. Specific instances are found in McAlister's report in the Richmond *Virginian*, Jan. 26, 1912.

already chartered in Virginia for such a "depot of supply" in Richmond. In 1911 with abundant financing they entered in a concerted participation in the state senatorial primaries, thereby securing seats for a number of their friends for the next four years.[21] With their aid the Jordan bill for a popular vote on state-wide prohibition was defeated in 1911-1912. Senator Jordan, highly indignant, asserted at the league convention that three men could have prevented this—Martin, Mann, and Byrd. Mann protested that he had been elected as a local optionist and that the state's financial condition would not permit the loss of so much revenue. Byrd offered appeasement in the form of legislative measures designed to prevent unfair voter registration and to protect dry territory. Martin kept quiet, for he had arranged to appease some of his enemies by making anti-machine Henry Stuart the next governor.

Meantime Dr. Cannon, believing that not over one-third of the voters[22] could be counted for state-wide prohibition, was vigorously seeking to strengthen his position. "It is evident," he told the league convention of January, 1910, "that the redemption of the state is largely dependent upon the amount of money which can be secured for the division of the work and the support of more workers."[23] Following a suggestion of national league officials three district superintendents were appointed who, by "quizzing" and other devices, participated actively in the election of federal representatives.[24] To diminish the respectability and the convenience of buying liquor by mail[25] he asked the legislature to put this business on a level with the older "jug trade" and denounced

21. L. H. Machen in *Times-Dispatch*, Jan. 25, 26, 1912, is particularly valuable.
22. Statement of Dr. Cannon to Dr. Pearson. The committee's report, said Cannon, was a "sincere document." The one-third estimate comes from J. G. Pollard. As late as 1914 Dr. Mitchell thought public opinion not yet ready for state-wide prohibition.
23. Superintendent's report, Virginia Anti-Saloon League *Proceedings*, 1910.
24. Richmond *Virginian*, Feb. 22, 1911.
25. *Ibid.,* especially statement by McAlister.

the wet newspapers for selling liquor for pay through their advertisements just like barkeepers.[26] The attack on the newspapers created a sensation. These ads had come as a logical result of the Byrd Law. They were now conspicuous, though occupying much less space than those of merchants or those of vendors of patent medicines, and presumably less influential in determining newspaper policies. The convention shared Dr. Cannon's opinion and ordered his report sent to all the voters. The editor of the *Times-Dispatch,* replying in a letter to the "brethren of the press," gravely declared that "the Rev. James Cannon, D.D.," was a wilful liar, a slanderer, and a fool.[27] On January 26, 1910, the first issue of the daily (except Sunday) Richmond *Virginian* appeared, whose motto was "A clean Paper for the Home," sponsored and owned by Dr. Cannon and a few other league supporters.[28] Appreciatively the convention of the league approved the establishment as a step of its executive committee. The other dailies welcomed the *Virginian* "as an intruder rather than a brother" because it "proclaims itself better in all respects than its contemporaries" and because it was expected to support the machine, which had no daily paper of importance. In the senatorial primaries of 1911 the *Virginian* lined up squarely behind Martin and Swanson notwithstanding some nasty disclosures made by their anti-machine opponents, William A.

26. In Jan., 1909, none were appearing in the *Times-Dispatch* or the Lynchburg *News.* In Jan.-Feb., 1914, three on Sunday was the average of the *Times-Dispatch* and only beer advertisements were in the Lynchburg *News.*

27. Feb. 25, 1911. The quarrel continued: in 1914 Dr. Cannon in the *Christian Advocate* said that the *Times-Dispatch* "raked into its owners' pockets the money paid by the accursed traffic to advertise. . . ." Richmond *Virginian,* Jan. 22, 1914. The *Times-Dispatch* passed from the hands of the Bryans to the Winston brothers in 1914 and the dries generally suspected them of being under the control of the liquor interests. The *Religious Herald* and many others deprecated the intemperate language used by both parties.

28. See Cannon, *Own Story,* pp. 137 ff., for his account of the founding of the paper. McDonald Lee, editor of the *Virginia Citizen* of Irvington and a well-known machine man, was president of the company.

Jones and A. J. Montague.[29] Senator Martin never forgot this service. And it was to be followed up two years later by an equally enthusiastic and successful support of Taylor Ellyson for lieutenant governor and by a well-understood preference for Samuel Williams for attorney general as against L. N. Machen and John Garland Pollard, though the dry records of Machen and Pollard were better.[30] The bond of machine and league was tightening.

Not all temperance men were happy over the developments since the Norfolk convention. Some were weary with fruitless labor, despondent. Some, like the *Religious Herald*'s editor, were shocked at "the extreme and violent language"[31] of Dr. Cannon in his attack on certain newspapers. Many anti-machine men, within and outside the league, complained bitterly of discrimination against them. There was much talk of "bossism," "management," "Pauline opportunism," and "running to Washington." Yet it was the wet leaders of Norfolk who celebrated in one of their own barrooms the temporary retirement of Dr. Cannon.[32]

In March, 1912, with the Richmond *Virginian* appearing regularly and Martin and Swanson safely seated in the Senate, the league's executive committee[33] began planning to compel the legislature of 1914 to pass an enabling act. It was

29. These concerned railroad campaign contributions at the time of Martin's first election to the Senate. *Times-Dispatch*, July 29, Aug. 8, 12, Sept. 7, 1911. Allen W. Moger, *Rebuilding of the Old Dominion, 1880-1902* (Ann Arbor, Mich., 1940), chap. 5, is good.

30. Pollard and his friends attributed the opposition to his refusal to join in the *Virginian* and his success to personal popularity and a local situation in the southwest. Stuart was unopposed for governor.

31. Feb. 23, 1911. Dr. Cannon was not the only offender.

32. Statement of J. A. Hough, Norfolk realtor and later league president. *Times-Dispatch*, Feb. 23, 1911. J. E. Price, N. B. Joynes, and John A. Lesner were named. Cannon's resignation supposedly was intended to save the league money during a time in which Cannon was fully engaged in promoting the Presbyterian assembly at Lake Junaluska, N. C.

33. Minutes of at least six meetings in 1912 and 1913 are preserved. Sometimes the headquarters committee was present. Securing a "guarantee fund," electing Cannon Superintendent again, and deciding to do no organizational work among Negroes were all decisions which were made. Cannon's reports were usually reduced to writing.

the third successive attempt and there were some who felt that it would be well to pause for further preliminary work. The committee determined to present as the issue "Shall the people be allowed to vote?" and instructed field workers to give special attention to counties in the districts whose senators had recently voted against the enabling act. The convention, meeting in Roanoke in February, 1913, approved the proposed issue and heard a suggestion that the selection of lieutenant governor and attorney general that year were very important.[34] As the legislature was assembling in January, 1914, it was generally admitted that the House would be distinctly favorable as the previous two had been, but none of the hostile senators were up for election. League leaders insisted that they must obey the will of their constituents as shown by the vote for House members in their districts; wise observers thought that they would stand pat. Sponsored by Judge Martin Williams, the Williams bill easily passed the House[35] and then (with anti-machine men Mapp and Walker leading) the Senate, but only after much wrangling and compromise and by the deciding vote of machine man Lieutenant Governor Ellyson. The matter was so mixed with politics that a substantial rumor was reported to league officials that anti-machine men of the Senate planned to let the bill die and the machine incur the odium. A rumor, well authenticated, had it that the essential vote of one senator was cast only after long-distance interposition of machine powers in Washington, the senator having been enticed into a spree at the critical time by wet friends. Four senators changed to the affirmative

34. Governor Mann opposed reading that part of the legislative report which related to plans. The following senators' names were read as having voted contrary to the will of their constituents in 1912: Bowers, Brock, Catron, Early, Echols, Fletcher, Hart, Massie, Moncure, Paul, and Watkins. Norfolk *Landmark*, Feb. 13, 1914.

35. G. Walter Mapp of Accomac and C. Harding Walker of Northumberland. Delegate Oliver of Fairfax and Senators Hold of Newport News and N. B. Early of Charlottesville assisted by Wendenburg of Richmond led the opposition.

as predicted[36] and the strategy of Dr. Cannon since 1909 and his more recent tactics were justified by success.[37]

The Williams Enabling Act[38] was thought by state-widers very satisfactory in the requirement that the ballots read "For Statewide Prohibition" and "Against Statewide Prohibition" instead of "For Statewide Prohibition" and "For Local Option" as the opposition wanted. Deemed helpful, too, was a provision against additions to the list of qualified voters after the bill's passage.[39] The league's executive committee, though pledging its support to whatever terms the legislative committee might find it necessary to make, was so alarmed at the partial exemption of the making of wine and beer from the contemplated prohibition that it voted not to accept responsibility for the law if this provision should remain in it. Resourceful Dr. Cannon persuaded the headquarters committee to approve with the understanding that, if the election was successful, he would ask the next legislature to eliminate the beer exemption.[40] The election was set for September 22, 1914.

From February 18 to September 22, 1914, Virginia voters had the issue of state-wide prohibition before them for their immediate decision. Though a memorable session of Congress was then in progress and the world war was having

36. Bowers of Culpeper, Fletcher of Loudon, Moncure of Fredericksburg, and Echols of Staunton. Governor Henry Stuart signed in accordance with his promise during the gubernatorial campaign.

37. Ed. J. Richardson of the league staff at this time assisted in making up this account. Dr. Cannon attested to the assistance of the machine at this critical time. The recent passage by Congress of the Webb-Kenyon Law to prohibit the shipment of liquor into dry areas probably weighed with many. Such an act had been long desired.

38. Act of Feb. 18, 1914.

39. Mapp said in the legislature that if additions to the existing lists after the passage of the bill were permitted, a telegram from Richmond to a dozen Virginia cities could mean 50,000 more voters provided in twenty-four hours: "He did not want the ignorant, the vicious and the purchasable vote put back on the books."—Lynchburg *News*, Feb. 6, 1914.

40. *Minutes* of executive and headquarters committees, Feb. 4, 26, 1914. This account is based on the principal newspapers and the official records of the league.

its dramatic beginnings, prohibition and anti-prohibition were "front page stuff." The issue was connected with no other issue; even party and factional alignments were ignored for the most part. The opportunity for a clear-cut decision was unusually good.

On the prohibitionist side the main body of forces was already largely assembled. Since 1908 they had been involved in almost unceasing local contests over licensing, over court voiding of elections, over making local regulations and their enforcement, and over the detection of bootleggers and speak-easies and their punishment. Methodist and Baptist state assemblies often tried to force the pace of the league in some areas[41] and other factors were important in the molding of sentiment. Occasionally professional prohibition orators came to the state such as John G. Wooley, who on three successive nights "swayed" a packed auditorium at the Newport News convention, and Richmond Pearson Hobson, who delivered his "Great Destroyer" speech in Lynchburg in 1913 and in Blackstone in 1914.[42] There was also direct pressure of ministers on their members[43] and the more frequent quiet attempts at forcing dry local optionists into line through half-identifying them with the liquor interests. Results were achieved by the pledge-signing campaign inaugurated by Cannon in 1913 and the efforts of Cannon and others to connect the liquor proponents with legalized prostitution in the fight for the anti-vice bill.[44] More dry votes came with the adhesion of sterling laymen such as quiet and conservative P. D. V. Conway, banker of Fredericksburg, and the excit-

41. E.g., the Methodists in 1909 and the Baptists in 1910-1911.
42. Roanoke *Times*, Feb. 18, 1913; Richmond *Virginian*, Jan. 9, 1914. E. C. Dinwiddie of Washington addressed the Virginia branch of the Woman's Temperance League of America (of which Mrs. J. Tyler Jobson of Richmond was president) on the "Call of the South" in Jan., 1914. The name was then changed to the Woman's Prohibition League.
43. E.g., W. A. Christian, "Vote Dry or Leave my Church," Richmond *Virginian*, Feb. 17, 1914. It was currently understood that Rev. G. W. McDaniel made the removal of liquor sellers' influence a condition of his acceptance of the pastorate of the First Baptist Church of Richmond.
44. Richmond *Virginian*, Jan. 26, March 5, 1914.

able but effective Dr. Livius Lankford of Norfolk,[45] and especially W. H. Hale, leader of the Valley Brethren Church, who had till now stayed out of politics.[46] Then these were all dramatized in the silent march of the 1914 league convention to the Capitol in a column, four abreast, that extended from the western gate to the southern portico, where Dr. Cannon read aloud the report of the legislative committee.[47] No one questioned that the league would lead a united front of dry voters when the test came.

It remained for the league to expand its organization and sound the bugle note. The former was planned in February. The headquarters committee was to consist of Cannon, Barbour, and Rev. E. T. Dadmun, Rev. J. W. Cammack, Rev. J. Sidney Peters, and Rev. W. Asbury Christian. Cannon was superintendent and Rev. J. D. McAlister, Rev. Ed. J. Richardson, and Rev. D. Hepburn were re-engaged as assistants with the munificent increase in salary of twenty dollars a month for the period of the campaign. Above these but meeting only rarely was the executive committee, a large body with J. W. Hough, president of the league, as chairman. The machinery designed for the campaign was new. For each county, city, and precinct there was a superintendent responsible directly to the state superintendent. For each ten voters there was a captain who should classify and report on the other nine. Rev. J. Sidney Peters was chosen as state organizer. Dr. Cannon was lauded in the *Virginian* for having "given time, thought and thousands of dollars of his money" for abolishing sins, especially in the cities, and to Mann for having readily laid aside affairs of state in order to lend his influence and his presence to the celebrations of churches, Sunday schools, schools, and social betterment groups. In the cities Cannon, McAlister, and others were

45. Virginia Anti-Saloon League Convention *Proceedings*, 1910. Richmond *Virginian*, Jan. 24, March 4, 1914.
46. Richmond *Virginian*, Jan. 23, 1914.
47. *Ibid.*, containing also a photograph of the procession. A figure appearing to be Cannon is in the foreground.

telling Sunday audiences in the churches that the real battle was to be between the church and the saloon. Then there was a pause to see what the opposition would do.[48]

Anti-prohibitionists arrived at 1914 without their old strong state political connections, without all-inclusive organization, without leadership, and without a well-considered and positive program. Governor Stuart signed the Enabling Act and was known to be beyond reach, politically or financially; Attorney General Pollard was an ardent state-wider; the machine was playing hands-off; and anti-machine leaders were divided. There were associations of liquor dealers but these could reach directly and openly only wet territory, which by this time the dries had so whittled down that only 10 towns and 20 counties were paying license charges of any kind.[49] Nor would their self-interested leadership be acceptable to many with whom business interest had little weight. Indeed, since 1909 liquor dealers had been fighting rearguard actions, relying on lawyers and courts and parliamentary obstruction. The wets did have strong newspaper support. In Richmond the *News-Leader* and the *Evening Journal* retained their customary aggressiveness, the former now receiving full attention from John Steward Bryan; the *Times-Dispatch* was passing through sale to a new ownership which many believed to conceal an outside control in complete sympathy with liquor. Some league leaders thought that though wet management was in Richmond its intellectual leadership was in strategic Roanoke. Virginia-born and broadly educated Alfred Brockenbrough Williams, Episcopalian, after years of experience as editor-in-chief of the *News-Leader*, was editor-in-chief and part owner of the *Morning Times* and *Evening World*. Recently "Alf" Williams had set out to examine in urbane fashion the stock arguments and current claims of prohibitionists

48. Virginia Anti-Saloon League Executive Committee *Minutes*, Feb. 4, 1914; Richmond *Virginian*, Jan.-Feb., 1914.
49. Annual Reports of Boards, Officers and Institutions: *Reports of the Auditor, 1913-1914* (Richmond, 1915).

in the light of ascertained facts and reason. His methods as well as his findings excited moderate dries to pangs of doubt.[50] But even Mr. Williams began with an admitted prejudice in favor of laissez faire in "sumptuary" matters and ended without discovering any other philosophy on which to build for human betterment. Not without reason did some shrewd men in early spring figure the odds as three to one in favor of prohibition.

To meet this situation anti-prohibitionists finally created two organizations. Most widely advertised was the Virginia Association for Local Self-Government. Sponsored by Charles V. Meredith, Dr. George Ben Johnston, Dr. Stuart McGuire, Egbert Lee (president of Richmond's Chamber of Commerce), M. C. Branch, and others representative of Richmond's best in the professions and in business as well as in society, this organization was brought into formal existence by a great mass meeting in Richmond, May 20. Judge George L. Christian, a well-known and highly respected Presbyterian, was its president and Ben P. Owen, Jr., whose tastes ran to politics, its secretary. Richmond's example was followed in other cities, notably in Norfolk where on July 31 a similar mass meeting was addressed by Robert Tunstall, Dr. Lomax Gwathney, and Dr. F. H. Hancock; and Walter H. Taylor, C. W. Grandy, Fergus Reid, and A. P. Thom were chosen vice-presidents of the association.

In Richmond the association published the *Trumpeter*, the initial issue appearing July 4. The object of the association was declared to be support for the existing policy of local option. Its promoters, mass meetings, and the *Trumpeter* insisted it had no personal interest in the liquor business; and local option, as Harry St. George Tucker emphasized, was not a device "invented to determine the liquor questions" but an age-old principle "imbedded in Virginia institutions as a bulwark of the Commonwealth's liberties." The argument of

50. See especially Jan. 14, 30, March 27, 1914.

the association was most fully set forth in a speech at the Richmond meeting by Royal E. Cabell. Mr. Cabell declared on the authority of his experience as commissioner of internal revenue under President Taft that the Virginia liquor laws were as good as any other state's and their enforcement as good and "far better than that obtained in any of the so-called prohibition states." He urged against prohibition, saying that it did prevent the sale and use of liquor, as the prevalence of blind tigers proved; that the states with the longest experience under it showed no economic improvement and some of them quite the reverse; that it destroyed regulation with the result that the vilest liquor and drugs were used and the social fabric consequently impaired; that it would cause a huge loss of revenue and a consequent increase of taxes, which would fall principally on the farmer; that the motive behind the whole movement was just a desire of some individuals and some communities to stick their noses into somebody else's business as had the old abolitionists—a desire utterly at variance with the ideas of Jefferson and Woodrow Wilson and amazing to the rest of the civilized world; and, finally, that temperance could be had only by inculcating the idea of individual sobriety.[51]

The other organization of anti-prohibitionists was the Brewers, Wine and Spirit Merchants' Association. It was led by Paul Garrett, successful wine-maker of the Norfolk region. In a "confidential letter to the trade" sent out in May this association announced its designs for an educational and organizing campaign. For arguments it pointed the "trade" to the recent uprisings of businessmen throughout the state against the attack on a cardinal principle of government and to the superiority of regulated over illegal and unregulated selling. It advised that dealers sit steady, pay their assessments, and keep quiet but ready for work. The organization of the

51. Richmond *Virginian*, Feb. 16, March 20, 1914; *Times-Dispatch*, May 21, Aug. 1, 1914; Cabell, *The Issues Involved in Statewide Prohibition* (reprint of speech, n.p., May 14, 1914).

state, the letter stated, "is moving along under the advice of most competent and experienced men," referring to professional organizers, copywriters, and managers brought in from Atlanta, Baltimore, and Chicago.[52] The Virginia retailers, including hotels and clubs, and the national liquor associations worked through this agency. But the work was severely handicapped by the success of the dries, largely due to Byrd, in securing legal restraints on late registration of voters. For it was among the poor and ignorant that liquor had always found its greatest strength and it was this element that failed to qualify to vote in the election.

The campaign was fought out with marked shrewdness and energy. Prohibitionists found they could not rely completely on machine help.[53] Their strategists saw their first duty was to hold together and enthuse the church forces. With perfect tactical skill they sought to identify the liquor business with the saloon and damn the saloon as social menace, crime, and sin.[54] The issue became a moral one. When it was seriously urged that the saloon could not be the issue in most of the counties and towns because there were no saloons, the reply was that those who talked had not shown their sincerity by helping to keep liquor from flowing into the "dry" territory and were, in most instances, but echoing the argument of liquor people or the liquor-subsidized press.[55] The Association for Local Self-Government was not to be taken very seriously. They were mostly nice old gentlemen with fine

52. The letter, dated May 30, 1914, and reprinted by the prohibitionists, is to be found in the collection made by L. H. Machen and hereinafter referred to as Machen Collection, now in the Virginia State Library.

53. It had not been forthcoming in the attempt to pass the enabling act in 1912 and Cannon's virtual threat to turn his power against the machine had not yet brought open support from Martin and the other machine leaders. Cannon, *Own Story*, pp. 146-152. Cf. original correspondence quoted here in Cannon Papers, Duke University.

54. Richmond *Virginian*, Jan. 26, 1914 (Cannon's sermon); and Sept. 15, 1914 (Rev. Claggett Skinner at the Second Baptist Church, Richmond); *American Issue, Virginia Edition*, May 1, 1914.

55. Richmond *Virginian*, Sept. 1 (citing *Religious Herald's* reply to *Times-Dispatch*), Sept. 2, 5, 1914 (charging direct but concealed liquor control in Richmond afternoon newspapers). Cannon in retrospect was not so harsh on the papers. Cannon, *Own Story*, pp. 154 ff.

names but altogether behind the times and mere figureheads who did not even know who liquor-propagandist Eddie Hirsh was or what he was doing at their headquarters. They were not altogether disinterested, however, for there was a letter from the son of the association's president soliciting liquor business.[56]

Anti-prohibitionists, though some of them clung to the local self-government argument and some found moral arguments of their own,[57] generally pushed to the front the economic questions or the unenforceableness of prohibitory measures. They contended that fully a million dollars annually would be lost directly and indirectly in taxes and would have to be made good principally through an increase of the burden on farmers.[58] The Richmond Tobacco Trade formally resolved to send out thousands of copies of their warning that tobacco would be attacked next. The *Trumpeter* played up a purported letter to Judge Martin Williams from his nephew introducing a man who was interested in prohibition and "the issue to come; namely the tobacco cigarette evil."[59] The failure of prohibition enforcement efforts in other states was shown in various ways: by the temperance journals' accounts of conditions in Nashville; by the direct testimony of prominent citizens who had been in Maine; by the *News-Leader*'s importation of liquor by express out of Georgia; by the Richmond *Journal*'s disclosure of whiskey conditions in Durham.[60] Indeed, A. B. Williams, after a Southern tour,

56. Richmond *Virginian, passim; Caught With the Goods*, a broadside in the Machen Collection.
57. See for example, Alexander Harrilton and Lassiter at the Petersburg meeting; also Eppe Hunton to Judge Christian, Richmond *Journal*, Sept. 12, 1915.
58. See Statement of Virginia Association in Richmond *Journal*, Sept. 19, 1914, and the *Times-Dispatch* editorial summary, Sept. 20, 1914. The estimate included a loss to the state of $532,000 in licenses and $200,000 to cities in license taxes besides twice as much in indirect losses.
59. Machen Collection; Richmond *Virginian*, Sept. 17, 1914 (Williams letter).
60. Richmond *Journal*, Aug. 31, 1914 (citing Major William A. Anderson and others), Aug. 24, 1914 (Taylor Robertson's article on Durham, N. C.); Richmond *Virginian*, Sept. 2, 1914.

asserted in the Roanoke *Times*[61] that prohibitory laws made no change in either drinking or its consequences. He argued that prohibition could not be a moral issue but only the economic one of whether the liquor business should be conducted with or without taxation of the dealers. Others, while accepting the economic argument, found in this certain and extensive illegal selling a moral evil of prime importance. Prohibition, said the *Times-Dispatch*, is "necessarily allied with a stratum of our population which is lower morally than the licensed retailers under the local option system." The issue, said the *News-Leader*, is not whether "the saloon must go" but whether "the speak-easy must come."[62] Prohibitionists minimized the tax danger to the farmers with whom it was a consideration to be weighed against their prevailing sympathy with prohibition, denied any plan as to tobacco, and produced masses of weighty testimony from businessmen and local officials in the neighbor states to show marked improvement under their state-wide laws. The force of the argument based on unenforceableness was admitted by John Garland Pollard in his statement that the voters were confused in the matter.[63]

Curiously enough the wets made little use of argument based on a philosophy of rational human pleasure and the individual's right to enjoyment, although this must have been most keenly felt by many of them.[64] The omission was probably due to a desire to emphasize the currently stronger argument of local option. The prohibitionists somehow let it be understood that if they succeeded the individual would still be able to procure his reasonable spirituous requirements. Neither side paid much attention to either the existing or any

61. Sept. 3, 1914.
62. Richmond *Virginian*, Sept. 4, 1914.
63. *American Issue, Virginia Edition*, May 1, 1914.
64. "Old-fashioned Virginia gentlemen, who saw their toddies and their 'night-caps' vanishing rapidly over the horizon, drove down to the Capitol to see if something couldn't be done"; Dabney, *Dry Messiah*, pp. 78-79; Dabney's is an excellent literary expression of the position of many Virginia wets.

possible future federal law on interstate shipment of liquors or to the nation-wide prohibition movement which the Virginia league had endorsed the year before.

In the dissemination of propaganda prohibitionists had the great advantage of access to many church meetings. Every Methodist district conference during the summer "made state-wide prohibition the order of the day."[65] The crusading spirit and the ever-ready women and children[66] made mass meetings easy for prohibitionists to hold. Consequently the league's management was able to maintain schedules for its speakers, native or imported,[67] and to bring its campaign to a whirlwind close after the orthodox fashion of political men. Anti-prohibitionists held fewer mass meetings: theirs, they said, was an educational campaign. They relied more on printed propaganda. Their chief medium was the city newspapers, most of which were "wet."[68] In this game, however, prohibitionists were quite at home and they had on their side the Richmond *Virginian*, the *American Issue, Virginia Edition*, the church papers,[69] and more than half the small-town and

65. Statement of Dr. Cannon in Richmond *Virginian*, Sept. 1, 1914.

66. The WCTU sometimes held mass-meetings, e.g., in the John Marshall High School building, Richmond. Richmond *Virginian*, Sept. 4, 1914.

67. The executive committee favored residents as speakers. *Minutes*, June 16, 1914. Among the outsiders who spoke were Sam Small, ex-Governor Hanly of Indiana, ex-Governor Glenn of North Carolina, and Dinwiddie and Baker of the National Anti-Saloon League.

68. The Roanoke *World*, the Lynchburg *News*, and the Bristol *Herald-Courier* continued dry.

69. The Richmond *Christian Advocate*, edited by Dr. Cannon, and the *Religious Herald*, edited by Dr. R. H. Pitt, were ardent. The *Presbyterian of the South*, Jan. 7, 1914, printed an objection to the church's addressing itself to the liquor question so far as the state's method of handling it was concerned and replied, first, that the paper had no ecclesiastical connection with the church and second that to exclude from discussion an ethical question because it has become a political issue would be to exclude serious discussion when most needed, and that "our various *church* courts have declared in favor of the *suppression* of the liquor traffic." The *Southern Churchman*, under Rev. Edward L. Goodwin, declared, Aug. 29, for state-wide prohibition despite its obvious distaste for "unwise leadership" and its disbelief in law alone, believing that in time the force of the people's "own strong will" would prevail and that the victory would be worth all that it would cost in "lawlessness and debauchery and seeming failure."

country papers. To the most effective of these newspapers[70] both managements entered subscriptions for a few issues or a few months by tens of thousands. There was circulated an unprecedented amount of handbills, broadsides, reprints, many of them illustrated. Whether from fear of antagonizing white people or from lack of trust, Negroes received no special attention. Otherwise this material was adapted to the loyalties and the prejudices of groups and was presumably so distributed. It was not of high quality in either concept or execution. Most striking were the portrayals of fanatical preachers who spread ruin and stirred up strife and of liquor men's wrongs to women and children. These went to the roots of the controversy and disclosed its deepest hates.[71]

Foremost among the anxieties of league leaders was the financing of the campaign. Without a war-chest or vested interests upon which to draw, dry leaders feared the ability and willingness of liquor people to spend on elections and often warned each other of the danger. Apparently the wets planned to set such a pace in expenditures as to force the league and its friends to quit or ruin themselves financially. In June the league's executive committee sent out a call for $75,000. At the same time it authorized a contract with the *Virginian* which apparently called for $25,000 to be spent for 25,000 copies of that paper daily for three months.

On September 1 Dr. Cannon said that $1,000 a day was

70. Special mention should be made of the reprinting in the September *Virginian* of the able and calm arguments of Representative R. Walton Moore in the Fairfax *Herald*.

71. In the Machen Collection are found: "Why Babies Die"; "Putting the Mortgage on the Cradle"; "The Empty Stocking"; "Notice to the Preachers: Keep off the Grass"; "Preachers Should Preach the Gospel and not Meddle with Outside Affairs"; "Home Rule and Local Self-Government. I fought for this in 1861. I will vote for this in 1914"; "The Price of State-wide Prohibition"—a staggering load of taxes; "Tennessee Pays the Prohibition Piper"; "Fanticism" with his sickle, "Hysteria," headed for tobacco fields; "Alcoholic Drink a Help to Mankind"—from *Harper's Weekly*; "How Kansas Farms Out its Poor"; "Illicit Distilling. A Prohibition Product"; "The Saloon A Social Institute" by G. E. Partridge; "Perils of Excessive Paternalism" from the *International Magazine*; "Voice of the Church not for Prohibition."

needed for the rest of the campaign to combat the outpourings of the liquor people. In the excitement the *Virginian* ran its extra issues to double the number contracted for and printed most of the other propaganda. Next year the league's treasurer reported expenditures of about $80,000 for 1914, the greater part of which had gone for printed propaganda. Most of this sum came from small gifts in cash or "subscriptions." There remained with the league a debt of about $14,000 owed to the *Virginian* on the contract. This was extinguished eventually through normal league collections. There is no record of expenditures not made through the league. Small sums were raised and spent locally and in the southwest coal operators were generous without publicity. The chief burden financially, however, fell upon the few who supported the *Virginian*, the net loss of which, Dr. Cannon afterward told the league's executive committee, was $250,-000. Apparently only the prospects of victory saved the dries from insolvency.[72] Of the oppositions' expenditures and the sources of their funds there seems to be no record although they appear to have had abundant financial resources. During the campaign word came to league headquarters that $75,000 had been spent for postage alone to send out wet propaganda. The *Virginian*, after the campaign, estimated the total anti-prohibition expenditures at nearly a million dollars. Private contributions to this side are not mentioned though there probably were some. Dr. Cannon stated later that two state and two national organizations of liquor people were the contributors. Each side made such use as it

72. Cannon's later estimates differ. He stated, "When our accounts were all paid, we owed the banks $24,000, for which I was personally responsible." Notes for this amount were signed by some prominent dries and the amount was paid off by normal league income during the next few years. Cannon, *Own Story*, p. 160. Virginia Anti-Saloon League Executive Committee *Minutes*, June 16, 1914, and undated communication of Dr. Cannon to this committee soon after the 1914 election; Richmond *Virginian*, Sept. 1, 1914. Virginia Anti-Saloon League Convention *Proceedings*, March 16, 1915. The conjecture as to expenditures in the southwest is scarcely more than an inference from statements of workers in that region.

could of the other's lavishness. The Richmond *News-Leader* suggested that the national league was paying the Virginia league's expenses and that therefore Virginia contributions were unnecessary. This apparently alarmed Dr. Cannon and he characterized it as "absolutely false." Since the Virginia liquor business had been estimated recently by liquor people at thirty million dollars annually, Dr. Cannon continued, the opposition's expenditures in the attempt to buy the election were obviously limited only by their judgment as to what it was politically safe to spend.[73]

As the campaign progressed the betting odds on the prohibitionists declined until no odds were offered. In the end, members of the old supporting churches stood together pretty solidly and with them the recent recruits from the politicians and a number of businessmen. The final word of the management on the two sides illustrates an important aspect of the campaign. Dr. Cannon stated that reports from every county and city from "reliable and unpaid leaders" indicated overwhelming victory. A bulletin from league headquarters urged discussion of the moral issue and "the relation which the saloon bears to the churches" on Sunday and prayer as well as personal work with doubtful friends on election day. The last reported message of the other side to the workers mentioned that there were 1,300 precincts "at each of which we must have one or two automobiles, besides several paid workers."[74]

At the election, September 22, 1914, 94,251 votes were cast "For Statewide Prohibition" and 63,886 "Against Statewide Prohibition." In studying the returns of this election one is impressed first by the extensiveness of the victory for state-

73. Recollections of Rev. David Hepburn, later superintendent of the league; Richmond *Virginian*, Sept., 1914; Richmond *News-Leader*, Aug. 1, 1914. The National Liquor Dealers' Association, the National Brewers' Association, the Virginia Brewers, Wine and Spirit Merchants' Association, and the Virginia Retail Liquor Dealers were mentioned as the contributors.

74. Richmond *Journal*, Sept. 19, 1914; Richmond *Virginian*, Sept. 1, 11, 1914.

wide prohibition. For a popular vote on a single issue to exceed, and by a large margin, the vote at presidential elections is by no means a frequent happening. The vote for prohibition was not only 50 per cent larger than that for the opposition but also was so well scattered as to constitute a majority in all but two congressional districts[75] and in 17 of the 19 towns and 78 of the 100 counties. The historically minded would say that this vote reflected directly the anti-liquor agitation of a century. But great as this agitation's effect was in 1914 the early seats of temperance work did no better than other places.[76] Not a single town or county west of the Blue Ridge was "wet." The west was much readier to try the radical experiment, all the readier because they were more attached to "useful virtues." The east was holding back because of vested interests, traditional beliefs, love of pleasure, disgust at agitation, and the sheer disillusionment of age. Since the west was overwhelmingly white whereas in the east many counties had Negro majorities and all of them a large Negro element, possibly the Negro was a deterrent to prohibition in accord with the earlier history of the movement. But this explanation is more economic than racial, for almost all the wet counties were deeply interested in making liquor or selling it to North Carolina, which already had state-wide prohibition.[77] The habit of voting against the machine was influential in some of these wet counties[78] and in the city of Richmond. In the next gubernatorial primary 17 of the 22 wet counties of 1914 voted anti-machine. It was important to the future of prohibition that the experiment was tried without the enthus-

75. The Alexandria and the Richmond districts. The former went wet by 10 votes, the latter, by 1,250. Virginia Anti-Saloon League Convention *Proceedings*, 1915, report of legislative committee.

76. Among the wet counties were Albemarle, Powhatan, Prince George, and Spottsylvania.

77. Warren, Page, Rappahannock, Greene, Albemarle, and Nelson constituted one block in the new fruit country. Patrick, Henry, Pittsylvania, and Franklin were old distilling counties close to North Carolina.

78. For example, in four of the six counties running out of the Northern Neck, Richmond, Westmoreland, King George, Spottsylvania, Stafford, and Prince William.

iastic endorsement of the principal cities. Alexandria was wet 3 to 1, Norfolk by 500, and Richmond by over 2,000 votes, but Danville, Fredericksburg, Newport News, Petersburg, Portsmouth, and Suffolk in the east all voted dry; the dissenting vote in them was over 4,000 and the total wet vote of these and the other cities named was over 15,000. Prohibitionists congratulated themselves on their showing in these ancient strongholds of liquor, but the "consent of the governed" in them was yet to be obtained.

## Chapter Fourteen

# REGULATION: ABANDONMENT AND RETURN

"Get on the Prohibition bandwagon, Gentlemen, it's going to win." North Carolina Governor Robert Broadnax Glenn thus addressed the December, 1908, meeting of the Virginia Anti-Saloon League. So the league abandoned the last vestige of regulation as an answer to the liquor problem and came out strongly for state-wide prohibition. After failing in 1910 and again in 1912, the legislature passed the Enabling Act in 1914 and on September 22, 1914, the dries won and it seemed that Virginia was on her way to becoming a totally dry state. Virginians approved state-wide prohibition by over 30,000 votes. As the news came from over the state the crowd that was assembled at the corner of Seventh and Grace streets, Richmond, grew more and more jubilant. At midnight Rev. James Cannon, Jr., recognized head of the anti-liquor movement in the state, announced that the struggle was won and the crowd sang hymns of victory "praising God for the great victory over one of the 'works of the Devil.' "[1] Cannon was exhausted and suffered a physical and emotional collapse, but the work had been accomplished. By careful labor through the years a dry sentiment was established in the state and this was turned into a powerful political force. This force merged with the Democratic machine of the state to form an unbeatable combination. Some estimates of the vote cast in the referendum went so far as to say that the outcome would have been different had it not been for the support of the machine. Others pointed to the fact that many who were local optionists at heart found it impossible to vote against prohibition without seeming to abandon their dry position. The wording of the ballot was "For Statewide Prohibition" or

1. James Cannon, Jr., *Bishop Cannon's Own Story: Life as I Have Seen It*, ed. R. L. Watson, Jr. (Durham, N. C., 1955), p. 158.

"Against Statewide Prohibition"; there was no opportunity to vote for local option, or so it seemed.[2]

The chief fear of careful people was that enforcement would be the primary problem. All were aware that one of the wettest elements of the state, the propertyless whites and Negroes, had not voted in the election and they were the ones who would find the legal acquisition of liquors of any sort impossible. The experiment was to be tried without their consent and they would form the greatest potential for law-breaking and the downfall of the principle of legislative prohibition. From the cities, from the anti-machine leadership, and even from those in the machine not content to have Cannon and Martin dominate every aspect of their lives, this organized opposition might rise.

Recognition of this fact came quickly from Cannon and some of the other leadership of the league when the state General Assembly convened some fifteen months after the referendum. Cannon called for "practical idealism—Pauline opportunism" in obtaining an acceptable prohibition law. Senators Walter G. Mapp and C. Harding Walker spent much time in conference with Cannon working to secure a bill that could pass the legislature. Cannon found that despite his 30,000 majority in the election it was going to be difficult if not impossible to get a state prohibition law passed in this session of the legislature without making some provision for the purchase of alcoholic beverages for personal use. Cannon and the league yielded on this point and the bill passed in both the House and the Senate in March, 1916, and was slated to go into effect on November 1 of the same year.[3]

The Mapp Law, as the prohibition act was generally known, defined ardent spirits as embracing "alcohol, brandy, whiskey, rum, gin, wine, porter, ale, beer, all malt liquors, absinthe and all compounds or mixtures of any of them with

2. Virginius Dabney, *Dry Messiah, The Life of Bishop Cannon* (New York, 1949), p. 102.
3. *Acts*, 1916, March 10, 1916.

any vegetable or other substance . . . all beverages containing more than one-half of one per centum of alcohol by volume, except as herein provided." It then prohibited the manufacture, sale, offering for sale, keeping for sale, and so forth, of such ardent spirits. This was done as "an exercise of the police power of the State for the protection of the State, for the protection of the public health, peace and morals, and the prevention of the sale and use of ardent spirits, and all of its [the law's] provisions shall be liberally construed to effect these objects." The law prohibited breweries which the Enabling Act had permitted and then carefully made provision for importation from other states where alcoholic beverages could be sold legally, a maximum for each person no oftener than once a month of a quart of distilled liquor or three gallons of beer or one gallon of wine. Thus the act in no way attempted to prevent individual drinking if such drinking were done under the rigid control of the state. This was done despite the fact that the Enabling Act made no such provision and those who voted dry had voted for "state-wide prohibition."[4]

The act provided elaborate regulations for enforcement and spelled out as fully as possible the numerous possible attempts to avoid the restrictions imposed by the law and made all these illegal. The framers of the act were assisted by a volume compiled by Lewis Machen, director of the Legislative Reference Bureau of Virginia, in which was presented *Extracts From Liquor Laws of Prohibition States* (Richmond, 1916). Enforcement machinery was to consist of a commissioner of prohibition appointed by the General Assembly for a period of four years at a salary of $3,500 a year. The commissioner was given the power to appoint deputies and inspectors and hire attorneys and clerical help.

The commissioner chosen by the assembly was Rev. J.

4. Dabney, *Dry Messiah*, p. 103, probably correctly adjudges Cannon's decision to allow such a provision: "He was always cautious lest he get ahead of public sentiment."

Sidney Peters, long-term associate of Cannon's in the prohibition fight and one of the leaders in the fight for approval of the Enabling Act and the framing and passage of the Mapp Act. Cannon professed to believe that one whose name was not so intimately associated with the dry cause might find greater acceptance among the wets of the state, but over his protests (the sincerity of which the wets doubted) Peters was chosen.[5]

Long before the movement toward state-wide prohibition had progressed this far the 1914 election in Virginia had an important effect on the developing national prohibition legislation. On December 22, 1914, eight of Virginia's ten representatives voted for a national prohibition amendment to the Constitution. The measure was defeated but the movement was to prove irresistible and by December, 1917, all ten of Virginia's representatives voted for the submission of the Eighteenth Amendment to the people.[6] Virginia's move toward prohibition was influential, too, in that after Tennessee went dry in 1909 a pause came to the prohibition drive broken only by West Virginia's action. Virginia began a new wave of victories for the dries and soon nine more Southern and Northern states were adopting state-wide prohibition.

Then the dries decided to take advantage of the wartime scarcity of food to press home their fight for a totally dry nation. Already they had thwarted the wets by passing the Reed Bill, which prohibited from the mails all liquor advertisements, orders, and even liquor itself if it were destined for a dry state. This was legislation further advanced than many dries desired since it gave dry states no choice. Cannon and other leaders of the National Anti-Saloon League dared not oppose such a "Bone Dry" law and Reed and the wets in Congress placed them in an awkward position. Virginia op-

5. "Absolutely False" said the *Times-Dispatch* of Cannon's protestations. March 10, 1916.
6. Peter H. Odegard, *Pressure Politics, the Story of the Anti-Saloon League* (New York, 1928), Appendixes A and C.

ponents of Cannon, including the very dry Carter Glass, suggested that Cannon's love for political power was being allowed to overpower his anti-liquor sentiments. This and the passage of the Reed Law were in part responsible for the turn against the dries in the Virginia gubernatorial election later that year.

Not to be stopped (even by presidential request) in their work for national prohibition, the dries seized on the Lever food-control bill then before Congress and amended it to the point that it prohibited the use of any foods or food materials for the production of alcoholic beverages except for very limited special uses. This brought immediate protests from the wets and promises from the brewers' representatives that unless beer and wines were exempted from the food control prohibitory bill the entire piece of legislation would be filibustered to death. To prevent this President Wilson called Senator Martin of Virginia[7] into his office and asked him to request of Cannon and the league that the measures be separated. Martin did so and after an exchange of letters making the President's request official Cannon and the legislative committee allowed the bill to be passed prohibiting the use of foods for distillation but permitting the use of such materials for the manufacture of beer and wine to continue at the discretion of the President.[8]

The willingness of Martin, the Southern dries, and the leaders of the Anti-Saloon League to modify their demands in the interest of the war effort and the unwillingness of the brewers to do the same influenced many senators and representatives to reconsider their position on the question of submitting a prohibition amendment to the Constitution to the people. Again the Virginians in Congress and Cannon as chairman of the league's legislative committee made their influence felt. Knowing that Wilson preferred the matter left in abeyance while more pressing war measures were pending,

7. Elected to the Senate in 1895 and served until his death in 1919.
8. Cannon, *Own Story*, pp. 188-190.

they could expect no help from the executive branch. Using their newly won respect they made a bargain with a small group of wets in Congress, which entailed the inclusion of a time limit for ratification for the prohibition amendment. The limitation finally approved was six years and Senator Warren G. Harding of Ohio, who agreed to vote for the measure with the time limit, informed the wets that he did not believe that the amendment could be ratified in such a period. Cannon was instrumental in convincing Harding to follow this course and Martin's leadership in Congress was instrumental in swinging enough votes to the dry side. The amendment was approved and submitted to the states on December 17, 1917.[9]

Virginia's influence on the submission of the national prohibition amendment and the role she played in the adoption of wartime prohibition was strengthened by the seeming success of her experiment in state-wide dryness. The years from 1916, when the Mapp Law went into effect, to mid-1919, when nation-wide legislation was added to the picture, form a complex but vital part of the story of Virginia's first three centuries of liquor legislation. Until 1916 the dependence was on regulation. After the Mapp Law became effective on November 1 the emphasis was on complete prohibition of manufacturing and selling and only consumption was left under the time-tested regulatory system. As a result of events taking place in the federal Congress even this vestige of regulation did not last.[10]

"Obey the Law" was the message of the Richmond *Times-Dispatch* of March 9, 1916 (the day before the final passage of the Mapp Law). The editorial continued:

It [the Mapp Law] should be enforced to the very limit of possibility. . . . An excellent measure in many respects, it has in the view of the *Times-Dispatch* obvious and serious defects. . . . If experience condemns certain of its provisions, they may be repealed or amended. But, meanwhile, obey the law. . . . For the

9. Cannon, *Own Story*, pp. 190-191; Richmond *Virginian*, Aug. 2, 1917.
10. When the Reed ("Bone Dry") Law became effective.

prohibition statutes to be flaunted in Virginia as they have been, for example, in Georgia would be an abomination. It would have an effect on character and conduct far more serious than the worst evils of the regulated liquor traffic.

This was the position of the leading elements of Virginia society. The law existed and was to be obeyed. From the Charlottesville *Daily Progress* in January of the next year came general approval of the effect of the law with only a hint of the heavier criticism which ultimately came.[11] An editorial entitled "Abolition of the Saloons Proving Popular" stated that the people of Virginia wanted to know what would be the effect of no saloons and for that reason voted for state-wide prohibition. Though some few wanted repeal and were laying plans for the next legislature, the drunken city bum and the noisy disgusting hobo were gone. At the end of the first year of state-wide prohibition the Richmond press unanimously admitted the success of the experiment and a striking array of businessmen agreed.[12] Prohibition, moderated by limited purchase rights from outside the state, seemed to be working for Virginia.

In February of 1917[13] Dr. Cannon reported that the effect of the Reed "Bone Dry" Law prohibiting the importation of liquors into dry states, even if state laws did not so provide, would "produce disaster in those states which have not yet forbidden all interstate shipments" and might "cause them to repeal or modify their present prohibition laws." He pointed out that many wets were willing to abolish the saloons as long as the laws did not force them to become dry as well. Cannon, with his usual astute knowledge of people, was accurately predicting the effect that almost total prohibition would have in Virginia.[14]

11. Jan. 31, 1917.
12. *Times-Dispatch*, Oct. 3, 1917.
13. Richmond *Virginian*, Feb. 24, 1917.
14. Shipments from out of state fell rapidly from 40,000 a month prior to July 1, 1917, to a few hundred in 1918. Commissioner's *Report*, 1918.

The first evidence of rejection of Virginia's experiment came in the gubernatorial election in the fall of 1917. The dries were so confident in their new-found power that they allowed two dry candidates to oppose one wet with the natural result of a victory for the wets in this race. Sentiment was such that wets were victorious in the legislative elections also. The candidates for governor were J. Taylor Ellyson, then lieutenant governor, John Garland Pollard, then attorney general, and Westmoreland Davis, editor of the *Southern Planter*. Cannon later stated that "I made a mistake in judgment which possibly resulted in the election of a candidate unfavorable to the prohibition laws."[15]

The league followed its usual practice of polling the candidates concerning their views of current and pending legislation relating to liquor and got favorable replies from Ellyson and Pollard and a dubious statement from Davis.[16] On August 2 the Virginian carried a statement by Cannon that the contest was between Ellyson and Davis. Davis opposed state-wide prohibition and so the wets were behind him. Davis' allies were encouraging Pollard to draw votes away from Ellyson. The next day Cannon denied attempting to draw votes from Pollard and throughout the Virginia Anti-Saloon League leaders insisted that they were working for Ellyson as individuals and not as officers of the league. On August 1, six days before the election, the Norfolk Anti-Saloon League adopted a resolution protesting the action of the *Virginian*, "the official organ of the temperance forces," in declaring for Ellyson over Pollard when both were dry. The Charlottesville *Daily Progress* attempted to analyze the candidates and their supporters by showing that the Reed Law turned the wets of the machine to support of Davis. Davis already had the farmers' support and would get the votes of many dries who opposed the tactics of the machine-

15. Cannon, *Own Story*, p. 164.
16. Richmond *Virginian*, July 14, 1917.

league coalition. Pollard would get the dry anti-machine elements and Ellyson would get the dry loyal machine votes. The result was as expected. The dry votes were split and Davis won.[17]

The dries were to find other difficulties before the next session of the legislature met and adjourned. For a time Cannon was not supreme even in the anti-liquor realm of the Old Dominion. He was made Bishop of the Methodist Church in May of 1918; the national prohibition movement was consuming more and more of his time and his new church duties almost precluded any time spent in Richmond. He relinquished his position as superintendent of the Virginia league in 1920 and sold the *Virginian*. With his absence the anti-liquor movement hesitated and seemed to falter. After the Mapp Law was strengthened in 1918 the trend was reversed for almost four years.

Another factor which contributed to the decline in prohibitionist sentiment was a series of complaints against the work of Commissioner of Prohibition Peters. The true worth of state-wide prohibition was determined when he "enlisted" the first year "five hundred and sixteen unpaid correspondents, well distributed through each of the counties and cities of the State . . . who were requested (and agreed) to keep this department promptly advised of any infractions of the law in their respective communities." Behind these were the WCTU, who contributed "time, talent, money and prayers," and "the Virginia Anti-Saloon League, with its wonderful and powerful organization covering every spot in the state with one of their representatives." Men of all political parties and even some Negroes were employed by the department to further its functions. In short, the Commissioner organized the Anti-Saloon League to enforce the law through the courts inde-

17. Jack Temple Kirby, "Alcohol and Irony: The Campaign of Westmoreland Davis for Governor, 1909-1917," *Virginia Magazine of History and Biography*, LXXIII (1965), 259-279, goes into Davis' Progressive background and concludes that only the circumstances of the prohibitionist struggle made it possible for Davis to win.

pendent of the ordinary police and law officers who were expected to co-operate and usually did.

From the standpoint of efficiency both the law and the department were reasonably successful. The state's courts, without delay but with due deliberation, sustained the law in all essentials. The ordinary machinery of justice set itself in motion—better on the whole in the cities than in the counties. The Commissioner made very detailed rules for drug stores and hotels and the sale of near-beer (a malt beverage permitted under the law).[18] In all of this the legal staff was invaluable and in checking on drugstores, hotels, and particularly the express companies, and in securing evidence against speak-easies and stills the inspectors and detectives were especially instrumental.

Violations of the law occurred everywhere. The inspectors investigated 1,359 complaints of violations the first year, 1,090 the second, and 2,911 the third. The number of investigations was limited only by the capacity of the investigators. Prosecutions numbered 2,009, 2,400, and 3,176; convictions, 1,320, 1,717, and 2,435. The Commissioner in his third report commented that the increase indicated "some improvement in official alertness . . . and . . . in jury service." It is interesting to note that the counties furnished less than one-third of the defendants the first two years but somewhat over one-half the third year. The counties had less trouble at first because they were already dry and the adjustment to the new law was easy. The Commissioner made no attempt to explain the rise in the third year. Perhaps city friends had learned that the county folk were not adverse to distilling a gallon or two for sale.

The charges the first year were varied, including drinking in public and giving as well as selling and transporting. The

18. The popular belief that the law could easily be evaded was illustrated by Peters in citing a current version of an old song, Commissioner's *Report*, 1917.

> Hush little barroom, don't you cry,
> You'll be a drug store by and by.

proportion of Negroes accused, and the proportion convicted, was very large. Private stocks and the quart-a-month safety valve together with an inherent respect for the law were holding the high class off; it was the rabble that caused trouble. When private supplies began to be exhausted and the Federal Wartime Prohibition which prevented the quart-a-month was approaching, the higher class began to join the lowest in the patronage of bootleggers. Importation from the North became a big business, especially out of Washington by rail and car and into the Norfolk region by boat. The Commissioner quickly concentrated on this and began the war with a new and definitely criminal profession. Here he was unfortunate enough to find himself arrayed against the powerful railroad influences and a great deal of public sentiment. When prices grew higher, home manufacture picked up. The war was being waged chiefly against the supply end when the department was abolished after a legislative investigation in 1921.[19] Such a supply business was clear evidence that Virginia had not eliminated drinking within its borders.

On January 11, 1918, before Cannon left Virginia and before the anti-liquor sentiment began to wane, Virginia became the second state in the nation to ratify the proposed prohibition amendment. With speed which surprised even the most ardent dries, the total ratifications reached the required 36 and the Eighteenth Amendment became a part of the Constitution.[20] Mississippi ratified first and Virginia followed almost immediately after the session of the assembly opened.

With ratification well under way the dries in the federal Congress rushed ahead in their drive to bring prohibition to the nation immediately. A Wartime Prohibition Act was passed in the summer of 1918 to become effective on July 1,

19. Peters was replaced as commissioner by H. B. Smith in 1920. This was another defeat for Cannon, who returned to Richmond to lead the fight to retain Peters' job. It could hardly be called a victory for the wets because Smith was bone dry personally and politically.

20. Nebraska ratified on Jan. 16, 1919, to become the thirty-sixth state. The amendment became effective Jan. 16, 1920.

1919. In May, 1919, the Volstead Act was introduced, passed, vetoed by President Wilson, and repassed over his veto to become effective on October 27. On January 16, 1920, the Eighteenth Amendment officially became a part of the Constitution and national prohibition became a reality. Reformers all over the nation celebrated this great event and Virginians joined in. Standing above all the ceremonies whether in praise or lamentation was the mock funeral observed in Norfolk by Rev. Billy Sunday. From the railroad station to Sunday's tabernacle the parade followed a carriage on which rested a coffin containing a corpse of John Barleycorn. Behind trailed a drooping devil in great anguish. When the crowd arrived at the tabernacle Sunday preached to the more than 10,000 people on the extermination of the saloon.[21] Virginia, after three centuries of regulation, had abandoned that policy and turned to prohibition for an answer to the long-standing problem of liquor and its consumption.

The relation of Virginians and liquor during the years following 1919 is technically beyond the bounds of this study. A very brief summary, however, may help show how the state turned away from prohibition and back to the regulation which she had practiced for almost three centuries.

The years of national prohibition saw a rising and falling of anti-liquor sentiment in Virginia.[22] The dries were content with the situation and generally praised the efficacy of enforcement. The wets, particularly in the old wet center of Norfolk, condemned enforcement and worked toward the seemingly hopeless task of repeal. After emasculating the amended Mapp Law in 1920 the state elected a dry governor and "the driest legislature the state has ever known."[23] To

---

21. Dabney, *Dry Messiah*, pp. 133-134.
22. The story of national prohibition in Virginia is covered, though from a somewhat wet point of view, by A. B. Clark, "Seventeen Years in the Desert: A History of the Prohibition Movement in Virginia," *Times-Dispatch*, Oct. 30-Nov. 21, 1933. Robert A. Hohner, "Prohibition in Virginia, 1901-1933" (Ph.D. dissertation, Duke University, 1965), throws much light on this period.
23. Anti-Saloon League *Year Book*, 1925, p. 153.

make enforcement more efficient the 1924 legislature passed the Layman Act, which was "one of the most drastic state prohibition codes in the United States."[24] Under it distilling was made a felony on first conviction, bootlegging and all other violations on second conviction of any violation of prohibition laws, and no judge could suspend sentence on cases involving more than one gallon of illegal whiskey.

The Democratic machine weakened and finally was completely destroyed by Bishop Cannon's success in turning the state (along with much of the rest of the "solid South") against the wet Al Smith and for the presumably dry Herbert Hoover in 1928. Hoover failed the Bishop, or at least the times and the nation did, and in 1932 both Roosevelt and Hoover urged repeal. Congress submitted a repeal amendment to the people which was quickly ratified and national prohibition came to an end. Virginia voted on October 3, 1933, to end prohibition and in 1934 adopted its present Alcoholic Beverage Control System (ABC). This permits whiskey in bottles to be sold in state-owned and operated stores regulated in theory by local desires. Beer and wine can be sold in licensed stores, restaurants, and road houses which like the old taverns often serve food as an afterthought. These are also regulated by the local community.[25]

Various movements to alter this system, both toward state-wide prohibition and toward more liberal regulations, i.e., liquor-by-the-drink, have been defeated several times since 1934. Prohibitory sentiment, though it did not die in the state with the death of Bishop Cannon in 1944, might easily have done so and, despite a great mass of dry voters, no current movement in this direction seems likely. Liquor-by-the-drink is more possible at the present time but the latent

24. *Ibid.*, 1924, p. 140.
25. Harold Wesley Ward, *The Administration of Liquor Control in Virginia* (Charlottesville, Va., 1946), p. 34. "The present system is, therefore, not a totally unprecedented venture in Virginia, but rather a combination of ideas with which the State had had some experience of its own."

sentiment of all the old prohibitionists and the confirmed feelings of many who prefer the strict regulation now practiced oppose this. Objection to changes to the law through the WCTU, the numerous church organizations, and their various boards is vocal. The whole temperance sentiment is directed by the Alcohol Education Council, Inc., of Virginia Churches with headquarters in Richmond. It publishes an *Information Bulletin* providing "facts about the problems of alcohol" and states that "Our staff works with people in practically every town and city of Virginia and feels that the majority of Virginia citizens do not want the present Alcoholic Beverage Control Act changed."[26]

The most striking fact about this entire survey of liquor and anti-liquor in Virginia is the persistence of the clash. From the very beginning there were those who regarded liquor as "good," to be enjoyed by mankind, and those who regarded its use as an evil which must be rigidly regulated or abolished altogether. Held strictly within their native elements in the Old Dominion neither of these positions could heavily outweigh the other. Both survived, each giving way as immediate events and opinions caused shifting emphasis. From time to time the anti-liquor faction would seize on some cause of the moment, intensify their efforts, and vitalize their organization, and for a period would be able to dominate the scene. Their attacks on liquor seemed to have no unity—the *cause célèbre* might be morality, social reform, or economics —and were connected only by that which they were opposing.

There is one unifying factor, the basically middle-class origin of the anti-liquor sentiment. The upper classes liked their liquor, felt they knew how to control its use, and rejected any idea of restrictions on themselves and their drinking. Only regulations which restricted drunkenness and abuses in selling were adopted while the gentry were in control. Those who were concerned about the effect of liquor devoted them-

26. *Information Bulletin*, XVIII, No. 1 (1964), 1.

selves to promoting the cause of voluntary temperance. The lower class did not do a great deal of thinking about the matter; they simply drank and opposed anyone who said that they shouldn't. But the middle classes were close enough to the lower groups to see the suffering caused by excessive drinking and not so far removed as to allow a concern for personal liberty to block action to bring the suffering to an end. They gained political and economic power and positions of leadership as the nineteenth century progressed and utilized this power to correct the evils they saw.

This corrective movement first entailed attempts to persuade the drinkers themselves to relinquish their costly habits. Through education, agitation, speeches, and pledging, they tried and failed to convert the drinkers. Then they turned to political action but did not meet much success. Later they took the old policy of legislative regulation, made it more restrictive and more effective, and began to organize support on a local level against the intemperate use of alcohol. Then came the national organizations with their outside leadership to provide new incentive and stimulus for action.

Local societies and a state society already existed as a result of indigenous movements. The Washingtonians, and later the Sons of Temperance, built temperance halls, appealed to sober men of the middle class and to the churches to support the war against drinking. After the Civil War, the Independent Order of Good Templars again brought native sentiment to a peak through a national organization. As the Templars grew in numbers so sentiment for local option grew in certain localities. Certain areas went dry and the Local Option Alliance was formed, uniting all workers in the temperance cause. As local option triumphed some attempted to get this sentiment behind the Prohibition party. This failed, but the work of the WCTU helped pave the way for the coming of the Anti-Saloon League in 1900. Rapidly the state increased its drive toward more and more dry territory under local option and began striving for state-wide prohibition. This came in 1916 and the Virginians assumed a position of leadership in the similar drive toward national prohibition.

The movements of the late nineteenth and early twentieth centuries fully utilized the state church organizations and under the leadership of the Virginia league joined with the state democratic machine to bring success to the cause of prohibition. Nation-wide dryness failed and, with its failure, the alliance between anti-liquor and the machine collapsed. A reaction came but the people of the state never fully turned to the side of the liquor interests. Instead they returned to the centuries-old method of regulation. Local sentiment embodied in state laws and administered by people in contact with the local situation proved over years of application to be the most successful answer to the struggle of liquor and anti-liquor in Virginia.

# APPENDIXES

*Appendix I*

# ACT OF 1619

Against drunkenness be it also decreed, that if any private person be found culpable thereof, for the first time he is to be reprooved privately by the Minister, the second time, publiquely, the thirde time to lye in boltes 12 houres in the House of the Provost Marshall & to paye his fees, and if he still continue in that vice, to undergo suche severe punishment, as the Governor & Councell of Estate shall think fitt to be inflicted on him. But if any Officer offende in this crime, the first time he shall receive a reproof from the Governour, the second time he shall openly be reprooved in the Churche by the minister, & the third time shall first be committed & then degraded. Provided it be understood, that the Governor hath alwaies power to restore him, when he shall, in his discretion thinke fitte.

(*J.H.B.*, 1619-1658/59, 9.)

*Appendix II*

# THE NORTHAMPTON PETITION
# OF 1676

That no drink may be sold within a mile of the Courthouse at any of the court sitting days. Considering the Detraction of time and the Rudeness of people where Drink is sold at Courts neglecting theire business spending and wasting theire Estates Abusing themselves, and Authorety. Quarreling and fighting with all Imagenary Illconviences and Evill consequences thereby accruing.

That no ordinary, or petty Tipling house may be allowed in our county; a means to keep young freemen and others from Running into Maryland.

(*J.H.B.*, 1659/60-1693, 100.)

*Appendix III*

# BACON'S LAWS, JUNE, 1676: AN ACT FOR SUPPRESSING ORDINARIES

Whereas it is most apparently found that the many ordinaries in severall parts of the country are very prejudiciall, and this assembly finde the same to be a generall grievance presented from most of the counties, *Bee it therefore enacted* . . . that no ordinaries, ale houses, or other tipling houses whatsoever, by any of the inhabitants of this country, be kept in any part of the country except it bee in James Citty, and at each side of the Yorke river, at the two great ferries of that river; *Provided*, and it is hereby intended that those at the ferries of Yorke river aforesaid, be admitted in their said ordinaries to sell and utter man's meate, horse-meate, beer and syder, but no other strong drinke whatsoever; and that all other ordinaries, ale houses and tipling houses whatsoever, in the country, (except as before excepted) be utterly suppressed, and whosoever shall presume to sell any sorte of drinke or liquor whatsoever by retail, under any colour, pretence, delusion or subtile evasion whatsoever to be drunke or spend in his or their house or houses, or upon his or their plantation or plantations, from and after the tenth day of September next, and be thereof lawfully convicted shall pay . . . one thousand pounds of tobacco, wherein no wager of lawe shall be admitted or allowed, any act, usage or custom to the contrary notwithstanding.

(Hening, W. W. [ed.] *Statutes at Large; Being a Collection of All the Laws of Virginia from the First Session of the Legislature in the Year 1619* [13 vols.; Richmond and Philadelphia, 1809-1823], II, 361.)

*Appendix IV*

# RATES SET FOR ORDINARIES BY THE LOCAL COURTS

RICHMOND COUNTY, April 8, 1755: per qt. Syder brandy, 6s.; Madiera wine, 2s. 6d.; New England rum, 9d.; English beer, 1s. 6d.; Virginia malt ale, 8d.; Near and Small beer, 1s.; lodging, 4½d.; Indian corn per gallon, 4d.

ROCKINGHAM COUNTY, May 6, 1778: per gallon. rum, 20s.; wine, 10s.; Good Whiskey, 16s.; good brandy, 20s.; good beer, 3s.; good cider, 4s.; hot meal with small beer, 3s.; cold meal without beer, 2s.; gallon of corn, 1s. 3d.; lodging in feather bed with clean sheets, 1s.

RICHMOND CITY, February 9, 1795: per qt. punch, 3s.; toddy, 2s.; Madiera, 6s.; strong beer, 1s. 3d.; cider or small beer, 6d.; per gill, rum or French brandy, 7s. 2d.; whiskey, 4d.; apple brandy, 4d.; dinner, 2s. 6d.; lodging, 1s.; corn, 1s.

HALIFAX COUNTY, September, 1838: per gallon. West India rum, $2.50; Northern rum, $1.25; apple brandy, $1.25; whiskey, $1.25; wines, $2.50 to $4.00; dinner, 37½ cents; dinner and drink, 50 cents; lodging, 25 cents.

*(from court records.)*

*Appendix V*

# CONSTITUTION, RESOLUTIONS, AND ADDRESS OF THE NORTHERN NECK (VIRGINIA) TEMPERANCE SOCIETY

At a meeting for the purpose of establishing a Temperance Society held at Kilmarnock Meeting-house, Lancaster, Va. on Saturday the first of September, 1827, the following preamble and constitution were adopted:

Whereas the undersigned have been convinced by painful and mortifying observation, that drunkenness is the most prevalent, loathsome, and pernicous vice, which haunts and afflicts the Northern Neck; that it is destructive to health, and brings thousands prematurely to the grave; fills the land with widows, and orphans; reduces multitudes of amiable families to poverty and wretchedness; populates our poor-houses, prisons, and penitentiaries; and tends to the subversion of all order, and the universal prostration of morals in society; and,

Whereas, it is undeniably evident, that drunkenness almost invariably originates in the temperate and habitual use of ardent spirits, and the common, but unfortunate practice of social drinking; and,

Whereas, we believe it to be the solemn and indispensable duty of every Christian, and every philanthropist, and every patriot, to combine their influence to arrest and exterminate the deadly, wide spread, and increasing evil, by discountenancing and opposing those customs which produce, and will produce, so long as they are cherished, the most alarming mischiefs in society,

Therefore, resolved, That we form ourselves into a society, under the title of the Northern-Neck Temperance Society, of which the following is the

## CONSTITUTION

It shall be the sole design of this society to discourage and prevent, by every lawful and laudable means, the habitual use of ardent spirits, and of wines.

This society will be composed of such persons as will solemnly agree to abstain entirely from using ardent spirits and wines, except as medicine, and the latter in the sacrament; from making vending and distributing them; and exert their influence to induce others to adopt the same course.

Any member wishing to withdraw from the Society, may do so at any time, provided he shall assign his reason for withdrawing in writing to the corresponding secretary.

This Society shall meet annually on the first Wednesday in May, at such place as they shall appoint.

The officers of this society shall consist of a president, a vice-president, a corresponding and recording secretary, and a treasurer, who shall respectively and faithfully discharge the duties of their office.

A Board of Managers shall be chosen; of which Board the officers of the Society shall be members and officers ex-officio. Five members shall constitute a quorum. The Board shall meet according to its own appointments, transact the business of the Society, and report its proceedings to the annual meeting.

The officers and managers shall be chosen at the annual meetings. Should an election not be made, they shall continue in office until another meeting.

A person shall be appointed at every annual meeting to deliver an appropriate sermon, or oration, to the following meeting.

The expenses of the Society shall be paid by voluntary contributions of its members and friends.

No alteration will be made in this Constitution, except at an annual meeting and by the concurrence of two thirds of the members present.

The following resolutions were adopted:

Resolved, that we will individually be encouraged and encourage one another, in the good and important cause in which we are engaged; and that we will labour by example, arguments, and persuasion, to constrain our friends and acquaintances to join the Society.

Resolved, that this Society recommend with the deepest sollicitude and earnestness, to our fellow citizens generally, and to the young and healthful especially, that they abstain from the habitual use of that bane, by which their property may be consigned to destruction, their bodies to the tomb, and their souls to perdition.

(Abner W. Clopton and Eli Ball, *Wisdom's Voice to the Rising Generation* [Philadelphia, *ca.* 1828], p. 158.)

*Appendix VI*

# SONS OF TEMPERANCE, "ODES"

### OPENING

Yes, we in those principles join,
And such shall our actions display;
Our hands and our hearts shall combine
To extend their beneficent sway.

Our laws we will ever respect,
Arise all contentions above—
And stand by each other erect,
On Parity, Friendship, and Love.

(Hutchinson Division, *Minutes.*)

*Appendix VII*

# MADISON, JACKSON, ADAMS
# TESTIMONIAL

Being satisfied from observation and experience, as well as from medical testimony, that ardent spirit as a drink, is not only needless, but hurtful; and that entire disuse of it would tend to promote the health, the virtue and happiness of the community, we hereby express our conviction, that would the citizens of the United States, and especially the *Young Men*, discontinue the use of it, they would not only promote their own benefit, but the good of the country and the world.

JAMES MADISON
ANDREW JACKSON
JOHN QUINCY ADAMS

(Lynchburg *Virginian*, November 27, 1834.)

# MASSIE ESTATE

An inventory of the estate of William Massie in 1862 estimated the value at $234,000. Liquors on hand and equipment for making it were put at $941, or a little over 4 per cent of the whole. There were on hand 2bbls., 33 bottles, and 20 gals. of brandy; 3 kegs (1 Cincinnatti and 2 "domestic") and 2 demijohns of whiskey; 6 demijohns of wine, madeira, and sherry; one-half bbl. ale; 1 jug of gin. A still house was valued at $186.

(Massie Papers.)

# SELECT BIBLIOGRAPHY

## MANUSCRIPTS

The two most important collections of manuscripts relating to the history of liquor and anti-liquor in Virginia are the John Hartwell Cocke Papers in the University of Virginia Library and the Bishop James Cannon, Jr., Papers in the Duke University Library. Other collections at the University of Virginia include the papers of William A. Anderson, Joseph C. Cabell, Westmoreland Davis, J. Taylor Ellyson, William A. Garrett, William Hodges Mann, Thomas S. Martin, and John B. and Lucian Minor. At Duke are also the plantation records of William Massie. The University of West Virginia has the Waitman T. Willey Papers. Innumerable legislative figures involved in the movement have some items in the manuscripts division of the Library of Congress but perhaps the most important are the Henry D. Flood Papers. Numerous items in addition to the records listed below are in the collections of the Virginia Baptist Historical Society Library. The C. C. Pearson Papers at Wake Forest College contain significant correspondence to Dr. Pearson from a number of figures involved in the temperance movement as well as G. W. Hawxhurst's sketch of the Virginia Good Templars.

## RECORDS OF TEMPERANCE ORGANIZATIONS
### (MANUSCRIPT AND PRINTED)

No complete collection of temperance society minutes exists. More (notably the reports of the Virginia Temperance Society) are in the Virginia State Library then elsewhere. Others are preserved by the University of Virginia Library, the Virginia Baptist Historical Society, the William and Mary College Library, and the Duke University Library. Dr. Pearson had access to the minutes of the Virginia Good Templars and the Virginia Anti-Saloon League, both of which are now unobtainable. Reports of many meetings are found only in newspapers. A number of circulars, cartoons, and other campaign literature of 1914 were assembled by L. H. Machen and some remain catalogued separately in the Virginia State Library.

The American Temperance Society *Reports*, and the American Temperance Union *Reports* and *Journal* are in the New York Public Library; the Anti-Saloon League of America *Proceedings* are in the Library of Congress.

## TEMPERANCE NEWSPAPERS

Despite the excellence of Winifred Gregory (ed.), *American Newspapers, 1821-1936; A Union List of Files Available in the United States and Canada* (New York, 1937), and Lester J. Cappon, *Virginia Newspapers, 1821-1935* (New York, 1936), many of the temperance newspapers have disappeared leaving not even a single copy. The papers of the Virginia Anti-Saloon League (*Christian Federation*, 1901-1904, *Civic Sentinel*, 1904-1908, *American Issue, Virginia Edition*, 1908-1919) are almost all at the Library of Congress. The Richmond *Virginian* (1910-1920), a political daily with prohibition sponsorship, is in the Virginia State Library and is available on microfilm. Scattered numbers of earlier newspapers are in the William and Mary College Library, the Virginia Baptist Historical Society, the University of Virginia Library, and the Duke University Library.

The files of the various newspapers of the state with dry or even wet tendencies carry extensive accounts of meetings of temperance organizations, their resolutions, and actions.

## CHURCH RECORDS

*Church Minutes.* For the Baptist organizations—Southern, state, and district—the collection in the Virginia Baptist Historical Society is ample. There is a fine collection of Methodist *Disciplines* in the Randolph-Macon College Library, where also the *Journals* of both General Conferences and the *Minutes* of the Virginia Annual Conference since 1868 may be had; but the minutes of the ante bellum Virginia Annual Conferences seem to have been burned during the Civil War without ever having been printed. Extracts from the minutes of the Holston and the Baltimore Annual Conferences are given by Richard N. Price, *Holston Methodism* (Nashville, 1903), and James E. Armstrong, *History of the Old Baltimore Conference* (Baltimore, 1907). The Presbyterian Virginia Synod *Minutes* are to be found in the Spence Library of the Union Theological Seminary, Richmond: Alexander's *Digest* (1922) covers both assemblies. Dashiel's *Digest of the Proceedings of the Conventions and Councils in the Diocese of Virginia* (1883) gives the scanty record of Episcopalians. There are some *Minutes* of the Christian Church in the office of the Missionary Society of that church in Richmond.

*Church Newspapers and Journals.* An excellent file of the Baptist *Religious Herald,* dating from the early 1830's, is in the Virginia Baptist Historical Society Library. *Circular Letters* of Baptists are in the *Minutes* of the district associations. Partial files of the Richmond *Christian Advocate* and its predecessors, notably the *Christian Sentinel* of the 1830's, are preserved in the office of the *Advocate* in Richmond, as are also a few numbers of the *Episcopal Methodist* of the late 1860's. Partial files of the *Central Presbyterian* and the Episcopal *Southern Churchman* are in the State Library. The Duke University Library and the William and Mary College Library contributed western *Christian Advocates* and odd numbers of the *Christian Sun* respectively.

### PUBLIC RECORDS AND DOCUMENTS

*Acts and Joint Resolutions Passed by the General Assembly of the State of Virginia.* Richmond, 1820-1919.

*Biennial Report of the Auditor of Public Accounts, 1858 and 1859.* Richmond, 1859.

*Executive Journals of the Council of Colonial Virginia,* ed. H. R. McIlwaine and W. L. Hall. 5 vols. Richmond, 1925-1945.

Hening, W. W. (ed.). *Statutes at Large; Being a Collection of All the Laws of Virginia from the First Session of the Legislature in the Year 1619.* 13 vols. Richmond and Philadelphia, 1809-1823.

*Journals and Documents of the Constitutional Convention, 1901-1902.* Richmond, 1902.

*Journals of the House of Burgesses of Virginia,* ed. H. R. McIlwaine and J. P. Kennedy. 13 vols. Richmond, 1905-1915.

*Legislative Journals of the Council of Colonial Virginia* [1680-1775], ed. H. R. McIlwaine. 3 vols. Richmond, 1918-1919.

*Minutes of the Council and General Court of Colonial Virginia, 1622-1632, 1670-1676,* ed. H. R. McIlwaine. Richmond, 1924.

*Proceedings and Debates of the Constitutional Convention, 1901-1902.* Richmond, 1906.

*Reports of the Cases Decided in the Supreme Court of Appeals of Virginia,* reporter, Peachy R. Grattan. 33 vols. Richmond, 1845-1881.

*The Revised Code of the Laws of Virginia* [1819]. 2 vols. Richmond, 1819.

*Supplement to the Revised Code of the Laws of Virginia; Being a Collection of all the Acts of the General Assembly . . . Passed Since the Year 1819.* Richmond, 1833.

United States Commissioner of Labor. "Economic Aspects of the Liquor Question," *Twelfth Annual Report, 1897.* Washington, 1897.

United States Department of Commerce, Bureau of the Census. *Historical Statistics of the United States, Colonial Times to 1957.* Washington, 1960.


UNPUBLISHED WORKS

Alexander, Ellen. "The South Carolina Dispensary System." Unpublished Master's thesis, Duke University, 1940.

Blake, N. M. "The Virginia Reform Convention of 1850-1851." Unpublished Master's thesis, Duke University, 1929.

Blanks, James B. "Social Control by Baptists in Virginia and North Carolina, 1775-1928." Unpublished Master's thesis, Wake Forest College, 1929.

Coyner, Martin Boyd. "John Hartwell Cocke of Bremo." Unpublished Ph.D. dissertation, University of Virginia, 1961.

Dozier, Richard. "Historical Notes Concerning the Planting of Baptist Principles in the Northern Neck of Virginia; Text Book from 1771. Sermons preached and heard by Richard Dozier, son of Thomas in (Westmoreland Co.) Virginia." Typescript copy in Wake Forest College Library.

Hall, Alvin LeRoy. "The Prohibition Movement in Virginia, 1826-1916." Unpublished Master's thesis, University of Virginia, 1964.

Hohner, Robert A. "The Anti-Saloon League in Virginia, 1901-1910; Prelude to Prohibition." Unpublished Master's thesis, Duke University, 1963.

———. "Prohibition in Virginia, 1901-1933." Unpublished Ph.D. dissertation, Duke University, 1965.

Horn, Herman L. "The Democratic Party in Virginia Since 1890." Unpublished Ph.D. dissertation, Duke University, 1949.

Steiner, Bruce E. "The Prelude to Conservatism, 1781-1822; An Account of the Early Life, First Ventures into Politics, and Legal Career of Benjamin Watkins Leigh." Unpublished Master's thesis, University of Virginia, 1959.

Thrift, C. Tinsley. "The Operations of the American Home Missionary Society in the South, 1826-1861." Unpublished Ph.D. dissertation, University of Chicago, 1936.

ARTICLES

Bean, W. G. "Anti-Jeffersonians in the *Ante Bellum* South," *North Carolina Historical Review*, XII (1935), 103-124.

Bruce, Philip Alexander. "Sir William Berkeley," *Dictionary of American Biography*, ed. Allen Johnson and Dumas Malone. (20 vols.; New York, 1928-1936), II, 217-218.

Carson, Gerald. "The Dark Age of American Drinking," *Virginia Quarterly Review*, XXXIX (1963), 94-103.

Edmonds, A. S. "The Henkels, Early Printers in New Market, Virginia," *William and Mary Quarterly*, 2nd ser., XVIII (1938), 174-195.

Gay, Constance. "The Campaign of 1855 in Virginia," *Richmond College Historical Papers*, I, No. 1 (1916), 309-335.

Gordon, Armistead C., Jr. "John Hartwell Cocke," *Dictionary of American Biography*, ed. Allen Johnson and Dumas Malone (20 vols.; New York, 1928-1936), IV, 253-254.

Harrison, Fairfax (ed.). "With Braddock's Army, (Diary of Mrs. Browne)," *Virginia Magazine of History and Biography*, XXXII (1924), 305-320.

Helderman, L. C. "A Social Scientist of the Old South," *Journal of Southern History*, II (1936), 148-174.

Hohner, Robert A. "Prohibition and Virginia Politics: William Hodges Mann Versus Henry St. George Tucker, 1909," *Virginia Magazine of History and Biography*, LXXIV (1966), 88-107.

Jeter, Jeremiah Bell. "Evils of Gaming," *The Baptist Preacher*, I (1842), 47-62.

Johnston, James H. "Negroes in the Government of Virginia from 1877-1888," *Journal of Negro History*, XIV (1929), 251-271.

Kirby, Jack Temple. "Alcohol and Irony: The Campaign of Westmoreland Davis for Governor, 1909-1917," *Virginia Magazine of History and Biography*, LXXIII (1965), 259-279.

Logan, William. "William Logan's Journal of a Journey to Georgia, 1745," *Pennsylvania Magazine of History and Biography*, XXXVI (1912), 1-16, 162-186.

Minor, Lucian. "The Temperance Reformation in Virginia," *Southern Literary Messenger*, XVI (1850), 426-438.

Morrison, A. J. "Virginia Works and Days, 1814-1819," *South Atlantic Quarterly*, XVIII (1919), 24-35.

N. R. "The Temperance Reform," *Virginia Historical Register*, April, July, 1850.

Newsome, A. R. "Twelve North Carolina Counties in 1810-1811," *North Carolina Historical Review*, VI (1929), 281-309.

Pearson, C. C. "Lucian Minor," *Dictionary of American Biography*, ed. Allen Johnson and Dumas Malone (20 vols.; New York, 1928-1936), XIII, 27.

"Progress of Temperance," *Southern Literary Journal*, I (1835), 85-91.

Robinson, William M. "Prohibition in the Confederacy," *American Historical Review*, XXXVII (1931-1932), 50-58.

Thorn, W. T. "The Negroes of Litwalton, Virginia: A Social Study of the 'Oyster Negro,' " *Bureau of Labor Bulletin*, No. 37. Washington, 1901.

Tucker, Beverley. "Temperance," *Southern Literary Messenger*, VIII (1842), 439-444.

W[ashington], H[enry] A. "The Social System of Virginia," *Southern Literary Messenger*, XIV (1848), 65-81.

### BOOKS

Abernethy, T. P. *From Frontier to Plantation in Tennessee*. Chapel Hill, N. C., 1932.

Adams, Henry. *History of the United States During the Administrations of Jefferson and Madison*. 9 vols. New York, 1890-1898.

Ade, George. *The Old Time Saloon*. New York, 1931.

Allen, Harvey. *Israfel, The Life and Times of Edgar Allan Poe*. New York, 1927.

Anderson, William H. *The Church in Action Against the Saloon*. Westerville, Ohio, 1910.

Andrews, Mathew Page. *Virginia, The Old Dominion*. 2 vols. New York, 1937.

Armstrong, James Edward. *History of the Old Baltimore Conference*. Baltimore, 1907.

Asbury, Francis. *Journal of Rev. Francis Asbury.* 3 vols. New York, 1852.

Bagby, George W. *John M. Daniels Latch-Key.* Lynchburg, Va., 1868.

Barclay, Wade Crawford. *Early American Methodism, 1769-1844.* New York, 1950.

Baron, Stanley. *Brewed in America: A History of Beer and Ale in the United States.* Boston, 1962.

Beebe, Benthal L. *A Compilation of Editorial Articles from the "Sign of the Times."* Middletown, N. Y., 1868.

Bennett, William W. *Memorials of Methodism in Virginia.* Richmond, 1871.

Blakey, Leonard Stott. *The Sale of Liquor in the South.* ("Studies in History, Economics and Public Law, Edited by the Faculty of Political Science of Columbia University," Vol. LI, whole No. 127.) New York, 1912.

Blanton, W. B. *Medicine in Virginia in the Seventeenth Century.* Richmond, 1930.

Bruce, Kathleen. *Virginia Iron Manufacture in the Slave Era.* New York, 1930.

Bruce, Philip Alexander. *Economic History of Virginia in the Seventeenth Century.* 2 vols. New York, 1896.

————. *History of the University of Virginia, 1819-1919; the Lengthened Shadow of One Man.* 5 vols. New York, 1920-1922.

————. *The Plantation Negro as a Freeman.* New York, 1889.

————. *Social Life of Virginia in the Seventeenth Century.* 2 vols. Richmond, 1907.

Bryan, John S. *Joseph Bryan.* Richmond, 1935.

Burton, H. W. *History of Norfolk, Virginia.* Norfolk, Va., 1877.

Byrd, William. *The Secret Diary of William Byrd of Westover, 1709-1712,* ed. Louis Wright and Marion Tinling. Richmond, 1941.

————. *The Writings of "Colonel William Byrd, of Westover in Virginia, esqr",* ed. John Spencer Bassett. New York, 1901.

Cannon, James, Jr. *Bishop Cannon's Own Story: Life as I Have Seen It,* ed. R. L. Watson, Jr. Durham, N. C., 1955.

Cappon, Lester J. *Virginia Newspapers, 1821-1935.* New York, 1936.

————, and Stella M. Duff (eds.). *Virginia Gazette Index*. 2 vols. Williamsburg, Va., 1950.

Chase, Simeon B. *A Digest of Law, Decisions, Rules and Usages of the Independent Order of Good Templars*. 10th ed. Philadelphia, 1874.

Chastellux, Francois Jean. *Travels in North America in the Years 1780, 1781, and 1782*, rev., trans., and ed. Howard C. Rice, Jr. Chapel Hill, N. C., 1963.

Cherrington, E. H., *et al.* (eds.). *Standard Encyclopedia of the Alcohol Problem*. 6 vols. Westerville, Ohio, 1925-1930.

Cherrington, Ernest Hurst. *The History of the Anti-Saloon League*. Westerville, Ohio, 1913.

Chitwood, O. P. *Justice in Colonial Virginia*. Baltimore, 1905.

Christian, W. A. *Lynchburg and Its People*. Lynchburg, Va., 1900.

Clopton, Abner W., and Eli Ball. *Wisdom's Voice to the Rising Generation*. Philadelphia, *ca.* 1828.

Colvin, D. Leigh. *Prohibition in the United States*. New York, 1926.

Cresswell, Nicholas. *The Journal of Nicholas Cresswell, 1774-1777*. New York, 1924.

Dabney, Virginius. *Dry Messiah, The Life of Bishop Cannon*. New York, 1949.

Davis, Arthur Kyle. *Folk Songs of Virginia*. Durham, N. C., 1949.

————. *More Traditional Ballads of Virginia*. Chapel Hill, N. C., 1960.

————. *Traditional Ballads of Virginia*. Cambridge, Mass., 1929.

Davis, D. Webster. *Life and Public Services of Rev. William Washington Brown*. [Richmond], 1910.

Davis, John. *Travels of Four Years and a Half in the United States of America*. London, 1803.

Delavan, E. C. *Temperance Essays*. New York, 1869.

Dorchester, Daniel. *The Liquor Problem in All Ages*. New York, 1884.

Eaton, Clement. *Freedom of Thought in the Old South*. Durham, N. C., 1940.

Eckenrode, Hamilton J. *The Political History of Virginia During the Reconstruction*. Baltimore, 1904.

————. *The Revolution in Virginia*. Boston and New York, 1916.

Ellyson, H. K. *Richmond Advertisements*. Richmond, 1851.

————. *Richmond Business Directory, 1845*. Richmond, 1845.

Evans, Philip S. *History of the Connecticutt Baptist State Convention, 1823-1907.* Hartford, Conn., 1909.

Evans, Thomas J. *A Digest of the Resolutions and Decisions of the National Division of the Sons of Temperance of the United States and of the Grand Division of Virginia.* Richmond, 1847.

Ezekiel, Herbert T. *Recollections of a Virginia Newspaperman.* Richmond, 1920.

Farish, Hunter D. *The Circuit Rider Dismounts, A Social History of Southern Methodism, 1865-1900.* Richmond, 1938.

Fithian, Philip V. *Philip V. Fithian's Journal and Letters, 1767-1774,* ed. John R. Williams. 2 vols. Princeton, N. J., 1930-1934.

Fletcher, James F. *A History of the Ashe County, North Carolina and New River Virginia Baptist Associations.* Raleigh, N. C., 1935.

Flippin, Percy Scott. *Financial Administration of the Colony of Virginia.* Baltimore, 1915.

———. *Herschel V. Johnson of Georgia.* Richmond, 1931.

Foote, William Henry. *Sketches of Virginia, Historical and Biographical.* 2nd ser. Philadelphia, 1855.

Forrest, W. S. *Historical and Descriptive Sketches of Norfolk and Vicinity.* Philadelphia, 1853.

Freeman, Douglas Southall. *R. E. Lee; A Biography.* 4 vols. New York, 1934-1935.

Furnas, J. C. *The Life and Times of the Late Demon Rum.* New York, 1965.

Gewehr, Wesley M. *The Great Awakening in Virginia, 1740-1790.* Durham, N. C., 1930.

Gladden, Washington. *Moral Gains and Losses of the Temperance Reformation.* Boston, 1895.

Gordon, Armistead C., Jr. *Virginian Writers of Fugitive Verse.* New York, 1923.

———. *William Fitzhugh Gordon.* New York, 1909.

Gough, John B. *Autobiography.* Springfield, Mass., 1871.

Gusfield, Joseph R. *Symbolic Crusade: Status Politics and the American Temperance Movement.* Urbana, Ill., 1963.

Hallock, William A. *"Light and Love," A Sketch of the Life and Labors of the Rev. Justin Edwards.* New York, 1855.

Hambleton, J. P. *A Biographical Sketch of Henry A. Wise.* Richmond, 1856.

Harman, John Newton. *Annals of Tazewell County, Virginia.* 2 vols. Richmond, 1922-1925.

Harrison, Fairfax. *Landmarks of Old Prince William.* Richmond, 1924.

Hatcher, Oranie V. *The Sneads of Fluvanna.* Roanoke, Va., 1910.

Hatcher, William E. *John Jasper, The Unmatched Philosopher and Preacher.* New York, 1908.

————. *Life of J. B. Jeter, D.D.* Baltimore, 1887.

Hawkins, William George (comp.). *Life of John H. W. Hawkins.* Boston, 1859.

Haygood, Atticus Greene. *Close the Saloons, a Plea for Prohibition.* Macon, Ga., 1880.

Hening, W. W. *The New Virginia Justice, Comprising the Office and Authority of a Justice of the Peace in the Commonwealth of Virginia.* 1st ed. Richmond, 1795.

Hill, Helen. *George Mason, Constitutionalist.* Cambridge, Mass., 1938.

Hundley, W. T. *History of Mattaponi Baptist Church, King and Queen County Virginia.* Richmond, n.d.

Ironmonger, Elizabeth Hogg, and Pauline L. Phillips. *History of the Woman's Christian Temperance Union of Virginia.* Richmond, 1958.

Jefferson, Thomas. *The Papers of Thomas Jefferson,* ed. J. P. Boyd *et al.* Princeton, N. J., 1950————.

Jeter, Jeremiah Bell. *The Life of Rev. Daniel Witt, D.D. of Prince Edward County, Virginia.* Richmond, 1875.

————. *A Memoir of Abner W. Clopton.* Richmond, 1837.

————. *The Mirror; or a Delineation of Different Classes of Christians.* Charleston, S. C., 1855.

————. *The Recollections of a Long Life.* Richmond, 1891.

Johns, John. *A Memoir of the Life of the Right Rev. William Bishop Meade.* Baltimore, 1867.

Johnson, G. G. *Ante-bellum North Carolina.* Chapel Hill, N. C., 1937.

Johnson, T. C. *The Life and Letters of Robert Lewis Dabney.* Richmond, 1903.

Jones, J. W. *Life and Letters of R. E. Lee.* New York, 1906.

Jones, J. William. *Christ in the Camp.* Richmond, 1887.

Kellock, Harold. *Parson Weems of the Cherry Tree.* New York, 1928.

Kennedy, John Pendleton. *Swallow Barn.* Philadelphia, 1832.

Kingsbury, Susan M. (ed.). *Records of the Virginia Company of London.* 4 vols. Washington, 1906-1935.

Krout, John A. *The Origins of Prohibition.* New York, 1925.

Lathrop, Elise L. *Early American Inns and Taverns.* New York, 1936.

*The Layman's Argument Against the Interdiction of Intoxicating Liquors by Church or State.* N.p., 1853.

Little, John P. *History of Richmond.* Richmond, 1933.

Lovett, O. I. *Plans Undertaken to Serve Seamen and Yeomen.* Middlesex, 1800.

McConnell, John P. *Negroes and Their Treatment in Virginia from 1865 to 1867.* Richmond, 1910.

McDaniel, R. C. *The Virginia Constitutional Convention of 1901-1902.* Baltimore, 1928.

McDonald, James J. *Life in Old Virginia.* Norfolk, Va., 1907.

McIlwaine, Richard. *Memories of Three Score Years and Ten.* New York, 1908.

McMaster, John B. *History of the People of the United States.* 8 vols. New York, 1888-1919.

Marsh, John. *Putnam and the Wolf; Or the Monster Destroyed.* Hartford, Conn., 1830.

Massey, John Edward. *Autobiography of John E. Massey,* ed. Elizabeth H. Hancock. New York and Washington, 1909.

Maxwell, William. *A Memoir of the Rev. John H. Rice, D.D.* Philadelphia, 1835.

————. *An Oration on the Improvement of the People Spoken Before the Literary and Philosophical Society of Hampden Sydney College.* Norfolk, Va., 1826.

Meade, William. *Old Churches, Ministers and Families of Virginia.* Philadelphia, 1885.

Minor, Lucian. *Reasons for Abolishing the Liquor Traffic* (pamphlet). N.p., 1853.

Moger, Allen W. *The Rebuilding of the Old Dominion, 1880-1902.* Ann Arbor, Mich., 1940.

Morton, Oren F. *History of Preston County West Virginia.* Kingwood, W. Va., 1914.

Morton, Richard L. *Colonial Virginia.* 2 vols. Chapel Hill, N. C., 1960.

Nevins, Allan. *American Press Opinion, Washington to Coolidge.* Boston, 1928.

————. *The American States During and After the Revolution, 1775-1789.* New York, 1924.

Neill, Edward D. *History of the Virginia Company of London.* New York, 1869.

Odegard, Peter H. *Pressure Politics, the Story of the Anti-Saloon League.* New York, 1928.

Olmsted, Frederick Law. *A Journey in the Seaboard Slave States.* New York, 1856.

Osgood, Herbert L. *American Colonies in the Seventeenth Century.* 3 vols. New York, 1904-1907.

Page, Thomas Nelson. *Social Life in Old Virginia Before the War.* New York, 1897.

Palmer, B. M. *Life and Letters of James Henley Thornwell.* Richmond, 1875.

Parrington, V. L. *Main Currents in American Thought.* New York, 1930.

Pearson, C. C. *The Readjuster Movement in Virginia.* New Haven, 1917.

Pell, Edward Leigh. *A Hundred Years of Richmond Methodism.* Richmond, 1899.

Pendleton, William C. *Political History of Appalachian Virginia.* Dayton, Va., 1927.

Peyton, J. Lewis. *Augusta County.* Staunton, Va., 1892.

Phillips, U. B. *Life and Labor in the Old South.* Boston, 1929.

Potter, Alonzo. *Drinking Usages of Society, Being the Substance of a Lecture Delivered in the Masonic Hall, Pittsburg, April 5, 1852.* Boston, 1852.

Powell, Mary G. *History of Old Alexandria.* Richmond, 1928.

Price, Richard Nye. *Holston Methodism.* Nashville, Tenn., 1903.

Rives, W. C. *Discourse before the Young Men's Christian Association of Richmond on the Ethics of Christianity.* Richmond, 1855.

Rogers, William B. *Life and Letters of William B. Rogers.* Boston, 1896.

Royall, Anne. *Mrs. Royall's Southern Tour.* Washington, 1830.

Rush, Benjamin. *The Drunkard's Emblem or An Enquiry into the Effect of Ardent Spirits upon the Human Body and Mind.* Printed by Ambrose Henkel and Co. at New Market, Va., *ca.* 1811.

Russell, John H. *The Free Negro in Virginia, 1619-1865.* Baltimore, 1913.

Russell, William Howard. *My Diary North and South.* London, 1863.

Sargent, Lucius M. *Temperance Tales.* New York and Boston, *ca.* 1830.

Scomp, H. A. *King Alcohol in the Realm of King Cotton.* Blakeley Printing Co., n.p., 1887.

Scott, Arthur P. *Criminal Law in Colonial Virginia.* Chicago, 1930.

Sellers, James Benson. *The Prohibition Movement in Alabama, 1702 to 1943* ("The James Sprunt Studies in History and Political Science," Vol. XXVI.) Chapel Hill, N. C., 1943.

Shanks, Henry T. *Secession Movement in Virginia.* Richmond, 1934.

Sheldon, William DuBose. *Populism in the Old Dominion: Virginia Farm Politics, 1885-1900.* Princeton, N. J., 1935.

Simkins, Francis B. *Pitchfork Ben Tillman.* Baton Rouge, La., 1944.

———. *The Tillman Movement in South Carolina.* Durham, N. C., 1926.

Sims, Henry H. *The Rise of the Whig Party in Virginia, 1824-1840.* Richmond, 1929.

Stanard, Mary Newton. *Colonial Virginia, Its People and Its Customs.* Philadelphia, 1917.

Stiles, J. C. *National Rectitude the Only True Basis of National Prosperity: An Appeal to the Confederate States.* Petersburg, Va., 1863.

Strong, Josiah. *Religious Movements for Social Betterment.* New York, 1900.

Stroupe, Henry S. *The Religious Press in the South Atlantic States, 1802-1865.* Durham, N. C., 1942.

Sullivan, Mark. *Our Times; The United States, 1900-1925.* 6 vols. New York, 1927-1935.

Summers, Lewis Preston. *History of Southwest Virginia.* Richmond, 1903.

Sweet, William Warren (ed.). *Religion on the American Frontier, 1783-1840.* 4 vols. New York and Chicago, 1931-1946.

———. *Virginia Methodism, A History.* Richmond, 1955.

Swem, E. G. *A Bibliography of Virginia.* 3 vols. Richmond, 1916-1955.

Sydenstricker, Edgar. *A Brief History of Taxation in Virginia.* Richmond, 1915.

Taussig, Charles William. *Rum, Romance and Rebellion.* New York, 1928.

Taylor, George Braxton. *Life and Times of James B. Taylor.* Philadelphia, 1872.

————. *Virginia Baptist Ministers.* 3rd and 4th ser. Lynchburg, Va., 1912.

Thomann, Gallus. *Real and Imaginary Effects of Intemperance.* New York, 1884.

Thomason, John W. *Jeb Stuart.* New York, 1930.

Thompson, S. H. *The Life of John R. Moffett.* Salem, Va., 1895.

Tigert, John James. *A Constitutional History of American Episcopal Methodism.* 2nd ed. Nashville, Tenn., 1904.

Timberlake, James H. *Prohibition and the Progressive Movement, 1900-1920.* Cambridge, Mass., 1963.

Tyler, Lyon G. *Williamsburg, the old Colonial Capital.* Richmond, 1907.

Waddell, Joseph. *Annals of Augusta County, Virginia, from 1726 to 1871.* Staunton, Va., 1902.

Walker, Cornelius. *Memoir of Rev. C. W. Andrews.* New York, 1877.

————. *Memoirs and Sermons of the Rev. William Duval, City Missionary, Richmond.* Richmond, 1854.

Ward, Harold Wesley. *The Administration of Liquor Control in Virginia.* Charlottesville, Va., 1946.

Washburn, Wilcomb E. *The Governor and the Rebel: A History of Bacon's Rebellion in Virginia.* Chapel Hill, N. C., 1957.

Wayland, John W. *History of Rockingham County, Virginia.* Dayton, Va., 1912.

Webb, Sidney, and Beatrice Webb. *The History of Liquor Licensing in England.* London, 1903.

Weisberger, Bernard A. *They Gathered at the River.* Boston, 1958.

Wertenbaker, Thomas Jefferson. *Norfolk: Historic Southern Port.* Durham, N. C., 1931.

————. *Torchbearer of the Revolution: the Story of Bacon's Rebellion and Its Leader.* Princeton, N. J., 1940.

Wheeler, Henry. *Methodism and the Temperance Reformation.* New York, 1882.

White, William Spottswood. *The African Preacher.* Philadelphia, 1849.

————. *Rev. William S. White, D.D. and His Times (1800-1873): An Autobiography,* ed., Rev. H. M. White, D.D. Richmond, 1891.

Whitener, Daniel Jay. *Prohibition in North Carolina, 1715-1945.* ("The James Sprunt Studies in History and Political Science," Vol. XXVII.) Chapel Hill, N. C., 1946.

Wiley, Bell I. *The Life of Johnny Reb.* New York, 1943.

Wingfield, Marshall. *History of Caroline County, Virginia.* Richmond, 1924.

Winslow, Ellen Goode. *History of Perquimans County* [N. C.]. Raleigh, N. C., 1931.

Wise, Jennings, C. *Ye Kingdome of Accawmacke or the Eastern Shore of Virginia in the Seventeenth Century.* Richmond, 1911.

Woods, Edgar. *Albemarle County in Virginia.* Charlottesville, Va., 1932.

Yearns, W. B. *The Confederate Congress.* Athens, Ga., 1960.

# INDEX

Abbot, Lyman, 202
ABC system, *see* Alcoholic Beverage Control System
Abingdon, 94, 112n, 144, 259n
Abolition: associated with temperance movement, 88, 136, 149; hurts Virginia temperance movement, 88-90; and John B. Gough, 92; mentioned, 135
Absinthe, 288
Accomac, 169, 173
Adams, John Quincy: and "pledge," 82, 310
Alabama, 170
Albemarle County: court records in, 32n; local societies formed, 61; Temperance Union debates use of cider, 88n; votes wet, 285n; mentioned, 173
Alcohol Education Council, Inc., of Virginia Churches, 300
Alcoholic Beverage Control System, 299-300
Alderman, Edwin A., 232
Ale, 288
Alexander, William, 98n
Alexandria, 38, 60, 69, 106, 112n, 168, 169, 189, 285n, 286
Alleghany County, 150n
Allen, Edgar, 177n
Amelia County, 61, 62n, 64, 150n, 187
American Colonization Society, 88n
*American Issue, Virginia Edition,* 244, 258, 281
American Temperance Society: activities aid Virginia Society, 74; Virginia Society joins, 76; mentioned, 55n, 58, 58n, 75
American Temperance Union: Virginia Society joins, 76; Cocke becomes president of, 85
American Temperance Union *Journal,* 121
Amherst County, 55n, 187n, 188, 225n

Anderson, William A., 229, 279n
Anderson-McCormick election law, 213
Andrews, C. W., 88n, 126, 127n, 128, 131, 137n
Andrews, Mrs. C. W., 88n, 127n
*Anti-Liquor,* 159n, 216
Anti-Saloon League: comes to Virginia, 222-224; early work under Mitchell, 224-231; Mann Law, 231-234; enforcement of Mann law by, 234-236; and James Cannon, Jr., 231ff.; local option and prohibition, 236-238; organization and propaganda, 239-249; joins the Democratic Party, 252-257, 259-261; passes the Byrd Law, 257-259; favors state-wide prohibition, 262-286; leads in enforcement, 287-290; does not oppose Reed Bill, 290; modifies demand for Bone Dry Law, 291-293; mentioned, 192, 210, 301
Apples, 83, 114, 209
Appomattox Baptist District Association, 68
*Arena,* 84
*Argus,* 159n
Armstrong, William, 75n, 77n
Asbury, Francis, 42, 52
Ash Camp Meeting-house, 55, 58, 73
Association for the Improvement of Public Schools, 233
Atkins, Henry P., 242n, 252
Atlanta, 278
Augusta County, 84, 134, 218

Bacon's Laws, 15, 15n, 16, 306
Bacon's Rebellion, 10, 15-16
Bagby, Mrs. T. B., 178, 200
Baldwin, J. C., 63
Ball, Eli: moves to Virginia, 59; as leader in first temperance society, 59ff.; publishes *Wisdom's Voice to the Rising Generation,* 65; church